TELLING IMAGES OF CHINA

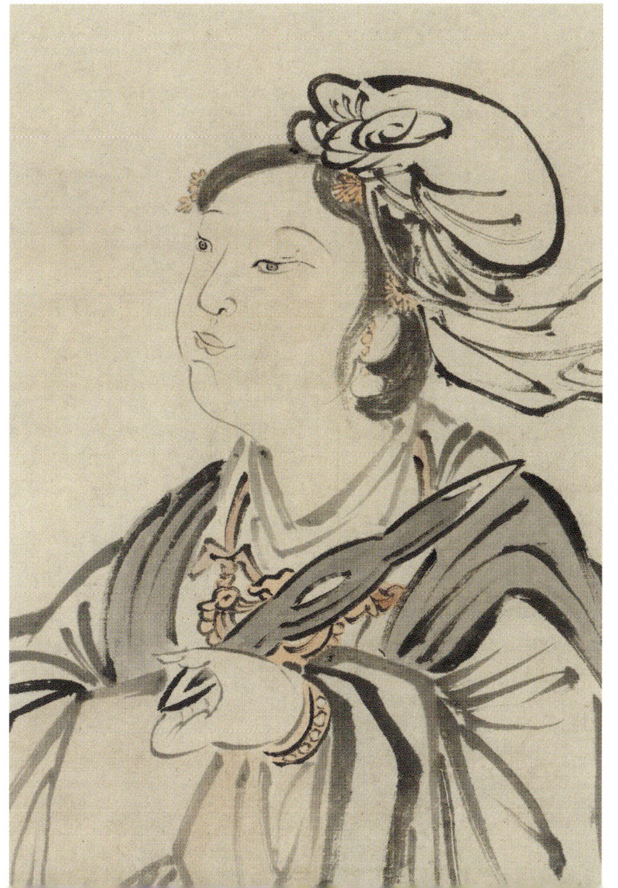

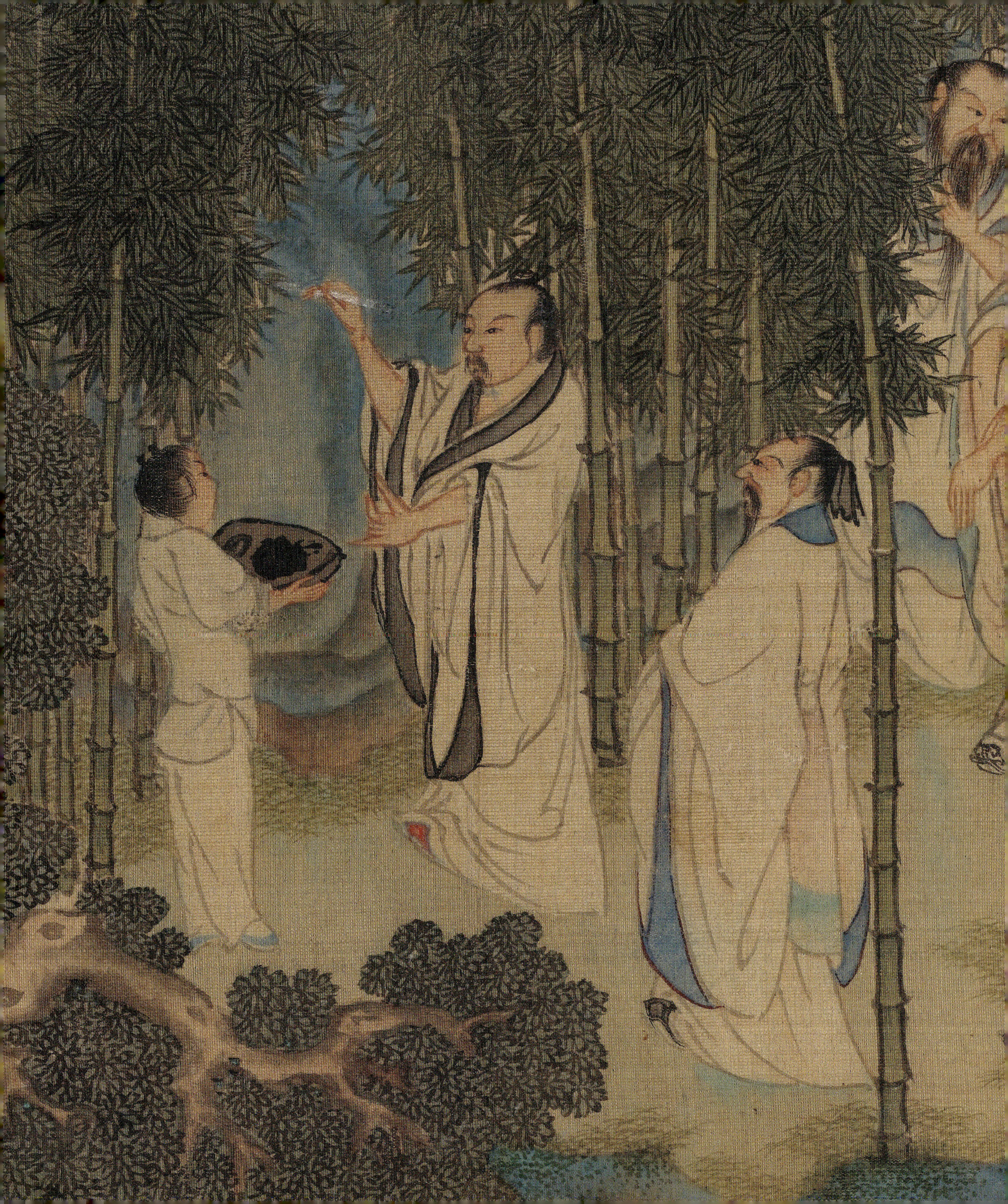

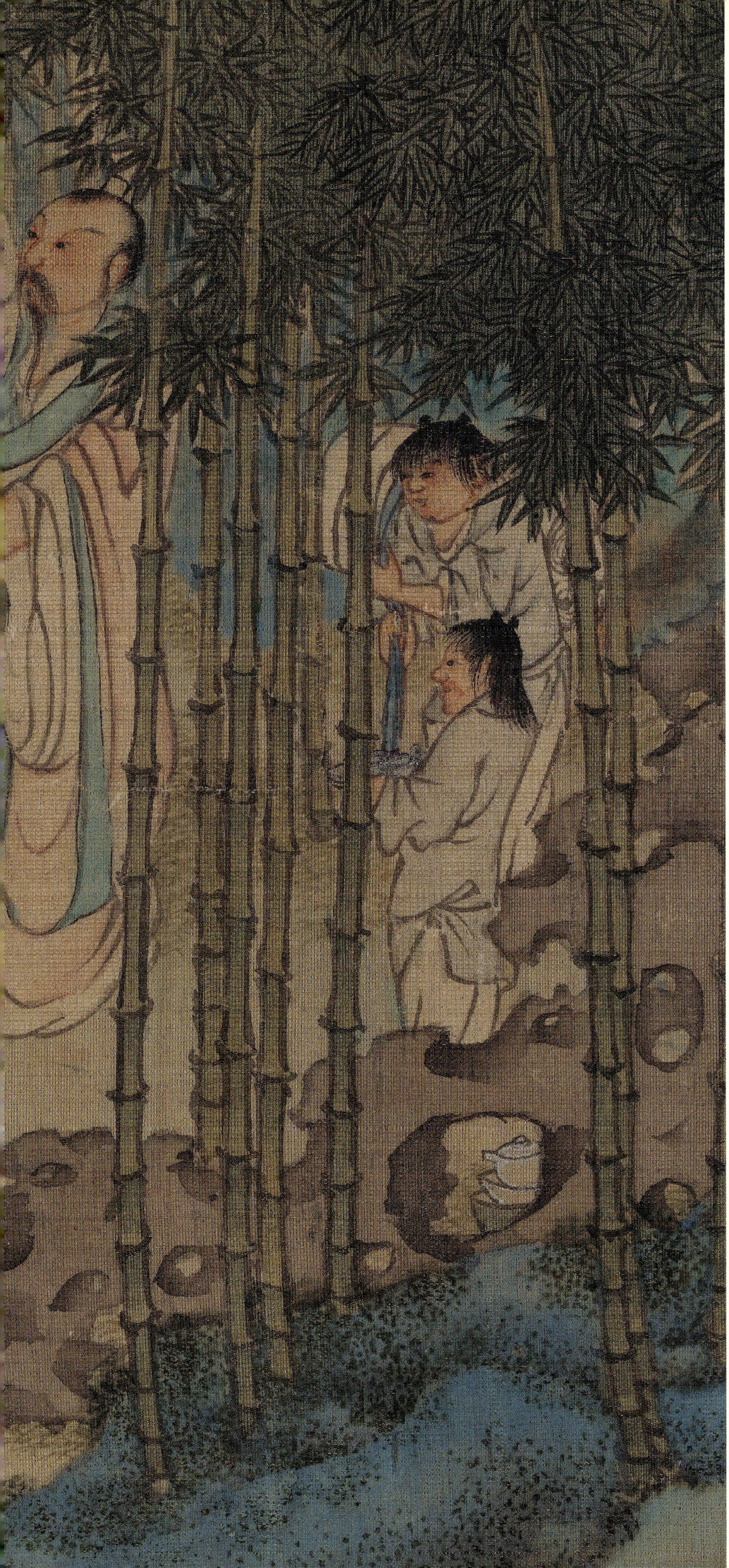

TELLING IMAGES OF CHINA

NARRATIVE AND FIGURE PAINTINGS

15th–20th CENTURY

FROM THE SHANGHAI MUSEUM

SHANE McCAUSLAND
LING LIZHONG

SCALA

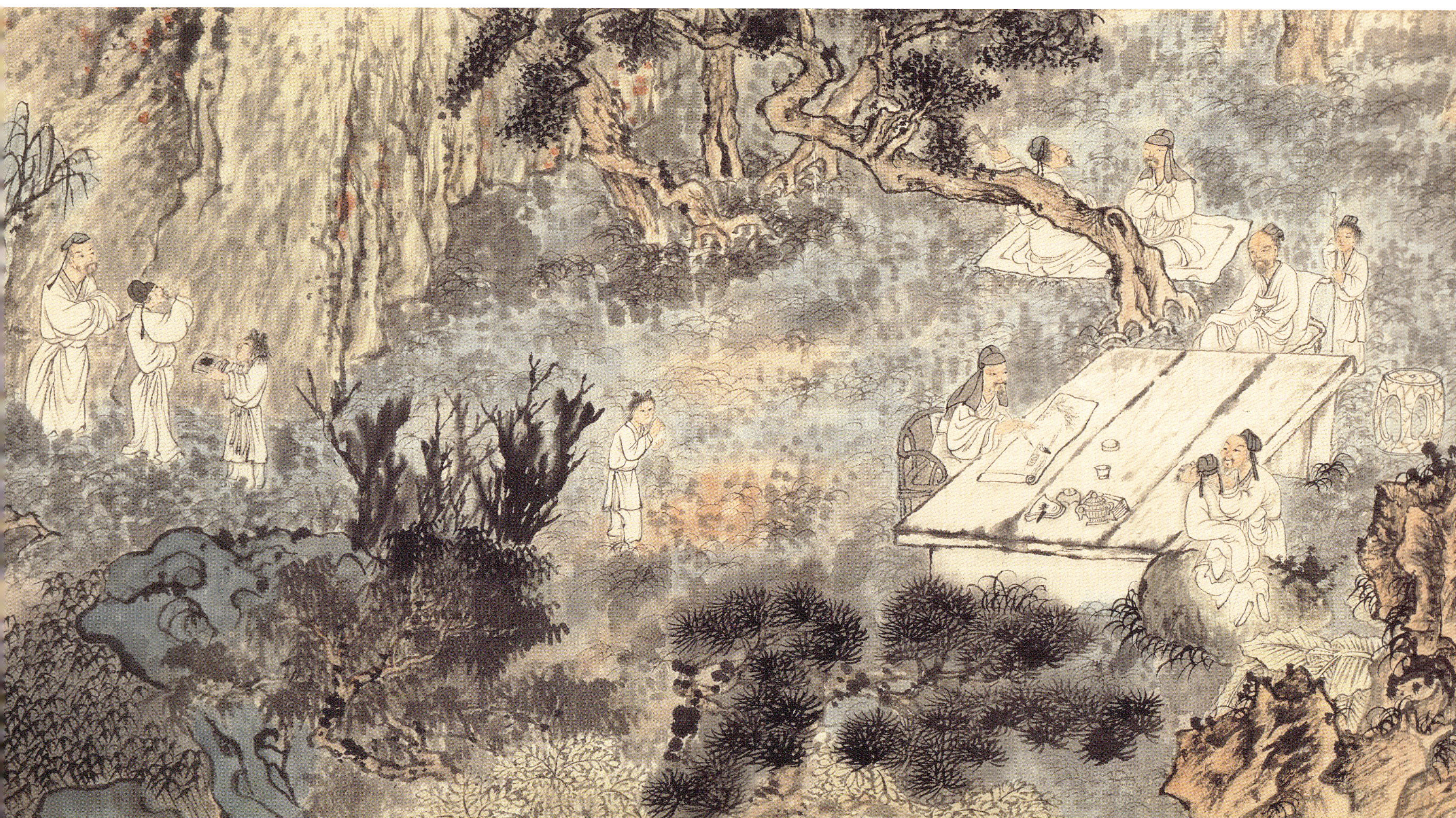

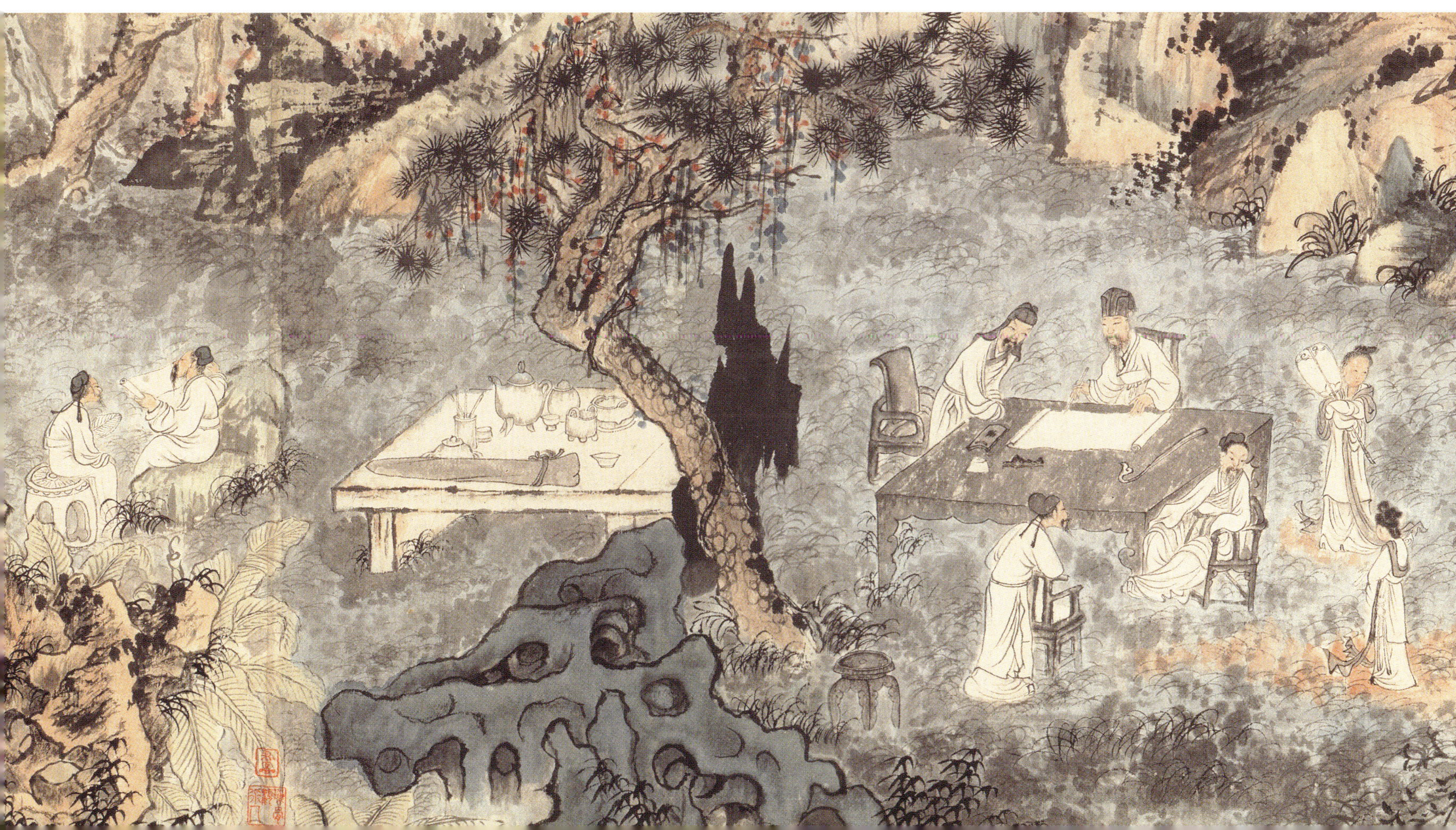

FOREWORD

I am delighted to introduce the catalogue of the exhibition *Telling Images of China*, which draws on the wonderful painting collection of the Shanghai Museum.

The idea of an exhibition from Shanghai began with a conversation with the Director of that splendid museum in the autumn of 2004, and the tentative arrangement reached then was taken up with enthusiasm by my colleague Dr Shane McCausland during his time as the Curator of the East Asian collections at the Library. He very wisely felt that the best way of creating an avenue to the understanding of the great traditions of Chinese painting was to use the power of stories which so many works illustrate – something which he felt would appeal particularly to an Irish audience. His colleagues in Shanghai embraced the concept enthusiastically and responded generously to his requests for loans and for participation in the writing of the catalogue. I wish to thank in particular Director Chen Xiejun for his warm welcome for the project, Ms Zhou Yanqun, general co-ordinator of exhibitions at the Shanghai Museum, and Mr Shan Guolin, Chief Curator of the Paintings and Calligraphy Department of the museum, whose friendly collaboration made Dr McCausland's task very much easier. The catalogue is enriched by an essay by Mr Ling Lizhong and by the photographs taken by Ms Zhu Lin, to both of whom we are deeply indebted.

As Shanghai prepares to welcome millions of visitors for Expo 2010 and its associated events, we are especially delighted here in Dublin to have in our care, for a brief period, such treasures of Chinese culture from the Shanghai Museum.

Michael Ryan
Director and Librarian, the Chester Beatty Library, Dublin

FOREWORD

China is one of the world's 'four great ancient civilisations' and its culture – unbroken through five millennia – is broad and rich, as well as deep-rooted. This has spawned some unique characteristics, including the temperament, ethics, values and ideals of its people, which are all manifestations of this enigmatic eastern civilisation.

The art of painting has a 2,000-year history and is an embodiment of traditional culture. When compared with landscape and bird-and-flower genres, we find that figure painting, because of its narrative element, is capable of reflecting the human, spiritual dimension of pre-modern culture more directly. The mounting of this exhibition demonstrates its curator, Dr Shane McCausland's insight into such aspects of Chinese culture.

The exhibition features a small selection – just thirty-eight fine paintings. What is more, they date to the Ming (1368–1644) and Qing (1644–1911) dynasties, a span of only six centuries, which is not long in Chinese history. Still, some of the ancient stories and figures illustrated long pre-date the paintings. In its scope, this exhibition encompasses philosophy and religious beliefs, art and culture, and folklore and customs. The subjects of the paintings are pleasingly varied, ranging from characters in religious lore and mythology to historical heroes and exemplars, from mainstream culture to folklore, from pivotal moments in history to everyday events, and from royal life to folk customs and manners.

I believe that visitors to this exhibition, beyond merely deriving aesthetic pleasure from the artworks on show, will also learn about the historical figures and stories behind the paintings, as well as their cultural contexts. I trust this exhibition will help advance understanding of the rich Chinese cultural tradition and that the universal human emotions, wisdom and aspirations to be found here will strike a chord with viewers.

I wish the exhibition every success.

Chen Xiejun
Director, Shanghai Museum

Chronology of Dynastic China

Shang Dynasty		**c.1600–c.1030 BC**
Zhou Dynasty		**c.1030–221 BC**
	Western Zhou	c.1030–771 BC
	Eastern Zhou	770–256 BC
	Spring and Autumn Period	770–476 BC
	Warring States Period	475–221 BC
Qin Dynasty		**221–206 BC**
Han Dynasty		**206 BC–AD 220**
	Western (Former) Han	206 BC–AD 8
	Xin dynasty (interregnum)	9–23
	Eastern (Later) Han	25–220
Three Kingdoms		**220–280**
	Wei (or Cao-Wei)	220–265
	Shu (Shu-Han or Western Shu)	221–263
	Wu (or Eastern Wu)	222–280
Jin Dynasty		**265–420**
	Western Jin	265–317
	Eastern Jin	317–420
Northern Dynasties		**386–581**
	Northern Wei	386–534
	Eastern Wei	534–550
	Western Wei	535–557
	Northern Qi	550–577
	Northern Zhou	557–581
Southern Dynasties		**420–589**
	Liu-Song	420–479
	Southern Qi	479–502
	Liang	502–557
	Chen	557–589
Sui Dynasty		**581–618**

Tang Dynasty		618–907
Five Dynasties		907–960
Liao Dynasty		907–1125
Song Dynasty		960–1279
	Northern Song	960–1127
	Southern Song	1127–1279
Xi Xia Dynasty		1038–1227
Jin (Jurchen) Dynasty		1115–1234
Yuan (Mongol) Dynasty		1271–1368
Ming Dynasty		1368–1644
	Hongwu	1368–1398
	Jianwen	1399–1402
	Yongle	1403–1424
	Hongxi	1425
	Xuande	1426–1435
	Zhengtong	1436–1449
	Jingtai	1450–1456
	Tianshun	1457–1464
	Chenghua	1465–1487
	Hongzhi	1488–1505
	Zhengde	1506–1521
	Jiajing	1522–1566
	Longqing	1567–1572
	Wanli	1573–1620
	Taichang	1620
	Tianqi	1621–1627
	Chongzhen	1628–1644
Qing (Manchu) Dynasty		1644–1911
	Shunzhi	1644–1661
	Kangxi	1662–1722
	Yongzheng	1723–1735
	Qianlong	1736–1795
	Jiaqing	1796–1820
	Daoguang	1821–1850
	Xianfeng	1851–1861
	Tongzhi	1862–1874
	Guangxu	1875–1908
	Xuantong	1909–1911

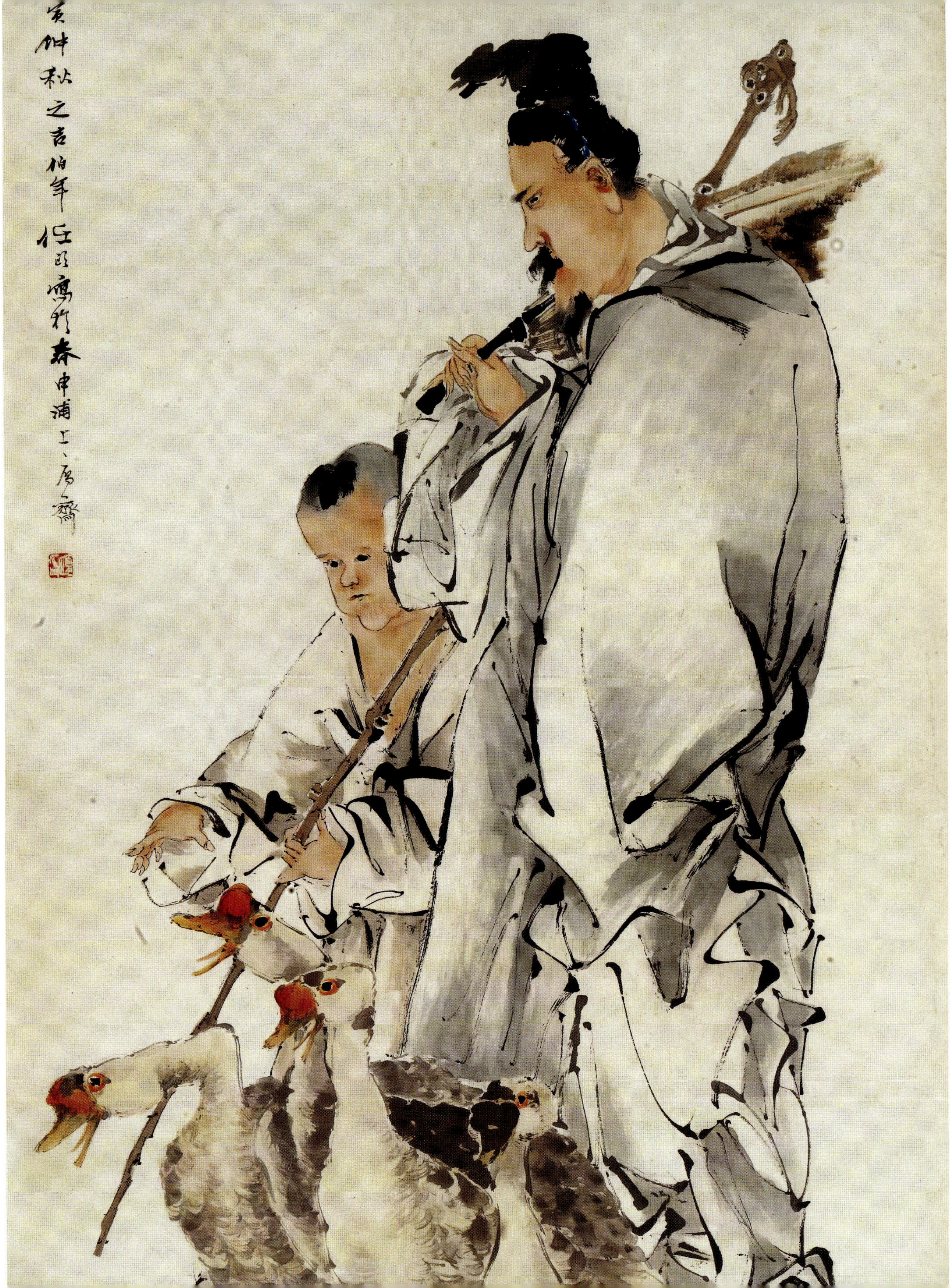

寅仲秋之吉伯年任頤寫於春申浦上

UNDERSTANDING TRADITIONAL CHINESE CULTURE THROUGH MING AND QING FIGURE PAINTINGS

With its 5,000 years of uninterrupted culture, China is the only surviving member of the world's 'four great ancient civilisations'. The long and rich cultural traditions of this mysterious Eastern people have given birth to a unique ethnic character with its own morals, values and ideals.

The art of painting in China dates back over 2,000 years and is an important embodiment of traditional Chinese culture. By comparison with the genres of landscape and bird-and-flower painting, the narrative features of figure paintings allow them to reflect ancient Chinese culture more immediately. The organisation and structure of this exhibition illustrates curator Shane McCausland's deep understanding of and close affinity with that culture.

From the thousands of ancient Chinese paintings that still exist today, thirty-eight masterpieces from the Ming (1368–1644) and Qing (1644–1911) dynasties have been selected for this exhibition. This period spanned less than 600 years, yet the people and stories depicted in the paintings date from hundreds and even thousands of years ago – back to the dawn of mankind. The contents of the paintings deeply reflect important elements of traditional culture in China, including philosophy, religious and folk beliefs, cultural arts and customs. More specifically, their subjects range from religious and mythological figures to historical personages, from mainstream culture to popular education, from great moments in history to the affairs of daily life, and from imperial lifestyles to folk customs.

It is fair to say that the highlight of this exhibition is the nature of the classic subject matter of the paintings coupled with the accessibility of their contents. I hope that all those who come to see it will not only appreciate the artistic skills of these painters but also find themselves closer to an understanding of Chinese culture through the figures, events and settings featured in the paintings. More than this, these ancient works testify to the universality of the human emotions, wisdom and desires that informed their creation.

Loyalty and filial piety have been Confucianism's greatest contributions to traditional culture. Confucians advocated the devotion and faithfulness of children towards parents, of ministers towards rulers and of a people towards its country. Taken one step further, this can be understood as universal love and allegiance to one's own land, people and even all of humanity. In this way, patriotism and ethnic integrity came to be highly

Ren Yi, *Wang Xizhi Admiring Geese* (Cat. 26, detail)

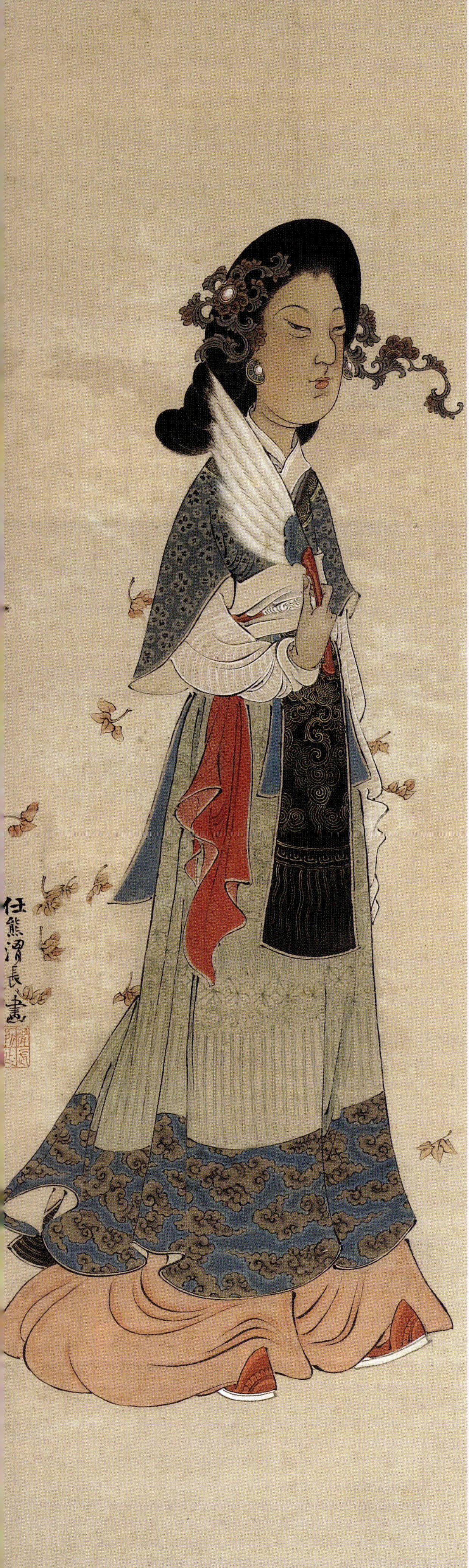

revered in the Chinese cultural tradition. In ancient China, there was no shortage of people who challenged those in power and fought for what they believed was right. Many would have met with persecution – some were even willing to risk their lives for their rulers, state and people. Their heroic feats have been recorded throughout history, as examples for later generations and to encourage lofty ideals.

Some of these stories feature in the exhibition, such as 'Lady of the Xiang river' (left), 'Su Wu tending sheep' (see Cat. 16), 'Wenji returning to China' (see Cat. 19) and 'Lady Zhaojun leaves China' (see Cat. 32). Depictions of these well-known, classic tales can be found throughout Chinese history, not only in paintings but also in drama, music and literature. The poem 'Lady of the Xiang river' was by Qu Yuan (339–278 BC), a minister of the state of Chu during the Warring States period (475–221 BC). It was written to show his loyalty to the King of Chu. However, despairing of ever reforming the government, Qu Yuan later drowned himself and was recognised as a great exemplar of patriotic conduct throughout Chinese history. The Han-dynasty envoy Su Wu was also recognised historically as a great exemplar of loyalty after he refused to defect to the Xiongnu during nineteen years of captivity on the steppe, despite extraordinary hardships and coercion.

While ancient Chinese history has men like Qu Yuan and Su Wu at its core, it also features patriotic women whose stories became legends. Only 100 years after 'Su Wu tending sheep' was written, a moving story called 'Lady Zhaojun leaves China' emerged. One of ancient China's Four Beauties, Wang Zhaojun was a woman of the Han imperial harem who was given away to a Xiongnu chieftain in 33 BC as part of a peace accord. Her patriotic self-sacrifice ensured more than sixty years of peace, and she came to be seen as a symbol of peaceful coexistence among ethnic groups.

While the theme of Zhaojun's story is quite clear, Guo Xu's *Album of Various Subjects* (Cat. 9) is not so transparent. His album of eleven leaves depicts immortals and historic figures who would seem to have little to do with loyalty or patriotism. However, by examining Guo Xu's life and the colophons written about the artwork, we find that in the remarkable leaf entitled 'An old lady feeds a hero' (opposite) he uses a classical story for contemporary commentary, and makes clear his loyalty towards his emperor. This story is about the early years of the great minister Han Xin (d. 196 BC), who helped Liu Bang unify China and establish the Han dynasty.

Guo Xu (1456–*c.*1529) came from Taihe, Jiangxi, and lived during the reign of Ming emperor Zhu Houzhao (Zhengde, 1506–21). During this period, Zhu Chenhao (1476–1519), the Prince of Ning in Nanchang, Jiangxi, started planning a rebellion, and apart from secretly preparing an army and supplies, he sought out many celebrated literati, including the well-known artists Tang Yin (1470–1524), Wen Zhengming (1470–1559), Xie Shichen (1487–*c.*1567) and Guo Xu himself. Tang Yin and Xie Shichen accepted gifts and money from the prince, and when his plot was later discovered, Tang Yin escaped death by feigning madness and fleeing. The Prince of Ning raised his army in revolt but was suppressed by military commander Wang Shouren (1472–1528) and his students Lei Ji and Liu Jie, who used the tactic of sowing discord among the prince's people, thereby ensuring national stability. Guo Xu had long since discovered the Prince of Ning's plot, as Wang Li points out in his colophon to the album: 'The emperor was gathering together all the best painters in the capital, and Zhu Chenhao wanted secretly

OPPOSITE: Ren Xiong, *Lady of the Xiang River* (Cat. 22, detail)

RIGHT: Guo Xu, 'An old lady feeds a hero', *Album of Various Subjects* (Cat. 9, leaf 6, detail)

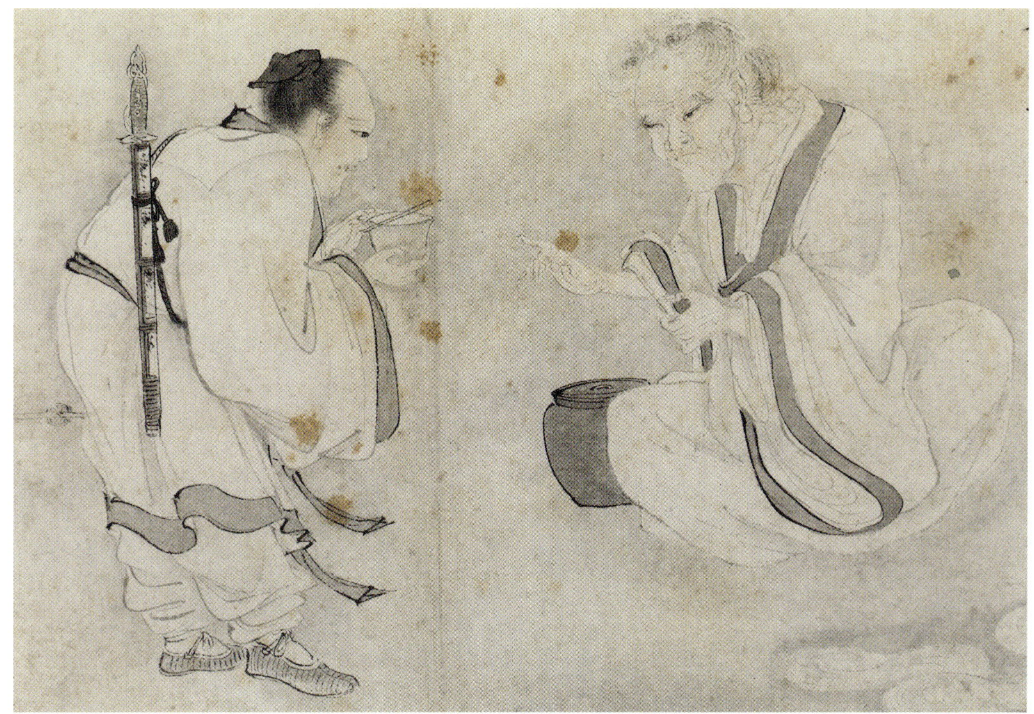

to bring Guo Xu over to his side, but Guo Xu politely declined. Guo Xu followed Wang Shouren's suggestion of offering an inscribed painting to show his intentions.' This painting was 'An old lady feeds a hero', and both Lei Ji and Liu Jie inscribed poems on it. They used the classic tale of Han Xin to secretly implore the Prince of Ning to give up his plot, at the same time expressing loyalty to the throne. The painting was made in 1503, and clearly the Prince of Ning did not heed Guo's warning. The prince's rebellion in 1519 was put down by the government and his entire family was wiped out as a punishment.

Another section of the exhibition concerns mythological tales and the Three Religions. The Confucian teachings of 'benevolence' (*ren*) and 'righteousness' (*yi*), and the non-conformist Daoist concept of 'inaction' (*wuwei*) lie at the heart of China's philosophical tradition. When Buddhism came to China from India in the Eastern (or Later) Han dynasty (25–220), these three teachings intermingled to form uniquely Chinese religious beliefs.

Buddhism flourished in China, and its adherents strictly followed its teachings. 'Bodhidharma meditating before a wall' (see Cat. 30) is a popular Buddhist story, and even though, at first, the Chinese resisted Bodhidharma's credo of not reciting sutras, not building temples and not transcribing Buddhist sutras, these were eventually incorporated into religious practice. As the teachings became more popular, so a distinctly Chinese form of Buddhism emerged – Chan (Japanese: Zen). Bodhidharma was recognised as the first patriarch of China's Chan sect, and Chan Buddhism went on to have a strong influence on later thought in China. The scholar-artists Su Shi and Mi Fu, who are depicted in Shitao's *Elegant Gathering in the West Garden* (Cat. 28; see p. 57 and p. 130), were both adherents of Chan Buddhism, which continued to have great influence on the artistic spirit in China.

Myths and legends have been around since early society, taking the form of spiritual concepts and mental attachments that arise in response to incomprehensible natural phenomena. As with gods in the ancient western world, in ancient China there was a deity corresponding to each type of natural phenomenon. For example, Pangu created the universe, the great inventor Fuxi and the goddess Nüwa created humans, and Shennong, the Divine Farmer, taught humans to cultivate the land and use medicine. There were also deities in charge of the wind, seas, mountains and rivers; a god of love who ensured happy marriages; and a god of luck who brought good fortune.

These gods (*shen*) had supernatural powers and were in charge of certain duties and tasks. Immortals (*xian*), who constituted a group apart from deities, lived forever, roamed about freely and often took an interest in the affairs of man, including deciding on the fate of people who had done wrong, and rescuing those in distress. For example, the Queen Mother of the West was in charge of human life and death, Iron-crutch Li (Li Tieguai) cured the ill and Celestial Master Zhang drove away demons. After the Ming and Qing dynasties, immortals and deities sometimes became intermingled; for example, the Two Immortals of Harmony were both immortals and deities (see Cat. 27).

Attaining the free and unfettered life of a deity or an immortal was a common pursuit of man in ancient China. In Chinese Daoism, one can become immortal through continual self-cultivation. Apart from ancient Daoist and Buddhist deities, and immortals and heroic figures who were deified, any person with the propensity to become an immortal can do so. This is represented in one of the paintings in the exhibition, Wang Zhao's *Iron-crutch Li* (Cat. 29), the subject of which is one of the Eight Immortals. Originally a handsome young recluse, Li was transformed into an immortal by the ancient Daoist sage Laozi. While travelling away from his body in spirit his body was burned, so his spirit occupied the corpse of a starved cripple, hence his moniker, Iron-crutch Li.

Because of their unwavering friendship and cheerful outlook in the face of adversity, the Tang-dynasty poet Hanshan and his friend Shide were called the Two Immortals of Harmony (see Cat. 27). As their story was passed down, they became the Gods of Love, representing harmonious marriage. Later, in the Five Dynasties period, the immortal Liu Haichan liked to play with the Golden Toad, which, according to folk legend, would spit out gold coins for humans (p. 15). This is why Liu Haichan became a god of wealth and auspiciousness in folk customs. These three individuals are depicted together in Shen Shao's painting, *Three Immortals* (Cat. 27).

Chinese mythology condenses the wisdom of powerful, fierce natural deities that the ancient Chinese humanised and made personal. For example, the figure of the Queen Mother of the West had a leopard's tail, a tiger's teeth and a fierce countenance that combined the characteristics of several animals, yet she evolved into a beauty unmatched on earth. And the many Chinese legends concerning ordinary people becoming immortals have a vernacular element, as their subjects illustrate common human traits far from any lofty ideal. This trend towards secularisation embodies the ancient Chinese philosophical notions of 'unity of heaven and man' (*tianren heyi*) and 'valuing harmony' (*he wei gui*), which differs from the tragic western sense of 'man conquering nature' and 'conflict'. As the modern scholar Xu Fuguan says: 'Among the world's ancient cultural systems there are no systematic cultures in which the relationship between man and nature is as harmonious as it became in China's antiquity.'

Throughout history there have always been people who were ahead of their time, whose extraordinary wisdom gave them insight into universal human truths, and whose sharp thinking sparked human understanding. They surpassed their origins to give spiritual value to all mankind.

For example, the Renaissance that followed the Middle Ages in the west resembled the 'awakening' period of the Wei-Jin era (3rd–6th century) in China. The Wei-Jin was the time of the most social turmoil and corrupt politics in Chinese history. The country fell apart, and from the need to strengthen their rule and protect their vested interests, its rulers championed the Confucian code, forcing ordinary people to abide by unfair social hierarchies, such as the nobility and hereditary systems. The result was that the ruling class lived extravagantly during this chaotic period, while the ordinary man was left destitute and hungry, and writers who spoke out were often persecuted.

It was during this time of extreme injustice that a number of educated recluses emerged, advocating freedom and spiritual independence, such as the Seven Worthies of the Bamboo Grove (see Cat. 18). It was at this time also that Tao Yuanming (also Tao Qian, 365–427), who is seen as China's greatest scholar-recluse, used his artistic imagination as a romantic poet to create 'Peach-blossom Spring' (see Cats 7 & 8), a vision of an ideal society, like the western Utopia. He proposed the emancipated ideology of 'standing aloof from the world' and 'retiring from public life'. His 'spiritual Eden' left

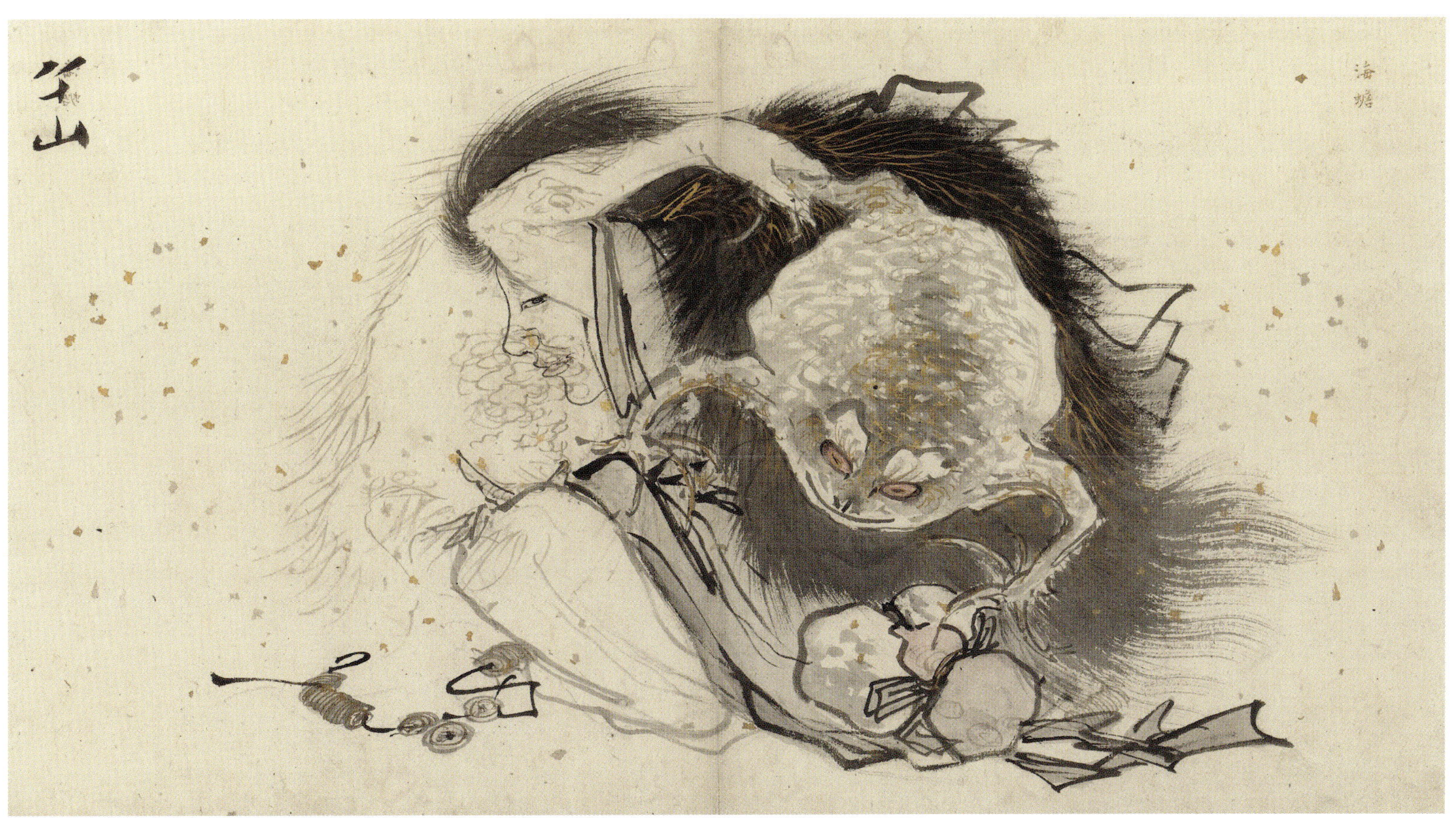

Zhang Lu, 'Liu Haichan and the Golden Toad', *Daoist Immortals and Natural Symbols* (Cat. 36, leaf 5)

a deep impression on traditional Chinese culture and was of much interest to later Chinese scholars.

The spiritual life and influential people were revered in traditional Chinese culture. Among those figures featured in the exhibition are the 'sage of calligraphy', Wang Xizhi, in *Purification Festival at the Orchid Pavilion* (Cat. 3) and *Wang Xizhi Admiring Geese* (p. 10); the 'poet immortal' Li Bai in Que Lan's *Li Bai Chanting Poetry* (Cat. 21); Li Gonglin, the creator of ink-outline painting, as well as Mi Fu and Su Shi, two of the 'four great Song-dynasty calligraphers', in *Elegant Gathering in the West Garden* (Cat. 28); as well as Mi Fu and Su Shi, two of the 'four great Song-dynasty calligraphers'; and Su Shi as the 'great writer' (*wenhao*) in the *Night Excursion to the Red Cliffs* (Cat. 15). The thoughts and actions of these prominent figures reflect the classic Chinese humanistic and cultural spirit, with traditional concepts appearing in their works, such as Confucian 'gentle, kind, courteous, modest and deferential' action; Buddhist 'endurance'; and the Daoist 'soft overcoming the hard'. Just as 'the Way is found in culture', these figures mastered various artistic forms, from poetry and calligraphy to painting and music. Whether bold or reserved, refined or broad, forceful, plain, innocent or broad-minded, the aesthetic concepts found in their works conform with and reach the heights of traditional mainstream culture and ethnic spirit.

China's long-standing feudal system allowed for long periods of imperialist rule. The rise of Chinese figure painting began with depictions of the lives of rulers and nobles, and these works represented the height of Han- to Tang-dynasty figure painting. During the Song and Yuan dynasties, painters turned towards everyday life for their subjects. Ming- and Qing-dynasty figure paintings took many forms, but especially feature antiquarian subjects. Some representative painters from this period include You Qiu (see Cats 32 & 33), Tang Yin and Qiu Ying (*c.*1494–1552).

In this exhibition, the works *Spring Morning in the Han Palace* (Cat. 33), *Consort Zhen at her Morning Toilette* (Cat. 11) and *Returning to the Academy by 'Golden Lotus' Lamplight* (Cat. 14) use classic themes centring on ancient palace life. The artists

You Qiu, *Spring Morning in the Han Palace* (Cat. 33, detail, scene 8)

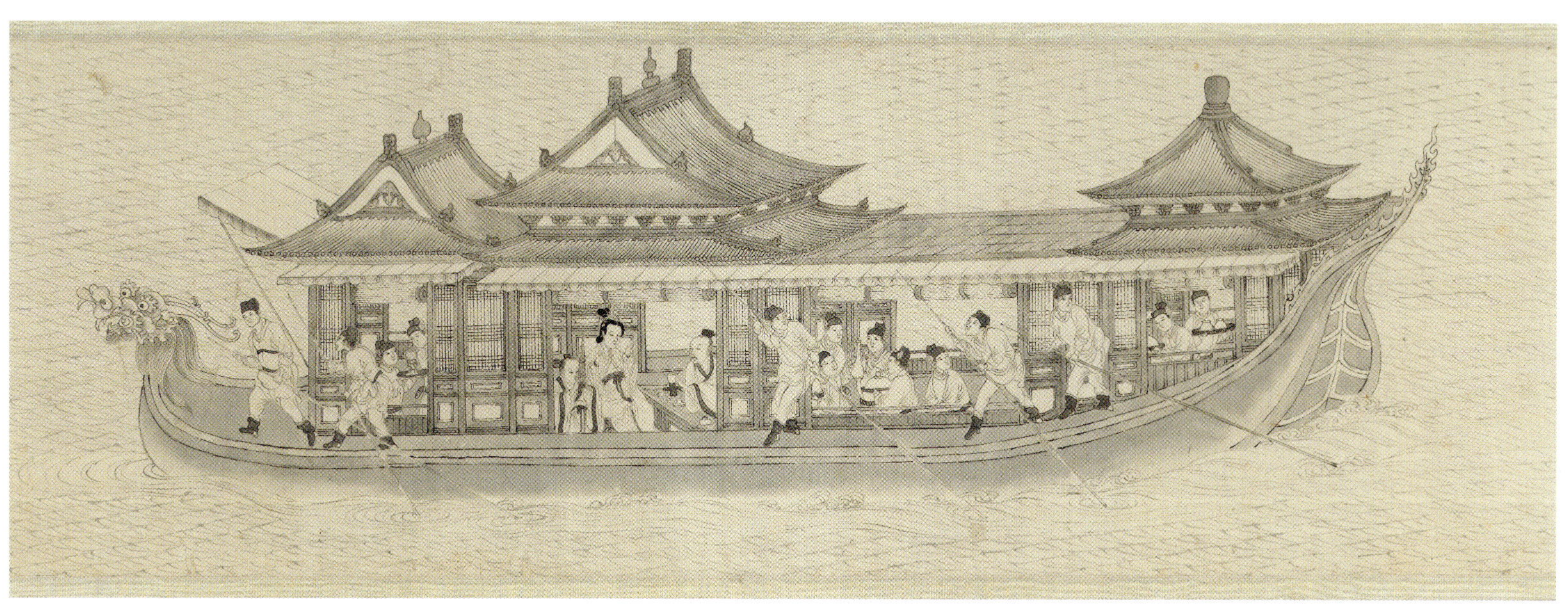

scrutinised ancient paintings to become familiar with palace culture of the time, including imperial architecture, palace decoration, fashion and the particular activities of palace inhabitants. For example, *Consort Zhen at her Morning Toilette* features Cao Pi's wife Zhen Mi rising early to apply her make-up; the revered imperial treatment of a talented minister is illustrated in *Returning to the Academy by 'Golden Lotus' Lamplight*; and the spring outing in *Women Enjoying the Spring Festival* (Cat. 13) shows noblewomen enjoying the zither, chess, painting and calligraphy.

There are works from the same period that appear to have antiquarian subjects which are used to express criticism of contemporary palace life. You Qiu's *Spring Morning in the Han Palace* (opposite) is based on the story known as 'Pair of Swallows in the Han Palace', about a ruler who neglects his country for music and women. The inscriptions were written by You Qiu's mentor Wen Zhengming and others who had lived during the reign of Ming emperor Zhengde. Like emperor Cheng of the Han dynasty in the story, Zhengde also favoured women and music over his palace duties, allowing the eunuchs to monopolise power. In this way, the painting reveals the artist's and the colophon writers' concerns over their country, and expresses their wish for the emperor to change his ways.

Just like stories from ancient imperial palace culture, tales from a genre known as 'scholar–beauty' romances were much loved by later (that is Ming and Qing) generations of readers. The talented scholar Cao Zhi of the Wei-Jin period (3rd–6th century) wrote his 'Goddess of the Luo River Ode' (*Luoshen fu*) in a burst of emotion arising from his love for Zhen Mi (see Cat. 23). This is ancient China's most romantic, yet sorrowful, love story. 'Romance of the Red Dust' is a romantic tale about the 'Red Duster lady', who had an eye for heroic men (see Cat. 25). Green Pearl, the heroine of *Golden Valley Garden* (Cat. 12), was not concerned with the moral quality of her lover but the loyalty she showed him when she leapt to her death to protect their love won over the hearts of countless people of culture. Even though Lin Daiyu (see Cat. 20), the heroine of the great eighteenth-century novel *Dream of the Red Chamber*, does not agree with Green Pearl's actions, she is not afraid to resist the Confucian system to achieve pure love and free marriage, and in the end sacrifices herself for love. The reason these scholar–beauty romances were retold throughout the ages is closely related to their instructional value and also the way they conveyed the passion that ancient Chinese people felt for true love.

In male-dominated, class-based ancient China, appearances and proper behaviour were valued in women. After the Ming and Qing dynasties, Chinese society opened up and became more accommodating and relaxed, and more and more women emerged from their boudoirs to receive cultural education. *The Female Disciples of Master Suiyuan* (Cat. 34) from this exhibition gives us a glimpse of this trend. Harmony Garden was the name of the famous Qing poet Yuan Mei's (1716–97) villa in Nanjing, where he took in women disciples from all over China. He bravely broke down the traditional feudal barriers against education for women and sought disciples of either gender, creating a new atmosphere and advancing the notion of equality between the sexes, which would have far-reaching implications.

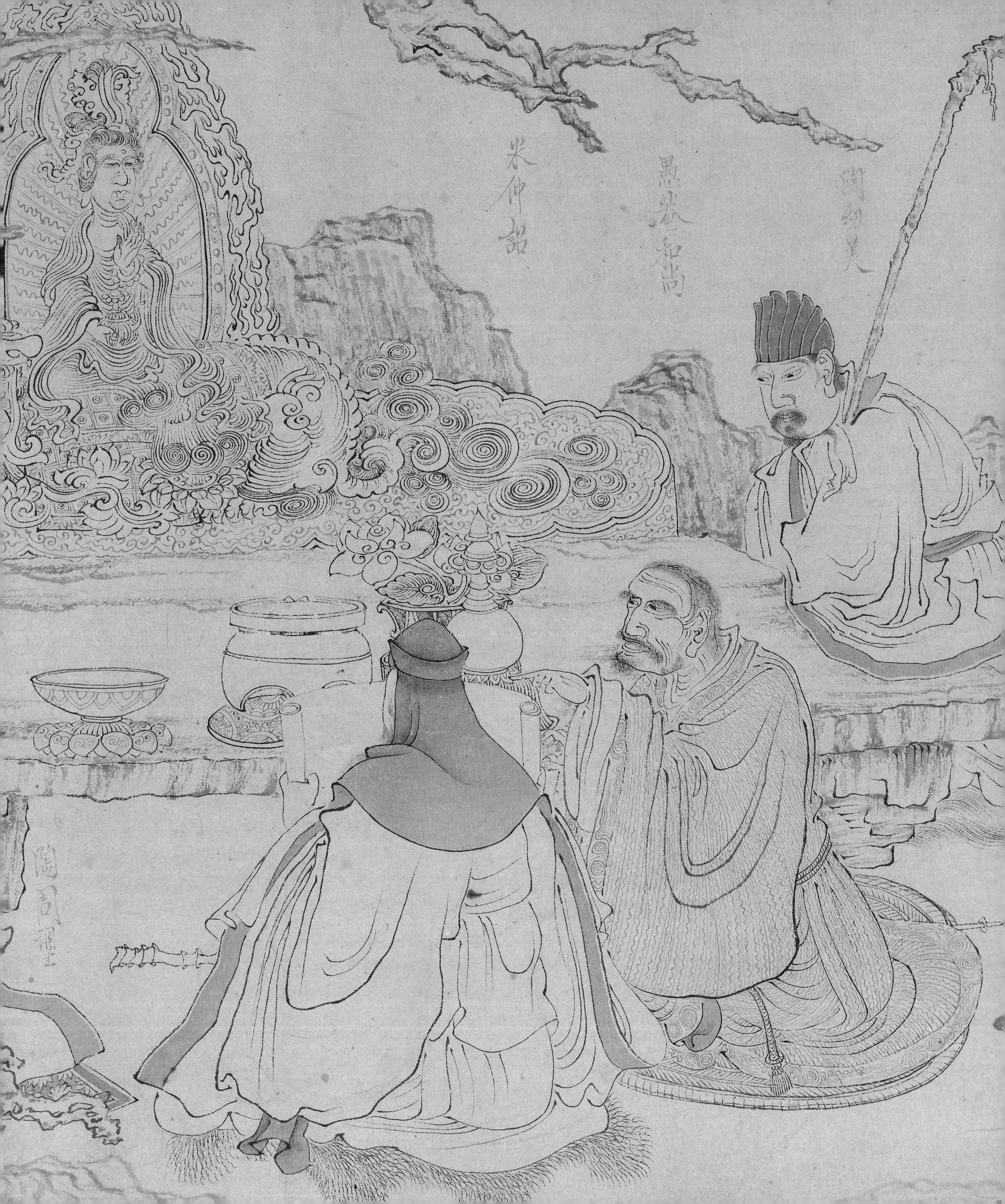
米仲詔
愚菴和尚
陶幼美
陶周望

TELLING IMAGES OF CHINA

Telling Images of China is an exhibition of narrative and figure paintings dating from the latter half of the last millennium, encompassing China's last two imperial dynasties – the native Chinese Ming dynasty (1368–1644) and the Qing dynasty (1644–1911) of the Manchu people – and the early Republican period (1912–) in the twentieth century. This time-span reflects the superlative quality of early modern and modern paintings in the Shanghai Museum collection, the sole source of this exhibition of thirty-eight figure paintings. Meanwhile, the subtitle 'narrative and figure paintings' is intended to point towards certain kinds of painting within the genre of figure painting, including works that might in general be called 'story paintings' (*gushi hua*), as well as more specifically 'narrative paintings' (*xushu hua*). This coincides with a new interest in the field of art history in visual narratives across Asia.[1] Broadly, each of the paintings in this exhibition retells some kind of story from Chinese legend, folklore, literature or history. While the source tales themselves are thematically and temporally diverse, ranging across mythology, folk and religious lore, epic, anecdote and romance, what unites them here is their presentation as pictorial images in works of painting.

In addition to being relevant to the idea of narrative art, paintings in this exhibition were identified for inclusion on the basis of their compelling visual quality and interest. A small number of them belong in the Shanghai Museum's highest designation of quality, including Shitao's *Elegant Gathering in the West Garden* and Hua Yan's *Golden Valley Garden*. In general, however, while making the selection with the museum's curators, Messrs Shan Guolin and Ling Lizhong, it emerged that paintings which carried traditional attributions to critically acclaimed artists did not always come up to the mark as 'story paintings', while, perhaps surprisingly, many accomplished works by less well-known and indeed obscure artists merited inclusion. In light of this, it is strongly hoped that the exhibition will demonstrate not just thematic coherence and depth, but also have a memorable visual impact.

Despite having this visual trait in common, however, the selected paintings exemplify a wide range of approaches to the illustration of source material. One Ming-dynasty handscroll offers a classic, collaborative model of the textual transcription by a calligrapher accompanied by a pictorial illustration by a painter, in this case a biographical text and a fully narrative painting comprising sequential scenes of images (see Cat. 33). Other paintings are more in the way of imaginary portraits of people based on pivotal biographical moments or events which are not necessarily inscribed on or beside the picture, as in the cases of some of the hanging scrolls. Sometimes, through iconography or attributes, actions or situations, or a combination of these with brief textual titles, figures may be recognised as characters from specific stories or

Chen Hongshou, *Elegant Gathering* (Cat. 4, detail)

OPPOSITE: An Zhengwen, *Yellow Crane Tower* (Cat. 1, detail)

legends. Some of these paintings must have been capable of functioning like triggers or *aides-mémoire* for the retelling of powerful stories, acting as the starting point for viewers' individual reminiscences on a figure's humanity or place in culture. Yet other paintings are more akin to genre scenes of palace life or customs, manners and festivals, which have a folkloric basis and a designated day in the traditional lunar calendar for display.

As a collection, these artworks recount exemplary stories from, and so provide a taste of, China's rich lyric tradition. As exhibits, these artworks reveal much about China's painting culture over six centuries. In its scope and size, this selection of thirty-eight paintings is perhaps just large enough to show an art-historical development of 'story painting' in China over this time-frame, and also to represent the lyric tradition in a meaningful way.[2] Indeed, the exhibition can be conceived of as a kind of thematic map, in that the same story might be the subject of more than one painting, or else a particular story, or part thereof, might be illustrated in one painting, while its author might be the subject of another.[3] Collectively, there are enough of these images to illustrate an adequately complex notion of China in cultural, political, social and religious, historical and regional terms. Yet, the artworks are not presented as a comprehensive group that define this China, but as a series of telling images.

It is also relevant to address some of the themes that emerge from this selection, which is the concern of the main body of this essay. This is no dogmatic approach: part of the attraction of 'unruly' artworks is that they are historical examples and events in and of themselves, which blur or disrupt the neat categories by which we would define them. Thus, the four themes-cum-exhibition sections need not be considered impermeable, and may be taken as points of departure for individual study and reflection, additional to the informative and thoughtful texts on the exhibits and their cultural setting by Mr Ling Lizhong. These themes are as follows: stories of crossings, including tales of exiles, loyalists, suicides and rustics; mythology, religious lore and the supernatural world; exemplary figures in cultural history; and finally, romances between emperors and concubines, and between scholars and beauties. Before attending to these in more detail, some introductory comments follow on the thematic structure in relation to chronology, and on historical ties between visual culture and literature in China.

Regarding the thematic structure and chronology, we have used a cartographic image – sketching a kind of map of themes – to outline one aim of this essay, but the thematic sections do not provide a chronology as such. That said, there is an historical or diachronic dimension to the exhibition that should be addressed. As the dating in the exhibition's subtitle – 15th–20th century – announces, all the artworks were produced by artists within this period. Here, 15th–20th century connotes, essentially, the Ming and Qing periods, categories employed by the Shanghai Museum and other official bodies in China for documentation and administrative purposes which may not be familiar to viewers in the west. The start of the Ming dynasty in 1368 is indubitably important for procedural reasons, but our purpose is not to downplay the early Ming reigns, Hongwu (1368–98) and Jianwen (1399–1402), which fall in the late fourteenth century, only to suggest a time-span in neutral fashion. No painting is specifically dated to the late fourteenth century, although it is not impossible that one of the early-Ming Zhe School paintings in the exhibition dates to before 1400 (opposite).

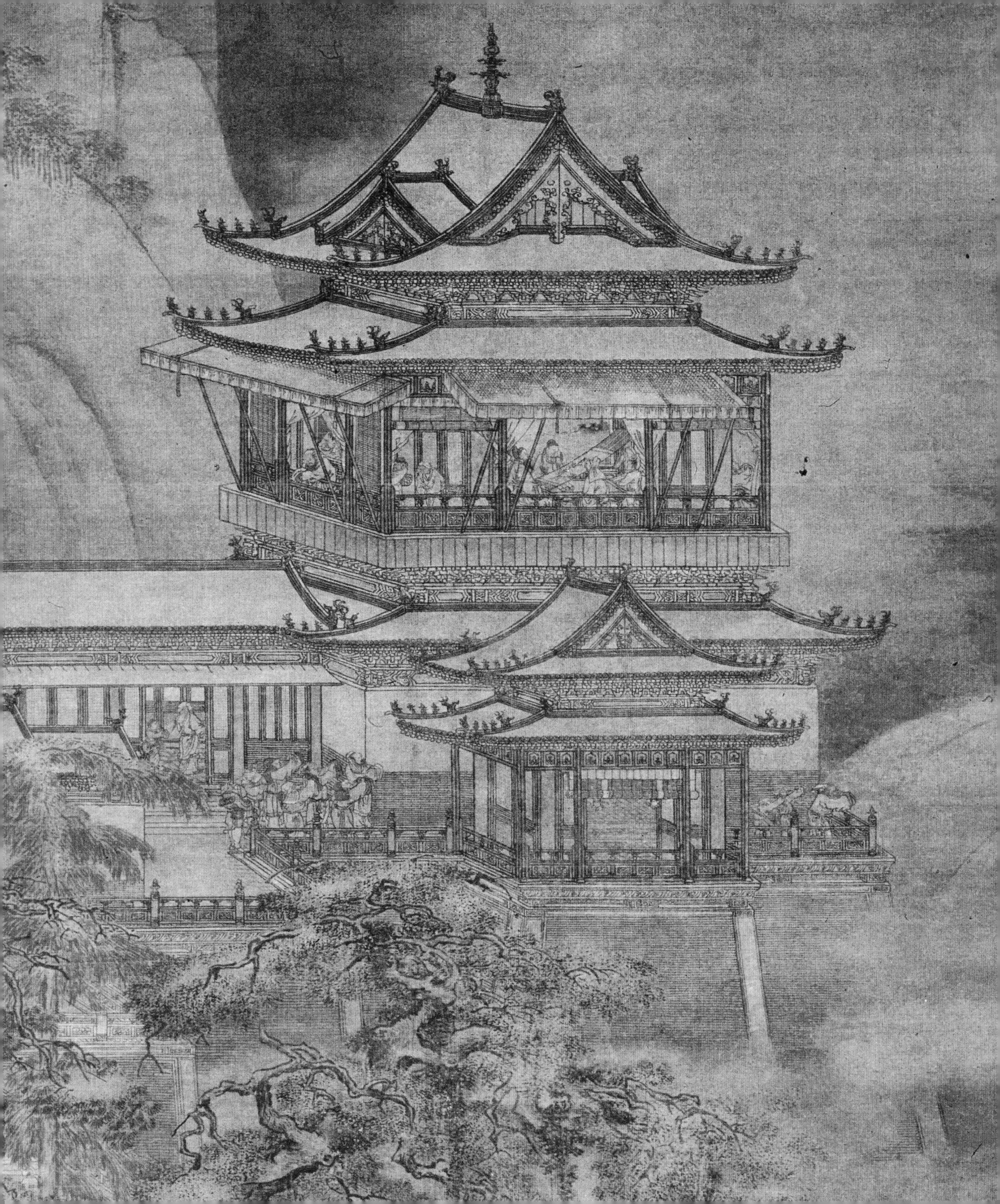

It might be said that this particular date-span – 15th–20th century – is rather cross-grained for Chinese art history, a field that tends to conceive of time in terms of a sequence of dynastic units following the transfer of the 'mandate of Heaven' from one royal house or political regime to the next. Thus, the great founding empires, Han (206 BC–AD 220) and Tang (618–907), roughly equate to the 'early' period; and the native Song (960–1279), the Mongol Yuan (1271–1368), the Ming and Qing dynasties correspond to the 'later' period. While the artworks in the exhibition date to the latter part of 'later Chinese art', no such limit is placed upon their contents, which poses a challenge of sorts to viewers unfamiliar with the broader patterns of Chinese history. Helpfully, some of these paintings treat themes from early history (from about 1500 BC) and mythology, the classical period of Confucius and others (the Warring States, 475–221 BC), the dawn of the imperial age in 221 BC and subsequent epochal moments. In addition, other paintings stand at the frayed edges of sanctioned history, by describing events which happened beyond the frontier of China proper, or stories deemed unsuitable for transmission in official records.

At the end of our time-frame, we have deliberately included early and mid-twentieth-century paintings by painters born under the Qing dynasty, partly for their own interest but also to serve as bridges into the dynastic past. The latest painting is by Qi Huang (Qi Baishi, 1864–1957), whose life spanned the end of the Qing dynasty, the founding of the Republic in 1912 and of the People's Republic in 1949. The marking of time can never be without some kind of subject-position, but the time-span which we give here in centuries is intended to be neutral, as noted, and accessible.

What about the links between visual culture and literature in China? The viewer is encouraged to explore these paintings on their own merits as artworks, but it is also useful to approach them and their types in relation to the critical apparatus of the Ming and Qing art world. There is no claim that 'story painting' existed as a category in pre-modern China comparable to landscape painting, the senior genre, or to figure painting, which is usually taken to include everything from genre scenes and portraits to figures-in-landscapes and animal paintings, as well as narrative painting.[4] The earliest masters in the painting tradition excelled as figural artists and story-tellers, as exemplified by the *Admonitions of the Court Instructress* picture-scroll attributed to Gu Kaizhi (*c.*344–*c.*406) in the British Museum, a probable fifth–sixth-century narrative work in his 'gossamer-thread' style.[5] During the early Song dynasty, figural painting lost some of its lustre to the new mode, monumental landscape painting. Although the pivotal scholar-artist Zhao Mengfu (1254–1322) in the early Yuan practised painting in a wide range of genres, by the late Yuan and early Ming, it was landscape that dominated in critical circles. It might be added that the scholar's art of calligraphy topped all genres of painting in the eyes of the influential Ming 'men of culture' (*wenren*), such as Wen Zhengming and Dong Qichang (1555–1636). Still, important Qing artists like the protean Shitao (1642–1707) and the Yangzhou painters are today studied primarily as painters, despite their facility as calligraphers and despite calligraphy's role in the historical development of painting during the Qing dynasty.

It might seem counterintuitive that figure painting, with its visual tie to humanity, was considered critically inferior to landscape, given the explosion of literacy rates and the rapid emergence of a commodity culture in the late Ming period (16th–17th century), but just as one can picture the idealised scholar-amateur hierarchy of art genres (predisposed towards landscape), so one can point to exceptions. For example, the eccentric Chen Hongshou (1598–1652), a scholar turned professional artist, is the outstanding torch-bearer of ancient figural traditions into the Ming–Qing transition in the mid-seventeenth century (p. 18). Chen and many of the other later artists represented in this exhibition not only executed paintings but also designed images – typically illustrations of dramas and novels – for reproduction in woodblock-printed books. Chen Hongshou established his name in the 1630s in part by designing illustrations to woodblock-print editions of the popular drama, *Story of the Western Wing* (*Xixiang ji*). It is small wonder that the interplay between 'popular culture' in print and 'high art' in painting intensified during this period, as the technologies of image reproduction became increasingly sophisticated, in spite of traditional critical discourse.

In practice, the growth of literacy in China in the early modern period implied an enormous range in literary abilities on the part of consumers of visual images, including

The poet Yuan Mei with his nephew's wife, Dai Lanying, and her son, Enguan, from You Shao and Wang Gong, *Female Disciples of Master Suiyuan* (Cat. 34, detail)

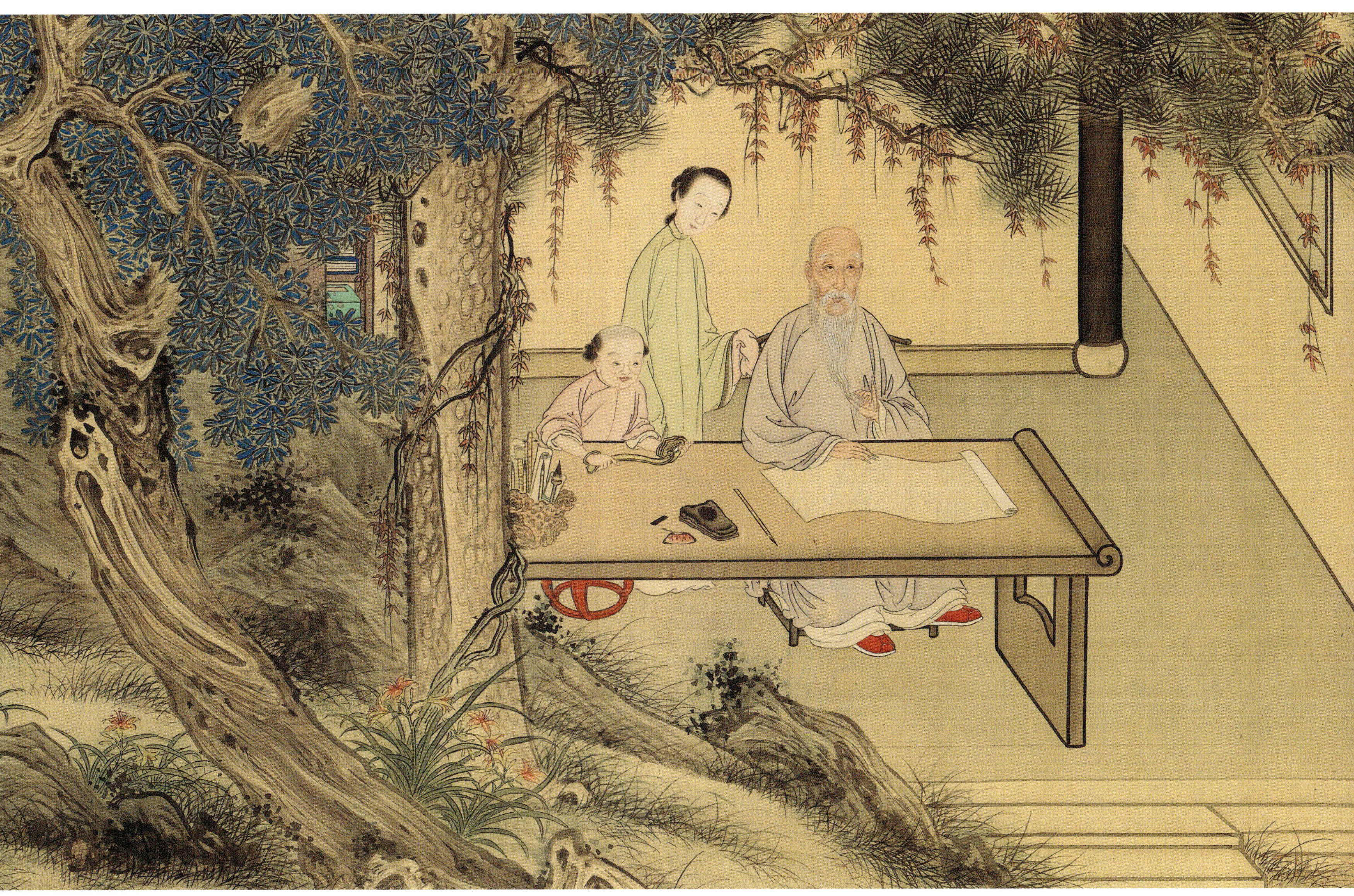

paintings. It is reckoned that some of the Ming professional and academic artists who worked under the rubric of the Zhe School were not particularly literate. Those who attained official positions at court were typically granted ceremonial ranks in the palace guards, such as An Zhengwen (see Cat. 1). The 'men of culture', individuals at the pinnacle of literati society who also rose to high rank in the civil bureaucracy, were for a long time the supreme arbiters of literary culture through their activities. As Ling Lizhong describes, a small number of late Ming courtesans were celebrated for their cultural accomplishments, whereas verse by the female half of genteel society, for instance, came to be valued more widely only in later eighteenth-century society, when the noted poet Yuan Mei (1716–97) assembled a coterie of female disciples around him in Nanjing (p. 23). In effect, when looking at the paintings in this exhibition, we should not always assume complete familiarity or facility with the textual sources of painting subjects on the part of early viewers. Indeed, the folkloric and/or genre content of some of these paintings, notably Ming paintings concerned with a specifically female culture, suggests the opposite.

In this book, the interweaving through history and across the China region, of many persons, iconographies and narratives, and of the artists who painted them, is at times complex; but this also represents the undiminished richness of the culture, which this exhibition commemorates and celebrates.

Stories of Crossings: Exiles, Loyalists, Rustics

Rather than speaking of boundaries in China, we introduce here the theme of crossings – because it keeps the focus on the active, human element in painting, and within that, the idea of the journey, transformation or developmental change.[6] The paintings grouped here offer examples of cultural patterns in the form of illustrated stories about crossings. We consider righteous suicides who crossed over into the afterlife out of loyalty or in protest, or both; people who crossed the border into 'barbarian' territory, how they came to do so, and what it meant to do so; we consider people who crossed figurative borders within China, including exiles, eccentrics and rustics.

The story linked to one of the paintings in this group dates to a foundational period of Chinese culture, the era of the sage-kings in classical antiquity. The hanging scroll *Lady of the Xiang River (Xiang furen*; Cat. 22) is by Ren Xiong (1823–57), one of the three highly successful members of the Ren family of painters in late Qing Shanghai. A portraitist and figural artist, Ren Xiong commonly depicted legends and historical stories in his paintings. Having made a name for himself, he died of tuberculosis at the age of just thirty-four, during the Taiping Rebellion (1850–64).

This richly coloured painting depicts one of the wives of the legendary ruler Shun, who according to tradition acceded to the throne in 2255 BC and reigned in exemplary fashion for fifty years. In legend, he died on a tour of his domain, whereupon his two grieving widows – the daughters of Shun's predecessor Yao, named Ehuang and Nüying – travelled to the spot by a river. Their tears stained the nearby bamboos, before they drowned themselves in the waters. Thus, local legends grew about how their spirits protected the Xiang River, and about how some types of bamboo there in the Hunan region of central south China come to have mottled leaves, including 'mottled bamboo' (*banzhu*), 'tear bamboo' (*leizhu*), 'Xiang bamboo' (*Xiangzhu*) and 'Xiang consort bamboo' (*Xiangfeizhu*).

The story of Shun's beautiful and loyal consorts has been the subject of many laments and poems since the Warring States period. Among the earliest are two, 'Lord of the Xiang' (*Xiang jun*) and 'Lady of the Xiang' (*Xiang furen*), the fourth and fifth of the 'Nine Songs' (*Jiuge*) group in the shamanistic poetry anthology, *Songs of the South (Chuci)*, attributed to the statesman Qu Yuan (*c.*339–278 BC).[7] For his part, Qu Yuan is known in Chinese history for his poetry, but also for his principled stand against injustice and corruption at court, after he committed suicide by drowning himself in the Miluo River in Hunan. It is no surprise, then, that the story of the Xiang consorts' suicides, with its link to the righteous, spurned minister Qu Yuan, carried with it strong political relevance and connotations of dissent throughout the dynastic period and beyond.[8] Ren Xiong's imaginary portrait was painted against the backdrop of widespread social unrest during the Taiping Rebellion period, in which over 20 million people are thought to have died.[9]

Stylistically, this richly dressed figure recalls the female figures of Chen Hongshou, the late Ming eccentric introduced above, known for his ironic and strange depictions of figures in bizarre, ancient styles (see Cat. 4). The points of overlap are many, including the body and facial type; the drapery with its richly decorated surface patterns, looping curves of the hemlines and scarves, and the gathered quality of loose fitting garments; and the antique effects, such as shoes with prongs on the toes to catch the robes, carved jade hair ornaments and the white feather fan. Despite these conscious archaisms, the visual references and the connotations of loyalty and virtue inherent in the subject are not laboured. The figure appears accessible to modern viewers, reflecting it would seem the look of well-heeled women among the artist's clientele, and one of the likely reasons for Ren Xiong's popularity among urban buyers of the increasingly cosmopolitan city of Shanghai. The picture of the *Lady of the Xiang* also introduces the theme of 'exemplary women' from history, which includes women who were notably chaste or unchaste, noble or ignoble of character, and who set standards through acts of outstanding selfish- or selflessness. Other such stories appear later.[10]

A handful of the tales illustrated in paintings in the exhibition are set in the Han dynasty, the first imperial regime to capitalise on the unifying conquests of the Qin dynasty (221–206 BC). While Qin is the root of the English word for China, Han is a byword in Chinese for China. Despite the Han dynasty's undoubted power and longevity, not to mention its new standards of statecraft and institutional sophistication, Han also endured moments of great instability, under threat from without by 'barbarian' invaders and from within by the abuse of power. Responses to those threats feature in stories that artists painted.

A painting by the Yangzhou master Huang Shen (1687–after 1770), *Su Wu Tending Sheep* (p. 27), has its origin in the story of two friends in the Former or Western Han: the imperial envoy Su Wu (140–60 BC) and the general Li Ling (d. 74 BC), who served under emperor Wudi (r. 141–87 BC). When Li Ling was defeated and his army destroyed in a campaign against the Xiongnu tribes bordering China to the north in 99 BC, he was captured and later defected, becoming a persona non grata in China. Su Wu was Wudi's

OPPOSITE: Huang Shen, *Su Wu Tending Sheep* (Cat. 16, detail)

envoy to the Xiongnu who was detained by them in 101 BC and thereafter banished and humiliated by being made to tend sheep and goats in the wilderness, as he is depicted in the painting by Huang Shen. He was ransomed in 81 BC after nineteen years. During that time, Li Ling was twice sent to try to persuade Su Wu to defect, but Su Wu remained loyal to the Han. After Han emperor Wudi died and was succeeded by Zhaodi (r. 87–74 BC), a Han Chinese embassy was sent to ransom Li Ling but he refused to change his allegiance again, having become one of the Xiongnu. The tale of the two men's friendship is sometimes depicted at the moment of their parting on the steppe, Su Wu having refused to defect. Here, Huang Shen focuses on Su Wu alone, a model of steadfast loyalty across the ages, in a painting which shares a title with a traditional tune, 'Su Wu tending sheep' (*Su Wu mu yang*).

Fractious Han–Xiongnu diplomatic relations are the background for two story paintings in the exhibition concerning women. You Qiu's *Lady Zhaojun Leaves China* (p. 28) recounts the tale of the righteous and beautiful Wang Zhaojun, one of the 'four beauties' of ancient China, along with Xi Shi, Diaochan and Tang emperor Minghuang's beloved Yang Guifei. Wang Zhaojun is the subject of many poems and legends, and has also been known by various names at different times because of the taboo on the name Zhao, including Mingjun (Bright Lady) and Mingfei (Bright Concubine).[11]

Wang Zhaojun was a court lady to Han emperor Yuandi (r. 48–33), but was never selected to be a concubine to the emperor. In later popular stories, it is said this was because she refused to bribe the imperial portraitist, Mao Yanshou, who made her look plain in the albums of the thousands of court ladies that he prepared for the emperor. A vignette in which Mao Yanshou is seen rendering the portraits of court ladies is often found in works depicting a related painting title, *Spring Morning in the Han Palace*.[12] Deceived, apparently, by the artist's impression, the emperor never laid eyes on Wang Zhaojun. Historically, however, she volunteered to be one of five palace women given in marriage to the Xiongnu chieftain (*Shanyu*), Hu Hanxia (d. 31 BC), in 33 BC. Back in the popular story, when she came before the emperor to be given away and he saw her for the first time, he realised what had happened and had the painter executed.

You Qiu depicts Wang Zhaojun at a most harrowing moment as she crosses out of China forever, into Xiongnu territory. The scroll opens to a depiction of an unworn trail meandering through a ragged forest, before opening out onto the steppe grasslands of 'barbarian' country. The story goes that Zhaojun left China carrying a *pipa* (stringed instrument), which, in You Qiu's painting, is carried for her by an attendant. Her mournful playing and physical beauty attracted the attention of the migrating geese, which were said to have fallen from the sky when they forgot to flap their wings. Thus, flying geese are part of the iconography of the tale in pictures. Zhaojun dutifully bore her Xiongnu husband two sons and a daughter, and after his death married his successor, bearing further children. Politically and diplomatically, Zhaojun's marriage alliance to the Xiongnu ruling family was a resounding success, ushering in more than half a century of peace between Han China and its northern neighbour. You Qiu organises the story so as to depict – in drawn-out form – the gut-wrenching moment that she arrives under escort in foreign territory, where she is awaited by her new husband and his entourage. Wang Zhaojun's story stands as a trope for what China must be prepared to offer in order to maintain peace and stability with her neighbours.

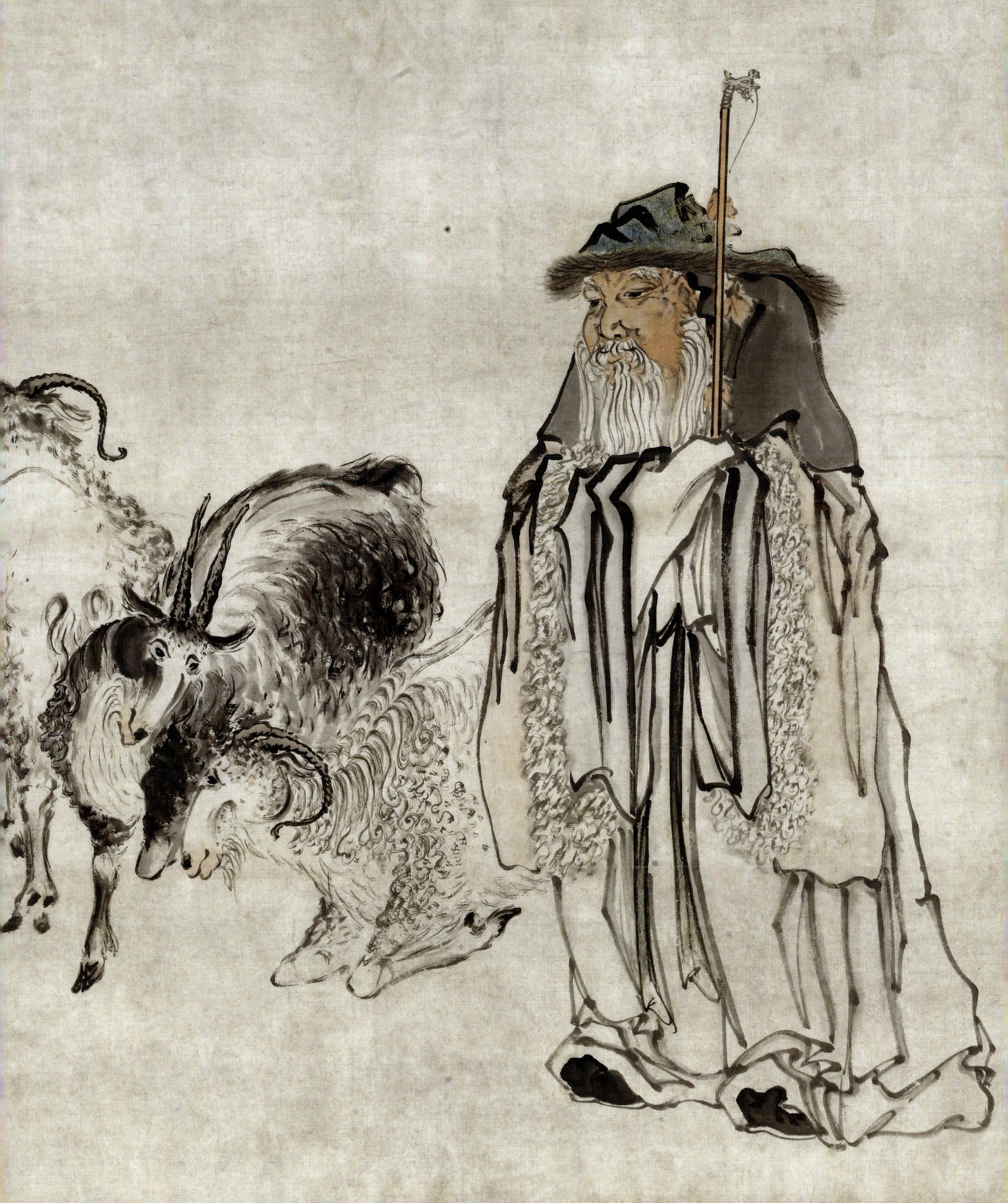

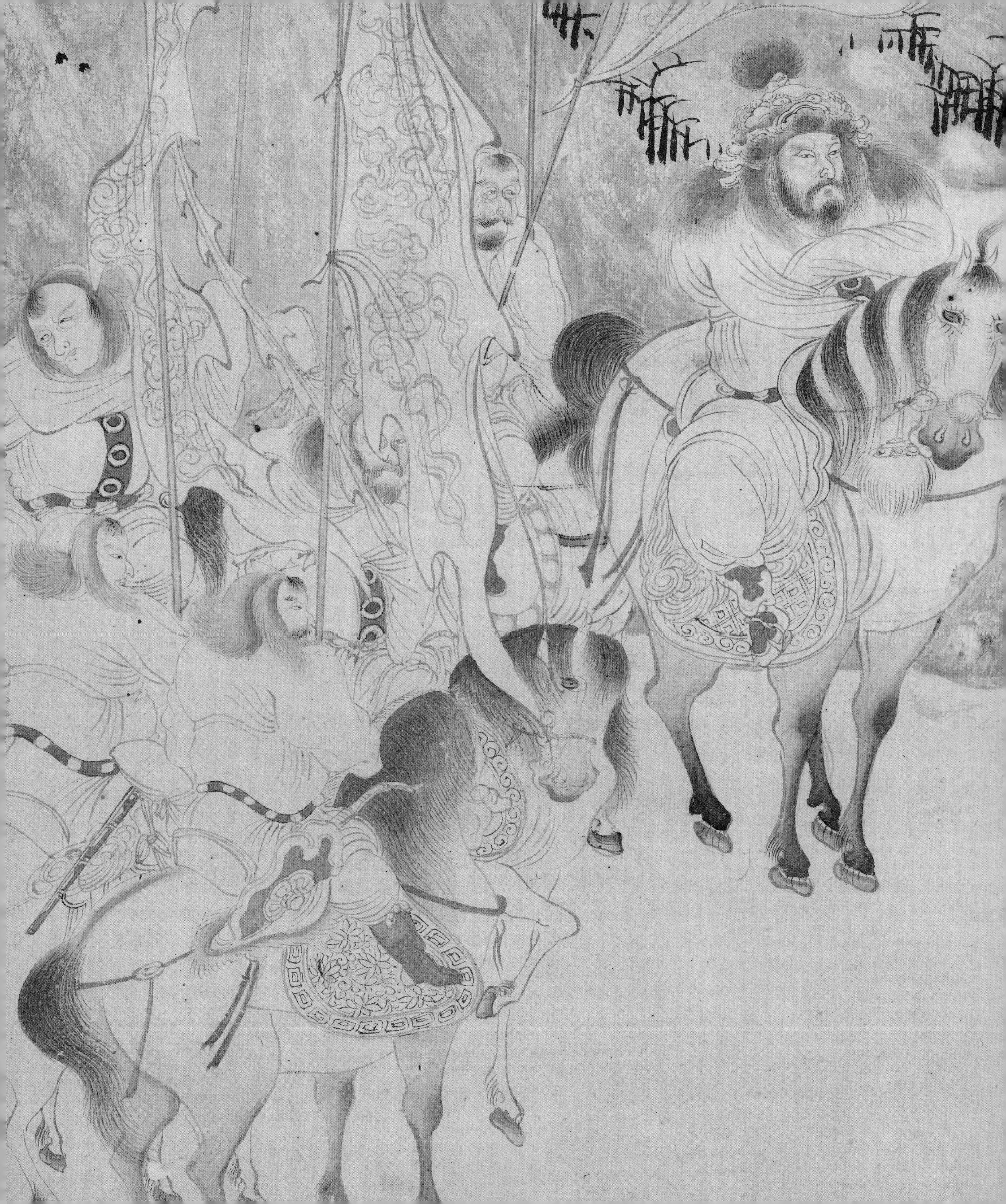

A linked but somewhat different Han narrative is provided by the hanging scroll, *Wenji Returning to China* (below), dated 1766, during the mid Qianlong period, by the little known painter Li Yao (active 1736–95). This refers to the story of the poet Cai Yan, also known as Wenji (b. 177), daughter of Cai Yong, a famous scholar of the Eastern (or Later) Han period (25–220). During the troubled break-up of the Han dynasty, she was abducted from her house during a raid on the capital in 195, ending up in the hands of the Xiongnu nomads. Thereafter, Cai Yan lived for twelve years in the steppe as a chieftain's wife, bearing him two children.[13]

After establishing his power base in north China, the notorious warlord Cao Cao (155–220), a friend of the late Cai Yong, wished her to return to China to participate in the compilation of the *Continuation of the Han History (Xu Han shu)*. He sent an embassy to ransom her, and she did return home – but without her children, who the Xiongnu would not permit to leave. Cai Yan is believed to have been the author of a

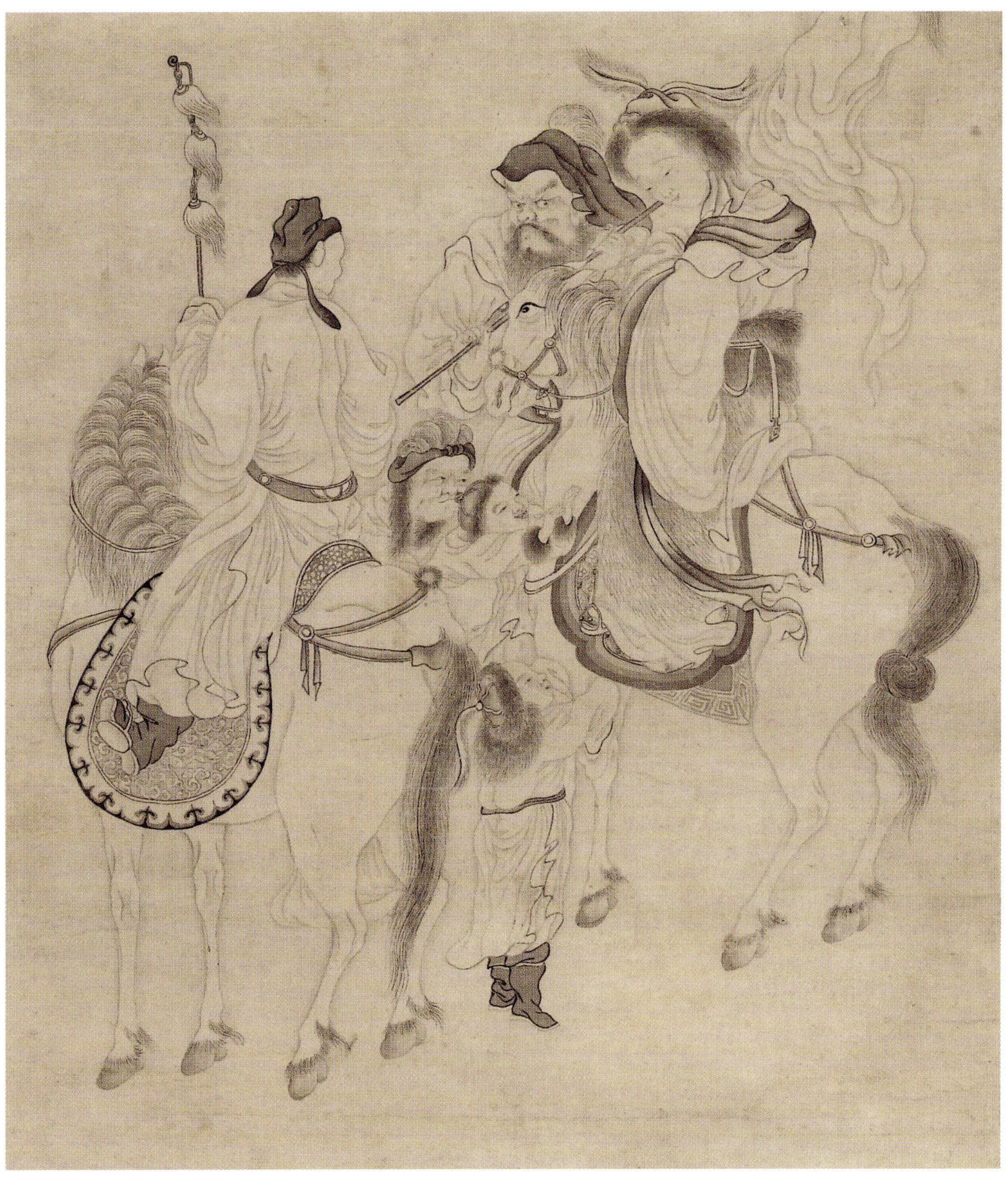

OPPOSITE: The Xiongnu chieftain and his retinue awaiting the arrival of Lady Zhaojun, from You Qiu, *Lady Zhaojun Leaves China* (Cat. 32, detail)

RIGHT: Li Yao, *Wenji Returning to China* (Cat. 19, detail)

OPPOSITE: Hua Yan, *Golden Valley Garden* (Cat. 12, detail)

famous set of classical tunes, 'Eighteen Songs of a Nomad Flute' (*Hujia shiba pai*), which is also the title of a number of narrative paintings dating from the Song period, illustrating the story of her abduction, captivity and ransom, and her harrowing decision to return 'home' to China without her beloved children.[14]

The final collapse of the Han dynasty in the early third century gave way to several hundred years of relative political instability, as a series of short-lived Chinese and non-Chinese regimes succeeded one another in north and south China. Yet, the Three Kingdoms and Wei-Jin periods were also times of richness and profound innovation in intellectual, cultural and religious life. Art and individualism flourished as new ideas arrived with Buddhism from the west, challenging and stimulating native systems of thought. The 'Seven Worthies of the Bamboo Grove' was a likely fictitious grouping of eminent figures of this period, a coterie of free-thinking, free-spirited neo-Daoist hermits of the Cao-Wei period (220–65) who gathered at the house of Xi Kang (223–62).[15] Their reclusive, dissipated lifestyles were seen as seditious in that they were effectively criticising the government by refusing to take part in it, and their supposed leader was later executed. The name of the group was recorded as early as in Liu Yiqing's (403–44) collection of anecdotes, *A New Account of Tales of the World (Shishuo xinyu)*,[16] and this was clearly a popular artistic subject in the southern capital, having been depicted in the later fifth century in a stamped brick picture found in 1960 near Nanjing.[17] In the present exhibition, the late Ming scholar-artist Li Shida's (1550–after 1623) *Seven Worthies of the Bamboo Grove* (pp. 32–33; also Cat. 18), dated 1616, is a technically accomplished, colourful illustration of the grouping.

The Suzhou artist Li Shida passed the elite 'presented scholar' (*jinshi*) examination in the second year of the Wanli reign (1574) and lived to be over eighty years old. This painting dates to late in the Wanli period (1573–1620), when the power of the Ming imperium was much weakened, in part by partisan politics and factionalism, but also by the refusal of the long-lived Wanli emperor to fulfil the traditional role of a monarch so cherished by the scholar-official bureaucracy. This was a period when strange and unusual styles and irony were prevalent in art, while art and culture were also fast becoming commodities. This painting can be interpreted as an autobiographic commentary on contemporary politics, since, like the 'seven worthies', Li Shida himself suffered as a result of showing disdain for the inner court. It is said that he refused to paint for the aristocracy. During the Wanli period, when the senior court eunuch Sun Long visited Suzhou, other literati answered his summons out of fear, and only Li Shida failed to pay his respects effusively. Not long later he was arrested, but luckily was released through the intervention of his friends.[18]

The issue of conflict between centre and periphery, or court and provinces, resurfaces in a later, Qing painting of another story from the Wei-Jin period, namely Hua Yan's (1682–1756) *Golden Valley Garden* (opposite), dated 1732. Although not a native of or permanent resident in the city of Yangzhou, Hua Yan is counted among the Yangzhou painters, and was one of the most distinctive artists active there during the first half of the eighteenth century. This painting dates to the late Yongzheng reign.

The story of the fabulously wealthy but unrestrained official Shi Chong (249–300) and Green Pearl, his dazzlingly beautiful concubine, also an accomplished flautist, is recorded in Shi Chong's biography in *Jin Dynasty History* (*Jin shu*).[19] After the Prince

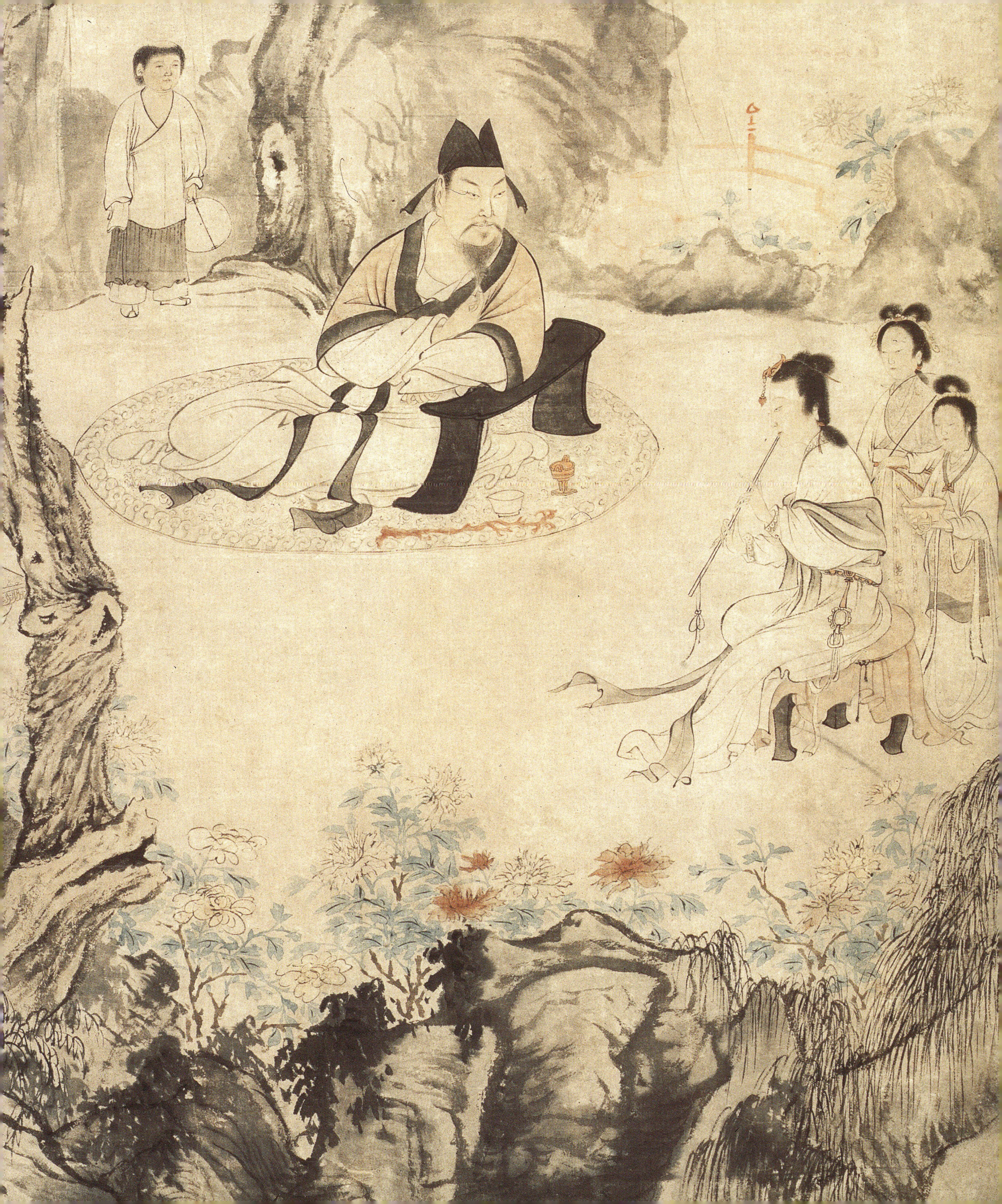

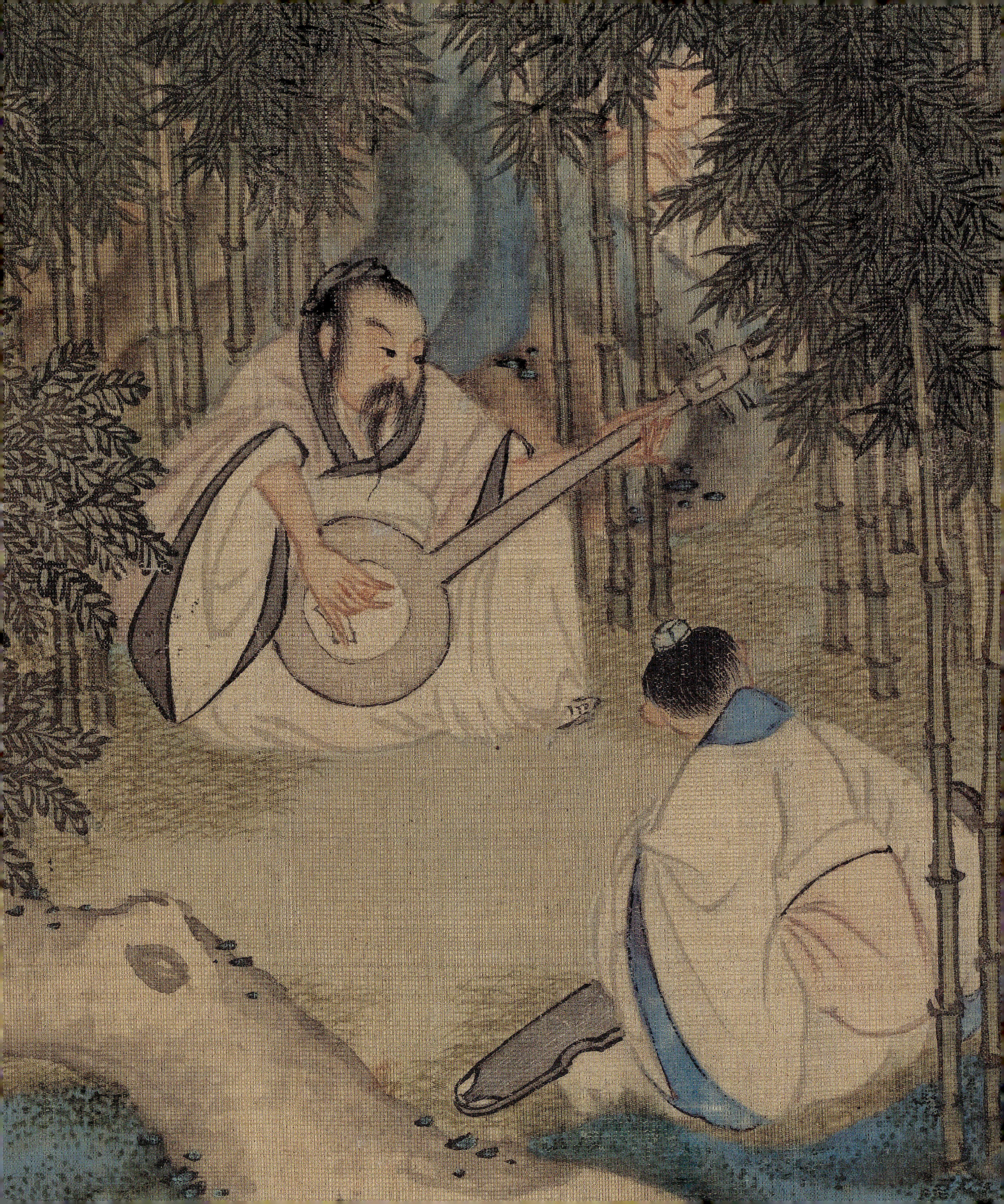

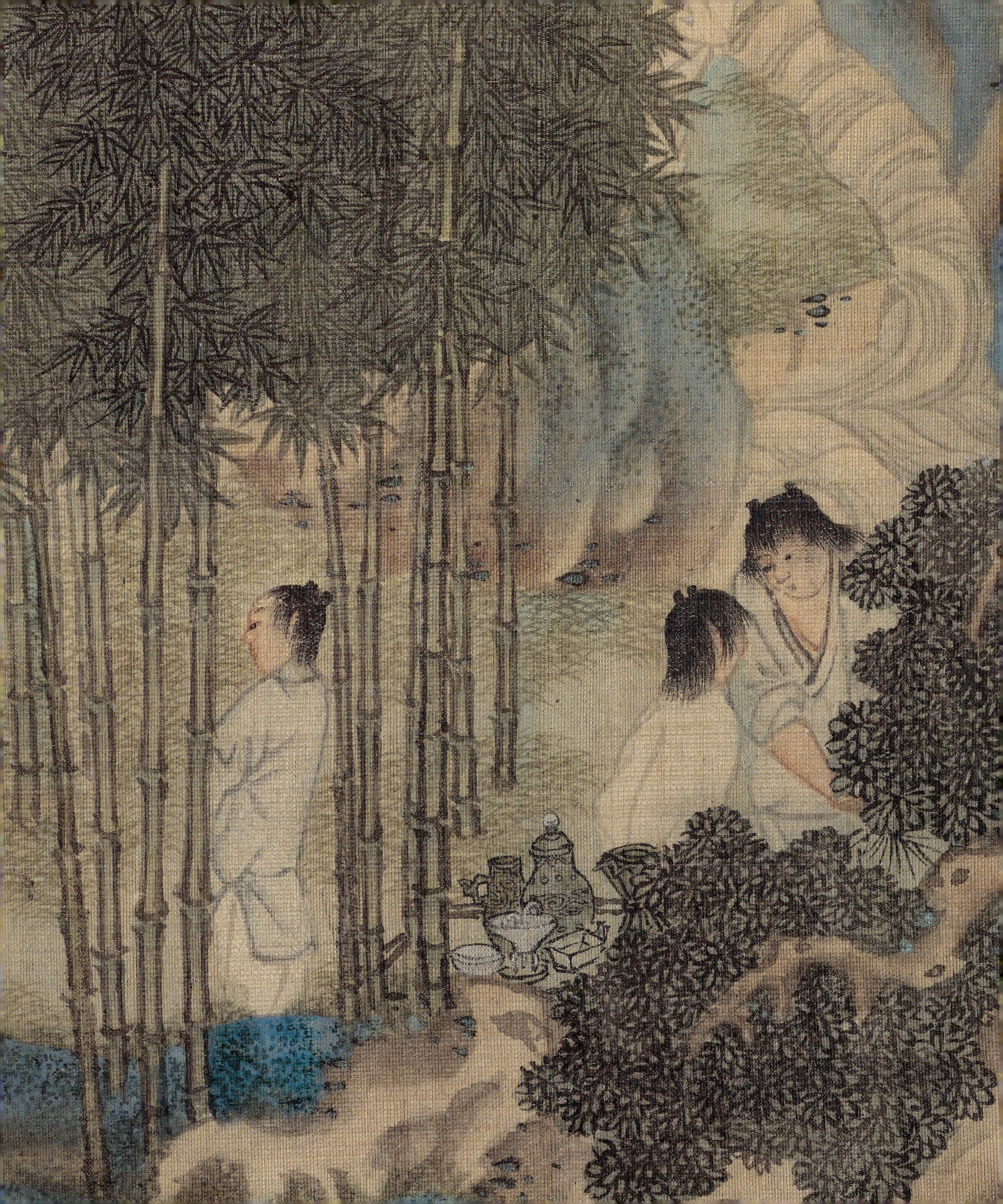

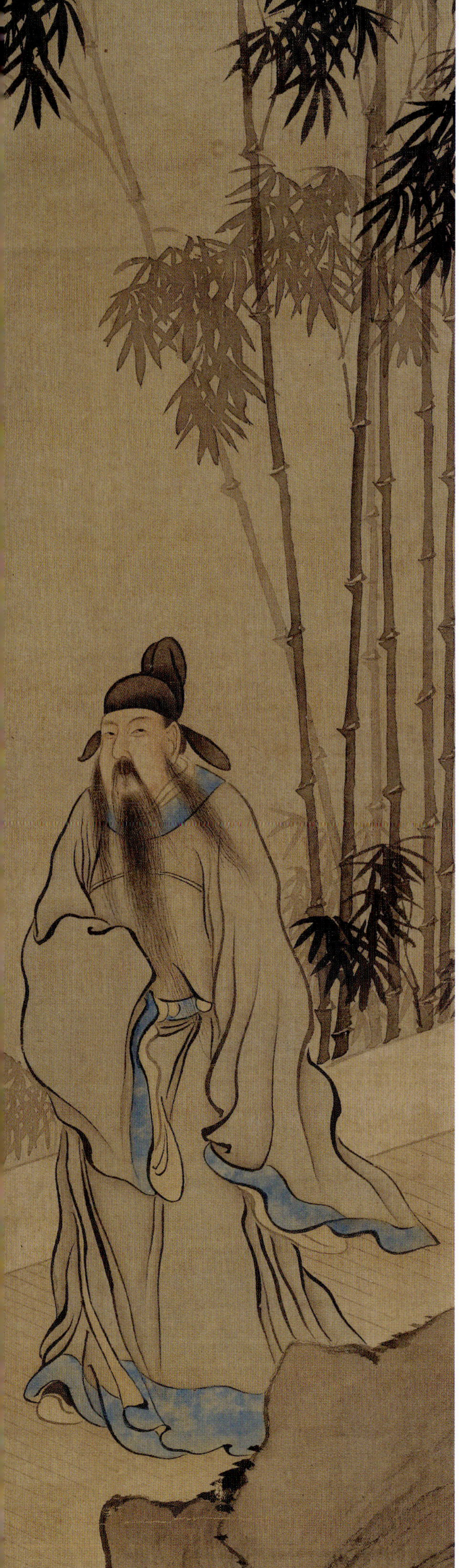

of Zhao, Sima Lun (d. 301), had usurped power at the Western Jin court, he quarrelled with Shi Chong's nephew. The prince's close ally Sun Xiu, seemingly taking advantage of the situation, sent an envoy to bring him Green Pearl. Shi Chong was staying at his summer villa at Golden Valley near Luoyang, where he was wont to entertain on a lavish scale, and to hold the elegant gatherings that were a model for Wang Xizhi's (321–79) Orchid Pavilion Gathering.[20] Shi Chong twice managed to dismiss the envoy, stating that he loved Green Pearl and that she was not available. Sun Xiu then accused Shi Chong of treason before the prince, demanding his arrest. Shi Chong was dining in a tower when the troops arrived to detain him. Rather than be taken, the loyal concubine Green Pearl threw herself to her death from the tower. Not long later, Shi Chong and his entire family were publicly executed.

In the painting, Shi Chong is seated in the centre leaning upon an armrest, and listening to Green Pearl playing her flute. Servant boys and girls stand about in attendance. The rounded scene is bounded by a circle of rocks and plants, as well as trees to the left, which form a kind of canopy in the distinctive mode of the artist. In an apt reference to very early painting, this circular device echoes the form of the 'space cell', a stylised circular space that early painters used to render small clusters of buildings, but also to highlight figures within the landscape. Yet, such is the sense of modernity in the painting, of freedom from the weight of tradition, that this might also be read as a purely formal visual play.

Although he could be capricious and cruel, Shi Chong is held up in history as a cultured man who deeply appreciated female beauty and poetry (he is the author of an 'Ode to Bright Lady Wang' (*Wang Mingjun ci*) about Wang Zhaojun, encountered above) – as well as music and fine food. He is also an example of how even extraordinary wealth, political connections and cultural achievements are sometimes not enough to protect an individual from those in power, and indeed how wealth and prominence may in themselves be what brings calamity upon oneself and one's family. Hua Yan was an artist in Yangzhou, a city made extraordinarily wealthy by its salt monopoly. The salt merchants were chief among the patrons of a distinctive 'eccentric' mode practised by the Yangzhou School artists. While many of the parallels between Shi Chong and these wealthy individuals would have flattered the latter, the painting also carried with it an implied warning about the limits to the influence of wealth and culture.

The exhibition includes two paintings entitled *Peach-blossom Spring* that might have been included in this section (they appear in the next), but it is worth introducing them here first for the insight they provide into another kind of journey or crossing within the world of the living. 'Peach-blossom Spring' (*Taohua yuan*) is the topic of a prose work by the early landscape poet Tao Qian (Tao Yuanming; 365–427) about a paradise world set within the real world, but nigh impossible to reach. The story, set in the Taiyuan period (376–96), during the reign of Xiaowudi of the Eastern Jin dynasty, relates how a fisherman of Wuling by chance discovered a cave, at the end of which lay a utopian world. After a stay there, he returned home, finding only disappointment in the real world; yet, he was unable to find his way back to the paradise again. The illustrations are a small fan painting by Ding Yunpeng and a jewel-like hanging scroll painting by Gu Fuzhen.

This section closes with a leap forward in time to the late Northern Song (960–1127).

PREVIOUS PAGES: Li Shida, *Seven Worthies of the Bamboo Grove* (Cat. 18, detail)

OPPOSITE: Huang Shanshou, *Returning to the Academy by 'Golden Lotus' Lamplight* (Cat. 14, detail)

A significant social and political development that took place over the tenth and eleventh centuries was the emergence, through a system of meritocratic appointments, of a new social class of scholar-officials, or literati (*shi*). These were classically or Confucian-educated men who, following success in the official examinations for the bureaucracy, filled the ranks of the civil service and acted as guardians of China's tradition of principled statecraft, where necessary by opposing the pragmatism of royal houses. The late Northern Song government is remembered for its partisan polity, involving a series of power struggles at court between conservatives and reformers.

Among the literati, a small minority of the most highly accomplished men of arts and letters were known as *wenren* ('men of culture'), including Su Shi (1037–1101), a towering poet, calligrapher, painter and statesman.[21] Part of the reason why Su Shi has been so admired in China is because of the vicissitudes of his political career, during which he was part of the conservative faction opposed to the reforms of Wang Anshi (1021–86). Later, we will come to a painting which marks his triumphant return to office following a period of exile, after the deaths of emperor Shenzong (r. 1068–85) and Wang Anshi (p. 34; also Cat. 14), and another about a literary gathering supposedly attended by Su Shi and the other maestri of the Northern Song art world (see Cat. 4). Here, we explore a painting that commemorates his life and poetry while in exile at Huangzhou on the Yangzi River in Hubei in the early 1080s, a banishment that resulted from a perceived slight towards the imperium in a poem. While in exile, Su Shi composed perhaps his best known pair of poems. The 'Former Red Cliff Ode' of 1082 recounts a boating excursion made with friends to the Red Cliff, a place steeped in history as the site of a famous battle at the end of the Han dynasty in which, against the odds, the allied forces of the south stopped the southern advance of the powerful northern warlord Cao Cao, encountered above. The melancholic 'Latter Red Cliff Ode' was composed a few years later after a solo visit.

The odes were first illustrated in literati painting by Qiao Zhongchang, in a version in handscroll format of about 1123.[22] Since then, the subject has been a standard of the literati repertoire, often in collaborative scrolls which include a calligraphic transcription of the text and a painting mounted together. Huang Shen's large hanging scroll painting, dated 1759, is entitled *Night Excursion to the Red Cliffs* (Cat. 15).[23] It shows Su Shi literally under the Red Cliff in a small covered boat with a single boatman for companionship. The particular quality of Huang Shen's painting practice is apparent, especially in the execution of the figures. The brushwork has a highly mannered appearance akin to the random-looking, but in fact highly specific forms of Chinese cursive calligraphy, yet, at the same time, these marks capture and convey the physical presence of the figures – the boatman as he struggles with his tiller and Su Shi as he bends his knees to the gentle strake of the boat's heel.

Religious Lore and Legends of the Supernatural

Many of the tales illustrated in these paintings are literary, having their sources in ancient poetry forms like the *Songs of the South*, or else in literary prose little related to the vernacular language. However, we also include paintings which illustrate folklore and legends, some of an explicit or else quasi-religious nature. To introduce this theme and emphasise the role of oral history, we might point to one notably vernacular picture in the exhibition, which stands somewhat apart from the set of educated, humanistic values we traditionally find in painting, namely *Quarrelling on Two Sides of a River* (below), by the little known Qing artist, Hu Fen.[24] Despite its title, it has no specific, identified tale as its subject. Rather, it is a kind of typical or genre scene from rural life in traditional China: a stand-off – across a stream – of raised voices and angry gestures between the people of two neighbouring villages. Ling Lizhong describes how such a scene of dispute barely short of violence could have come about – through a simple disagreement between village children, and he suggests how the trope of a stream as a boundary line between villages, as the symbol of division and strife between rural communities, is common the world over. But beyond its genre-like quality, the painting also has a mini-narrative or narratives taking place inside it, with numerous vignette-like scenes happening simultaneously on either side of the stream. The sting implied

Hu Fen, *Quarrelling on Two Sides of a River* (Cat. 10, detail)

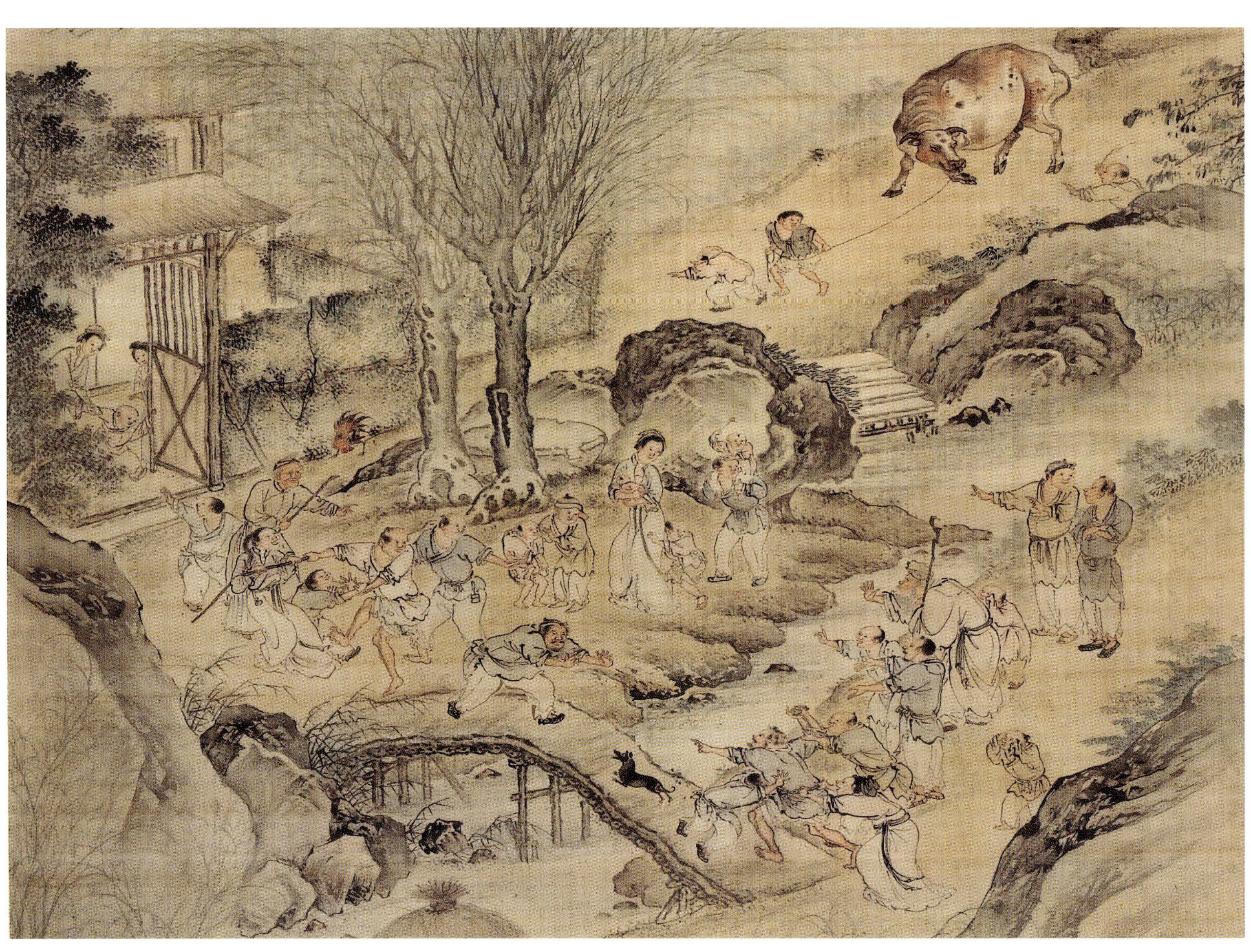

by the threat of violence is somehow drawn by the presence of children, and especially by their antics. In one humorous and naturalistic moment, a small boy is raising his skirts in order to urinate in the direction of the 'enemy'; this has been noticed by an adult close at hand, who puts out an arm to restrain the boy, as if the act of urination were crossing a line of acceptability, even in the context of this heated situation. There is a terrific sense of fun, here, in the finely observed detailing, which is wholly refreshing in an artwork.

Zhang Ling's (?–before 1529) *The Weaver Girl* (Cat. 35), painted in the mid-Ming Hongzhi reign in 1504, is an example of a folkloric tale illustrated in a painting. It presents an image of the heroine from the legend of the Cowherd (Niulang) and the Weaver Girl (Zhinü), who are the stars Altair and Vega, which lie on either side of the Milky Way. There are different versions of this ancient tale, but in essence it begins when the two fall in love, marry and have children.[25] However, the Weaver Girl's father, the god of heaven (sometimes her mother), becomes angered that she has ignored her heavenly duty of weaving clouds. He creates the Milky Way across the sky, separating the couple forever – a scene depicted in an album leaf in the exhibition (below). However, once a year on the 'night of sevens' (*qixi* – the seventh night of the seventh month in the lunar calendar) they are reunited, an occasion celebrated across East Asia in a manner akin to Valentine's Day in the west. Zhang Ling's painting was likely enough

The creation of the Milky Way in Guo Xu, *Album of Various Subjects* (Cat. 9, leaf 11)

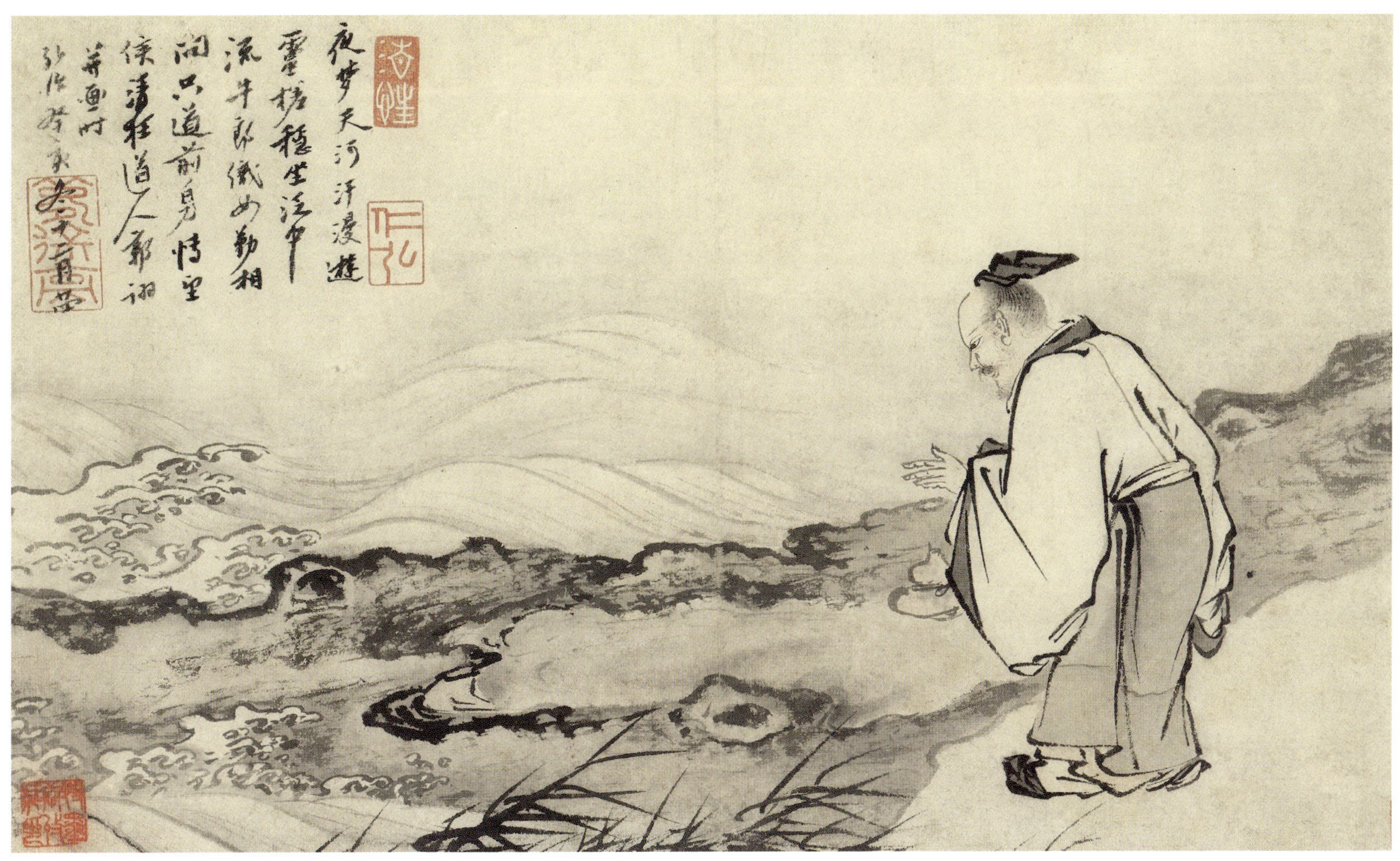

done for this occasion in 1504, since it is dated 'the beginning of autumn', referring to the start of the seventh month in the lunar calendar.

In dynastic China, this festival was especially observed by young women who used the opportunity to 'plead for skills', such as in embroidery and other handicrafts, which would help them secure a good husband or else advancement within a polygamous, strictly hierarchical household. Ding Guanpeng's court painting is an imperial Qianlong commemoration of the festival (below). The festival is strongly associated with court romance, as its inclusion in the famous ballad, 'Song of Lasting Sorrow' (*Chang hen ge*), by the Tang poet Bai Juyi (772–846) attests. 'Song of Lasting Sorrow' retells the story of the passionate love-affair between Tang emperor Minghuang (r. 712–56) and his consort, the *femme fatale* Yang Guifei, mentioned earlier. Historically, Yang Guifei was executed during the An Lushan rebellion in 756 and the emperor abdicated in favour of his son, but in this romantic ballad the mournful retired emperor sends a wizard to bring her spirit back to him. The wizard finds her in the isles of the

Ding Guanpeng, *Ladies on the 'Night of Sevens' Pleading for Skills* (Cat. 6, detail)

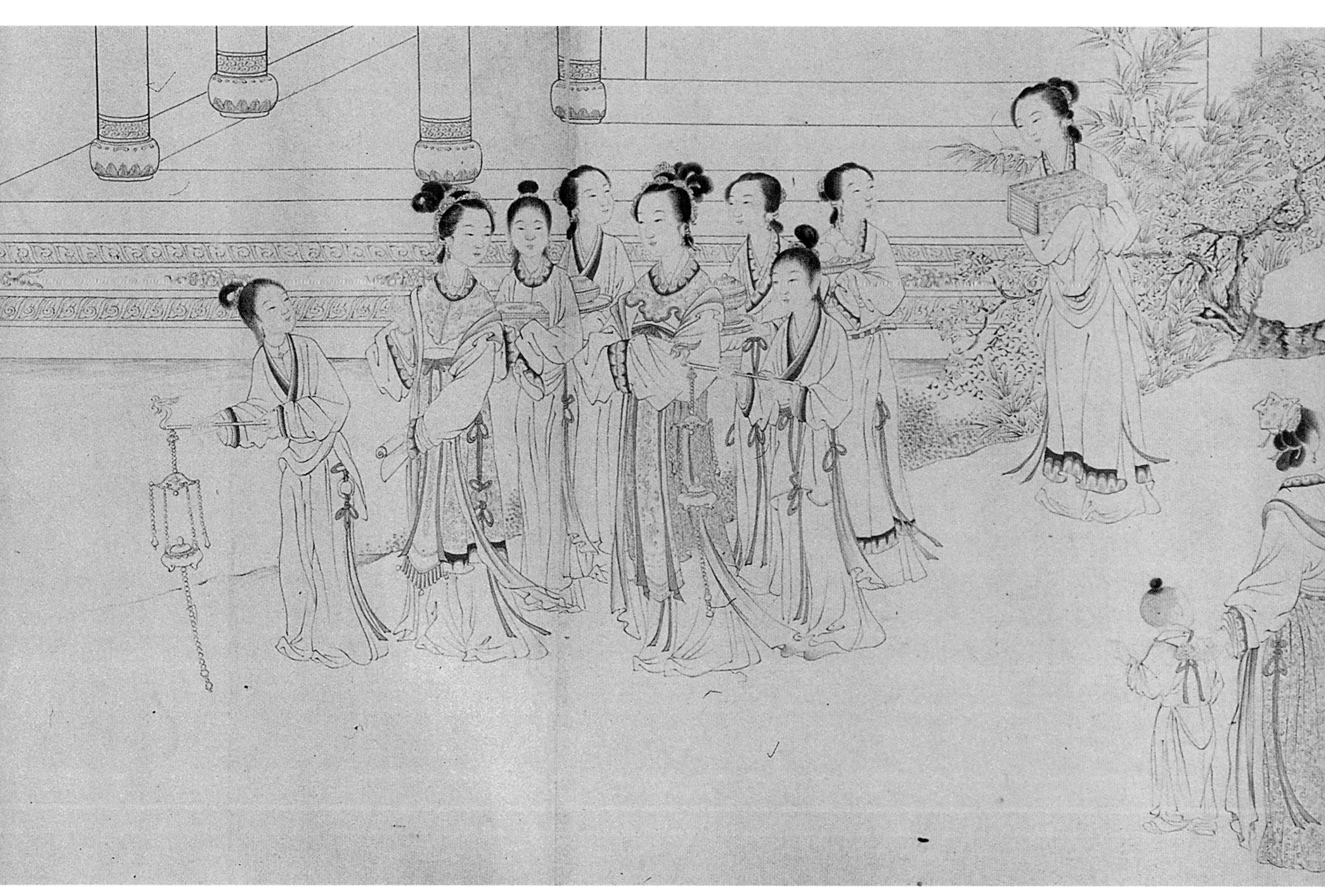

immortals but is unable to return with her. Instead, she gives him love tokens to present to the retired emperor.

According to the companion piece, 'An Account to Go with the "Song of Lasting Sorrow"' by Bai Juyi's friend Chen Hong (early ninth century), when the wizard then asks Yang Guifei for a private memory as proof for the emperor, recalling this legend, she replies:[26] 'Back in the tenth year of the Tianbao Reign [752], I was attending on His Majesty, who had gone to the palace on Mount Li to escape the heat. It was autumn, in the seventh month, the evening when the Oxherd and the Weaver Star meet. It was the custom of the people of Qin on that night to spread out embroidery and brocade, to put out food and drink, to set up flowers and melons, and to burn incense in the yard – they call this 'begging for deftness'. Those of the inner palace hold this custom in particularly high regard. It was almost midnight; and the guards and attendants in the eastern and western cloisters had been dismissed. I was waiting on His Majesty alone. His Majesty stood there, leaning on his shoulder, then looked up at the heavens and was touched by the legend of the Oxherd and the Weaver Star. We then made a secret vow to one another, a wish that we could be husband and wife in every lifetime. When we stopped speaking, we held hands, and each of us was sobbing. Only the Emperor knows of this.' The envoy returns and relays this to Minghuang. Much afflicted by grief, he dies shortly afterwards. Paintings like this one, which we may imagine were brought out for display on the 'night of sevens', had the power to evoke such archetypal romances.[27]

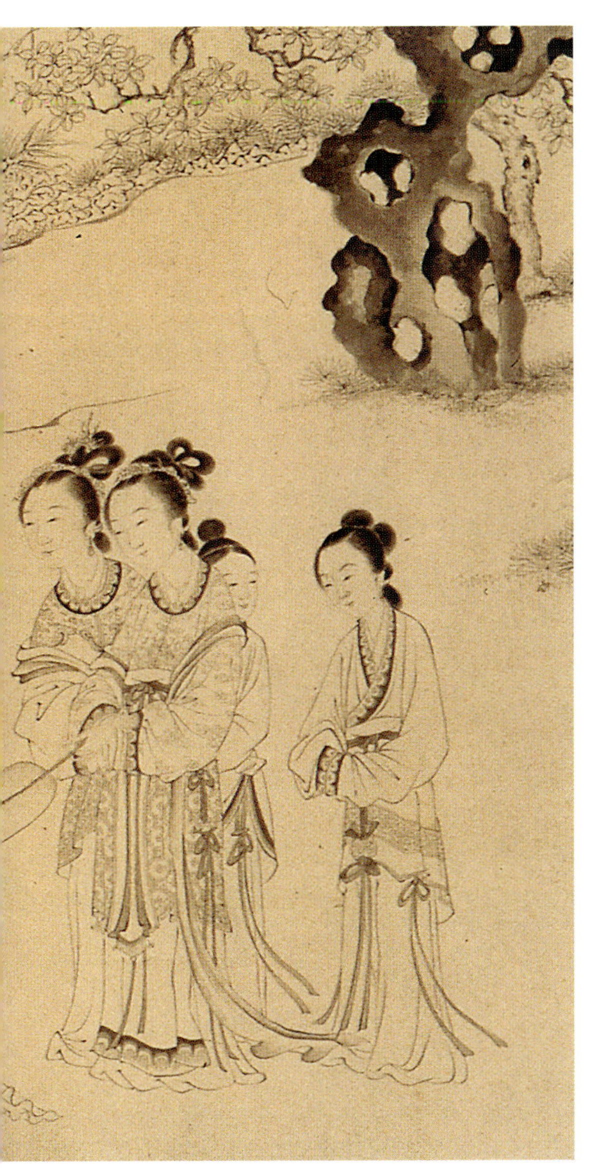

Reflecting the rich exchange of ideas over many centuries between China's three leading religious traditions, Confucianism, Buddhism and Daoism, as well as syncretic practices of worship and resistance to ideas of apostasy, the notion of 'Three Religions united as one' (*San jiao he yi*) became increasingly popular in the Song dynasty (960–1279). Seemingly, the idea of combining neo-Confucian virtue-ethics, Daoist mystical thought and Buddhist teachings on emptiness and rebirth, which were already somewhat interwoven, had broad appeal. In visual culture, this manifested in imaginary triple portraits of the three, roughly contemporary founders of the religions – Confucius, Laozi and the historical Buddha, Siddhartha Gautama. These, in turn, formed the basis of many later picture titles popular across East Asia, such as the 'three vinegar tasters' (*sansuan*), in which the three all tasted one beverage, but each reacted differently, according to their respective religions. Another similar subject was the 'three laughers of Tiger Ravine' (*Huxi sanxiao*).[28]

A number of paintings relate to both elite and popular Buddhist tales and lore. The stories date from the time of Buddhism's arrival in China – Ren Yi's picture of the stylish monk Zhidun, for instance (see Cat. 24), to which we come later.[29] The late Ming artist Li Lin (1558–after 1636) provides a charming scene of children surrounding the so-called laughing Buddha, Budai, in *The Laughing Buddha Budai Surrounded by Children* (Cat. 17). The popular story of Budai, a Chinese monk who became known by the quirky nickname 'cloth-bag', as Ling Lizhong describes, is informative about how Buddhist beliefs and values that originated in India became, over many centuries, 'domesticated' in the context of Chinese society.

Another Buddhist story painting, an artwork dating from the early twentieth century, is Wang Zhen's (1867–1938) *Bodhidharma Meditating Before a Wall* (p. 41).[30]

OPPOSITE: Wang Zhen, *Bodhidharma Meditating Before a Wall* (Cat. 30, detail)

Wang Zhen began his career working in a scroll mounting shop, where he was able to copy works by Ren Yi, then Shanghai's leading painter.[31] He later worked his way up in banking and shipping and, after the turn of the twentieth century, became a representative for Japanese trading firms in the city, including Mitsubishi. An influential businessman and philanthropist, he used the growing financial rewards of his business success to support artists in Shanghai and political change, including the 1911 revolution which overthrew the Qing, all the while continuing to paint and to adhere as a devout layman to Buddhist teachings.

Wang Zhen's *Bodhidharma* of 1923 depicts the Buddhist monk from southern India who brought Chan Buddhist teaching to China in the early fifth century, and became China's first Chan Buddhist patriarch. Bodhidharma travelled to the Northern Wei, after his teaching did not find favour in southern China; this is why he is sometimes portrayed in China and Japan crossing the Yangzi River on a reed. Here, he is seated on a powerful boulder overhanging a rock-strewn mountain torrent. The inscription contains a poem in four couplets of four lines on the spiritual dimensions of Bodhidharma's decade spent meditating in silence before a wall of stone. Echoing in places the *Heart Sutra*, it begins, 'Facing a wall for ten years, the five *skandhas* [causes of suffering] are all empty', and describes how, 'With his body he spoke the way', in his reaching enlightenment or spiritual awakening. A popular legend about this period of meditation relates that on one occasion when he fell asleep, he cut off and discarded his eyelids, which grew into tea bushes. Thereafter, drinking tea became the Chan or Zen monk's way to stay awake during long periods of meditation.[32]

Like the boulder, the figure is executed in outline by coarse broad brushstrokes; only the boulder is filled in, textured by the dots of repeated stabs with a wet brush. The patriarch's robe is pure white. His shoulders hunched and his foreign, bearded face assuming a look of fierce concentration, the figure is silhouetted by the white vapours behind and hemmed in by the overhanging cliff and two-column inscription to each side. The calligraphically painted strokes of the figure-in-landscape seem to waver – in our perception – between forms that render pictorial images and those that disintegrate into vibrant abstractions of the media.

As with the Buddhist tales, the Daoist-themed 'story paintings' range in date and social appeal across Chinese history. *Yellow Crane Tower*, an early Ming court painting by An Zhengwen (Cat. 1), commemorates one of the great architectural towers of southern China, which stands on a hill over the Yangzi River in Hubei Province, and was associated historically with a tale of a Daoist immortal who flew from there on a crane, never to return. In the painting, this story is made real by being depicted in the present, for the immortal on his crane is seen flying off, a scene witnessed by many of those in and about the tower. Such a painting would have been made to hang in a palace or official building in the early Ming capital. From the same academic school of painting, the Zhe School, and also related to Daoist themes, are the anonymous Ming painting of Zhuge Liang emerging from mountains at the end of the Han dynasty (*Kongming Leaving the Mountains*; Cat. 2) and the later Ming Zhe-School artist Wang Zhao's picture of the popular immortal, Li Tieguai of the Sui dynasty (581–618), in *Iron-crutch Li* (Cat. 29).[33]

Daoist immortals, as well as Daoist deities (they were often confused in later times), were also the subject of popular groupings, such as the so-called Eight Immortals,

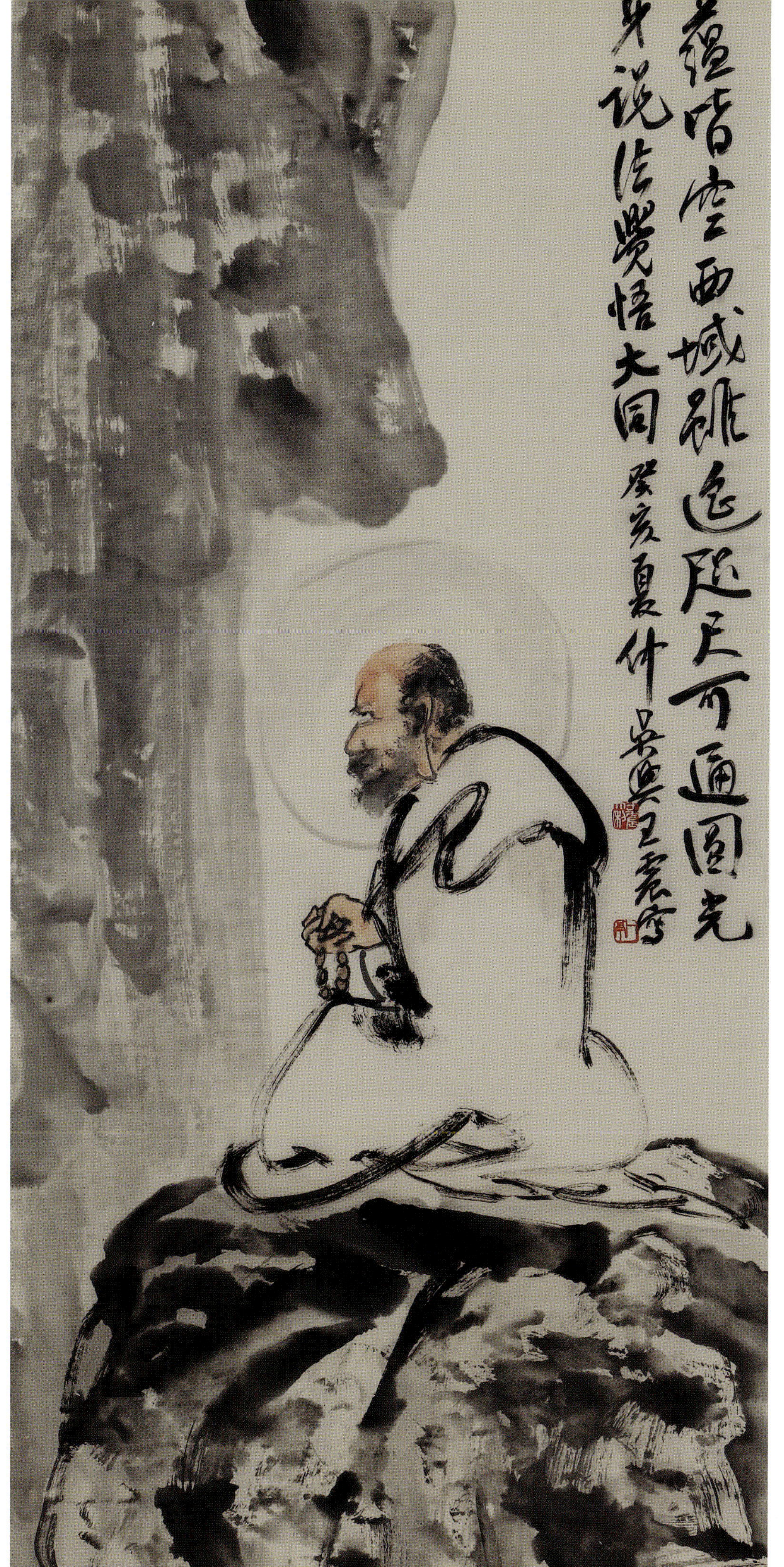

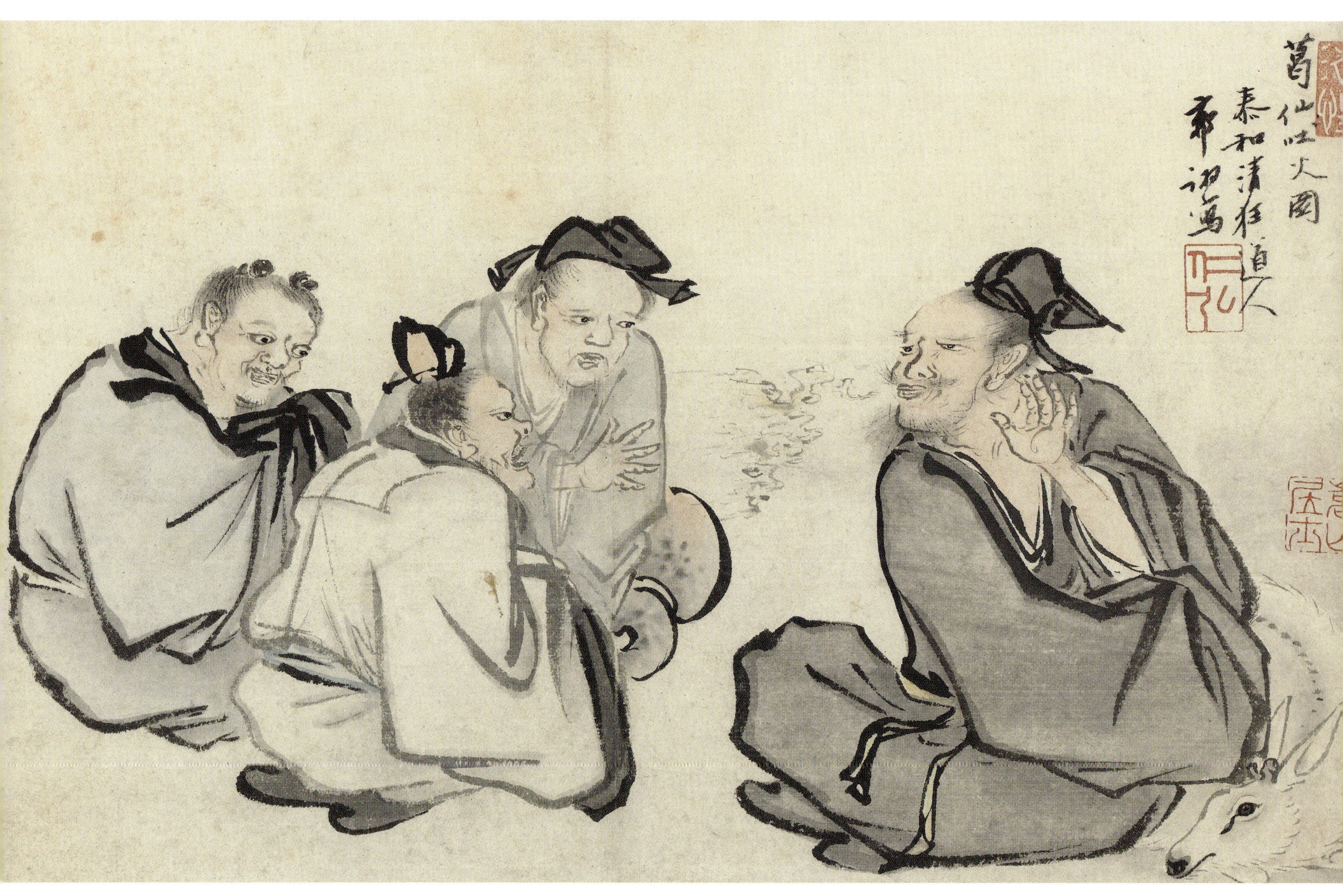

Guo Xu, 'Immortal Ge spitting fire', *Album of Various Subjects* (Cat. 9, leaf 7, detail)

although there were more than this number. Two pictorial albums in the exhibition, both dating to about the mid-Ming dynasty, depict the serried ranks of Daoist immortals and deities, but under generic Chinese titles like 'album of miscellaneous paintings' (*zahua ce*). These are *Album of Various Subjects* by Guo Xu (1456–*c.*1529) and Zhang Lu's (1464–1538) *Daoist Immortals and Natural Symbols.*[34]

Guo Xu's album (Cat. 9) contains scenes of Daoist immortals and figures from history and legend, including: 'Immortal Ge spitting fire' (above), about Ge Xuan (164–244), the renowned scholar and Daoist adept, who was able to transform food when he spat it out; the legendary Fuxi, who discovered the eight trigrams (*bagua*) that were the basis for ancient divination and early writing handed down in the Confucian classic, *Book of Changes (Yijing)*; 'Immortal Qiu', a picture of Qiu Chuji, one of the Daoist patriarchs of north China – a saviour of lives who is remembered for his benign influence on Genghis Khan; 'Playing a flute, riding a buffalo'; 'Northern frontier'; 'Drunken immortal', a portrait of a Zhong Kui-like immortal staggering along with the support of one of his demon helpers; 'Seeking a suitable phrase' (Mi ju); 'Mi Fu admiring a rock', a picture of the Northern Song literatus and calligrapher; 'Night's dream – river of Heaven', about the legend of the Weaver Girl and Cowherd; 'Shennong', the legendary father of agriculture; and 'An old lady feeds a hero', an anecdote from the impoverished early life of Han Xin (d. 196 BC), later a military commander under Liu Bang, founder of the Han dynasty, in which Han Xin is fed by an old woman who takes pity on his hunger.

Similarly, Zhang Lu's album of eighteen leaves (Cat. 36) contains named figures associated with specific stories, as well as generic figures. Leaves 3 and 4 portray, respectively, the gods of fortune (*fu*) and longevity (*shou*). Leaf 5 shows the popular figure of Liu Hai and his three-legged toad; leaf 6 illustrates an immortal riding a white deer; leaf 7 is a portrait of Liezi, the fifth-century-BC philosopher and author of an ancient text of the same name; leaves 8 and 9 show groupings of old men, respectively, the Four Greybeards of Mount Shang and 'five old men', referring to the Five Planets (p. 44). Most of the remaining leaves depict individuals from among the Eight Immortals. Leaf 10 features Immortal Woman Ma (p. 45 bottom); leaf 11, Li Tieguai, or Iron-crutch Li (p. 45 top); leaf 12 has a boy writing; leaf 13 shows an immortal sleeping on a rock – this is Cao Guojiu; leaf 14 depicts a seated immortal with double gourd, namely Zhongli Quan, usually dubbed the leader of the Eight Immortals and the teacher of Lü Dongbin (also known as Chunyang), who is pictured in leaf 15; leaf 16 has Lan Caihe; leaf 17 shows an old man seated on a skin, who is Elder Zhang Guo (Zhang Guo Lao), a man who had the ability to jump inside a gourd. The last leaf (18) shows an immortal, Qingyang Xianzi (literally, Green Goat Immortal), riding a long-haired goat.

The painting entitled *Three Immortals* (Cat. 27) is an imaginary triple portrait by the early Qing artist, Shen Shao (active 1662–1722), of immortals of the Tang period. The subjects are described by Ling Lizhong in his essay (see p. 14). Not much is known about the painter Shen Shao, other than that he was a pupil of the eminent portraitist Zeng Jing (1568–1650) but the fact that he has signed his painting 'Dizi Shen Shao', or 'Disciple Shen Shao', tells us that it was likely painted as a devotional act under the rubric of the Daoist religion. Another work by Shen Shao in the Shanghai Museum is a portrait of a Daoist deity, Guan Yu, who was a general under Liu Bei (161–223), whose forces defeated Cao Cao at the Battle of the Red Cliffs.[35]

Among the Daoist paintings of women in the exhibition is Cui Zizhong's (*c.*1574–1644) *Jade Woman among Clouds* (Cat. 5). The title of this painting, set in the heavens, tells us only that it is of a 'jade woman', a beautiful immortal of the skies. Her body robed in a voluminous white gown, which closes only loosely over her breasts, she stands on top of a vast cloud. Her hair is tied up in a topknot, and she wears a small hat tied under her chin with strings, and slippers on her unbound feet. Her body faces somewhat to the left but arcs gently to the right, almost like a waning crescent moon, as she gazes down over the cloud on the world. Her skin is pale and unblemished, and her face wears an expression of compassion and concern. The numinous cloud-form, echoing the hems and folds of her robe, descends to the lower right of the picture, meandering back and forth in piled up layers which are built up and textured by many feathery brush-strokes under light and dark washes. The continual and endless transformation of the cloud in this rarefied setting is suggestive for the interpretation of the image and its potency before viewers.

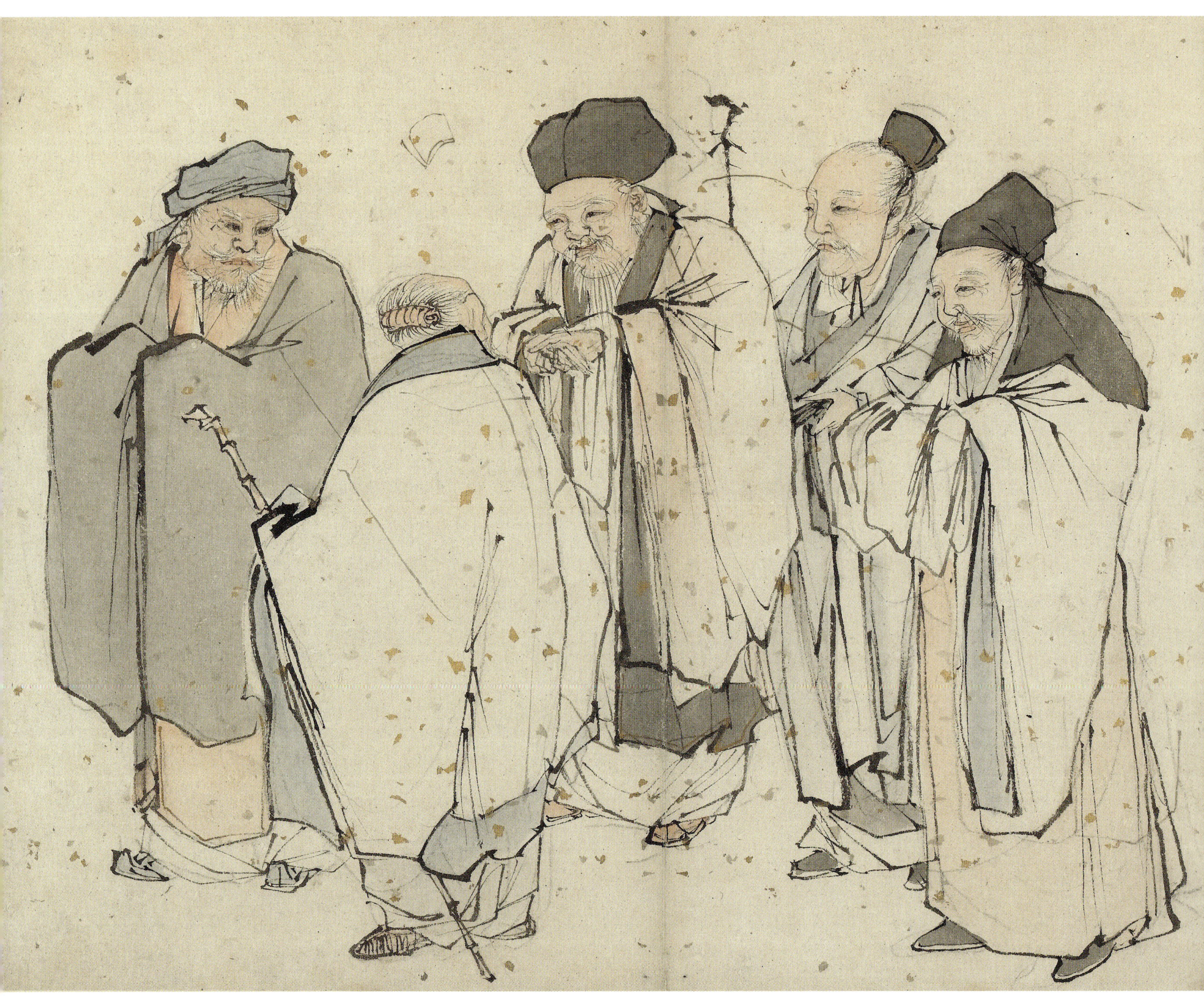

ABOVE: Zhang Lu, 'The Five Planets', *Daoist Immortals and Natural Symbols* (Cat. 36, leaf 9, detail)

OPPOSITE TOP: Zhang Lu, 'Li Tieguai', *Daoist Immortals and Natural Symbols* (Cat. 36, leaf 11)

OPPOSITE BELOW: Zhang Lu, 'Immortal Woman Ma', *Daoist Immortals and Natural Symbols* (Cat. 36, leaf 10)

According to the artist's inscription above the figure, she is the Queen Mother of the West (Xiwangmu), a royal among the pantheon of immortals in ancient legend who dwells among rainbow-coloured clouds.[36] Belief in some kind of potent, fearsome royal deity of the west probably dates to prehistoric times in China, while the earliest textual sources describe a human figure with the teeth of tiger, a leopard's tail and an awesome cry, indicating that she has undergone many transformations in the popular imagination over thousands of years, gradually becoming linked with the cult of

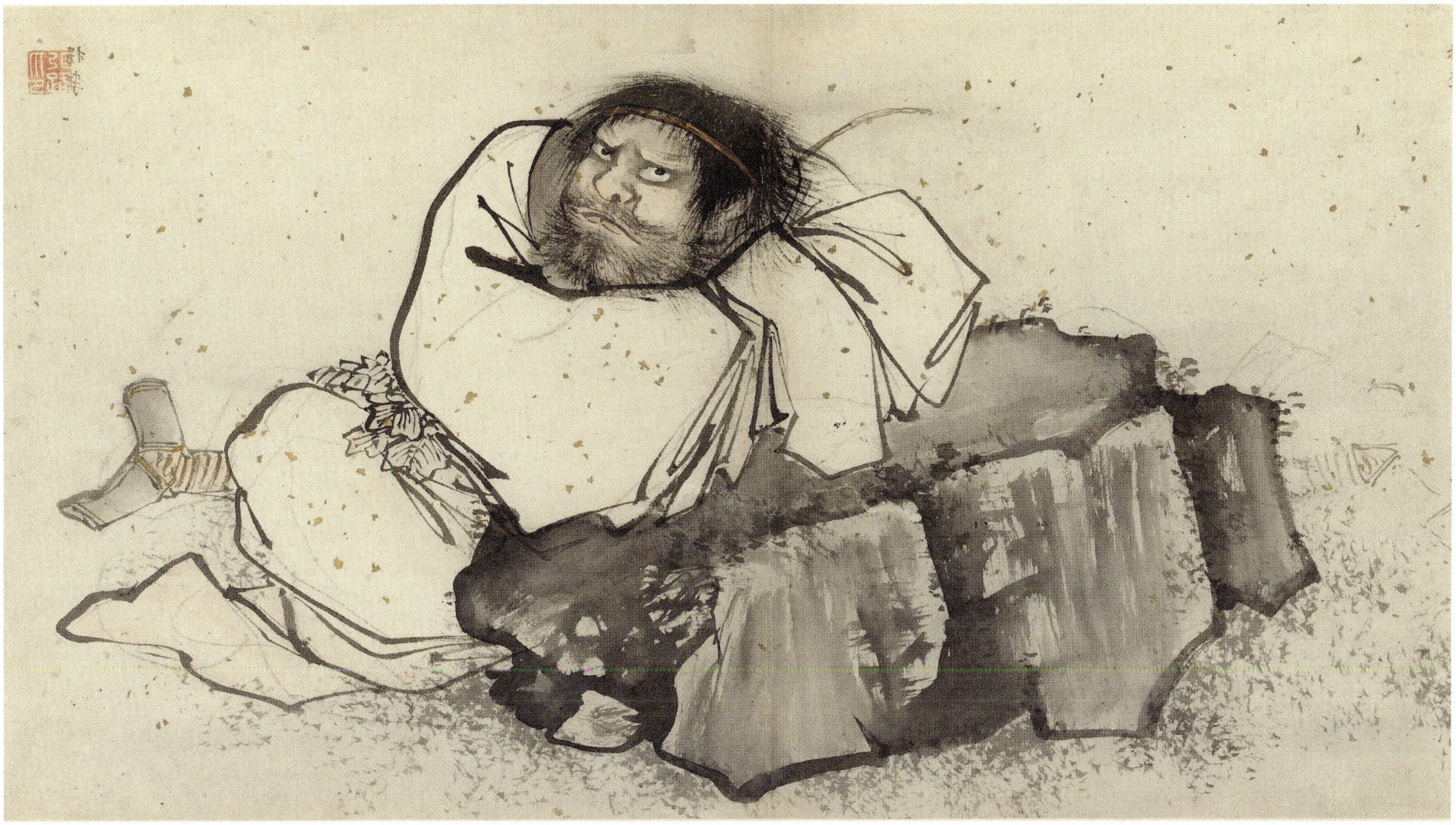

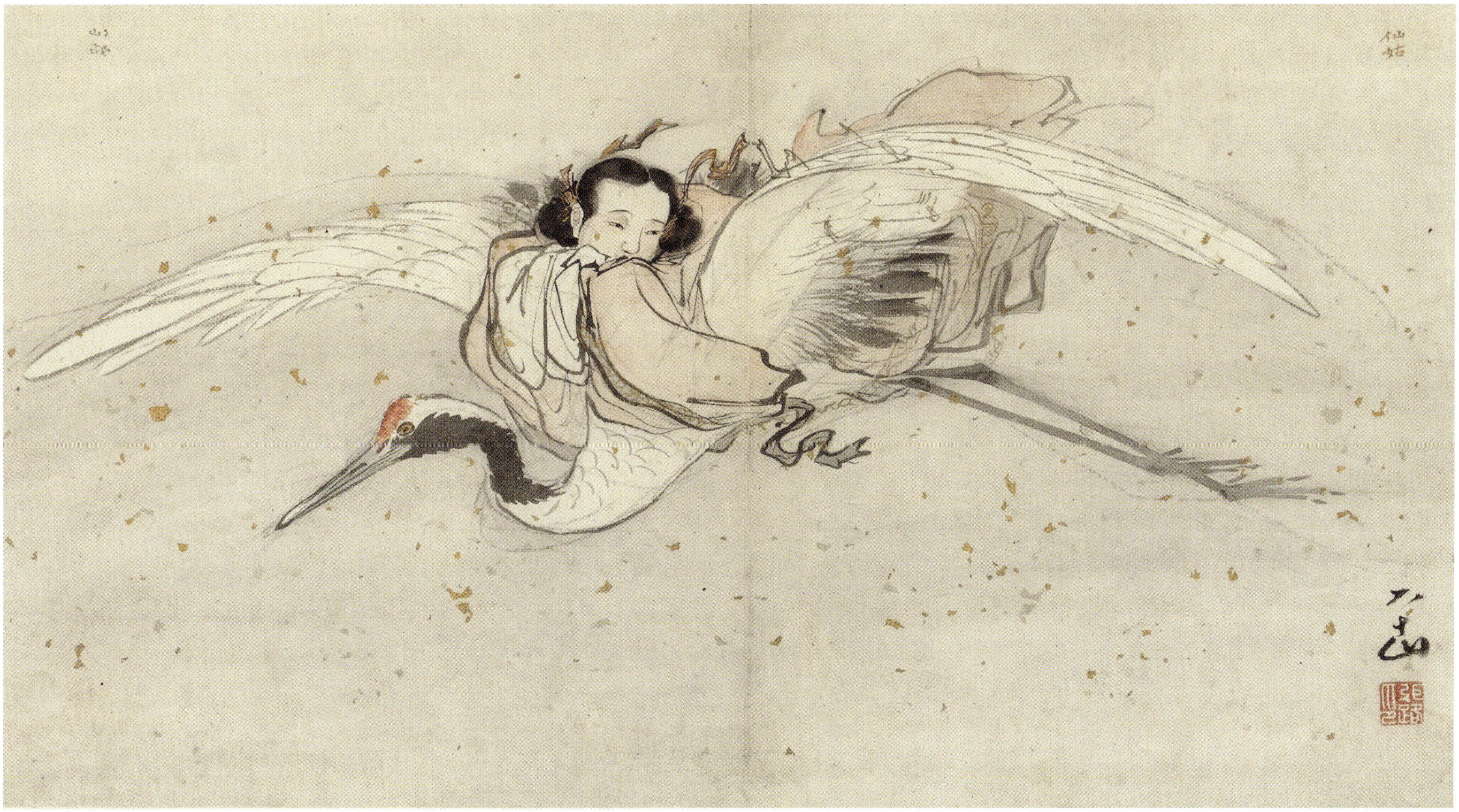

longevity and the pursuit of immortality.[37] By the early medieval – or post-Han – period, people from the emperor down prayed to her as the bringer of blessings and of sons. In later periods she is sometimes depicted with a peach or peaches in her elaborate headdress. In Daoist religious lore, eating one of these peaches, which grow in her orchard in the western mountains (referred to in the inscription), confers immortality on the eater, but the peach trees produce them only once every eon. Xiwangmu is also known as the mother of three beautiful daughters, and associated with a text about achieving sexual bliss.

Cui Zizhong is the late Ming painter paired with Chen Hongshou in the expression, 'Chen of the south, Cui of the north' (*Nan Chen bei Cui*), which identified them as two of the leading artists of their time. Cui was active in the capital region, while Chen was mainly active in his native Hangzhou region. If Chen Hongshou was celebrated for his eccentricity and consummate ink-outline technique, Cui Zizhong was appreciated for the detached, archaic mood his paintings created, whereby his subjects, while ancient, had a certain timeless quality to them. A distinctive feature of his pictures, seen here in the folded cloud formation, is the use of layered washes covered by many short pale brushstrokes to render dominating cloud, vapour or water forms – giving them a magical quality that clearly appealed to the patrons and viewers of his art. Cui Zizhong is also remembered historically for having starved to death when the Ming-dynasty capital, Beijing, fell in 1644.[38]

We have touched, above, on the story known as 'Peach-blossom Spring', a work of prose by Tao Qian, a man who is equally celebrated in Chinese literature for his limpid landscape poetry. Two paintings in the exhibition treat this subject, under the title *Peach-blossom Spring*: a fan mounted as an album leaf by the late Ming master Ding Yunpeng (1547–1628) (Cat. 7), and a small hanging scroll by the underrated late seventeenth-century painter Gu Fuzhen (1634–after 1716) (Cat. 8). According to Tao Qian's text, *Taohua yuan ji*, the story begins when a fisherman chances to find himself travelling along a river, its banks lined with blossoming peach trees.[39] He then finds the entrance to a cave, which he follows into the mountain, eventually discovering that it opens out, at the other end, to an idyllic world, where the people all live happy, peaceful lives as farmers. They tell him their ancestors escaped to this place from China during troubled times, and claim to have had no knowledge of the outside world for many years. After some time the fisherman returns home, carefully marking his path, but mysteriously he is unable ever to find his way back to the paradise world of Peach-blossom Spring. Although this tale does not necessarily have to be read as a Daoist one, it still has strongly Daoist connotations in the ideas of escape from mundane reality and of personal transformation. Medieval writers in China liked to imagine that this idyllic community was inhabited by immortals.[40]

In Gu Fuzhen's meticulous painting, the peach-blossom-lined river appears in the lower right corner. The fisherman's empty boat is moored there, below the domed entrance to a cave. Enhancing the air of mystery and suspense, the cave roof is studded with stalactites. This corner of the painting is clearly marked off from the rest of it by a chain of mountains and hills. Beyond, we, the viewers, can see the utopian world of Peach-blossom Spring, where the fisherman is now. There are neatly laid out fields full of crops. There are small clusters of houses. All around are the mountains which have cut this place off from the real world for decades. Gu Fuzhen's mountains are executed in a stylised manner, making appropriate use of the ancient blue-and-green landscape technique developed at about the time this story originated. Yet, there is another curious element: the receding ground plane is more reminiscent of optical or vanishing-point western landscape art than tiered, layered Chinese landscape – which employed a mobile perspective whereby forms were piled-up in the picture plane. On one hand, this recalls the more unifying spatial approach in the long handscroll depiction of *Peach-blossom Spring* ascribed to the great Suzhou professional Qiu Ying (*c.*1498–1552) (Museum of Fine Arts, Boston).[41] Yet it is also reminiscent of the receding western ground plane as a new device that would have been familiar to artists in Kangxi China via the landscape paintings and engravings which European Jesuits and others had started to bring to China from the late sixteenth century. There is no suggestion that its use here equated Europe with Utopia, rather its relative novelty may have been an effective means to suggest the remoteness, unfamiliarity and wonder of the paradise world.

Two Daoist paintings in the exhibition have an almost talismanic quality to them. Dating from the Kangxi period, one is *Celestial Master Zhang* (Cat. 37) by the little-known Zhou Xun (1649–1729). This is a portrait of the founder of the Tianshi (Celestial Masters) sect of Daoism. Also himself the first Celestial Master, Zhang Daoling (or sometimes Zhang Ling), lived in the Later Han period (2nd century AD). Although the Celestial Masters sect was popular at this early date, many other successful sects later grew up. Zhang Daoling's significance in religious Daoism is that, in legend, in the year 142, he was visited on Mount Heming ('Crane's cry') in Sichuan by Laozi, the reputed author of the founding text of Daoist mysticism, *The Way and its Power* (Arthur Waley's translation) (*Dao de jing*).[42] Zhang received a revelation from Laozi and was conferred healing powers as a sign. He organised the first community, and the patriarchy then passed from father to son over the succeeding generations. As the Zhengyi sect, it still continues today as one of the two main sects of Daoism, along with Quanzhen Daoism. Celestial Master Zhang is usually depicted wearing a sword, and sometimes he has a foreign appearance, as is suggested here by his bushy eyebrows and strange bulbous nose. His fierce expression, as he eyes the bat above him, suggests the supernatural powers he has at his disposal.

The other painting is an image of the demon-queller Zhong Kui in the early eighteenth-century work *Zhong Kui and Spiders* (Cat. 38), also by Zhou Xun.[43] This painting may be likened to quasi-religious talismans that had the power to ward off evil but also to bring good fortune and beneficence. As Li Lizhong describes, the painting's title, *tianxi* (literally, 'adding spiders') is a pun on 'heavenly good-fortune'. Woodblock prints of Zhong Kui have been displayed in Chinese households since the Song dynasty at around new year, and again at the summer solstice (Duanwu, the fifth day of the fifth month), to keep at bay the five noxious or poisonous creatures (*wudu*) – the snake, centipede, scorpion, lizard and toad or spider.[44] In this deluxe painted form of talisman, the fearless Zhong Kui wears red, a colour demons are averse to.

The story of Zhong Kui and his magical demon-defying powers originates in the Tang dynasty.[45] According to legend, he was a young scholar who, when he failed to advance in the bureaucracy through the civil service examinations, committed suicide, vowing to serve the emperor as a ghost. There are many popular stories about Zhong

Guo Xu, 'Drunken immortal', *Album of Various Subjects* (Cat. 9, leaf 3)

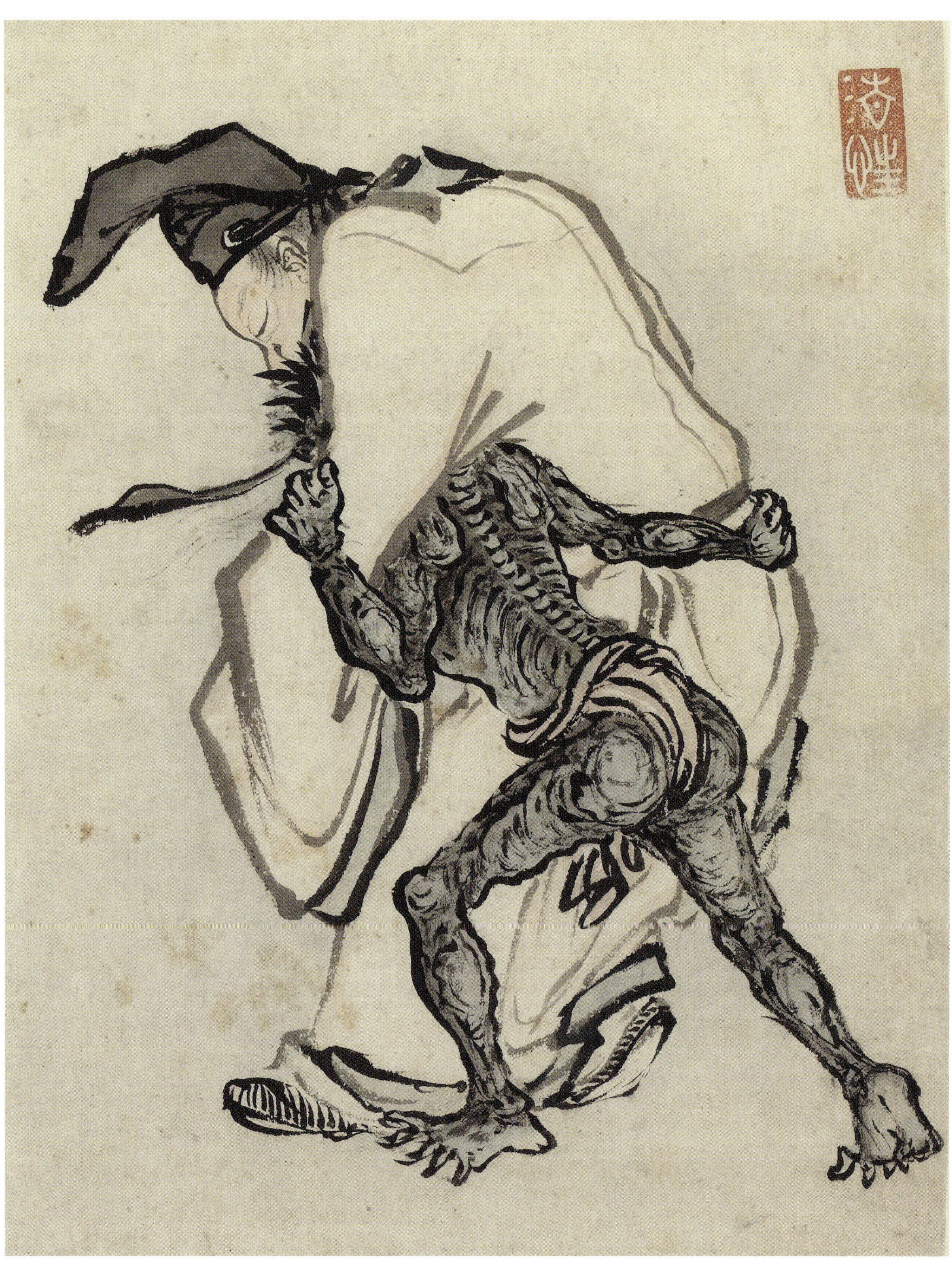

Kui's adventures in the underworld, including one often illustrated in paintings in which the demons trick him into getting drunk so they can steal his magical sword (which can slay them), and his boots. He is rescued by his loyal helpers, who included demons. A similar scene is found in one of the leaves in the album by Guo Xu, entitled 'Drunken immortal' (above), in which the tottering immortal, his eyes closed and his clothing awry, is being helped to walk by a demon, a grotesque-looking near-naked figure of muscle and bone. As the corpulent figure of the immortal loses his balance and stumbles heavily backwards, the small but powerful demon puts his head under his master's shoulder and wraps an arm around his back in support.[46]

Some Models in History and Culture

A third theme of the exhibition highlights exemplary contributions to the formation of Chinese culture. We group some of these models here and in the process of juxtaposition, come to observe some of the common themes in their depiction. Here is where we find what is, arguably, China's historical core identity, as formed and maintained by the guardians of China's great traditions of statecraft and literary culture – the scholar-official or literati class, which existed between the eleventh and early twentieth centuries. Chief among their models are individuals of self-cultivation in the mould of the ancient sage Confucius. The stories told around these men, and the ways they were illustrated at different moments in history, are both very telling about the humanistic ideals extolled by the scholar class in later dynastic China.

A useful starting point is the painting *Educating a Son* (Cat. 31) by the Ming-dynasty artist Wu Shien. Executed in bold, vigorous brushstrokes on a dark silk ground, this painting belongs stylistically in the category known as the Zhe School, which included academic and professional artists, and was associated with the Ming-dynasty capitals Nanjing and Beijing.[47] The subject of the painting is the education of one of Confucius' most revered followers, the Warring States-period (475–221 BC) moral philosopher Mengzi, whose philosophy stressed what he believed was the basic innate goodness and benevolence of human nature.[48] As with Confucius (Kongfuzi or Master Kong), Mengzi has been better known to westerners, since the arrival of European Christian missionaries in China in the late sixteenth century, by his Latinised name, Mencius. It was a celebrated fact that although he would become one of the great minds of early Chinese thought, and an advisor to the court of the state of Qi in the 310s BC, Mencius had a difficult childhood and schooling. He is one of the models of the trope of the son raised by a widow (*guamu jiao zi*). A number of well-known historical figures were raised by their widowed mothers, including the statesman Yan Zhenqing (709–85) and poet Yuan Zhen (799–831) in the Tang, and, in the Yuan, the scholar-artist Zhao Mengfu.

In Mencius' case, he famously was unable to focus on his studies. When he lived near a graveyard, his mother lamented that he was too focused on the dead. When they moved close to a market, his mother deplored that he became too concerned with commerce. Finally, it was only when she moved him near a school, did the boy begin to show a love of learning. This painting illustrates an imaginary moment when the young Mencius and his mother are moving house. The all-important books and stationery for his education are carried by an elderly female servant, who is eyed severely by Mencius' mother. One can easily imagine this painting as the focal point for a retelling of Mencius' early life-story, but it is also a well-observed and witty rendition of the social exchange between an ambitious but impecunious mother and a proud, wily servant transposed from antiquity into the early Ming empire.

The period most admired as the age of style during the dynastic period is the Eastern Jin dynasty (317–420), one of the vibrant but short-lived regional court regimes which thrived in the several centuries between the Han and Tang empires (3rd–6th century), sometimes referred to variously as the Period of Disunion, or Northern and Southern Dynasties, or Six Dynasties. A time of individualism, non-conformity and artistic experimentation and spontaneity, this period also witnessed the spread of elite forms of Buddhism, in addition to renewed interest in the mysticism of native Daoism, especially at southern courts. Among the great artists to emerge in this period were the figure painter Gu Kaizhi, to whom the *Admonitions* scroll in the British Museum is attributed, and the calligrapher Wang Xizhi, who became known as the 'sage of calligraphy', and is the ancestor of the 'classical tradition' of Chinese calligraphy.[49] Traditionally the first calligrapher to capitalise on the new expressive possibilities of the writing brush, Wang Xizhi forged cursive forms of the Chinese script, in which strokes and lines of characters resembled ribbons which seemingly twisted and turned in space, emancipated from the static frontality and scribal connotations of Han-dynasty clerical script.

Wang Xizhi's calligraphy masterpiece was a preface he composed and transcribed to a collection of poems composed at a famous literary gathering held on the day of the 'purification festival' in the spring of 353 at his Orchid Pavilion, believed to have been situated at Kuaiji in modern Zhejiang Province. An anonymous late Ming painting entitled *Purification Festival at the Orchid Pavilion* (below) is a fine example among the hundreds of later pictorial celebrations of this event. Typically, in these paintings, the

The Sage of Calligraphy, Wang Xizhi, composing the 'Orchid Pavilion Preface', from Anonymous (Ming), *Purification Festival at the Orchid Pavilion* (Cat. 3, detail)

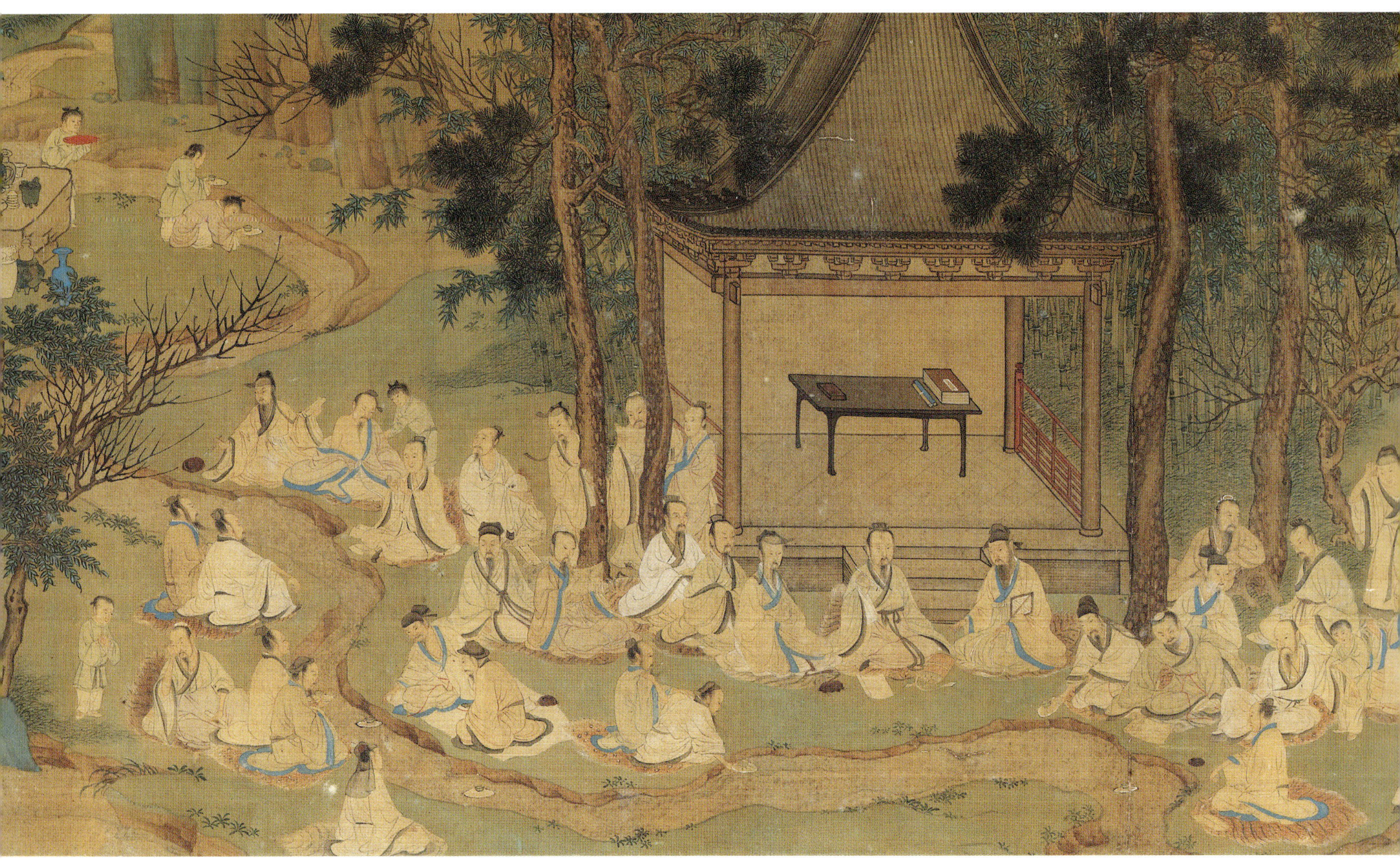

various cultured guests are seated along the banks of a small stream engaged in 'pure conversation' (or 'pure talk', *qingtan*). Servant boys float wine-cups placed on leaves down the stream. When a cup stopped by a guest, he was expected to compose a poem or, if he failed, to drink several cups in forfeit. At the end of the day, Wang composed and transcribed a text to head the resulting poems, known as the 'Preface to the Orchid Pavilion Collection'.[50] The fate of the original preface by Wang Xizhi is the stuff of legend: it supposedly was buried in the tomb of the early Tang emperor Taizong (r. 629–49), a passionate admirer of Wang's calligraphy, but not before it had been copied and engraved in stone for transmission to later generations.

Such is his cultural significance as the ancestor of the classical tradition of Chinese calligraphy, that Wang Xizhi is the subject of colourful stories that have circulated throughout history. Many of these originate in *New Account of Tales of the World*, a collection of tales and anecdotes about the behaviour and activities of the most stylish individuals of this period.[51] One of the most popular stories associated with Wang Xizhi concerns his love of geese. The Shanghai painter Ren Yi's (1840–96) *Wang Xizhi Admiring Geese* (Cat. 26) illustrates an anecdote in which Wang agreed to exchange a specimen of his calligraphy for a flock of geese.[52] It has always been assumed that Wang Xizhi liked watching geese because the graceful curves of their necks were a source of inspiration for his innovative curving strokes in calligraphy – their neck movements were apparently a model for his manipulation of the writing brush through the wrist. It is possible that he was also partial to roast goose. The anecdote is also relevant in art history since it established – at least retroactively – a lofty amateur ideal, among the artists of the elite, of exchanging one's art for things, rather than receiving payment in cash as in a mere business transaction.[53] Indeed, artists, including professionals working in the amateur tradition, did not advertise cash prices for their paintings until the eighteenth century. Active in late nineteenth-century Shanghai, Ren Yi was assuredly a professional painter working for a cosmopolitan clientele;[54] for Ren Yi, the depiction of this particular tale no doubt had a pleasantly ironic/nostalgic ring.

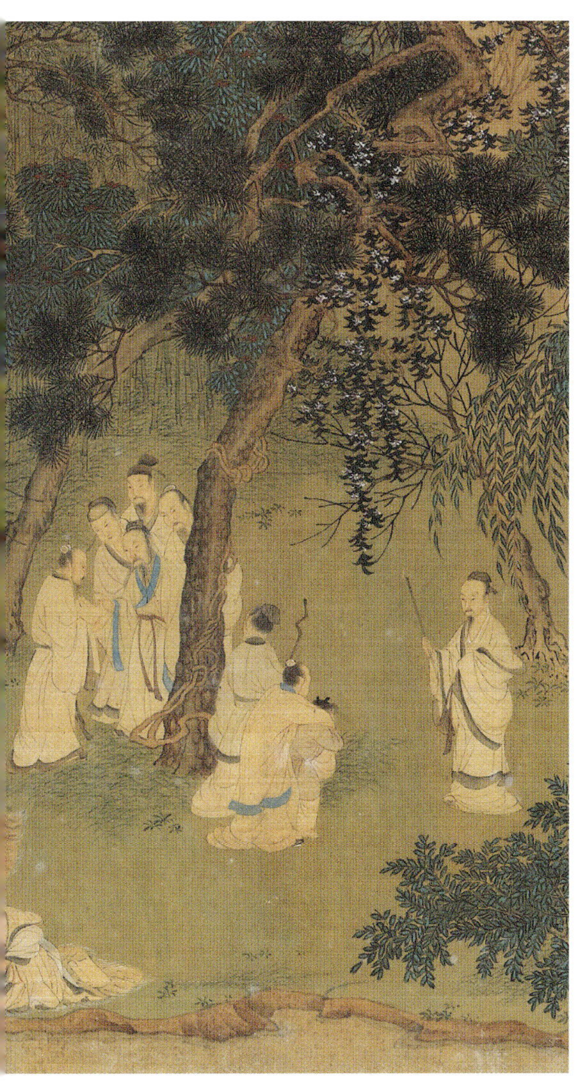

A member of Wang Xizhi's circle, and another celebrated figure in the *New Account of Tales of the World*, was a Buddhist monk called Zhidun (314–66), a greatly admired and respected member of the educated Jiangnan clergy during the Eastern Jin period.[55] An anecdote in the *New Tales* describes how Zhidun was inordinately fond of fine horses, which he seems to have bred:[56] 'The monk Zhidun always kept several horses. Someone remarked, "A holy man and raising horses don't go together." Zhidun replied: "This humble monk values them for their divine swiftness [like that of the human mind]."' This story is the source of Ren Yi's masterly hanging scroll, *The Monk Zhidun Admiring a Horse* (p. 52), one of the finest and most visually exciting works in the exhibition. The painter Ren Yi, better known as Ren Bonian, trained in Suzhou under Ren Xun (1835–93), one of the trio of Ren family artists referred to above (Ren Yi was not related), but moved in 1868 to Shanghai, where he would become the city's most prominent painter. Ren Yi's early style was clearly shaped by knowledge of his illustrious predecessor in figural art, the late Ming eccentric Chen Hongshou (see Cat. 4), but Ren Yi later became a master in his own right, drawing liberally on sources and modes from a diversity of visual media – from ink rubbings to foreign prints to painting to photography – in the development of a distinctive modern artistic voice.

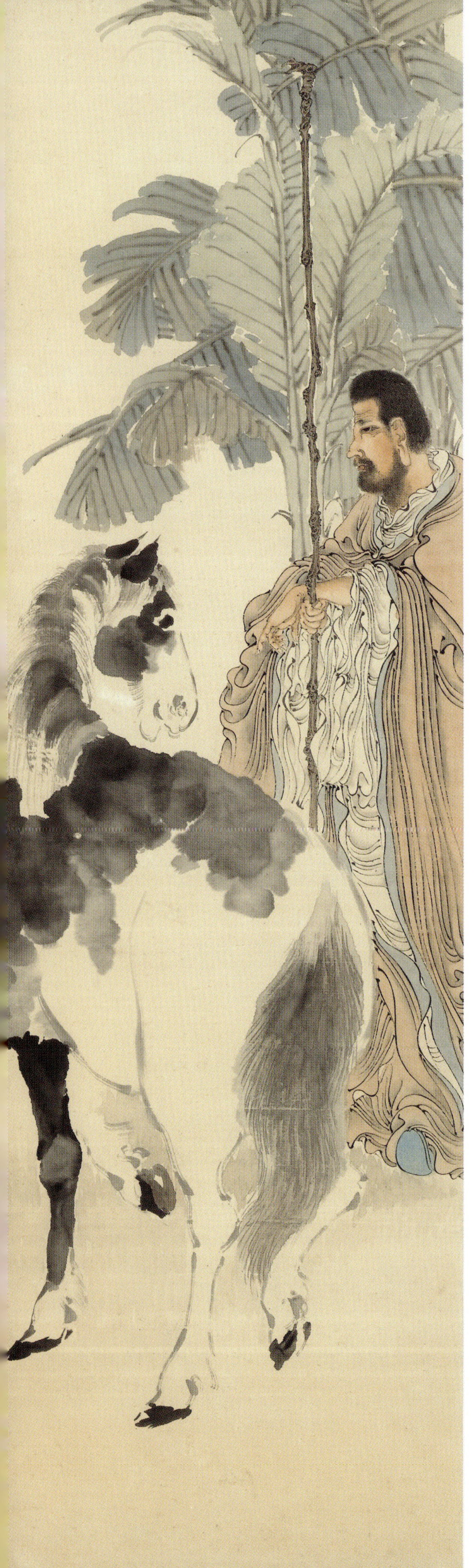

The story of the 'divine thoroughbred' (*shenjun*) admired by Zhidun has been depicted probably since the Tang dynasty, but it is apparent that these specific old-master sources or their copies did not mean much to Ren Yi.[57] Rather, this painting brilliantly integrates a host of competing ancient and modern visualities, which combine with and seem to comment on the narrative element of its subject. There is the extraordinary visual appearance of the horse itself. His head and mane are depicted realistically, and his neck appears to turn in space. His hind quarters, however, are like an exercise in Chinese ink abstraction, a flat, formalistic play of the media, reminiscent of the mode of the eccentric Yangzhou painters of the later eighteenth century, who included Hua Yan and Huang Shen (see Cats 12,15 &16). The depiction of the figure of Zhidun is another intrigue. The intense, narrow folds of drapery done in an agitated ink-outline style must be a deliberate reference to the style of the Tang-dynasty Central Asian artist Weichi Yiseng (late 7th–early 8th century), the foreignness of this style being a culturally and temporally appropriate image to depict Zhidun from a late Qing perspective. The face of the monk is another fascinating exercise in art-historical referencing. The foreign facial features and the exaggerated manner of their depiction clearly recall the model for this type of figure known to Ren Yi, namely ink-rubbings made from the stone engravings of the Temple of the Sacred Cause (Shengyin si) in Hangzhou, which recorded the images of the sixteen arhats by the monk-painter Guanxiu in the tenth century. Layered on top of, or perhaps within this reference is another – to the art of the Yangzhou master Luo Ping (1733–99), who also used these same Guanxiu figures as the models for portraits of his contemporaries.[58] However, what distinguishes this painting as a work of late Qing art is another striking effect, seen especially in the vicinity of the gnarled staff. The staff itself is portrayed in sharp focus, while the banana leaves behind are rendered in wet ink washes of pale blues and greens, creating the sense of a shallow depth of field as in studio photography of this period.[59] The compelling matrix of visual effects and philosophical concepts, of lofty antiquity and exciting modernity in this painting convey a vibrant and uplifting picture of cosmopolitan culture in late Qing Shanghai. Still, it seems that Ren Yi was at heart a conservative, and a nationalist, as one of his occasionally quoted statements suggests: 'I have often lamented that today's officials seek after barbarians' culture to transform China and alter her ways. Some have gone so far as to promote such ideas as democracy and freedom. It is to take our esteemed moral principles and let the flippant youths have a field day… How the world has changed, so much and daily, to such a degree of ferment!'[60]

We come in a moment to another of Ren Yi's paintings, but turn first to the anonymous Ming work which bears the title *Kongming Leaving the Mountains* (Cat. 2), one of two paintings illustrating epic military themes of the early empire. If the title is correct, this is an illustration of a pivotal historical moment from the Three Kingdoms period, when the great military strategist Zhuge Liang (known as Kongming, 181–234) emerged from the wilderness in Hubei Province, where he had been farming and studying, to become an advisor to Liu Bei, eventual founder of the Shu-Han dynasty (221–63). (Liu Bei was one of the two leaders who defeated Cao Cao at the Battle of the Red Cliffs; see page 43.) Popularly known as Crouching Dragon (Fulong) or Sleeping Dragon (Wolong), Zhuge Liang has long been admired as one of early dynastic China's

OPPOSITE: Ren Yi, *Monk Zhidun Admiring a Horse* (Cat. 24, detail)

shrewdest military minds – a reputation anchored and popularised by the accounts of his daring in the epic *Romance of the Three Kingdoms (Sanguozhi yanyi)* traditionally ascribed to the writer Luo Guanzhong (*c.*1330–*c.*1400). Executed in the early to mid-Ming style of the Zhe School, this painting, we can imagine, was created at the Ming court in the wake of the appearance of that novel.

Keeping with the military theme, Ren Yi's *Three Knights in Wind and Dust* (p. 55) depicts the three leading characters from the 'Romance of the Red Dust', a tale about three knights-errant who fight for social justice at the end of the Sui dynasty. Ren Yi liked painting folkloric subjects, as well as epic stories and legends, mythology and history, but he was especially drawn to this subject, which he painted a number of times.[61] The story takes place in around the early seventh century, under the despotic rule of the powerful but short-lived Sui regime (581–618). Hongfu nü (Red Duster lady) was trained as an assassin in service of the most powerful minister and general, Yang Su (d. 606). The brilliant warrior Li Jing (571–649) also hoped to serve, and visited Yang Su with that aim, only it was Hongfu who was deeply impressed by him and the two eloped. Hongfu nü later helped Li Jing to befriend a stranger known as Curly-bearded Stranger (Qiuran ke), and together they pledged to assist Li Shimin (599–649), the eventual founder of the Tang dynasty and later emperor Taizong.[62]

The style of the painting, in contrast with *Monk Zhidun Admiring a Horse*, relates to a 'layered' mode that Ren Yi developed in the 1880s. Dated to 1880, this painting may be seen as a precursor of that mode. The Curly-bearded Stranger, the figure in red on the donkey in the foreground, resembles a kind of cut-out, silhouetted against the flat bridge, white background and fence. The powerful tree similarly occupies a single plane. Behind, again silhouetted by the pale toned background, Li Jing and Hongfu nü lurk, gesturing in a covert manner to their mounted fellow conspirator, who it seems is now taking his leave.[63] One recent study has argued that this layering effect was a 'surreptitious appropriation' of this technique in Japanese woodblock prints circulating in Shanghai. Such was the demand for pictures of Chinese historical figures and episodes, argues Lai Yu-chih, that artists like Ren Yi, having exhausted Chinese sources, resorted to borrowing Japanese depictions of Chinese themes which were unknown in Shanghai.[64]

Two of the iconic figures of literature in dynastic China, men who bridged the worlds of politics and poetry, are the Tang poetic genius Li Bai (701–62) and the Northern Song literatus Su Shi. Li Bai – or sometimes Li Bo – has long been a household name in China, along with his near contemporary Du Fu (712–70), on account of his brilliant poetry, but also for his unconventional behaviour.[65] Hailing from Sichuan in the southwest, Li Bai briefly enjoyed imperial favour at the court of emperor Xuanzong in the mid-eighth century, after the emperor appointed him scholar in the prestigious Hanlin Academy. While enjoying peonies by night with his favourite, Yang Guifei, the emperor summoned Li Bai to compose verses to a tune the court ladies played. Li Bai arrived drunk but managed to compose 'Three verses to the Qingping melody' (*Qingping diao, sanshou*). However, in the process he managed to offend the powerful eunuch Gao Lishi, first by asking him to remove his boots in front of the emperor. Then, Gao Lishi resented a line in the third verse, which he believed likened Yang Guifei to a woman who topples kingdoms.[66] Other colourful stories about Li Bai abound, many concerning his drinking – he was one of the figures in Du Fu's poem

OPPOSITE: Ren Yi, *Three Knights in Wind and Dust* (Cat. 25, detail)

'Eight Immortals of the Wine Cup' (*Yinzhong baxian*). He is also the subject of a Ming illustrated drama, Tu Long's (1542–1605) *Tale of the Colourful Brush (Caihao ji)*, about his life in Xuanzong's time.[67] According to legend, he died by drowning when he tried to embrace the moon reflected in water.

Li Bai has been a portrait subject since at least the Song dynasty.[68] His life-story, or tales from it, would have been called to mind merely by imaginary portraits such as *Li Bai Chanting Poetry* (Cat. 21), a large hanging scroll by Que Lan (1758–1844). A distinctively late Qing court or court-style painting, in which the great poet is transposed from the Tang into an elegant, opulent Qing-period garden setting surrounded by beautiful young women, this may illustrate the incident of Li Bai's drunken composition of verses to the Qingping melody.[69]

It is a dramatic modernisation, in terms of visual culture. The artist has made striking use of a shifting perspectival technique. In the fore-, middle- and background areas, the lines converge towards a distant vanishing point, creating overall a composite, stylised illusion of depth. In between these spaces, pitted rocks and gnarled trees in leaf feather across the picture surface in more traditional Chinese fashion. The vanishing-point perspective technique, along with *chiaroscuro* or shading, had been standard practice for some of the Jesuit artists and their pupils active at court under the Qianlong emperor (r. 1736–95), among them Giuseppe Castiglione (1688–1766). They commonly employed it in hybrid ways, like here, using Chinese media and sometimes in collaborative works with Chinese artists.

The period of activity of this painter, Que Lan, late in the Qianlong reign to early in the succeeding Jiaqing (1796–1820), falls several decades after the highpoint of court painting under the Qianlong emperor in the mid-eighteenth century, but the incorporation of this localised Chinese interpretation of European technique, in combination with generic Chinese methods to portray the rock and trees, as means to create a lively, up-to-date setting for a distant historical figure, suggests they were still unfamiliar enough in the visual culture of the elite in Qing China to command attention – to bring the colourful Li Bai to life again in the present. What is also in keeping with the modus operandi of the technically accomplished Qianlong court painters is the sanitising treatment of the subject. This is nothing like Su Liupeng's portrait, dated 1844, in the Shanghai Museum, of a drunken Li Bai who needs the help of two men to walk;[70] indeed, the figure of Li Bai here is a model of sobriety (this is echoed by the pictorial style), and only one small wine cup is in evidence.

We have encountered, above, aspects of adversity connected with the Song literatus Su Shi. In this section of the exhibition, we introduce two paintings which relate his achievements as a scholar-official in government. The first of these is *Elegant Gathering in the West Garden* (pp. 56–57), by the distinguished seventeenth-century artist Shitao (1642–1707). It depicts a literary gathering, possibly fictitious, hosted in 1087 by Wang Shen (*c.*1048–*c.*1104), son-in-law of the former emperor Yingzong (r. 1063–67), and attended by Su Shi, his brother Su Che (1039–1112), and more than a dozen fellow poets, painters, calligraphers, friends and political allies, all scholar-officials in the government. Among them, Li Gonglin (1049–1106), was said to have recorded the event in a painting, while Mi Fu (1051–1107) wrote an 'Account', *Xiyuan yaji tu ji*,[71] which is transcribed by Shitao in an inscription following the painting. Although such

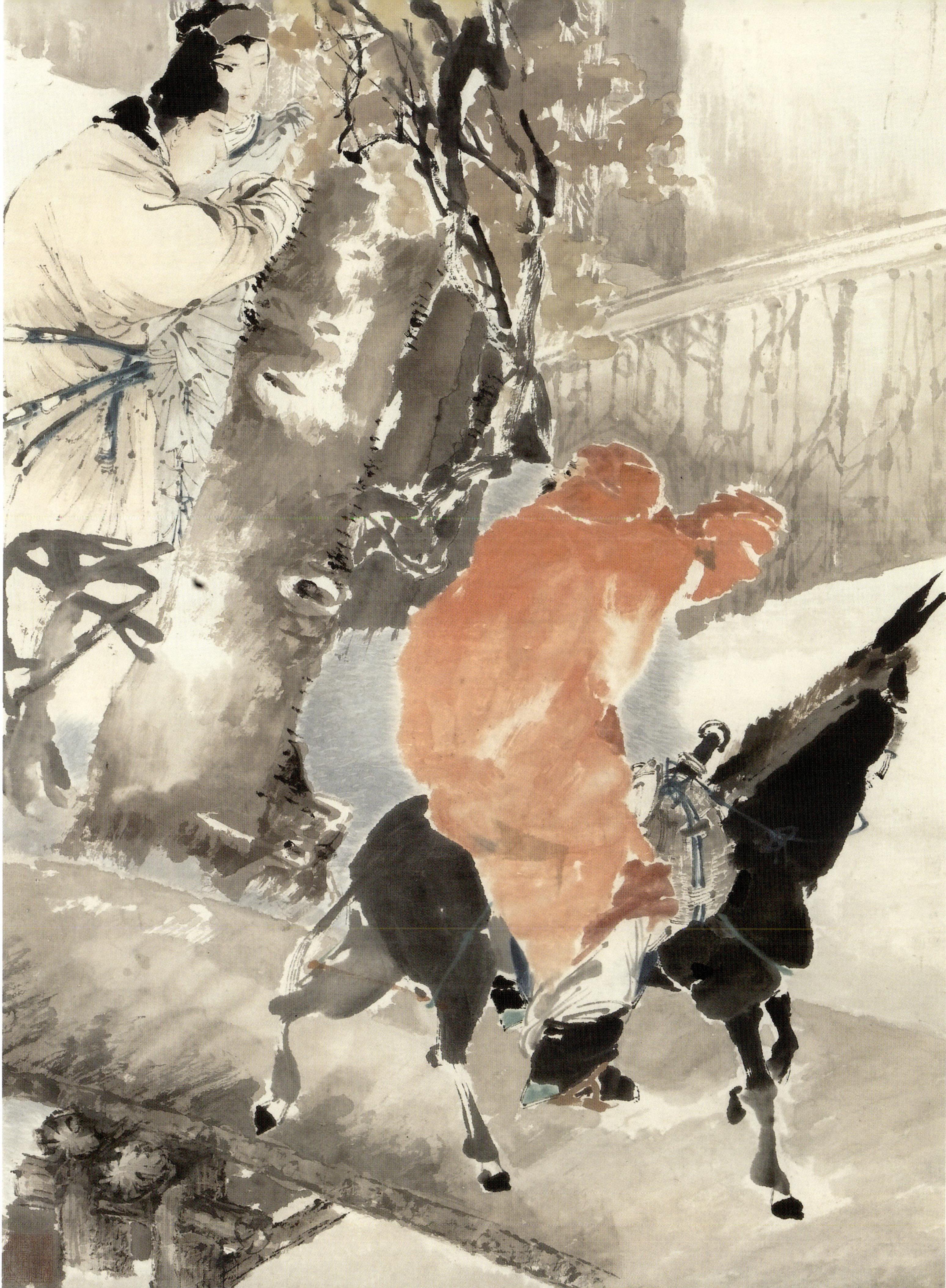

a gathering of the leading lights of late Northern Song literati culture represented a cultural ideal in itself, historically, such a gathering would also have come to mind as a latter-day restaging of that famous earlier 'elegant gathering' (*yaji*) hosted by Wang Xizhi at his Orchid Pavilion on the occasion of the purification festival (see Cat. 3), itself modelled on the gatherings hosted by Shi Chong at Golden Valley Garden (see Cat. 12).

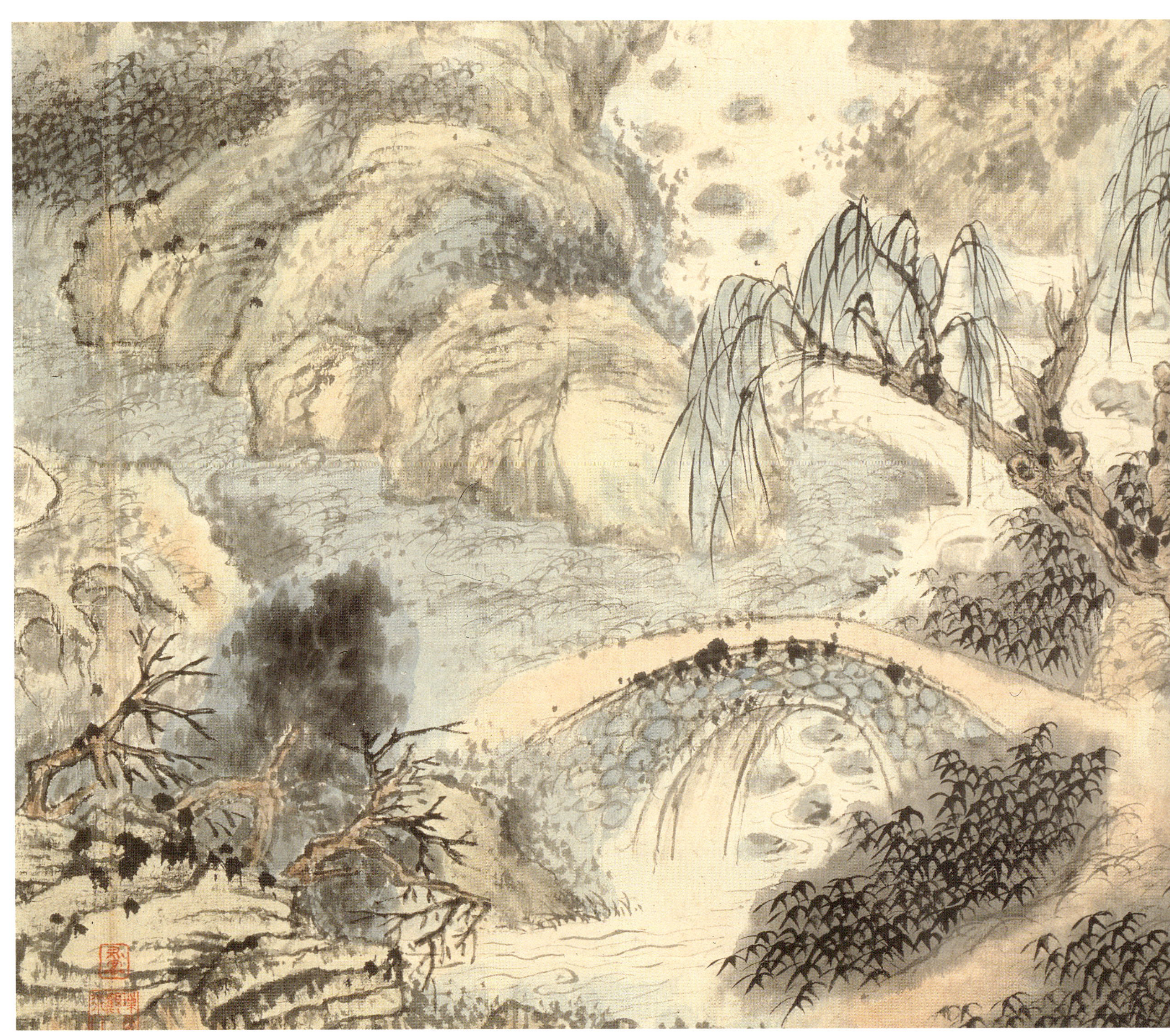

Sometimes labelled an eccentric and a precursor to the Yangzhou eccentrics of the eighteenth century, Shitao, or Zhu Ruoji, was a minor member of the Ming royal family, who survived the establishment of Manchu rule in China in the decades after 1644 by becoming a Buddhist monk (Shitao – 'stone wave'), and went on to become a professional painter, one of the era's great individualists, along with his distant relative Bada Shanren (1626–1705). A protean artist, Shitao famously questioned why he should imitate or learn from the old masters: the legend of one of the artist's seals on this painting

The calligrapher Mi Fu inscribing a rock, from Shitao, *Elegant Gathering in the West Garden* (Cat. 28, detail)

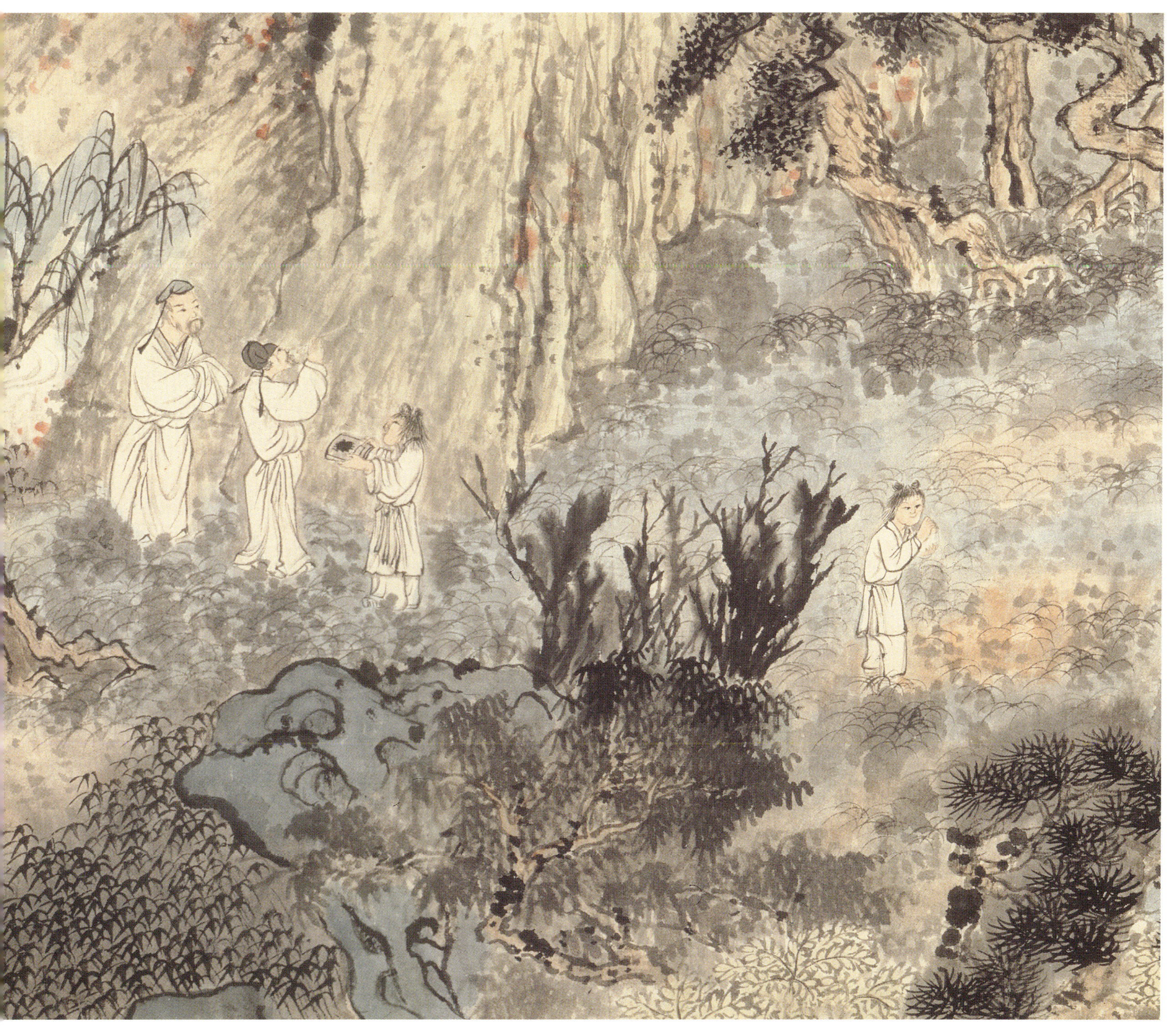

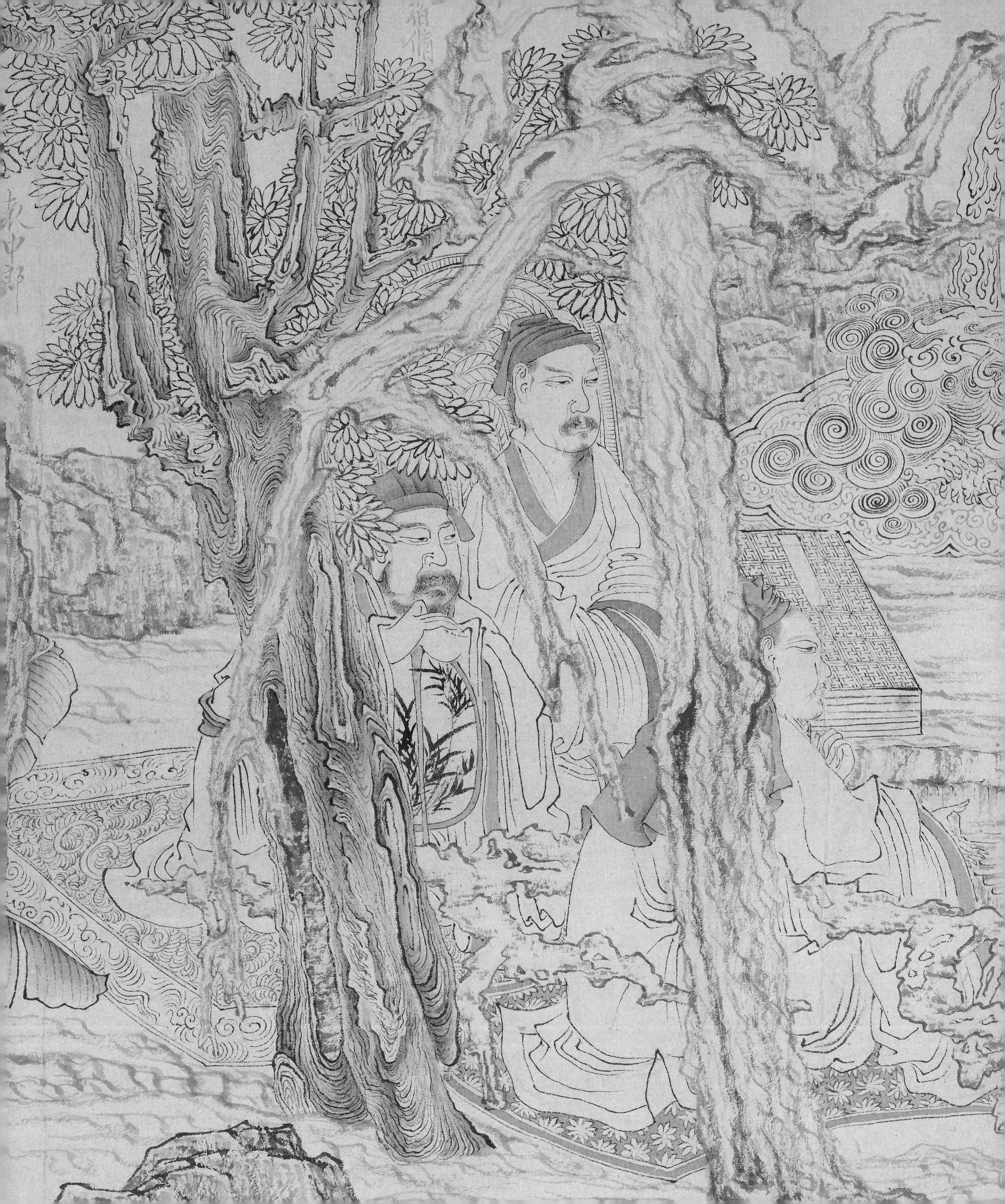

OPPOSITE: Chen Hongshou, *Elegant Gathering* (Cat. 4, detail))

reads, 'Regretful the ancients did not see [me], Dadizi, Ji' (*Hen guren bu jian Dadizi Ji*). The painting style that developed, as he moved from city to city in south China during the Kangxi reign (1662–1722), was indeed entirely his own. Jonathan Hay's study of the artist explores his work as a function of early modernity in China.[72] In this painting of the renowned West Garden literary gathering, there is no obvious stylistic reference to its first illustrator, Li Gonglin; it is, rather, exemplary of Shitao's lively brush style and colour handling.

A short handscroll painting entitled simply *Elegant Gathering* (opposite) by Chen Hongshou (1598–1652) is wonderfully representative of the artist's late figural style, notable for its looping shapes and the pulsating quality of the calligraphic outlines. However, the proper subject of this painting, executed for a patron named Tao Sheng in 1647,[73] is a topic of debate. One of the prominent figures portrayed in the painting is Mi Wanzhong (1570–1628), an influential calligrapher and taste-maker active in the capital in the Wanli reign. New research by Li Lan of the Shanghai Museum suggests, however, that Mi Wanzhong is not the main character as such. Rather, the painting commemorates a literary gathering hosted by Tao Yunjia (Youmei, 1556–1622), grandfather of Tao Sheng, which took place in Beijing between 1590 and 1600.[74]

A second painting, which may be associated with Su Shi, is entitled *Returning to the Academy by 'Golden Lotus' Lamplight* (Cat. 14), dated 1892, by Huang Shanshou (1855–1919), whose period of activity spanned the end of the Qing dynasty in 1911 and the founding of the Republic of China in 1912.[75] It depicts a well-known anecdote, which was a fairly common topic in both prints and paintings in the later dynastic period,[76] about a scholar-official who is summoned for an audience late at night, and is then given an imperial escort by 'golden lotus' lanterns back to the Hanlin Academy. Huang Shanshou's painting is a moonlight scene showing the honoured scholar-official being escorted from his late-night audience by a lamp-bearing servant along a paved path between tall, over-arching bamboos and an ornate garden rock. The bearded minister eyes the viewer askance as he strides purposefully back to his office, his way lit by the scampering lamp-bearer.

This story may be interpreted as the re-appointment of Su Shi to high office following his return from exile at Huangzhou in the early 1080s. One night he received an imperial summons from emperor Zhezong (r. 1085–1100) while on duty in the Hanlin Academy. On his arrival in the audience chamber, Su Shi was informed of his promotion by the Dowager Empress Gao (1032–93), and then told by the emperor that it was really the late emperor Shenzong who had wanted to promote him (but for political reasons could not). The three were all moved to tears at this recollection. Later, the emperor even allowed Su Shi to sit in his presence and offered him tea. He was then sent back to the Academy with the emperor's own 'golden lotus' lanterns.[77]

The political backdrop to Huang Shanshou's painting of 1892, and the pressing issue of modernising the government and the nation at that time, is complex. Even though the reform-minded Guangxu emperor (1871–1908; r. 1875–1908), just twenty-one years old, was the titular head of state, the real power still lay in the hands of the Empress Dowager, Cixi (1835–1908), his former regent and a staunch conservative. The Guangxu emperor's initiative, the Hundred Days Reform, was stopped in a *coup d'état* by Cixi in 1898, and Guangxu was effectively deposed. That Cixi was opposed to any wholesale political reform along the lines of the Meiji Restoration of 1868 in Japan, may have precipitated the fall of the Qing dynasty in 1911, shortly after her death.

Viewers might have been expected to recognise a story or anecdote from a picture, and perhaps a brief title or caption, but what they would have gleaned from the particular twist put on the story by the illustration is a more difficult question, and one that becomes harder to recover with time. One can imagine Huang Shanshou's painting being presented as a gift to a recently elevated official by someone who wished to be remembered, or else hanging as an auspicious or aspirational image in a house or office. Plausibly, it also had a political motive, or served a political end. What is of such interest in the stories presented through images in this way is not just the narratives in and of themselves, but rather the ways they are narrated or manipulated for changing times in the picture-making process.

Romances and Tales of Talent and Beauty

The purpose of illustrating stories and figures in early painting of the Han and post-Han period was linked to prevailing notions of the didactic function of art. The oeuvre of early painters like Gu Kaizhi has historically consisted of works illustrating didactic texts such as *Biographies of Exemplary Women (Lienü zhuan)* and *Admonitions of the Court Instructress (Nüshi zhen)*. The *Admonitions* comprises illustrations of a didactic poem widely studied by elite women in later times, written by the polymath and courtier Zhang Hua (232–300) in the year 292, about how court ladies should behave. Some of these twelve admonitions cite exemplary women, good and bad, from history; others are abstract lessons, such as reflecting on one's conduct or reminding other women of their duty.

In the medieval period, under the Tang dynasty, the genre of the 'scholar and beauty' tale took shape. The 'Story of Oriole' (*Yingying zhuan*) by Yuan Zhen plots the illicit love-affair between the impoverished but brilliant young scholar Zhang and Oriole (Yingying), the beautiful daughter of a late chief minister.[78] There is no happy ending, but rather the tale highlights the shabbiness and dubious morality of late Tang society. The story is a useful touch-stone of changing literary tastes, however: it was reborn as a drama with a happy ending in the thirteenth-century playwright Wang Shifu's celebrated *Story of the Western Wing (Xixiang ji)*.[79] This classic tale of a 'scholar and beauty' features the attempted abduction and rape of the heroine Oriole by a rebel leader, erotic poems, assignations and a protracted liaison between Oriole and Student Zhang. A racy tale, it was also among the most popular subjects of print-illustrated books published in the vibrant late Ming period (late 16th–early 17th century), and illustrated print editions (one was illustrated by Chen Hongshou) were widely available to and avidly consumed by the reading public. However, it seems that the subject matter was too risqué to be a suitable topic for paintings, and it is not known as a painting topic.

By the more conservative standards of the high Qing period in the eighteenth century, the *Story of the Western Wing* was even considered unsuitable reading for well-brought-up girls – at least, according to the dialogue in Cao Xueqin's (1716-63) great mid-eighteenth-century novel, *Dream of the Red Chamber (Honglou meng)*.[80] Written in the vernacular in the context of the Qianlong literary inquisition (and originally published anonymously), this semi-autobiographical work charts the changing fortunes of one family and features hundreds of characters. Extolled for its vivid and insightful portrayal of characters, particularly the women, it became enormously popular in the late Qing period and was frequently illustrated in print form.[81] A painted scene from the novel is included in the exhibition, in the modern artist Qi Baishi's (Qi Huang; 1864–1957) *Daiyu Buries Flowers* (Cat. 20) dated to the artist's eighty-seventh year (1950).[82] The painting concerns a poem about burying flowers by the beautiful, emotional Lin Daiyu, first cousin and love interest of the protagonist Jia Baoyu, in which she reflects melancholically on her own fading beauty and her constrained existence as a woman within patriarchal, feudal society. In Qi Baishi's inscription to his painting, Daiyu's lament about flowers is borrowed as an image for the artist's reflection on his own ageing: 'I still care that flowers bloom and flowers fall. How that makes me think longingly of my younger days.' Qi Baishi's painting shares some characteristics with the many late Qing period print illustrations of this moment in the novel. Daiyu holds a hoe to dig with and the bag of wilted flowers she means to bury in the 'clean' dirt – symbolically a way for her to remain unsullied by the shabby value system of contemporary society. Yet, in the manner of its execution, the painting is more psychologically penetrating as a portrait of a still-young woman lamenting her fading beauty, than any print. Although the figure is a somewhat stylised late imperial type-form for a beauty, the wavering outlines of the drapery and the tentative quality of the folds, and indeed the forlorn facial expression, are all visually evocative of the subject's fragile emotional state.

We may observe how the spread of literacy in the late Ming period was mirrored by the growth and sophistication of print publishing in that period, and how certain subjects seemingly not deemed appropriate subject matter in the genteel art of painting were nevertheless illustrated in mildly pornographic printed books. Against this background, the long handscroll painting *Spring Morning in the Han Palace* (pp. 62–64) by You Qiu, goes against the norm. Although one of the major professional artists practising in Suzhou in the sixteenth century, You Qiu is not in the first tier, but is rather known for having continued the traditions established by more accomplished predecessors like his father-in-law, Qiu Ying. Still, he enjoyed the friendship of leading literati including Qian Gu, the brothers Wang Shizhen (1526–90) and Shimou (1536–88), and Mo Shilong. Yet, in contrast with Qiu Ying and others, You Qiu, at his best painting Buddhist and Daoist figures and women, preferred to work in the *baimiao* technique, in delicate ink-outline without colours, a mode associated with early literati masters like Li Gonglin.[83]

This fully narrative painting in twelve scenes depicts the story of the torrid love triangle between Han emperor Chengdi (r. 33–7 BC) and two of his favourites, the sisters Zhao Feiyan and Hede. The first of these was a famously slender beauty and the third of the Four Beauties of ancient China, who started out as a dancing girl and earned the moniker, 'Flying Swallow' (Feiyan). She became empress, only to lose imperial favour to her younger sister Hede, who became Bright Consort, second in rank only to the empress.[84] In becoming imperial favourites, the Zhao sisters successfully ousted Lady Ban, one of the most upright and virtuous exemplars among

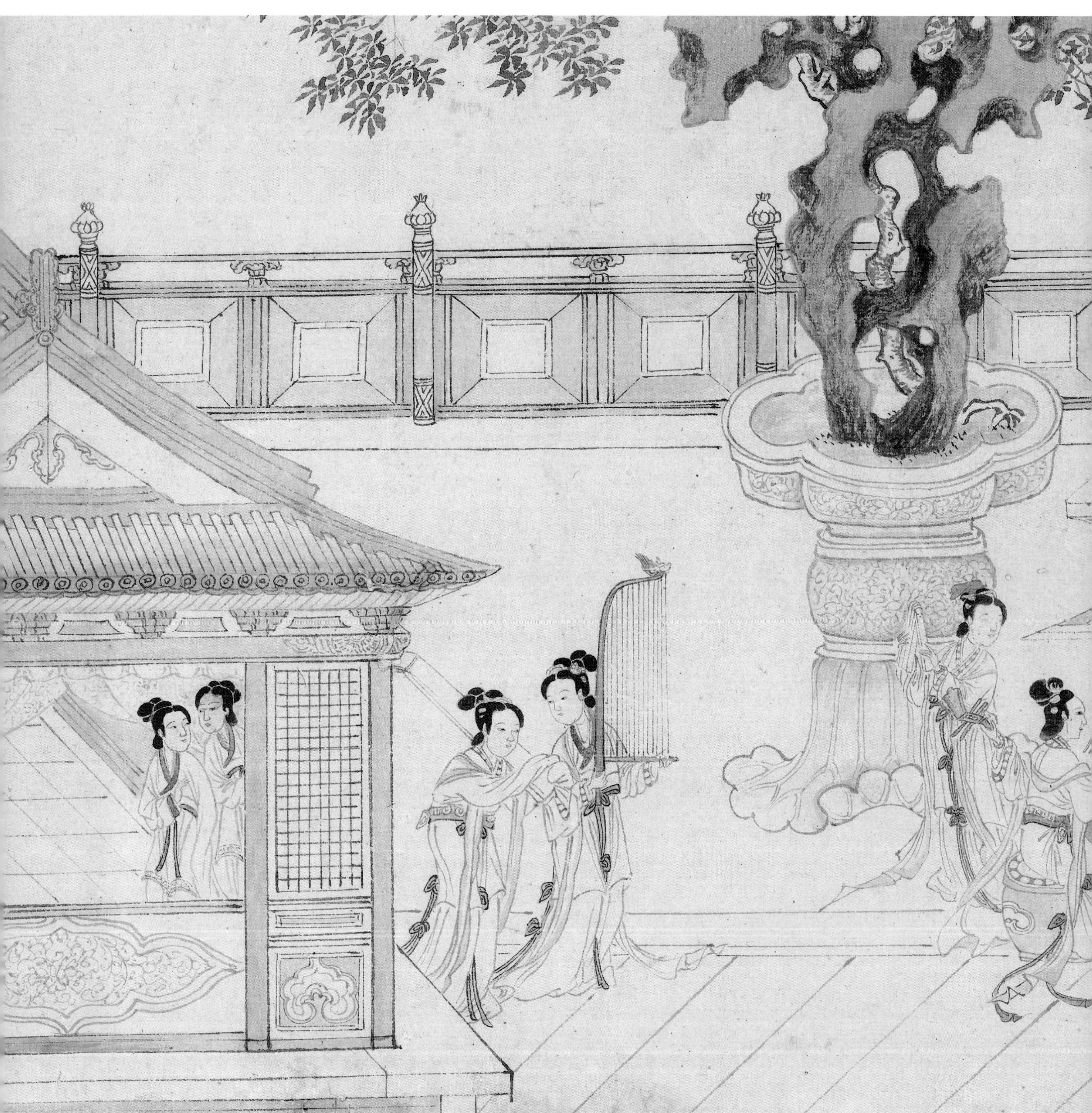

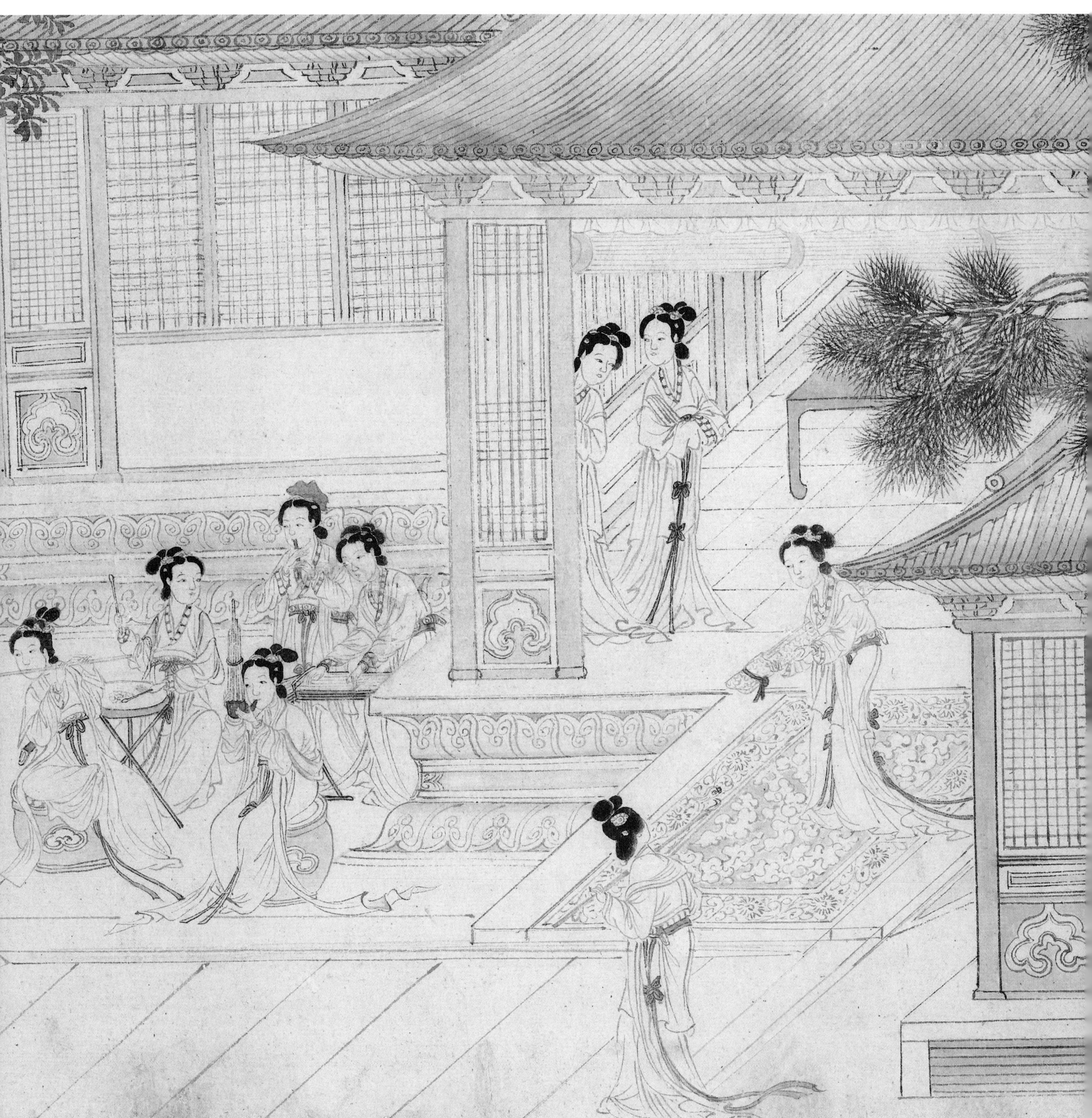

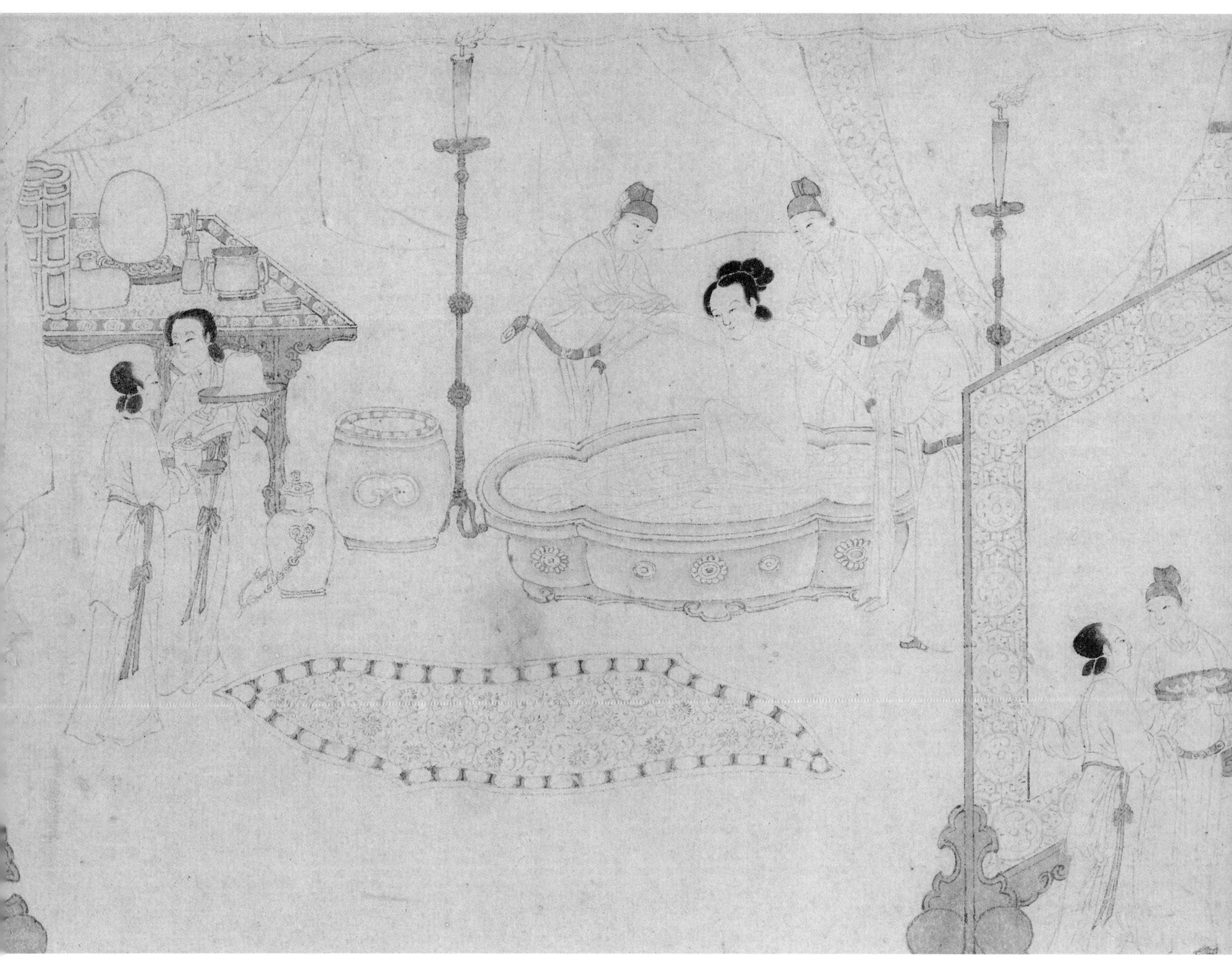

PREVIOUS PAGES AND ABOVE: You Qiu, *Spring Morning in the Han Palace* (Cat. 33, details, scenes 1 and 11)

Han women, and a frequent subject in early didactic paintings. She was commonly portrayed in a scene entitled 'Lady Ban declining to ride in the imperial palanquin', after she refused to accompany the emperor in his carriage on a pleasure outing lest by her presence at his side she made him appear frivolous, like bad rulers in ancient paintings. The witty and insightful illustration of this scene in the *Admonitions* scroll attributed to Gu Kaizhi suggests that Lady Ban's loss of imperial favour was less due to her far-sighted observation of protocol than to the superior charms of a younger and less admonitory beauty – the one depicted beside the emperor in the palanquin, who may have been Zhao Feiyan.

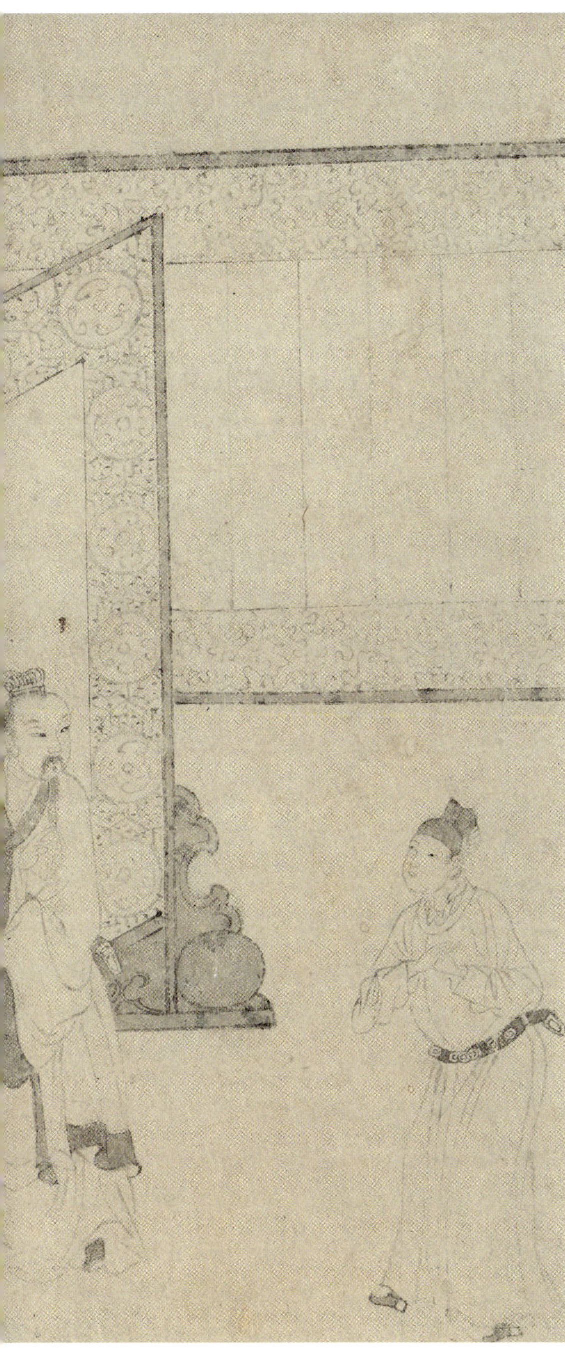

Although official and sanctioned versions of the lives of the Zhao sisters were recorded in dynastic history and in the *Biographies of Exemplary Women*, what You Qiu illustrated here was an alternative source of history, not deemed fit, presumably due to its salacious and sexually explicit content, for the category of biography proper, and hence entitled the 'Outer Biography of Feiyan'. According to the inscriptions in the scroll, the patron acquired a fine calligraphic transcription of this text by the Suzhou eminence Wen Zhengming, and in about 1568 he commissioned the professional artist You Qiu to illustrate it.[85] In plotting the vicissitudes of the women's lives at the pinnacle of the mid-Han-dynasty polity, the painting stands out for its near-explicit depiction of vignettes from the 'Outer Biography', including two scenes of female nudity which are extremely rare in the history of Chinese painting outside the little-studied genre of erotica.[86]

In outline, the story is illustrated as follows. Scene 1 shows the sisters learning the arts of dance and music as serving girls in the household of the emperor's sister. The sisters are poorly quartered and in winter share a bed for warmth. In scene 2, Feiyan has risen from her bed to answer the door to her lover, a huntsman of the woods who is startled by her naked beauty. On an imperial visit, Feiyan comes to the emperor's attention and he recruits her to his harem, although at first, as shown in scene 3, she chastely declines the imperial favour. Cohabiting with Feiyan, the emperor's health deteriorates, and he summons her sister, Hede, who eventually displaces Feiyan for the emperor's favour (scene 3 and on). The remainder of the scroll illustrates various vignettes in the subsequent history of the love triangle, including the sisters' unsuccessful attempts to conceive and bear the emperor a male heir by illicitly taking bullish lovers. In the penultimate scene, the emperor is portrayed in the role of sexual voyeur, getting his thrills from watching Hede at her bath by candlelight through a hole in a screen. The last scene is typically oblique, depicting the emperor and Hede happily enjoying genteel activities in an elegant garden setting. The text actually describes a night of drunken and amorous revelry, during which Hede mistakenly gives the emperor a fatal overdose of aphrodisiac, for which mistake she later commits suicide by taking poison. The painting was commissioned shortly after the Jiajing emperor himself died from such an overdose early in 1567, and, in drawing parallels between the past and the present, may have been intended as a form of coded warning to the court against this kind of imperial conduct. The painting was not likely to have been seen at court, but rather to have been appreciated by the influential scholar-official circle of Suzhou.

Dating to the late Ming or early Qing period (mid-17th century), and belonging in the category of genre or folklore painting, is a delicately executed handscroll, *Women Enjoying the Spring Festival* (p. 66), by Huang Juan (active 1630–56), a little-known artist in painting history.[87] Despite having no specific storyline, but rather a folkloric content relating to women's activities at the New Year festival, the scroll is nevertheless carefully plotted as a work of visual art. It comprises a series of genre-type scenes done in a plain, impersonal style cleverly suited to the subject matter – women at leisure honing their virtues. This type of painting vaguely recalls the style of Qiu Ying, whose *Spring Morning in the Han Palace* (Palace Museum, Taipei), a long handscroll depicting women at leisure in palace gardens, is a masterpiece of the genre.[88] Within the context of very late Ming professional painting in the Jiangnan region, Huang Juan's scroll is generic,

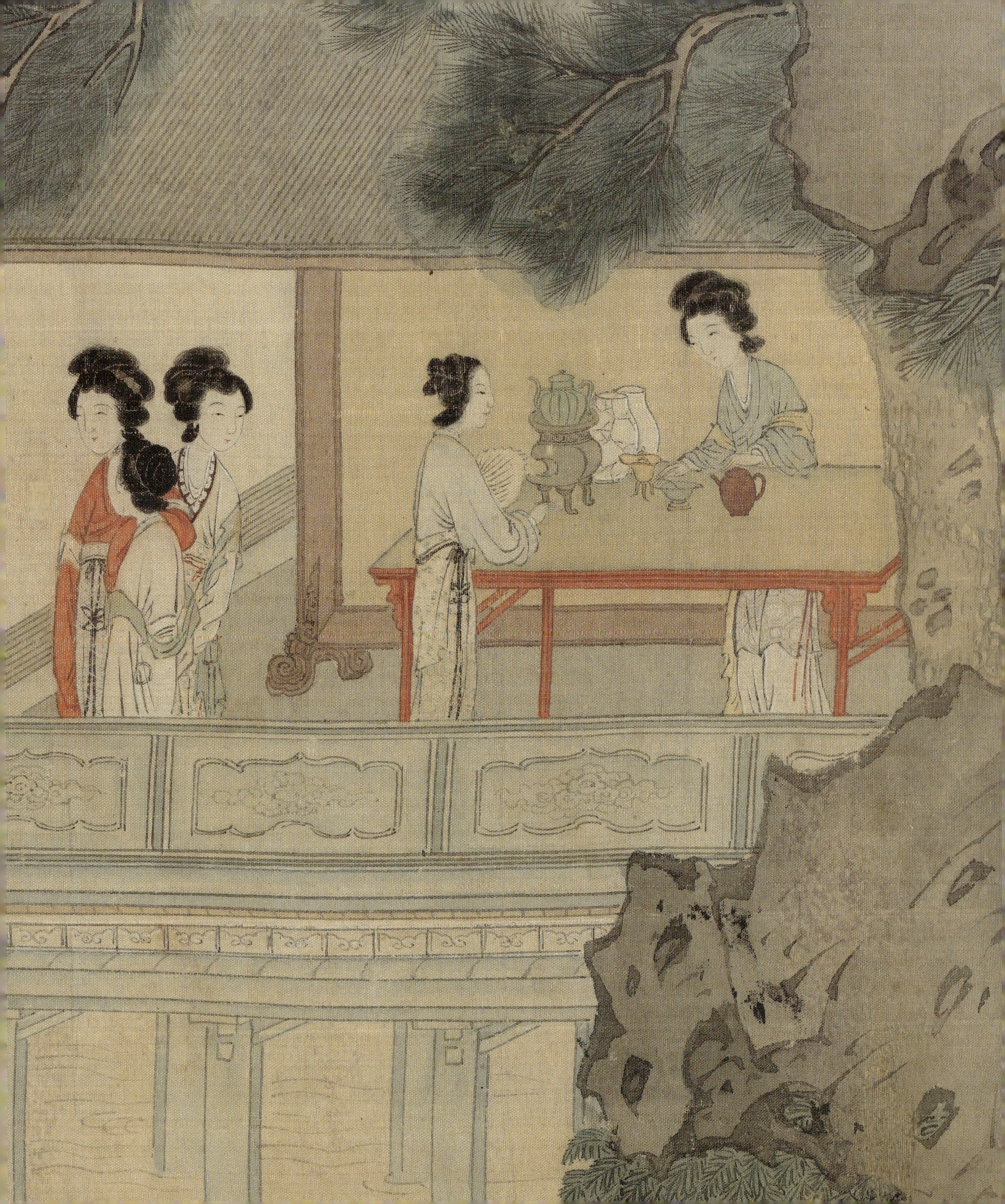

OPPOSITE: Huang Juan, *Women Enjoying the Spring Festival* (Cat. 13, detail)

in terms of its brush style and its plotting. The figures of the women conform to types, being barely distinguishable as individuals. There are no very strident colours, the strongest being the reds and blues, which accent a rather uniform green-blue setting. The scroll is plotted by presenting a series of standard formal motifs, including (in order) pines, willows, bamboos, cypresses, bananas and wutong trees, as the pillars and posts in a sequence of scenes. These scenes are linked in the scroll in two movements or acts divided, or linked, by a stone arched bridge. In the first movement, the scenes shift back and forth across the water in a zigzag, from a pavilion over water at the back, to a boat at the front, to an island at the back, to the bank at the front. After the bridge, this is varied, as the scenes progress on land as follows: women standing on open ground at the front, women seated on a mat or under trees at the front, women seated in a pavilion at the back, and on open ground at the front.

In this idealised setting some of the gentle womenfolk discuss antiquities, while others are reading or boating; yet others are situated in proximity to bamboo of the feathery kind associated with accomplished women in history like Guan Daosheng (1262–1319), wife of the Yuan-dynasty scholar-artist Zhao Mengfu.[89] Elsewhere, musicians are playing together, or are apparently engaged in cultured conversation known as 'pure talk'. There is no indication of a hostess, whose husband or father this fine property might belong to, or whether it is a private or public garden or park. It is hard to say whether the scroll charts the meanderings of a small social gathering of women who engage in a series of activities over the course of a day, or whether these are selected episodes from a much larger event. Possibly, the re-appearance in various scenes of one woman with a red top and another with a blue top indicates a series of activities.

In some sense, a painting like this is actually a kind of anti-narrative, a kind of 'lofty' reaction to the grubbier aspects of contemporary culture – like celebrity courtesans and racy literature. Relative to men, the names of few women are recorded in Chinese history, and yet we know the names of many accomplished courtesans from this period, including Ma Shouzhen (Xianglan, 1548–1604).[90] Seen against the late Ming cultural landscape, Huang Juan's painting stands in contrast to this vibrant late Ming commodity culture, holding its own because of its deep historical roots. In a somewhat sanitised form, it relates to the genre-cum-didactic tradition of the *Admonitions* scroll and *Biographies of Exemplary Women*. As is sometimes remarked, the illustration of and later attention to such didactic works as the *Admonitions* and *Biographies* indicates that their precepts and lessons were perennially ignored, rather than obeyed.

We may observe, in this vein, that far greater note was being taken by Ming-dynasty scholar-officials (who compiled official history) of cases of 'exemplary women' (*lie nü*) than had been the case with their pre-Ming predecessors. Cases of 'exemplary women' to be considered for inclusion in the official history of the Ming (which by tradition would be compiled under the succeeding dynasty) numbered in the hundreds.[91] Since the category of exemplary women existed to call attention to both positive and negative role-models, it is not necessarily the case that Ming women were more virtuous than their forebears, but rather that Ming historians wished to highlight female morality and virtue through increased reportage. Arguably, this was because they believed that female mores were degenerating. Huang Juan's painting, which champions the demure

OPPOSITE: Hua Xu, *Consort Zhen at her Morning Toilette* (Cat. 11, detail)

ideal of womanhood, is perhaps as interesting for what it is, as for what it seeks not to be.

A related handscroll painting, executed by one of the great talents of the Qing emperor Qianlong's court atelier, Ding Guanpeng (d. after 1770), is entitled *Ladies on the 'Night of Sevens' Pleading for Skills* (Cat. 6), dated 1748.[92] Like many other Qianlong court paintings, this one is ostensibly a reprise of a celebrated earlier work, in this case, Qiu Ying's *Ladies in the Han Palace Pleading for Skills (Hangong qiqiao tu).* The subject is a celebration of the legend of the Cowherd (the star Altair) and the Weaver Girl (the star Vega), lovers who, according to legend, meet just once a year on this night, the seventh day of the seventh month in the lunar calendar, as noted above. Traditionally, Chinese girls 'plead for skills' from the Weaver Girl to help them secure a good husband. The painting describes precisely this: elegant court ladies celebrating the festival in appropriate ways. There are thirty-one of these exquisitely painted ladies in the scroll, all rendered in an authoritative and precise figural manner – some are making preparations, moving utensils or candles, while others read or enjoy the moonlight. Mounted after the painting is a poem by the Qianlong emperor. This painting is exactly the kind of moralising artwork that the Qianlong emperor would have commanded to be made for the edification of the women of his back palace. Of course, they were not Chinese, since intermarriage between Manchus and Chinese was forbidden. However, the existence of this artwork suggests that they, like the emperor, were expected to act as models in appropriate roles and guises for the Chinese subjects of the Qing empire.

Another painting in the exhibition is testament to a somewhat different ideal of feminine accomplishment in the mid-Qing period, and also a sign of a growing modernity in late imperial China. Actually, this painting could just as easily be a part of the section, above, on models of culture. Rather than polishing traditional feminine virtues, the numerous young women depicted in You Shao and Wang Gong's *The Female Disciples of Master Suiyuan* (Cat. 34) are accomplished in poetry and literature, traditionally the preserve of male literati. The Master Suiyuan referred to in the title is the pre-eminent literatus Yuan Mei, a vigorous advocate of classical verse by women poets, who assembled a well-known coterie of students. Yuan Mei is the elderly gentleman seated in a garden pavilion at the end of the scroll surrounded by his female pupils. The painting is dated in Yuan Mei's inscription to the first year of the Jiaqing reign (1796), shortly after the Qianlong emperor's retirement from the throne after sixty years in favour of his son. Not wishing to remain on the throne longer than his grandfather, the Kangxi emperor (r. 1662–1722), the Qianlong emperor abdicated in a public act of filial piety (*xiao*), one of the most important of all Confucian virtues. Despite the conservative views usually ascribed to the artists, and in spite of Yuan Mei's great age at this time, this painting can be seen as ushering in a new and somewhat more liberated era for culture and society, and as a kind of commentary on changing literary values in mid-Qing China.

With the last two paintings in this part of the exhibition, we return to the theme of women in the context of romantic liaisons. Both concern the celebrated early poet Cao Zhi, author of the 'Goddess of the Luo River Ode' (*Luoshen fu*), also known as the 'Consort Zhen Ode' (*Zhenfei fu*), about an encounter between the poet and the beguiling goddess.[93] The painting *Consort Zhen at her Morning Toilette* (opposite), by a relatively obscure Qing-dynasty artist, Hua Xu, portrays the beautiful lover of Cao Zhi.[94]

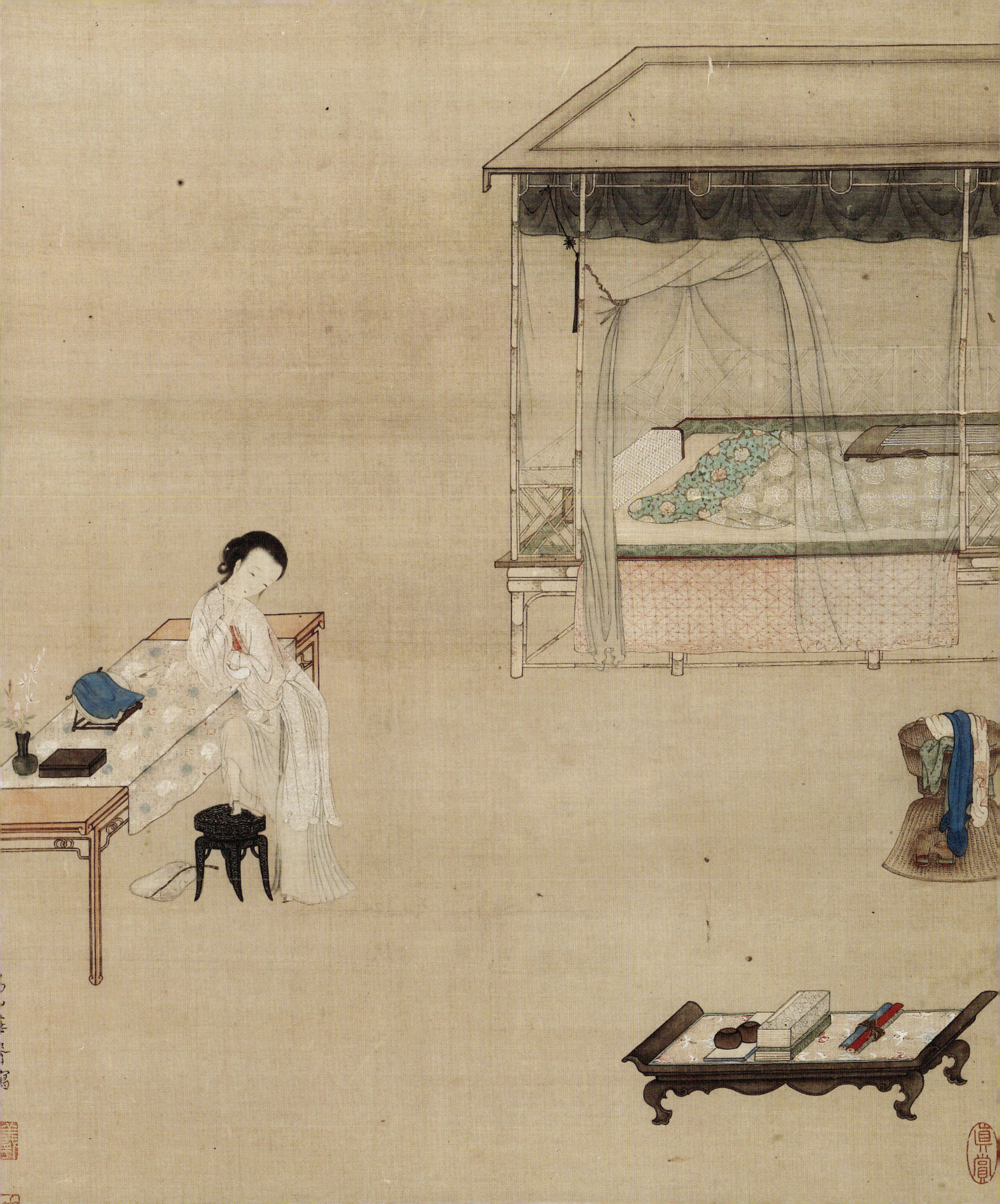

That the lady, Zhen Mi, has just got out of bed is clear from the rumpled bedclothes, half pulled back bed curtains, and the covered mirror on the table. She also wears no shoes over her (anachronistically) bound feet. Her tiny shoes, and yesterday's clothes, lie strewn across the wicker basket to the right. Although alone, the lady assumes a sexually provocative pose, her head cocked to one side, her chin on her hand, and her bound foot plain to see on the stool, as she lets her left arm play across her bust. Who is the object of her desire? On the floor below her lies a discarded fan on which is painted a dragon, the symbol of her husband, Cao Pi, the emperor. She closely eyes the table – identified as *her* table by the inlay pattern of phoenixes, which are symbols of the empress. Her gaze seems to fix not on the books on this table, for they are neatly squared, but on the bundle of scrolls with coloured wrappers that lie askew, which may be letters.

This is not such a straightforward scene as a woman performing her morning toilette, but rather a nuanced evocation of Consort Zhen's predicament as lover of the emperor's brother, Cao Zhi. The instrument in the bed might represent her loneliness and longing for romantic fulfilment. The emperor does not visit her, and she has rejected him (the dropped fan); rather, she gazes longingly at the scrolls – the writings or letters that may be her only means of communication with Cao Zhi. Notably, the figure of Consort Zhen is transposed into the present, not just by dint of the contemporary (Qing) furnishings, material culture and bound feet, and indeed her figural type, but also pointedly through the insinuations of her literary accomplishments.

We have already encountered, above, the ground-breaking mid-nineteenth-century artist, Ren Xiong, who is also the painter of the hanging scroll *Goddess of the Luo River*, an imaginary portrayal of the goddess after whom Cao Zhi's ode is entitled (see Cat. 23).[95] This well-known ode describes Cao Zhi's romantic but ultimately frustrating encounter with this ethereal, beautiful figure on his journey home following his dismissal from court after Consort Zhen's enforced suicide. It is often interpreted as Cao Zhi's encounter with her spirit. In the painting, the goddess is depicted as a beribboned beauty wearing colourful multi-layered dresses, carrying a garlanded, feathered staff over her shoulder, standing among the lush vegetation of her domain in the Luo River. Historically, Cao Zhi's ode was believed to have been illustrated in its entirety by Gu Kaizhi in the fourth century. Although a number of Song-dynasty handscroll paintings of this title survive, they are no longer connected with him by modern scholars. Still, Ren Xiong's painting draws upon the early iconography of the female beauty with her trailing, fluttering tassles and layered tresses found in such early paintings.[96] It might seem like Ren Xiong's painting was just yet another opportunity to re-traditionalise culture, to reassert the antiquity of Chinese culture in the face of growing foreign intervention in China, but it is also important to recognise that it was through such active re-engagements that artists pioneered new artforms appropriate to the times. One of the challenges of looking at paintings from nineteenth-century China is learning to recognise and interpret the sometimes difficult to quantify effects of a Chinese modernity.

Notes

Some of the stories featured in this exhibition exist in multiple versions. In other cases, the plot lines of tales have evolved with reiteration over time. The narrative accounts provided in this book are sometimes simplified, schematic or indicative.

The measurements used in the Catalogue section of this book refer to the size of the painting medium (paper or silk) rather than the scroll mounting.

1 Narrative painting was, for instance, a topic of the conference, 'Rethinking Visual Narratives from Asia: Intercultural and Comparative Perspectives', organised by the Department of Fine Arts, University of Hong Kong, on 8–9 June, 2009.

2 On the link between Chinese lyric aesthetics and narrative painting, see Dore J. Levy, 'Vignettism in the Poetics of Chinese Narrative Painting', in Alexandra Green (ed.), *Rethinking Visual Narratives from Asia: Intercultural and Comparative Perspectives.*

3 The idea, here, of a thematic map in Chinese art history owes to Jonathan Hay, 'Shitao's late work (1697–1707): a thematic map', PhD diss., Yale University, 1989.

4 For the Shanghai Museum's exhibition and study of pre-modern figure painting, see *Shimao fengqing: Zhongguo gudai renwuhua jingpin ji (Highlights of Ancient Chinese Figure Paintings from the Liaoning Provincial Museum and the Shanghai Museum*); hereafter *Highlights of Ancient Chinese Figure Paintings*. The current exhibition is drawn from the same area of the Shanghai Museum collection as the 2001 exhibition, *Ancients in Profile: Ming and Qing Figure Paintings from the Shanghai Museum* (hereafter *Ancients in Profile*), but is specifically concerned with narrative painting and addressed to a western audience.

5 For a volume of essays on this artwork, see Shane McCausland (ed.), *Gu Kaizhi and the Admonitions Scroll.*

6 Cf. John Hay (ed.), *Boundaries in China* (London: Reaktion Books, 1994).

7 Tr. David Hawkes, *Ch'u Tz'u: The Songs of the South, an Ancient Chinese Anthology.*

8 On this theme, see for example, Alfreda Murck, *Poetry and Painting in Song China: the Subtle Art of Dissent* (Cambridge, Mass.: Harvard University Asia Center for the Harvard-Yenching Institute, 2000). Images of the two consorts were painted by Fu Baoshi (1904–65) as a way to decry the lack of a unifying leader in a time of national crisis; see Alfreda Murck, 'Images that Admonish', *Orientations* 32.6 (June 2001), pp. 52–57.

9 A study on the artist's milieux is Britta Lee Erickson, 'Patronage and Production in the Nineteenth-Century Shanghai Region: Ren Xiong (1823–1857) and his Sponsors', PhD diss., Stanford University, 1997.

10 For a study of women in early modern narrative art in China, see Marion S. Lee, 'Narrating Historical Women and Fictional Characters in Ming and Qing China: A Matter of Encoding Remembrances and Contemporaneity', in Green (ed.), *Rethinking Visual Narratives from Asia.*

11 Zhao was the personal name of the posthumous emperor Wendi of Jin, Sima Zhao (211 65). The painting is featured in *Highlights of Ancient Chinese Figure Paintings*, no. 60; *Ancients in Profile*, no. 8.

12 A well-known example by Qiu Ying is in the Palace Museum, Taipei; illustrated in Wen C. Fong and James C. Y. Watt, *Possessing the Past: Treasures from the National Palace Museum, Taipei*, pl. 203.

13 Featured in *Ancients in Profile*, no. 28.

14 See for example, Irene S. Leung, 'The Frontier Imaginary in the Song Dynasty (960–1279): Revisiting Cai Yan's "Barbarian Captivity" and Return', PhD diss., University of Michigan, 2001; and Robert A. Rorex and Wen C. Fong, *Eighteen Songs of a Nomad Flute: The Story of Lady Wen-chi.* For another translation of the songs by Dore J. Levy, see Kang-i Sun Chang and Haun Saussy (eds), *Women Writers of Traditional China: An Anthology of Poetry and Criticism.*

15 The others included Ruan Ji (210–63), Shan Tao (205–83), Wang Rong (243–305), Ruan Xian (234–305), Xiang Xiu and Liu Ling.

16 Tr. Richard B. Mather, *A New Account of Tales of the World by Liu I-ch'ing*, ch. 23, pp. 371ff.

17 On the painting subject, see Ellen Johnston Laing, 'Neo-Taoism and the "Seven Sages of the Bamboo Grove" in Chinese Painting', pp. 5–54.

18 See *Ancients in Profile*, no. 12; *Highlights of Ancient Chinese Figure Paintings*, no. 29. This story of the 'Seven Worthies of the Bamboo Grove' is also the title of a work of video art by the contemporary Shanghai-based artist Yang Fudong (b. 1971), to be shown during the run of the exhibition. Rendered in a slightly different translation as *Seven Intellectuals of the Bamboo Forest*, Yang Fudong's 300-minute, five-part work is a kind of ironic romanticisation of the past, yet it also contains beguilingly beautiful images of figures engaged in spontaneous, impulsive living in the mountains – and, later, in the metropolis.

19 *Jin shu, juan* 33 (Beijing: Zhongua shuju, 1999), pp. 654–57, esp. p. 657; tr. Helmut Wilhelm in John Minford and Joseph S. M. Lau (eds), *Classical Chinese Literature: An Anthology of Translations*, vol. 1, p. 478.

20 See Mather, *New Account of Tales of the World*, ch. 16.

21 On Su Shi's poetry, see Stephen Owen, *An Anthology of Chinese Literature: Beginnings to 1911*, pp. 663–83. On the 'cult' of Su Shi, see Alfreda Murck, 'Spiritual Communion: The Cult of Su Shi', in *Eccentric Visions: the Worlds of Luo Ping* (Zurich: Museum Rietberg, 2009), pp. 80–87.

22 A handscroll in ink on paper, 30.48 x 566.42 cm, in the Nelson-Atkins Museum, Kansas City. For this scroll, see Richard K. Kent, 'Ch'iao Chung-ch'ang's *Illustration of Su Shih's "Latter Prose Poem on the Red Cliff": Pai-miao* (Plain Line Drawing) as Heuristic Device', *Taida Journal of Art History*, no. 11 (September 2001), pp. 95–132; see also Jerome Silbergeld, 'Back to the Red Cliff: Reflections on the Narrative Mode in Early Literati Landscape Painting', *Ars Orientalis* 25 (1995), pp. 19–38. For an exhibition of Red Cliff paintings, see *Chibi fu shuhua tezhan* (*The Red Cliff: Special Exhibition of Calligraphy and Painting*), exh. cat. (Taipei: National Palace Museum, 1984).

23 Published *Liangtuxuan shuhua jicui (Liangtu Studio Calligraphy and Painting Collection*); hereafter *Liangtuxuan shuhua jicui*, p. 77.

24 Published *Liangtuxuan shuhua jicui*, p. 93.

25 The sources in the Han-dynasty text, *Gushi shijiu shou* (*Nineteen Ancient Poems*), and other texts are listed in *Ancients in Profile*, no. 7. See also *Highlights of Ancient Chinese Figure Paintings*, no. 43.

26 Translation by Owen, *Anthology of Chinese Literature*, p. 451.

27 On the pictorial illustration of the 'Song of Lasting Sorrow' in East Asia, see Shane McCausland and Matthew P. McKelway, *Chinese Romance from a Japanese Brush: Kano Sansetsu's Chōgonka Scrolls in the Chester Beatty Library*.

28 For a painting of this topic in the Shanghai Museum, attributed to Wang Zhao, see *Ancients in Profile*, no. 4.

29 On Buddhist art in China, see also Marsha Weidner (ed.), *Latter Days of the Law: Images of Chinese Buddhism, 850–1850*; Helmut Brinker and Hiroshi Kanazawa, *Zen Masters of Meditation in Images and Writings* (Zurich: Artibus Asiae Publishers, 1996).

30 Published *Liangtuxuan shuhua jicui*, p. 128.

31 For studies, see Hsing-yuan Tsao, 'A Forgotten Celebrity: Wang Zhen (1867–1938), Businessman, Philanthropist, and Artist', *Art at the Close of China's Empire: Phoebus*, vol. 8 (Tempe: Arizona State University, 1998), pp. 94–109; Xiao Fengji, 'Haishang huajia Wang Zhen shengping shiji' (The Shanghai painter Wang Zhen's life-story), *Duoyun*, no. 49 (1996), pp. 49–51. Also relevant are Wang Zhen's *Buddhist Sage* of 1928 in the Metropolitan Museum of Art, a portrait of Bodhidharma, illustrated and discussed in Wen C. Fong, *Between Two Cultures: Late-Nineteenth- and Early-Twentieth-Century Chinese Painting from the Robert H. Ellsworth Collection*, pl. 21 and pp. 66–67; and *Limitless Longevity Buddha* (1925), published in Julia F. Andrews et al., *Between the Thunder and the Rain: Chinese Paintings from the Opium War through the Cultural Revolution, 1840–1979*, no. 66.

32 A scene of Bodhidharma meditating amid crumbling walls is included in Yoshitoshi Tsukioka's 1885–92 woodblock-print series, *One Hundred Aspects of the Moon*, illustrated at: http://www.internationalfolkart.org/exhibitions/past/moonweb/section1/026.htm

33 On Daoist arts in China, broadly, see Stephen Little with Shawn Eichman, *Taoism and the Arts of China*; for Li Tieguai and his description in *Complete Biographies of the Assorted Immortals* (*Liexian quan zhuan*; comp. Wang Shizhen, 1598), see no. 125.

34 The albums are featured in *Highlights of Ancient Chinese Figure Paintings*, nos 22 and 41, respectively.

35 See *Ancients in Profile*, no. 49.

36 For a transcription, see *Ancients in Profile*, no. 16. See also, *Highlights of Ancient Chinese Figure Paintings*, no. 46.

37 The Queen Mother of the West is mentioned by the Daoist adept Tao Hongjing (456–536) in *Zhen gao* (*Statements of the Perfected*), *juan* 2, pp. 10b–11a (*Zhen gao* is part of the Daoist canon, *Zhengtong daozang*, text no. HY 1010 in the numbering system of Weng Dujian (comp.), *Daozang zimu yinde* [1935; reprint, Taipei: Xinwenfeng chuban she, 1988]). For this and other references, see Little, *Taoism and the Arts of China*, nos 24–27; and Zhou Xiyao in *Shimao fengqing: Zhongguo gudai renwu hua*, p. 120. The Daoist canon is reprinted in *Zhengtong daozang* (*Daoist Canon of the Zhengtong Reign; 1444–45*), 61 vols (Taipei: Xinwenfeng chubanshe, 1988). See also, Suzanne Cahill, *Transcendence and Divine Passion: The Queen Mother of the West in Medieval China*.

38 For a study on the oeuvre, see Julia F. Andrews, 'The Significance of Style and Subject Matter in the Painting of Cui Zizhong', PhD diss., University of California, Berkeley, 1984.

39 Tr. in Owen, *Anthology of Chinese Literature*, pp. 309–10.

40 Owen, *Anthology of Chinese Literature*, p. 644.

41 On the topic, see Richard M. Barnhart, *Peach Blossom Spring: Gardens and Flowers in Chinese Painting*.

42 Arthur Waley, *The Way and Its Power: A Study of the Tao Te Ching and its Place in Chinese Thought* (London: Allen & Unwin, 1934).

43 Published *Liangtuxuan shuhua jicui*, p. 70.

44 Ronald G. Knapp, *China's Living Houses: Folk Beliefs, Symbols, and Household Ornamentation* (Honolulu: University of Hawai'i Press, 1999), p. 76ff.

45 The source in *Tang yishi* (*Left-Over Affairs of the Tang*), a lost text cited in Chen Wenzhu, *Tianzhong ji* (*Record of Heaven's Centre*; 1589) is translated in Little, *Taoism and the Arts of China*, no. 92; another translation by Mary H. Fong, 'A probable second "Chung K'uei" by Emperor Shun-chih of the Ch'ing Dynasty', *Oriental Art* 23, no. 4 (1977), pp. 427–28.

46 On Zhong Kui in mid-Ming paintings, see for example, Stephen Little, 'The Demon Queller and the Art of Qiu Ying', *Artibus Asiae* 46, nos 1-2 (1985), pp. 5–128.

47 For studies, see Chen Jie-jin and Lai Yu-chih (gen. eds), *Zhuisuo Zhepai* (*Tracing the Che School in Chinese Painting*), exh. cat. (Taipei: National Palace Museum, 2008); and Richard M. Barnhart, *Painters of the Great Ming: the Imperial Court and the Zhe School*.

48 Tr. James Legge, *The Works of Mencius* (reprint, New York: Dover, 1970).

49 For a study, see Lothar Ledderose, *Mi Fu and the Classical Tradition of Chinese Calligraphy* (Princeton: Princeton University Press, 1979).

50 Tr. by H. C. Chang, in Minford and Lau (eds), *Classical Chinese Literature: An Anthology of Translations*, pp. 479–82.

51 Tr. Mather, *New Account of Tales of the World*.

52 *Ancients in Profile*, no. 47.

53 In the sixteenth century, Qiu Ying painted *Zhao Mengfu Writing the Heart Sutra in Exchange for Tea*, now in the Cleveland Museum of Art (1963.102), in a latter day reprise of the Wang Xizhi anecdote above. Illustrated at www.clemusart.com (search: collections; artist: Qiu Ying; title).

54 For a study of Ren Yi's artworld circle, see Roberta May-Hwa Wue, 'Making the Artist: Ren Bonian (1840–1896) and Portraits of the Shanghai Artworld', PhD diss., New York University, 2001.

55 Biography in Mather, *New Account of Tales of the World*, pp. 508–09, citing Zhu Faji (4th c.), *Gaoyi shamen zhuan* (*Biographies of Lofty and Detached Monks*).

56 *Shishuo xinyu, yanyu* (*Speech and conversation*), no. 63; tr. Mather, *New Account of Tales of the World*, p. 61. Zhidun was also fond of cranes (see no. 76 and p. 66, respectively).

57 See for example, the ancient (Song-dynasty?) handscroll *Divine Thoroughbred* (*Shenjun tu*), attributed to either Han Gan or Han Huang, in Liaoning Provincial Museum.

58 See for example, the portraits of Yuan Mei, Jin Nong and Ding Jing, illustrated in *Eccentric Visions* (as n. 21), nos 14, 13 and 11, respectively. See also Patricia Berger, 'Public Spectacle and Private Devotions: Buddhist Art in Eighteenth-Century Yangzhou', *Eccentric Visions*, pp. 40–49.

59 On the link between photography and Ren Yi's portrait style, see Richard Vinograd, *Boundaries of the Self*, pp. 143–44. See also Yu-chih Lai, 'Remapping Borders: Ren Bonian's Frontier Paintings and Urban Life in 1880s Shanghai', *The Art Bulletin* 86 (September 2004), pp. 550–72; and Chia-ling Yang, *New Wine in Old*

Bottles: The Art of Ren Bonian in Nineteenth-Century Shanghai (London: Saffron, forthcoming).

60 From an essay of 1907 by Zhang Jingfu citing Ren Yi's words, entitled 'Ren Bonian xiansheng Yuzu wubun tuji' (A record of Master Ren Bonian and his painting: Five Relations among the Featured Category); cited in Ding Xiyuan, *Ren Bonian* (Shanghai, 1989), *nianpu* section, pp. 47–48; tr. Claudia Brown and Ju-hsi Chou, *Transcending Turmoil: Painting at the Close of China's Empire*, pp. 181–182.

61 One 1882 painting is in the Palace Museum, Beijing, and another, dated 1867, is in the Suzhou Museum.

62 The original Tang story featuring these three, and the likely source of numerous later dramas and plays, is *Qiuran ke zhuan* (*Story of the Curly-bearded Stranger*).

63. You Qiu also depicted Hongfu nü, but the two paintings bear little relation. For You Qiu's monochrome 1575 painting, *Red Duster* (*Hongfu tuzhou*), see *Zhongguo lidai huihua, Gugong Bowuyuan cang huaji*, vol. 6 (Beijing: Renmin meishu, 1990), p. 20.

64 See Yu-chih Lai, 'Surreptitious Appropriation: Ren Bonian (1840–1895) and Japanese Culture in Shanghai, 1842–1895', PhD diss., Yale University, 2005, p. 262ff; see also her 'Remapping Borders' (as n. 59).

65 For Li Bai, see, for example, Kathlyn Maurean Liscomb, 'Li Bai, a Hero among Poets, in the Visual, Dramatic, and Literary Arts of China', *The Art Bulletin* 81.3 (September 1999), pp. 354–89; Owen, *Anthology of Chinese Literature*, p. 397ff; and for Du Fu, see pp. 413–40.

66 For a study on the reception of Li Bai's poetry, see Paula M. Varsano, *Tracking the Banished Immortal: the Poetry of Li Bo and its Critical Reception* (Honolulu: University of Hawai'i Press, 2003).

67 Tu Long, *Caihao ji* (reprint, 2 vols; Shanghai: Shangwu yinshuguan, 1954).

68 A well-known portrait attributed to Liang Kai (late 12th–13th c.) is in the Tokyo National Museum. Illustrated at www.tnm.jp (search: paintings; Chinese; figures).

69 Shan Guolin in *Ancients in Profile*, p. 11.

70 *Ancients in Profile*, no. 43.

71 See Ellen Johnston Laing, 'Real or Ideal: The Problem of the "Elegant Gathering in the West Garden" in Chinese Historical and Art Historical Records', *Journal of the American Oriental Society* 88.3 (July–September 1968), pp. 419–35.

72 Jonathan Hay, *Shitao: Painting and Modernity in Early Qing China.*

73 The date of about 1647 is proposed by Weng Wange [Wan-go Weng] in his *Chen Hongshou: His Life and Art*, (see vol. 1, p. 188; vol. 2, no. 70), on the basis of the signature and seals.

74 Li Lan, 'Chen Hongshou "Yaji tu juan" chutan' (A Preliminary Discussion of Chen Hongshou's *Elegant Gathering* handscroll), in *Shimao fengqing: Zhongguo gudai renwuhua guoji shuxue yantaohui* (*Customs and Manners: An International Scholarly Symposium on Ancient Chinese Figure Painting*), n. p. The painting has also been read as a 'pictorial manifesto' of Pure Land Buddhism among late Ming literati, including the influential Gong'an School literary theorists, the brothers Yuan Hongdao (1568–1610) and Zongdao (1560–1600), pictured at the left end; see Hsing-li Tsai, 'Ch'en Hung-shou's "Elegant Gathering": A Late Ming Pictorial Manifesto of Pure Land Buddhism', PhD diss., University of Kansas, 1997.

75 Published *Liangtuxuan shuhua jicui*, p. 126.

76 See for examples, the mid-16th-century handscroll painting by the professional artist Zhang Lu (*c.*1490–*c.*1563), *Su Dongpo Returning to the Hanlin Academy* (Jingyuanzhai Collection at University Art Museum, Berkeley), and the 1593 print in *Guwen zhengzong* (*The Orthodox Transmission of Antique Prose*) (Anhui Zhengshaozhai edition), illustrated in Craig Clunas, *Pictures and Visuality in Early Modern China*, figs 12 and 13.

77 Another scholar-official to be so honoured by the Tang emperor Xuanzong was the Head of the Hanlin Academy, Linghu Tao. The emperor once kept him up most of the night discussing matters of business, by which time the candles of his own escort had burned down. The emperor conferred on him the imperial escort by 'golden-lotus candles'. On his arrival at the Academy he was mistaken for the emperor. See the biographies of Linghu Tao in *Jiu Tang shu (Old Tang History), juan* 172 (Beijing: Zhongua shuju, 1999), pp. 3039–40; and *Xin Tang shu* (*New Tang History*), *juan* 166 (Beijing: Zhongua shuju, 1999), pp. 3961–62, esp. p. 3962.

78 Tr. James Hightower, 'Yuan Chen and the Story of Ying-ying', *Harvard Journal of Asiatic Studies* 33, pp. 93–103; Owen, *Anthology of Chinese Literature*, pp. 540–49.

79 Tr. Steven West and Wilt Idema, *The Story of the Western Wing.*

80 Tr. by David Hawkes as *The Story of the Stone.*

81 An example by a well-known figural artist is Gai Qi's (1779–1824) *Honglou meng tuyong* (China: Huai pu ju shi, 1879).

82 Published *Liangtuxuan shuhua jicui*, p. 132.

83 Wang Shizhen (1526–90) likens You Qiu's *baimiao* style to Li Gonglin and Zhao Mengfu's in his colophon to *Spring Morning in the Han Palace* (Cat. 33), a painting he commissioned of You Qiu in 1568. For a transcription of the colophon, see *Shimao fengqing* (as n. 4), Zhumulu, no. 9, p. 16.

84 For a translation of Empress Zhao's biography in *Han shu (History of Han), juan* 97 (Beijing: Zhongua shuju, 1999), pp. 2933–36, see Burton Watson (tr.), *Courtier and Commoner in Ancient China*, pp. 265–77. Studies on Zhao Feiyan include Barbara Bennett Peterson (ed.-in-chief), *Notable Women of China* (Armonk: M. E. Sharpe, 1999), pp. 87–90.

85 For a transcription of the texts in this handscroll, see *Highlights of Ancient Chinese Figure Paintings*, vol. Zhuluji (Catalogue Entries), no. 9.

86 On this painting, in comparison with a roughly contemporary Japanese narrative, see Shane McCausland, 'Visual Narratology in China and Japan around 1600 – A Comparative Study', in Green (ed.), *Rethinking Visual Narratives from Asia.*

87 The painting is featured in *Highlights of Ancient Chinese Figure Paintings*, no. 11; *Ancients in Profile*, no. 18.

88 Cited above, in n. 83.

89 See for example, the handscroll attributed to her, *Bamboo Clumps in Mist and Rain*, in the Palace Museum, Taipei.

90 Others include Liu Rushi, Guan Baimen, Gu Hengpi, Li Xiangjun, Wang Yue, Bian Yujing and Wang Wei.

91 This issue is explored in Yin Ji'nan, 'Late Ming Collectors and Connoisseurs, and the Making of the Modern Concept of "Gu Kaizhi"', in McCausland (ed.), *Gu Kaizhi and the Admonitions Scroll*, pp. 249–56.

92 Featured in *Ancients in Profile*, no. 33.

93 Tr. Owen, *Anthology of Chinese Literature*, pp. 194–97.

94 *Ancients in Profile*, no. 36.

95 *Ancients in Profile*, no. 46.

96 See for example, the work of Chen Pao-chen, including: 'Three representational modes for text/image relationships in early Chinese pictorial art', *Taida Journal of Art History*, no. 8 (March 2000), pp. 87–135; and 'The Goddess of the Lo River: A Study of early Chinese narrative handscrolls', PhD diss., Princeton University, 1987.

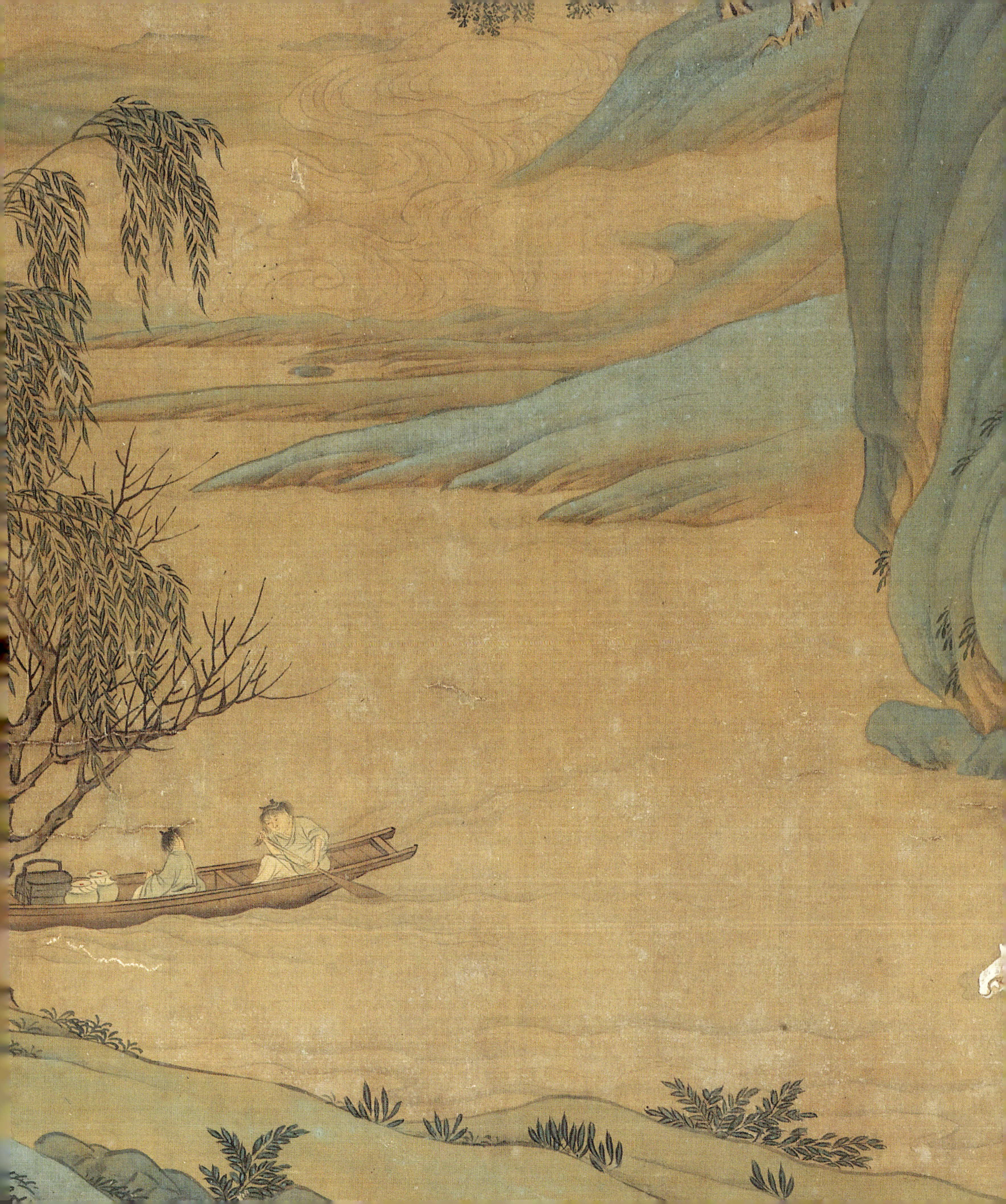

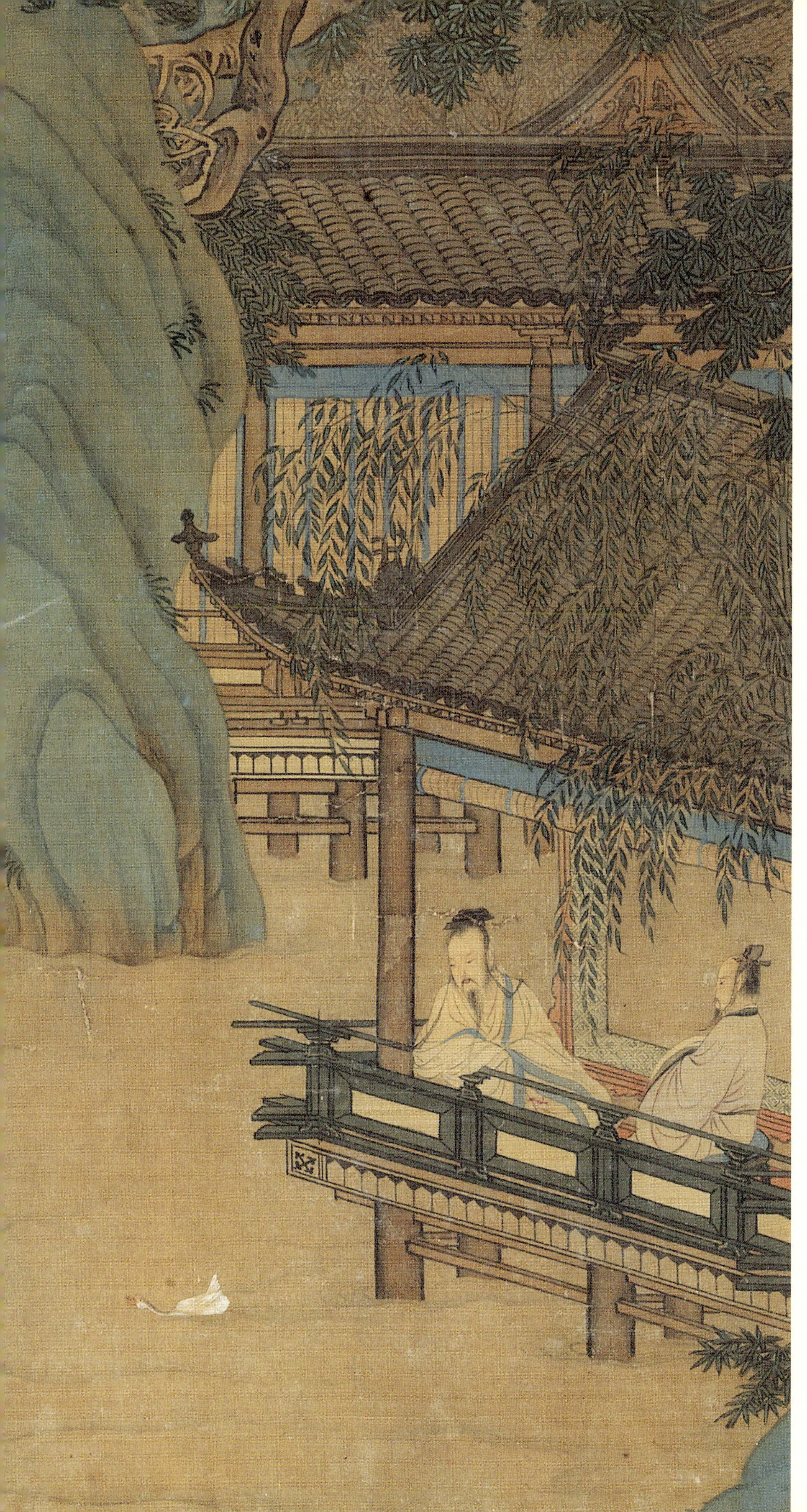

CATALOGUE

1

明 安正文 《黄鶴樓圖卷》

An Zhengwen (early Ming, late 14th–early 15th c.)
Yellow Crane Tower
Hanging scroll; ink and colours on silk
162.5 × 105.5 cm

The subject of this painting, Yellow Crane Tower (*Huanghelou*), is one of China's 'Three Great Towers of Jiangnan' (Jiangnan refers to the broader region around modern Shanghai), along with the Yueyang Tower (*Yueyanglou*) and the pavilion of Prince Teng (*Tengwangge*). The Yellow Crane Tower overlooks the grand Yangzi River on Snake Mountain in Wuchang, Hubei Province. It was constructed in the year 223 for Sun Quan (see Cat. 15), the King of Wu during the Three Kingdoms period (220–80). The original three-story building was around 30 metres high and had a military function, namely as a lookout tower for the city. After the Tang dynasty (618–907), it grew in popularity as a venue for literary gatherings among men of culture. The poets Li Bai, Bai Juyi and Jia Dao were among those who climbed the tower and composed many celebrated verses about it. Cui Hao wrote the following majestic lines about a Daoist immortal who is said to have flown from the tower on a crane:

> An ancient rode off on a yellow crane, leaving
> behind this Yellow Crane Tower.
> The yellow crane left never to return, traversing
> the white clouds for a thousand years.

The tower featured strongly in the literary and historical imagination of the Chinese people, so much so that it was always rebuilt following the numerous occasions on which it burnt down. The current building, reconstructed in 1957, is an imposing five-story tower that rises 51 metres and commands a magnificent view.

The Yellow Crane Tower was a favourite subject of painters such as Xia Yong in the Yuan dynasty (1271–1368) and Xie Shichen (1487–*c.*1560) in the Ming dynasty (1368–1644). This painting portrays an immaculately maintained, grand and imposing tower and shows the painter's exceptional technique in architectural painting. Little is known about the artist, other than that he was a court painter in the early Ming dynasty, in the ranks of the Embroidered Uniform Guards of the Hall of Honesty and Benevolence.

PREVIOUS PAGES: The Sage of Calligraphy, Wang Xizhi, admiring geese, from Anonymous (Ming), *Purification Festival at the Orchid Pavilion* (Cat. 3, detail)

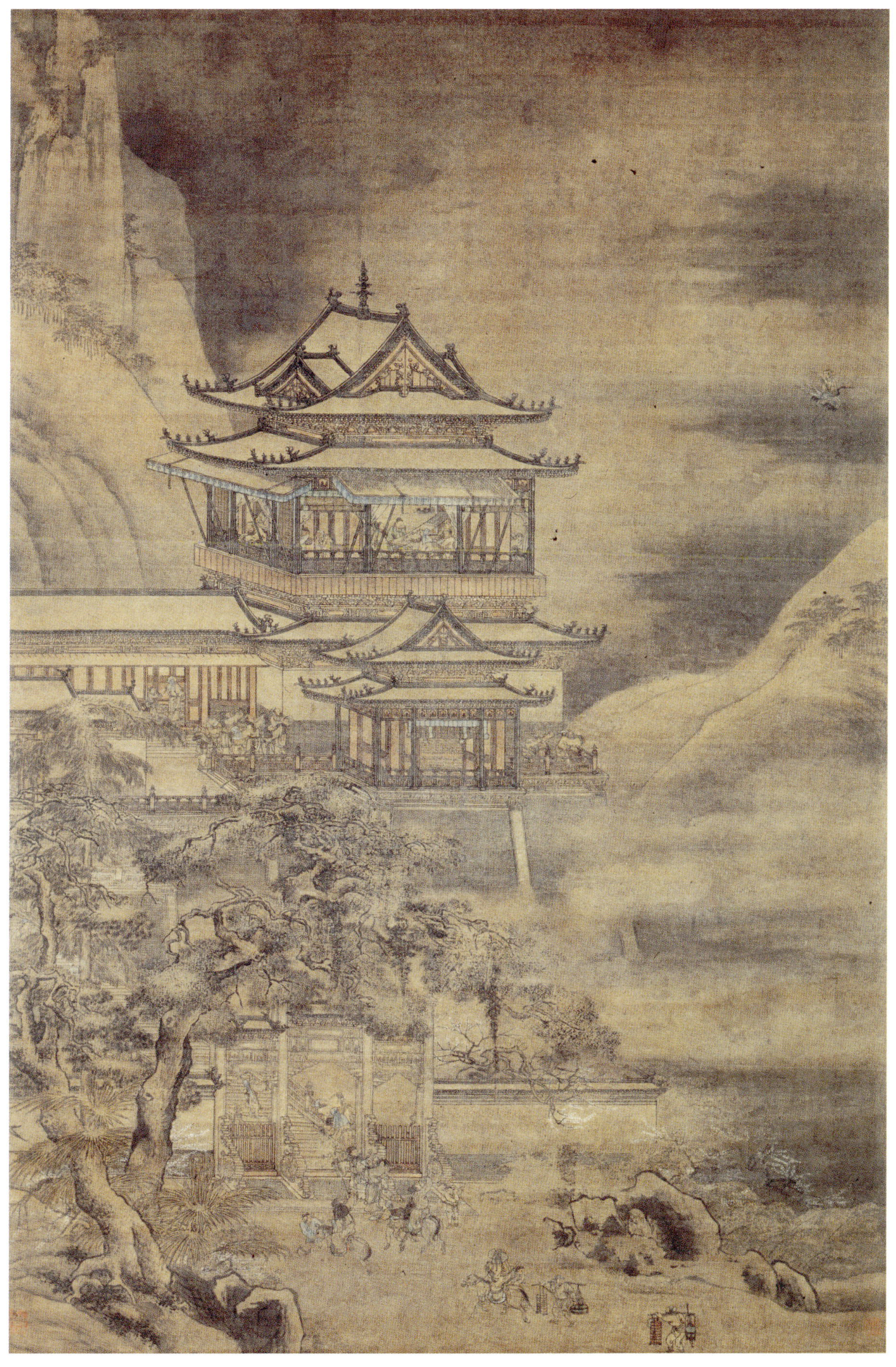

2

明 無款《孔明出山圖軸》

Anonymous (Ming, 1368–1644)
Kongming Leaving the Mountains
Hanging scroll; ink and colours on silk
192.7 × 142.1 cm

After the Han dynasty (206 BC–AD 220) fell in the early third century, China was divided among the rival regimes of the feudal lords. Zhuge Liang (181–234), whose style-name was Kongming, was perhaps the most renowned strategist, politician, diplomat and prose writer of this era, known as the Three Kingdoms period (220–80).

The story, 'Kongming leaving the mountains', describes the warlord Liu Bei's three visits to Kongming's thatched hut to try and persuade him to leave the mountain and assist him. Zhuge Liang was moved by Liu Bei's perseverance, and finally agreed to help him, going on to become his most valued advisor. Prior to this, Zhuge Liang had been a recluse in rural Nanyang, Henan Province. He was, however, an avid reader of military books and therefore familiar with the political situation of the day. Believing that Liu Bei was the rightful heir of the House of Han led to Zhuge Liang's decision to help him restore the Han dynasty and reunite China.

Subsequently, Zhuge Liang went on to mastermind numerous battlefield victories. He was a master of stratagems, such as 'Fire at the Red Cliffs', 'Borrowing the enemy's arrows' and 'Burning a line of camps', all of which were classic examples of the few defeating the many. He helped Liu Bei establish the Western Shu dynasty (221–63), which solidified China's division into the Three Kingdoms of Wei, Wu and Shu.

The figure on the left of the painting, with a headband and flowing robes, calmly spurring on his horse, is Kongming. Liu Bei is the figure respectfully accompanying him to his left. The two other men on horseback are Liu Bei's fellow generals, Guan Yu and Zhang Fei.

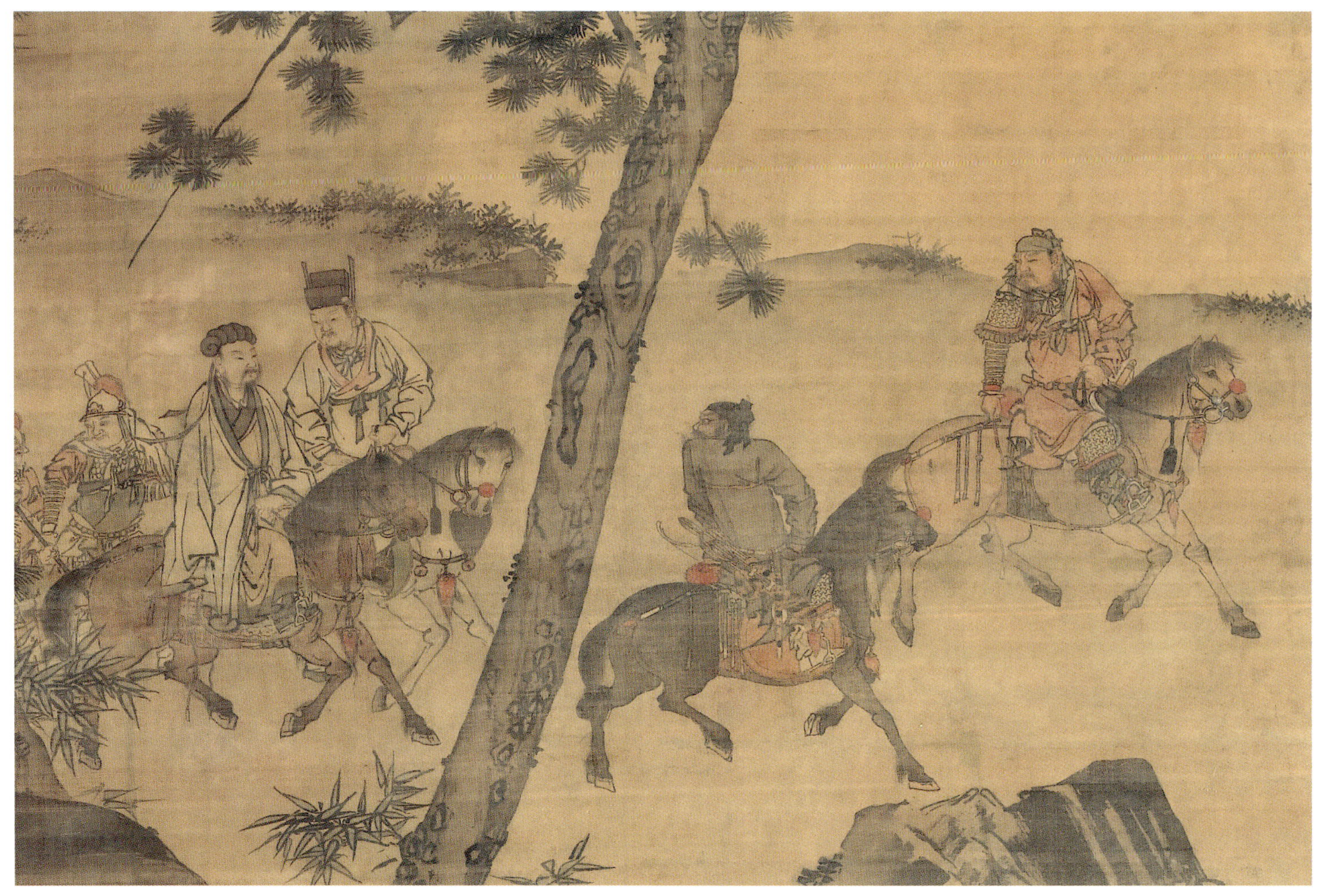

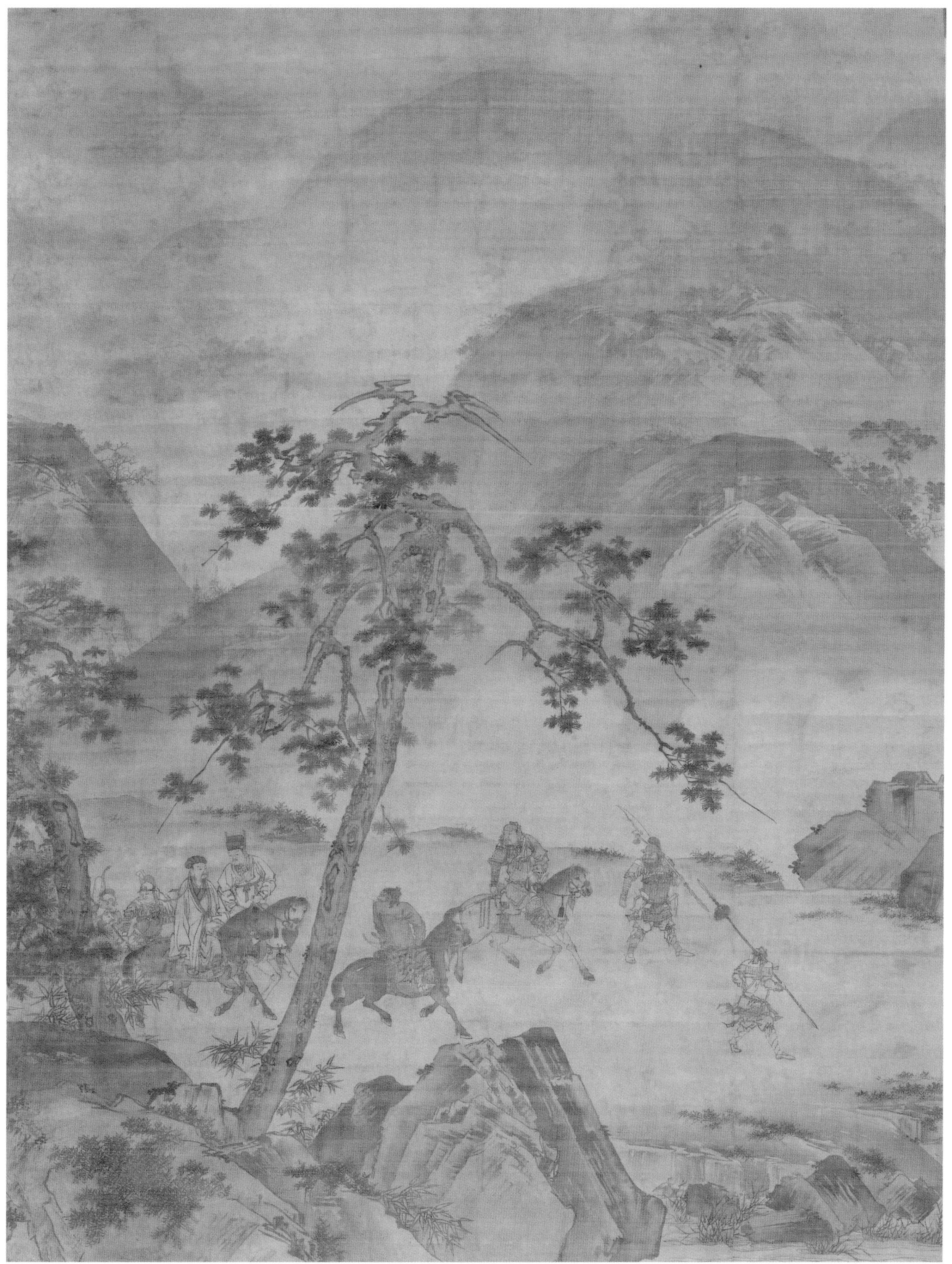

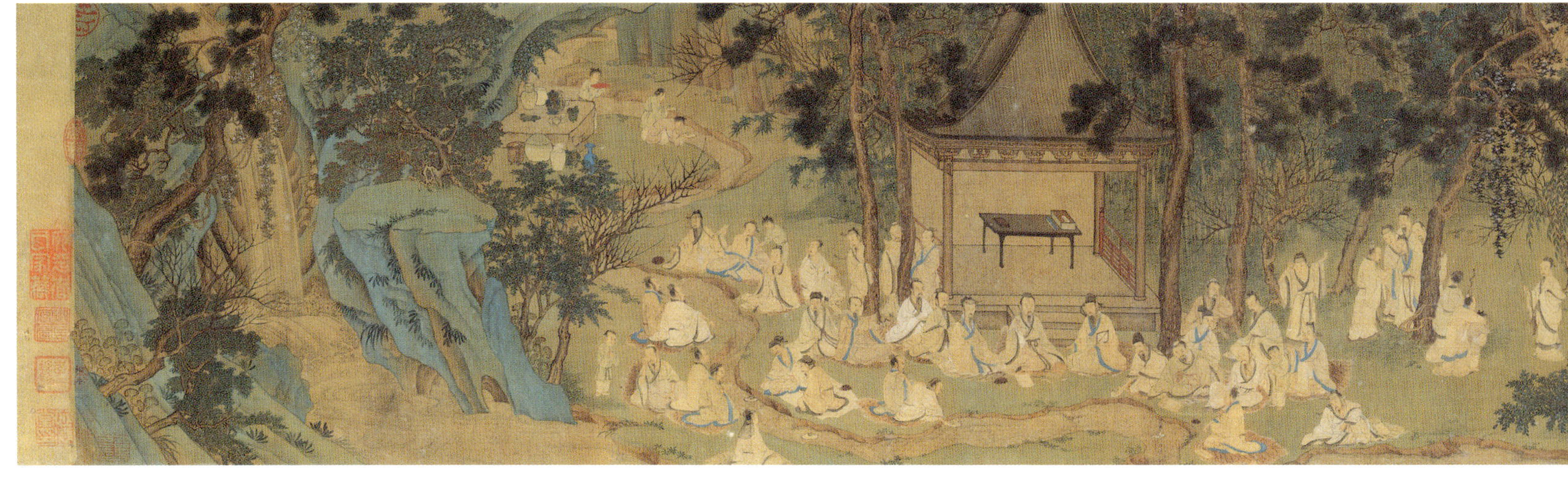

3

明 無款 《蘭亭修禊圖卷》

Anonymous (Ming, 1368–1644)
Purification Festival at the Orchid Pavilion
Handscroll; ink and colours on silk
27.7 × 177.7 cm

The springtime Purification Festival is an ancient custom, observed on the third day of the third month in the lunar calendar, whereby people gather beside water to bathe – the idea being to wash away evil spirits and to ward off disaster. On this day in the year 353, Wang Xizhi (321–79), the 'sage of calligraphy' (see Cat. 26), invited some forty fellow men of culture to an 'elegant gathering' at his Orchid Pavilion in Shaoxing, Zhejiang Province. They sat on mats on both sides of a stream and played a drinking game. They floated wine cups on the water, and wherever one happened to stop, the person sitting closest would have to compose a poem, or else drink several cups as a forfeit. By the end of the day, twenty-seven men had succeeded and fifteen forfeited. To head the collected poems, Wang Xizhi composed and transcribed his 'Orchid Pavilion Preface' *(Lanting xu)*, celebrated as the greatest ever piece of running script calligraphy. The 'Preface' survives only in Tang-dynasty copies, which are held in the Palace Museums in Beijing and Taipei. It is said that the original manuscript was buried in the Zhaoling, the tomb in present-day Xi'an in Shaanxi Province of the Tang emperor Taizong (r. 626–49), who was an ardent devotee of Wang Xizhi's calligraphy. This tomb has not yet been excavated, so it may be that Wang Xizhi's only surviving original work is buried within it.

The elegant gathering at the Orchid Pavilion produced a masterpiece of calligraphy and a celebrated work of literature, both of which have been passed down through the generations since antiquity. The story, 'Orchid Pavilion gathering', therefore came to represent a spiritual Eden revered in Chinese culture throughout the ages.

This painting is notable for its delightful colouring and for its soaring artistic conception, which evokes a sense of nostalgia.

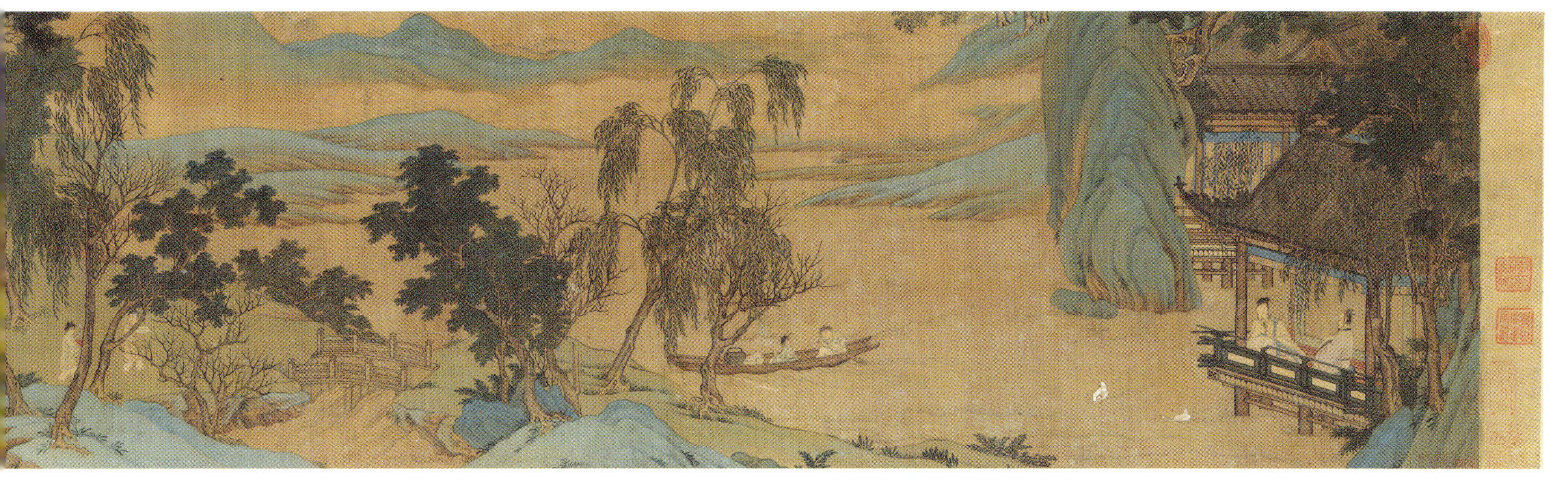

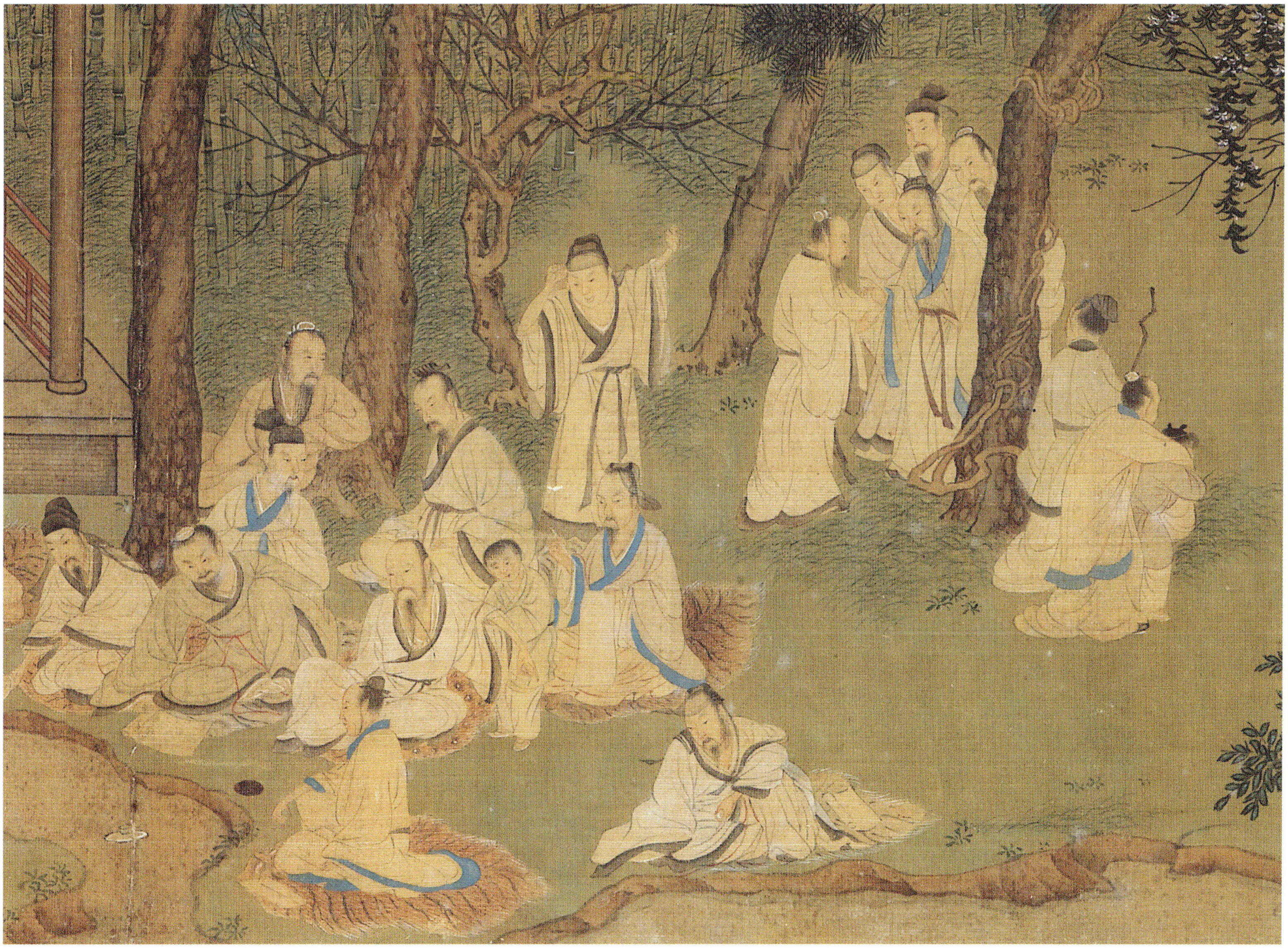

4

明 陳洪綬 《雅集圖卷》

Chen Hongshou (1598–1652)
Elegant Gathering
Handscroll; ink on paper
29.8 × 98.4 cm

Born into a scholar-official family in Zhuji, near Shaoxing in Zhejiang Province, Chen Hongshou showed precocious talent as a painter from childhood. He was known chiefly as a prolific and highly eccentric figural master, who developed a distinctive swirling ink-outline technique in revival of ancient styles, and revelled in strange and exotic portrayals. At times, his pulsating drapery lines double, self-consciously, as strokes of calligraphy – the scholar's art. However, he saw himself as a literatus, and tried in vain for some forty years to enter the civil bureaucracy by passing the relevant provincial examinations. Finally, in around 1640, he purchased his qualification and moved to Beijing, but was disappointed by the low-level post he received and soon quit. Already a famous painter, he had been assigned to making copies of imperial portraits. Returning home to the south, he resigned himself to living off his art as a professional. In this later period, after the fall of the Ming dynasty in 1644, Chen Hongshou became a Buddhist monk and began to sign his paintings 'Regretful Monk' (as here).

In fact, having been selling paintings and book illustrations since at least the 1620s, and having developed an active studio practice in the 1630s, he already had numerous patrons in his home region. These men included Tao Sheng of Zhuji, for whom this painting was done in 1647. It commemorates an 'elegant gathering' of nine men, each identified by name in a caption above his head, who are assembled in a rock garden around a Buddhist shrine. Among the famous individuals gathered here is Mi Wanzhong, the Beijing calligrapher and taste-maker depicted reading in the middle, but the patron's link is through his grandfather, who is portrayed in the wicker seat to the right.

Such was Chen Hongshou's fame in his day that he became known, along with the Beijing artist Cui Zizhong (see Cat. 5), in the phrase 'Chen of the south; Cui of the north' (*nan Chen bei Cui*).

SMcC

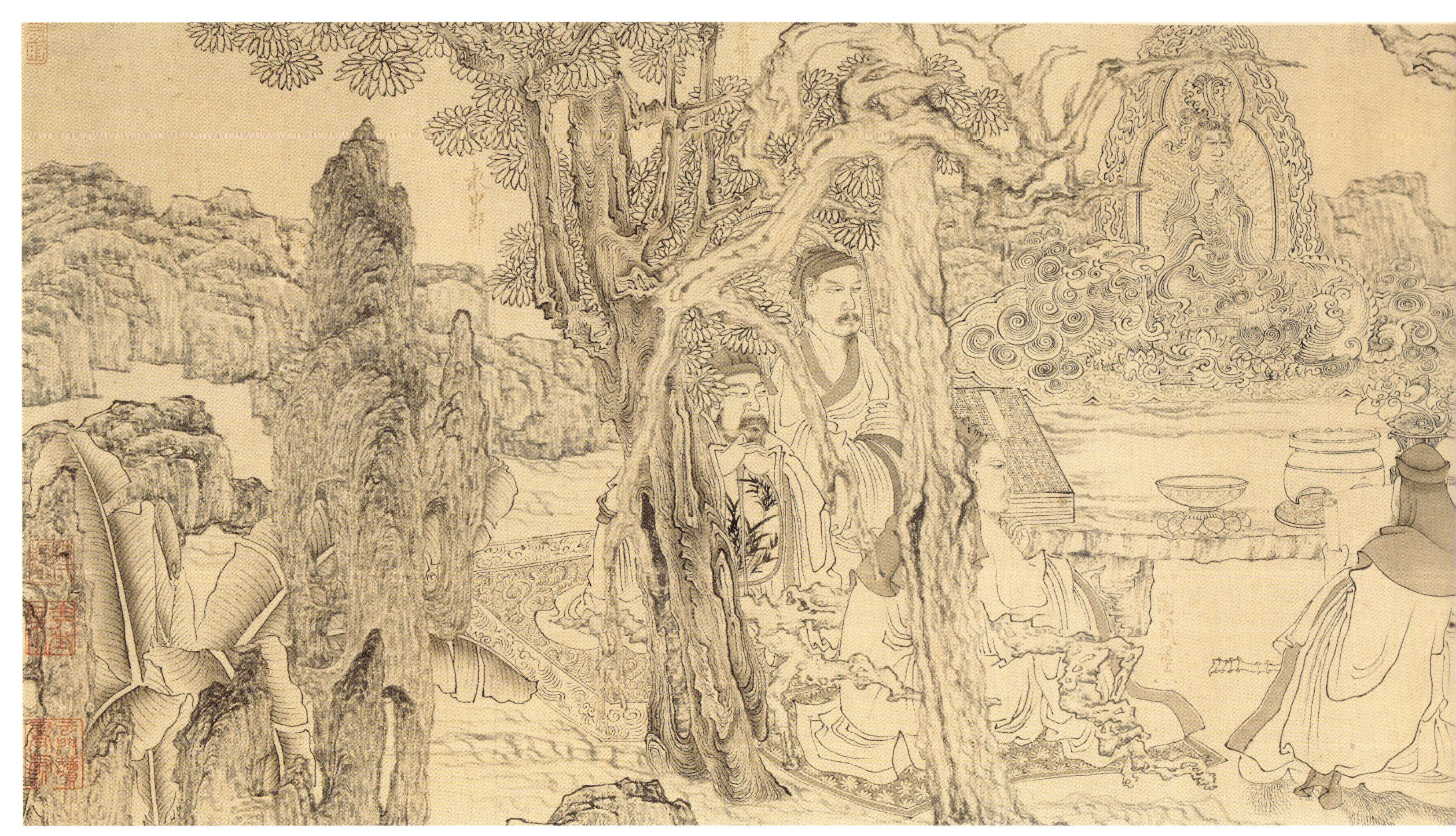

陳老蓮居士无上神品真迹

同治十年歲在辛未嘉平月出浣爲
轉畫龕主人題
方濬益記

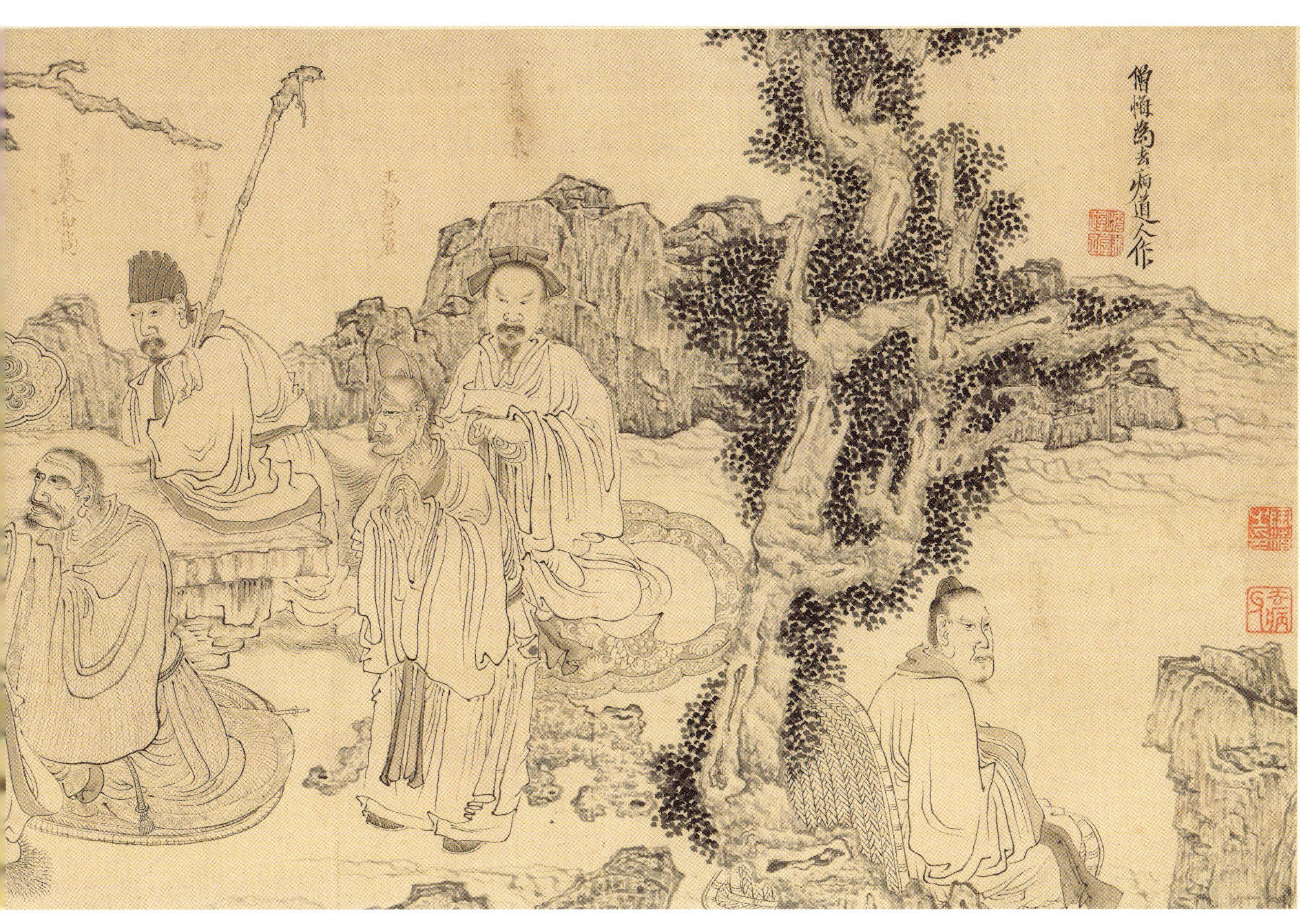

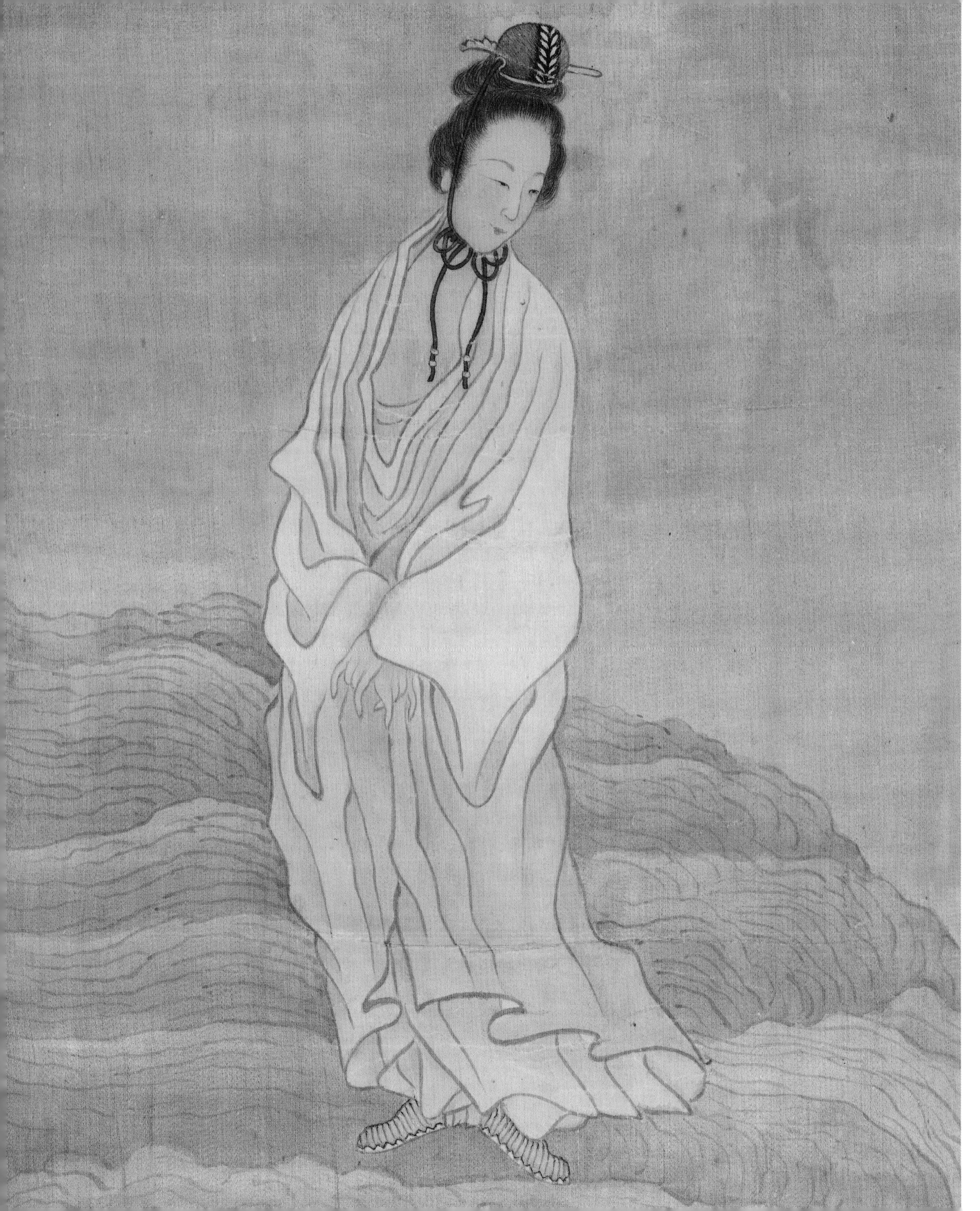

5

明 崔子忠 《雲中玉女圖軸》

Cui Zizhong (*c.*1574–1644)
Jade Woman among Clouds
Hanging scroll; ink and colours on twill-weave silk
168 × 52.5 cm
Donated by Chen Daoxi

The 'jade woman' evolved from the early Chinese legend of the Queen Mother of the West (Xiwangmu). The Queen Mother of the West lived on Mount Kunlun in the south of the Western Sea and had power over the lives of humans. She had a leopard's tail, a tiger's teeth and a fierce countenance that combined the characteristics of several other animals. During the Warring States period (475–221 BC), people believed that the Queen Mother of the West could extend people's lives, and stories spread about emperors seeking the elixir of immortality from her. Legend had it that she gave Han emperor Wu a flat peach (of immortality) that grew only once every 3,000 years, which could confer immortality on the eater. By the Han dynasty, the Queen Mother's image had changed into that of a heavenly beauty, or 'jade woman'. Her status among the pantheon of the immortals rose, and she gained the additional powers to bestow good fortune and children. By the Tang dynasty, the Queen Mother was as revered as ever, and after a period of time she was named the head of all the female immortals and an auspicious deity.

This painting features misty clouds, a graceful 'jade woman' and a supernatural aura. The style is self-consciously unsophisticated but also classical and elegant. Cui Zizhong was from Laiyang, Shandong Province. He excelled at painting figures, especially elegant women, and adopted a simple, 'lofty and ancient' style. He made his name alongside Chen Hongshou (see Cat. 4) in the saying: 'Chen of the south, Cui of the north' (*nan Chen bei Cui*).

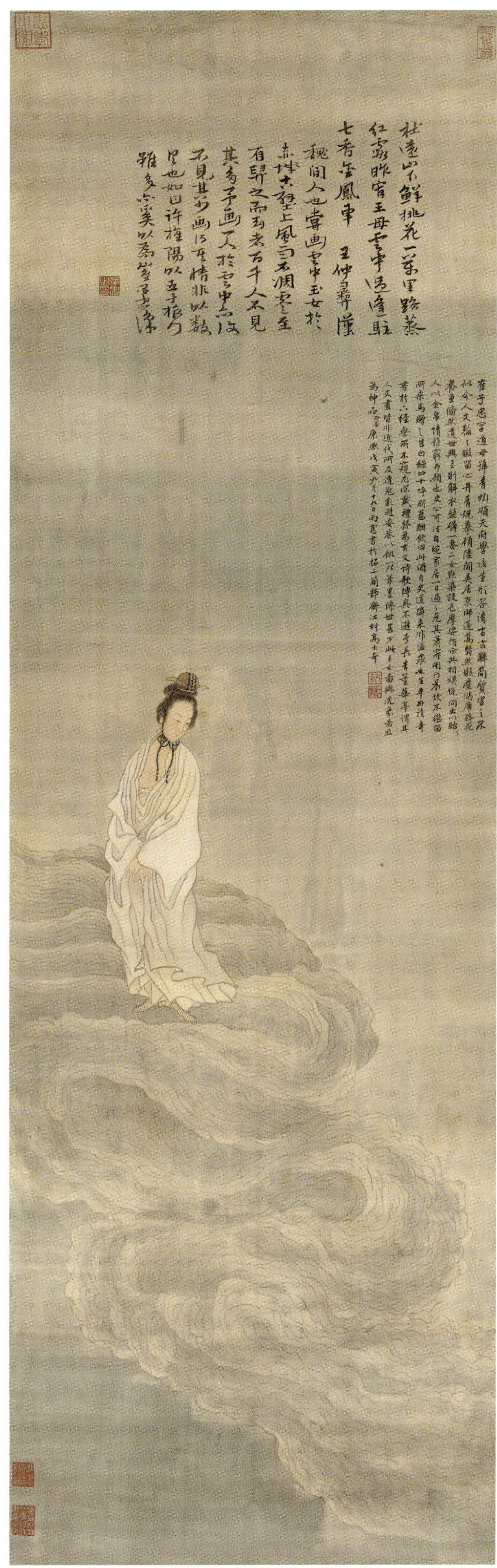

6

清 丁觀鵬 《乞巧圖卷》

Ding Guanpeng (d. after 1770)
Ladies on the 'Night of Sevens' Pleading for Skills
Dated 1748
Handscroll; ink on paper
28.7 × 386.5 cm

The Weaver Girl (see also Cats 9 & 35) was beautiful, intelligent, spirited and skilled, making her the idol of many women in ancient China. Each year on the Night of Sevens (the seventh day of the seventh month in the lunar calendar), young women gathered together to play games. They dressed in new clothes and gathered in courtyards, where they would set up an incense table on which they would place fruit and make-up. Then they would 'plead for skills' from the Weaver Girl. They took part in competitions, for instance, to see who could thread the most needles by candlelight. The winner would be a good seamstress or slipper-maker. In another game, 'Fancy Treats' (*Qiaoguo*), lotus, peach and fish moulds were used to cut dough which was then fried, and whoever produced the best looking treat won the game. In 'Fancy Lamps' (*Qiaodeng*), participants made lamps that featured chrysanthemums or orchids, or were modelled to depict set themes like the 'Eight Immortals Crossing the Sea' and 'Immortal Blessings for Long Life'. The food and lanterns made at the festival were then given to relatives and friends for good luck.

In Chinese, the word 'skills' (*qiao*) means 'agile' and 'nimble', and these were traits that were

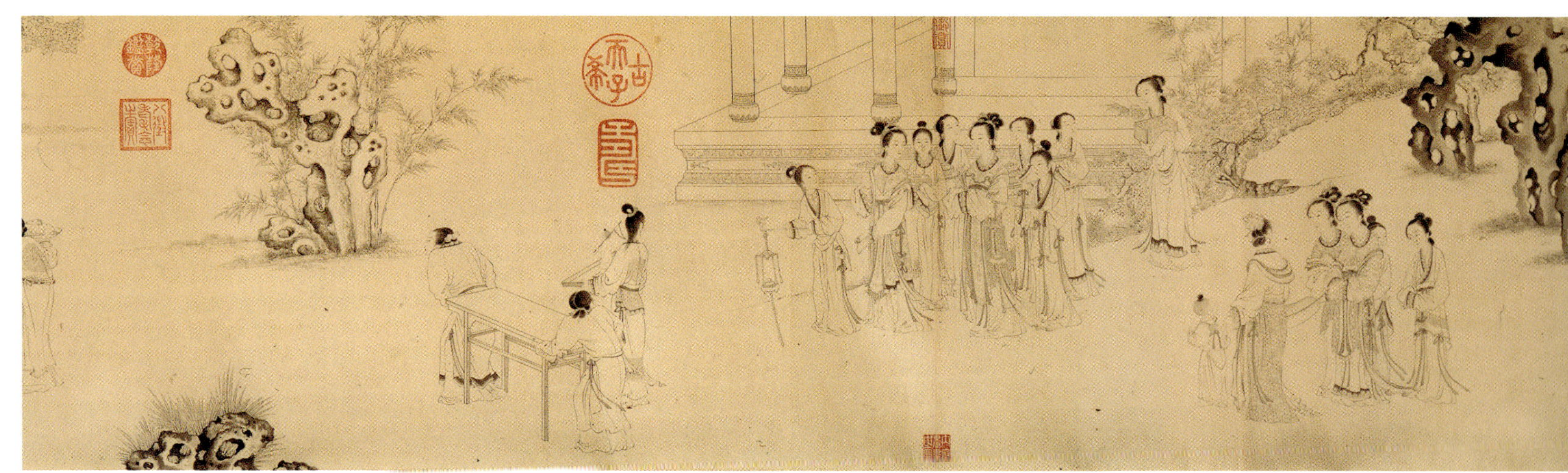

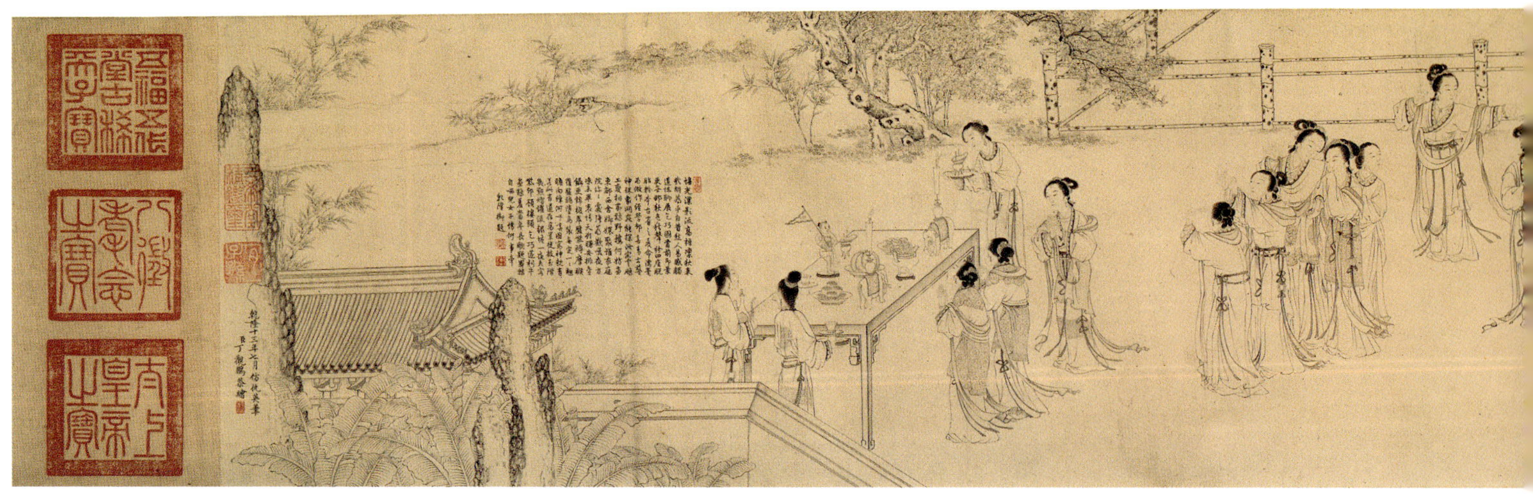

traditionally highly valued in women. This festival was, therefore, also called the Women's Festival, an auspicious occasion on which it was appropriate to pray for good fortune, skills and long life. There are seventy-six women in the painting, participating in activities such as setting up the incense table, laying out fruit, tying up colourful ribbons, threading needles, praying to the Longevity Star and pleading for skills.

Ding Guanpeng was a court painter during the Qianlong reign (1736–95), and excelled at portraying religious figures.

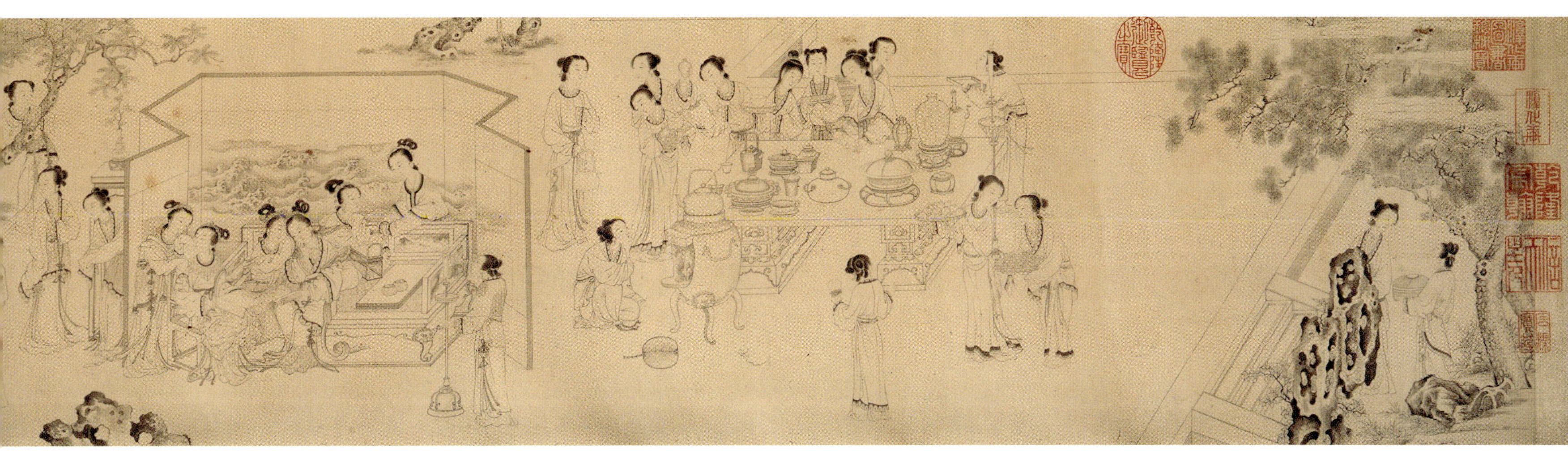

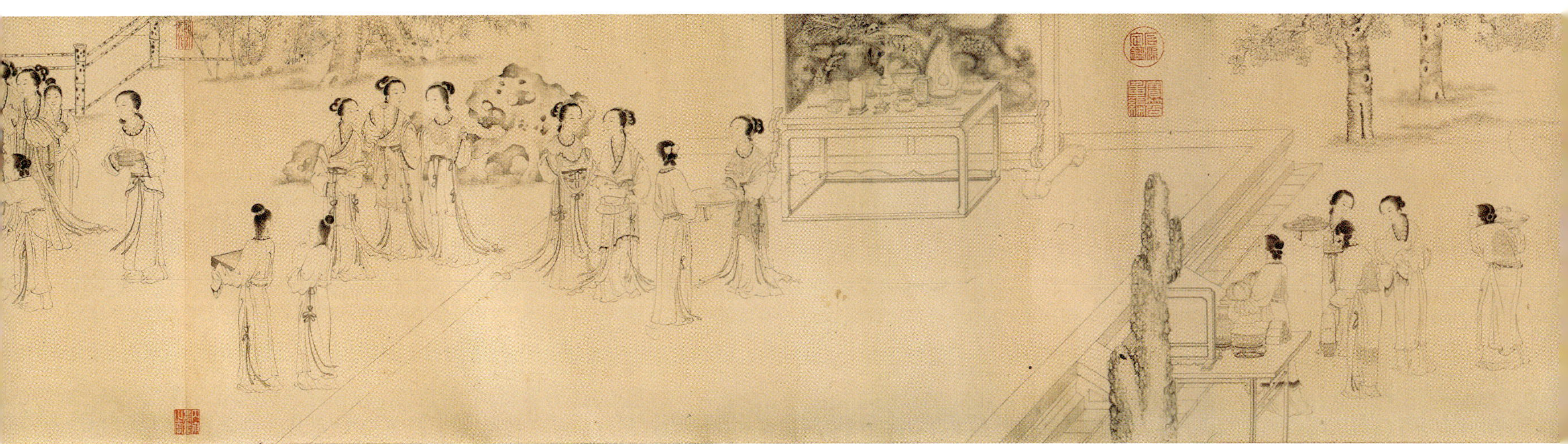

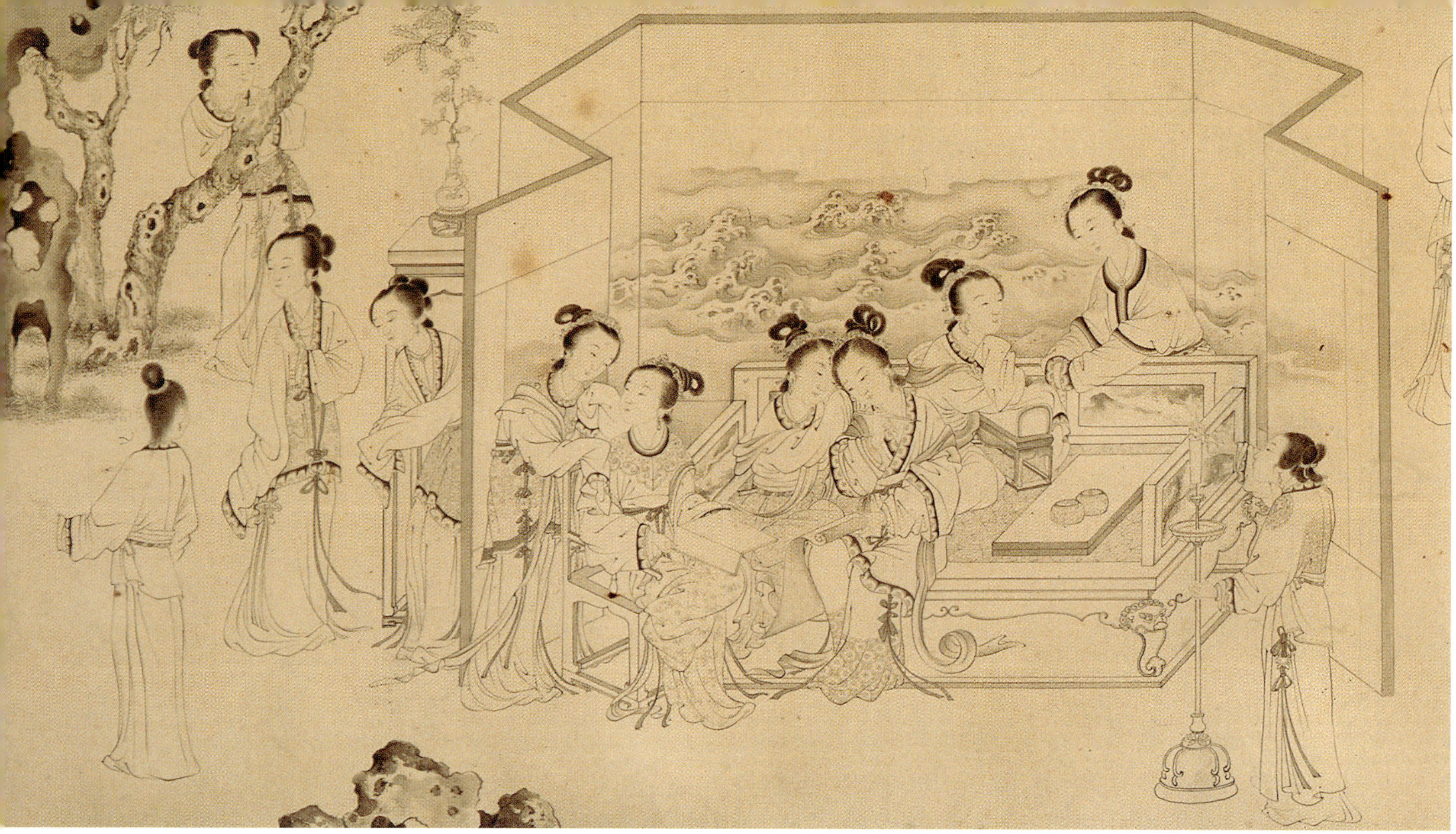

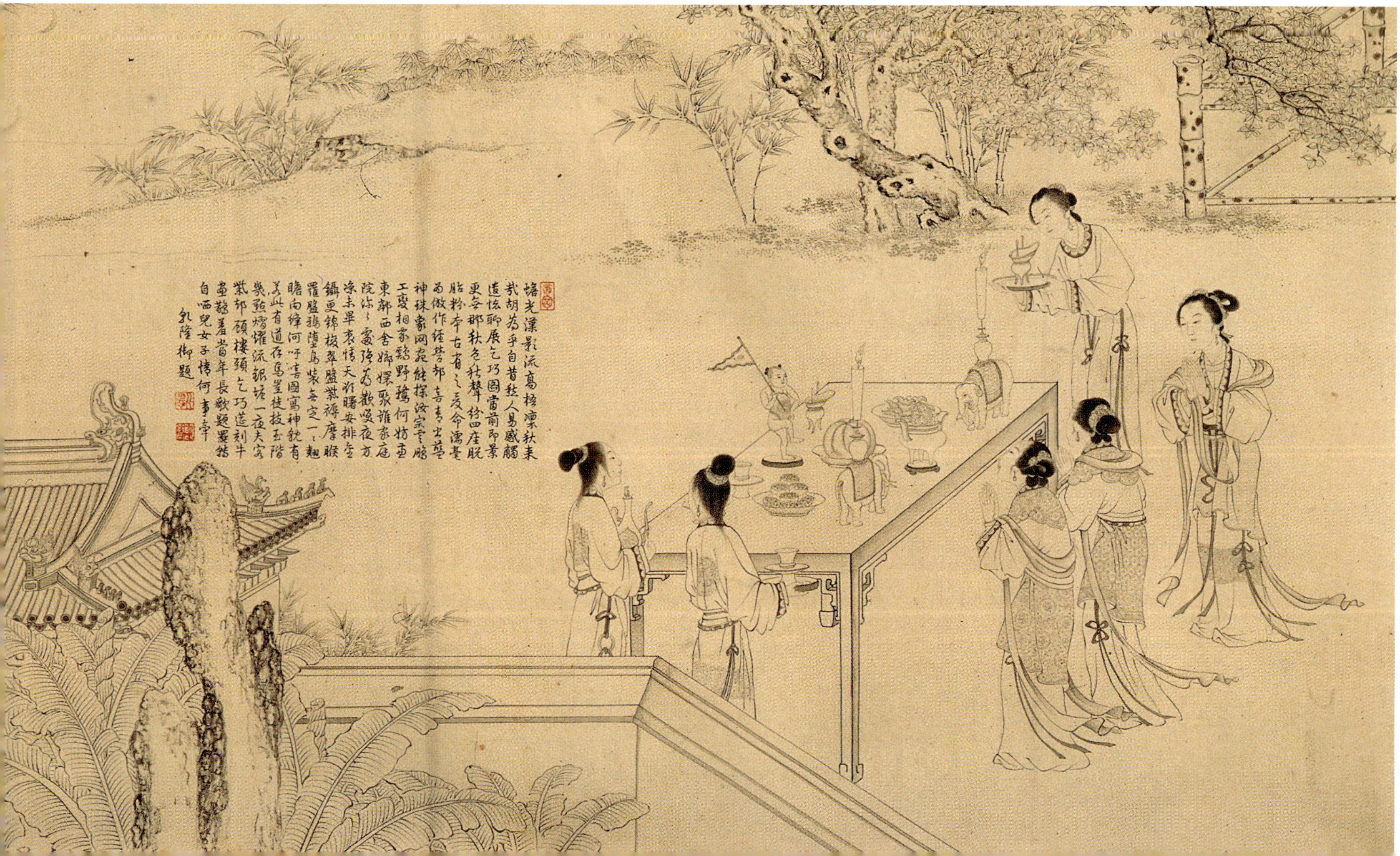

蟾光漾影流高梧凜秋來
哉胡為乎自昔愁人易感觸
遠依聊展乞巧圖當前即景
更安排秋色秋聲紛四座脫
胎粉本古有之爰命濡毫
而傚作經營郤喜青出藍
神珠象罔宛能探汝宗今勝
工變相家鷄野鶩何妨垂
東鄰西舍娜嫋聚誰家庭
院深深露強為歡娛夜方
涼未畢哀情天孫曙安排金
鑷更錦梭翠盤紫褥摩睺
羅盤鵲墮烏紫無定一一翻
瞻向緯何呼嗟圖寫神就有
美此有道存焉豈徒技玉階
幾點螢爐流銀燭一夜夫家
紫郤頓樓頭乞巧遙刻牛
畫鵲羞當年長歌題罷話
自哂兒女子情何事乎
乾隆御題

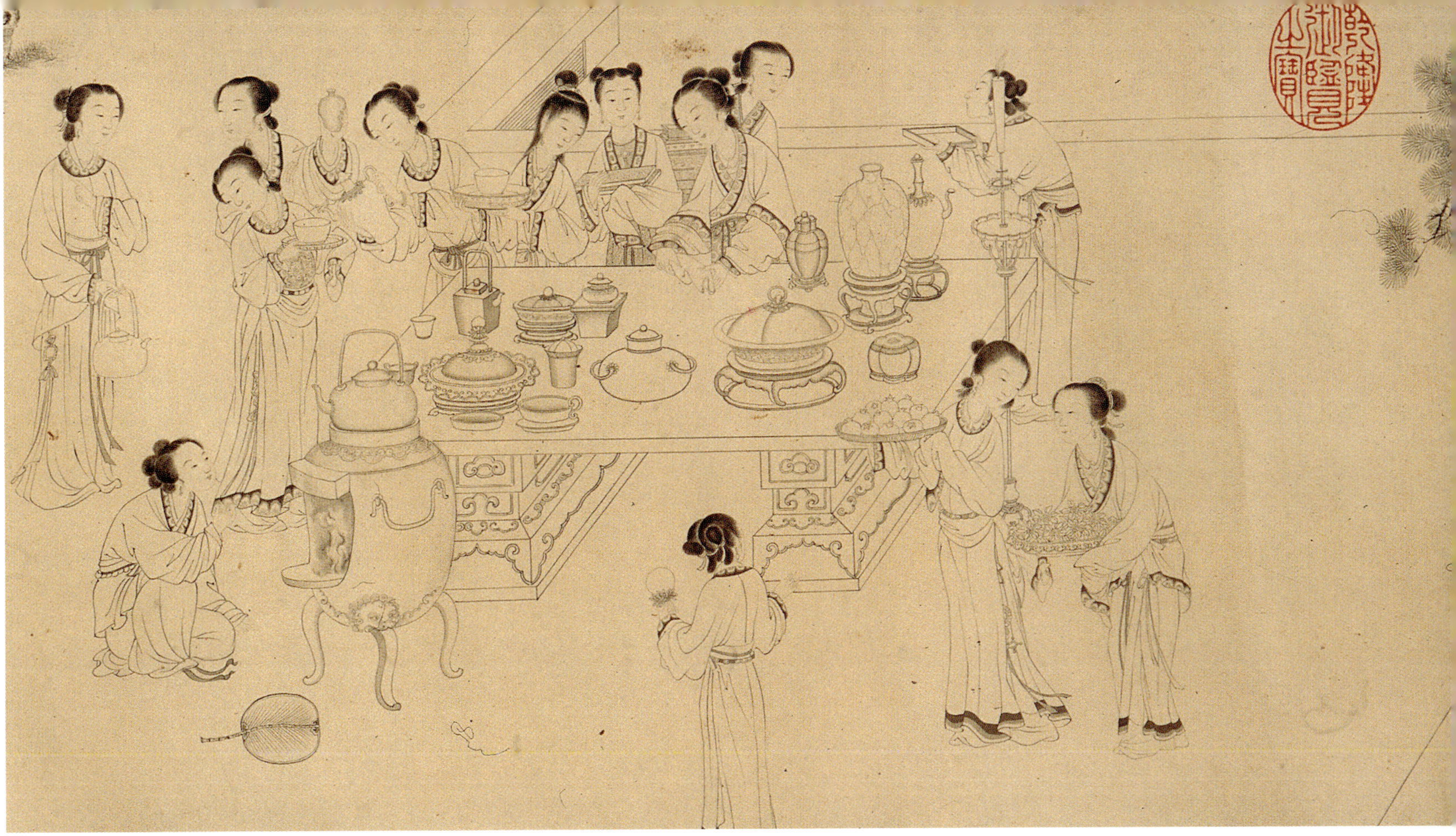

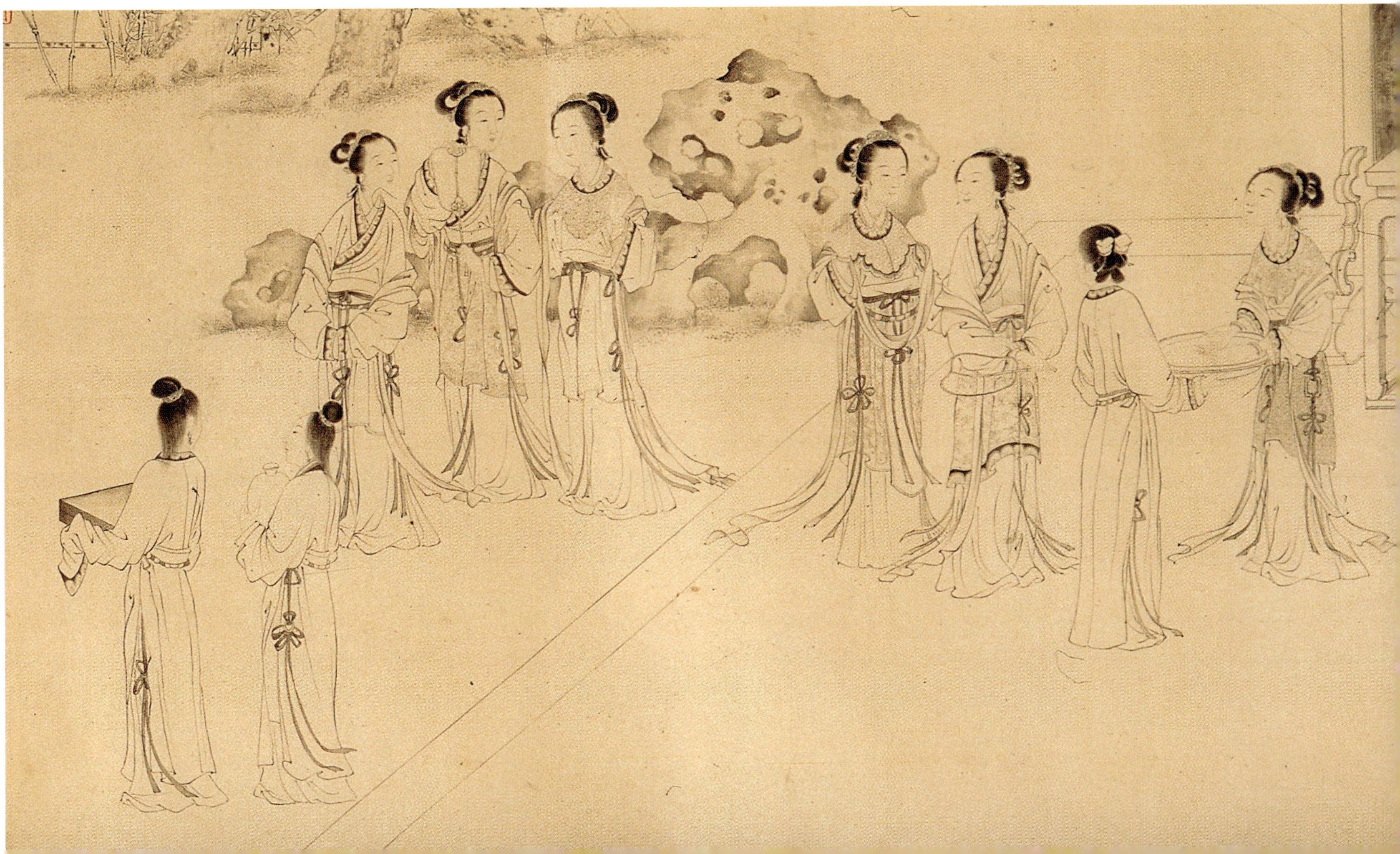

7

明 丁雲鵬 《桃源圖扇》

Ding Yunpeng (1547–1628)
Peach-blossom Spring
Dated 1582
Folding fan mounted as an album leaf; ink and colours on paper
16.1 × 50.8 cm

'Peach-blossom Spring' is a unique allegory in Chinese culture that has its origins in the short story 'Tale of the Peach-blossom Spring' (*Taohua yuan ji*) by the Eastern Jin-dynasty (317–420) scholar and poet Tao Qian (or Tao Yuanming). In this tale, a fisherman is rowing his boat along a river when he suddenly loses his way and enters an enchanting peach-blossom forest. At the end of the forest the fisherman discovers a cave in a mountain, which he enters. When he emerges on the other side he discovers a small village with neat rows of houses and abundant fields. Men and women are working in an orderly fashion together, while everyone enjoys a life of comfort and happiness. When the villagers hear that a fisherman has arrived, they eagerly invite him into their homes. They tell him that their ancestors came to this place to escape wars, and that nobody has since left, so that they know nothing of events in the outside world. The fisherman leaves the village and marks his path, hoping to be able to return, but try as he might, he never finds the spot again.

Tao Yuanming was deeply affected by the turbulent social conditions that uprooted so many people during his time. He used his romantic imagination to create this self-sufficient village cut off from the world, where there was no fighting or exploitation, and where everyone was equal. Through this story he expressed his dissatisfaction with the cruel realities of life he saw around him, and created an ideal society that man could aspire to – like the western Utopia.

This painting's bright colours and careful brushwork create a feeling of loftiness. Ding Yunpeng was from Xiuning, Anhui Province.

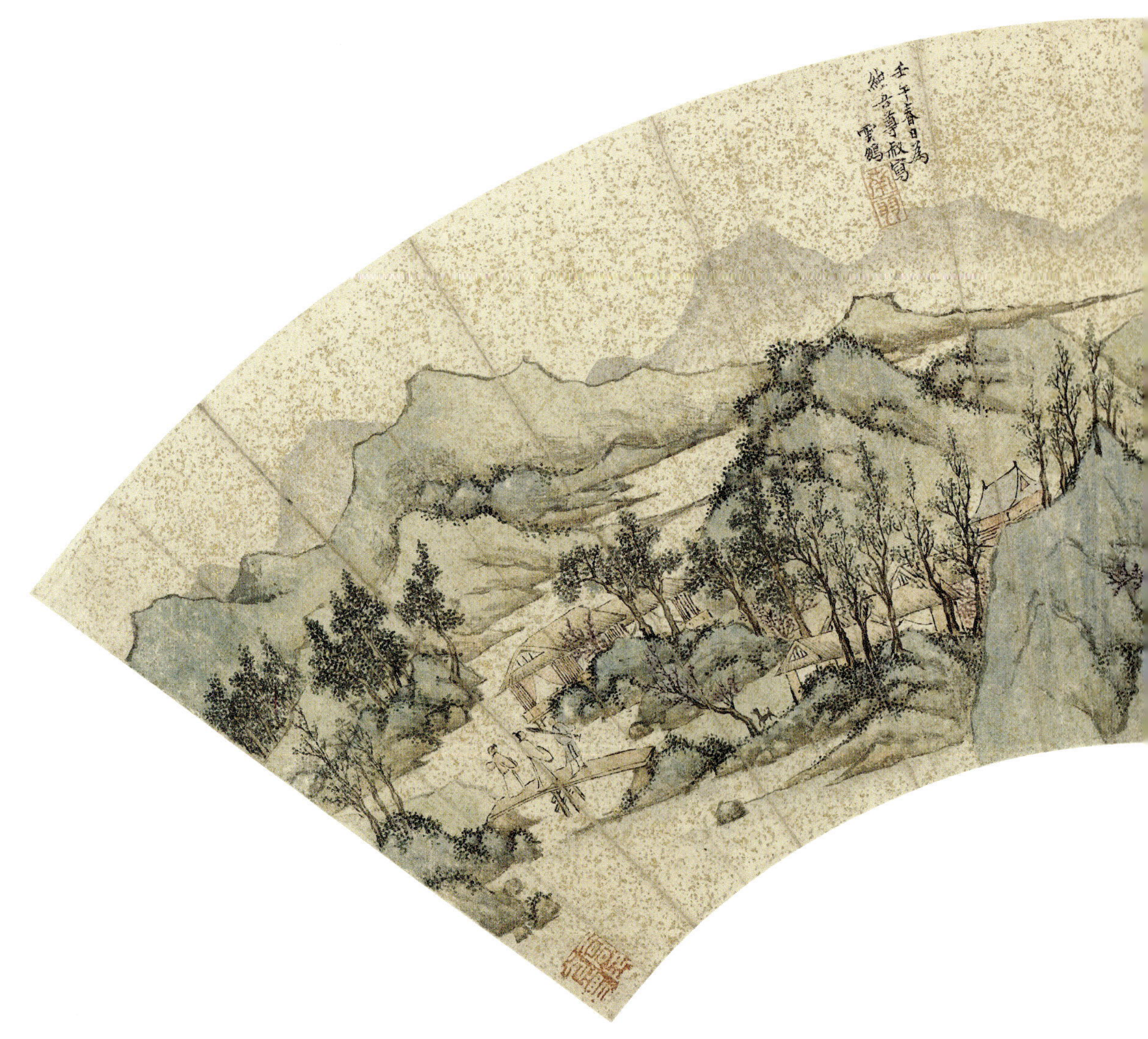

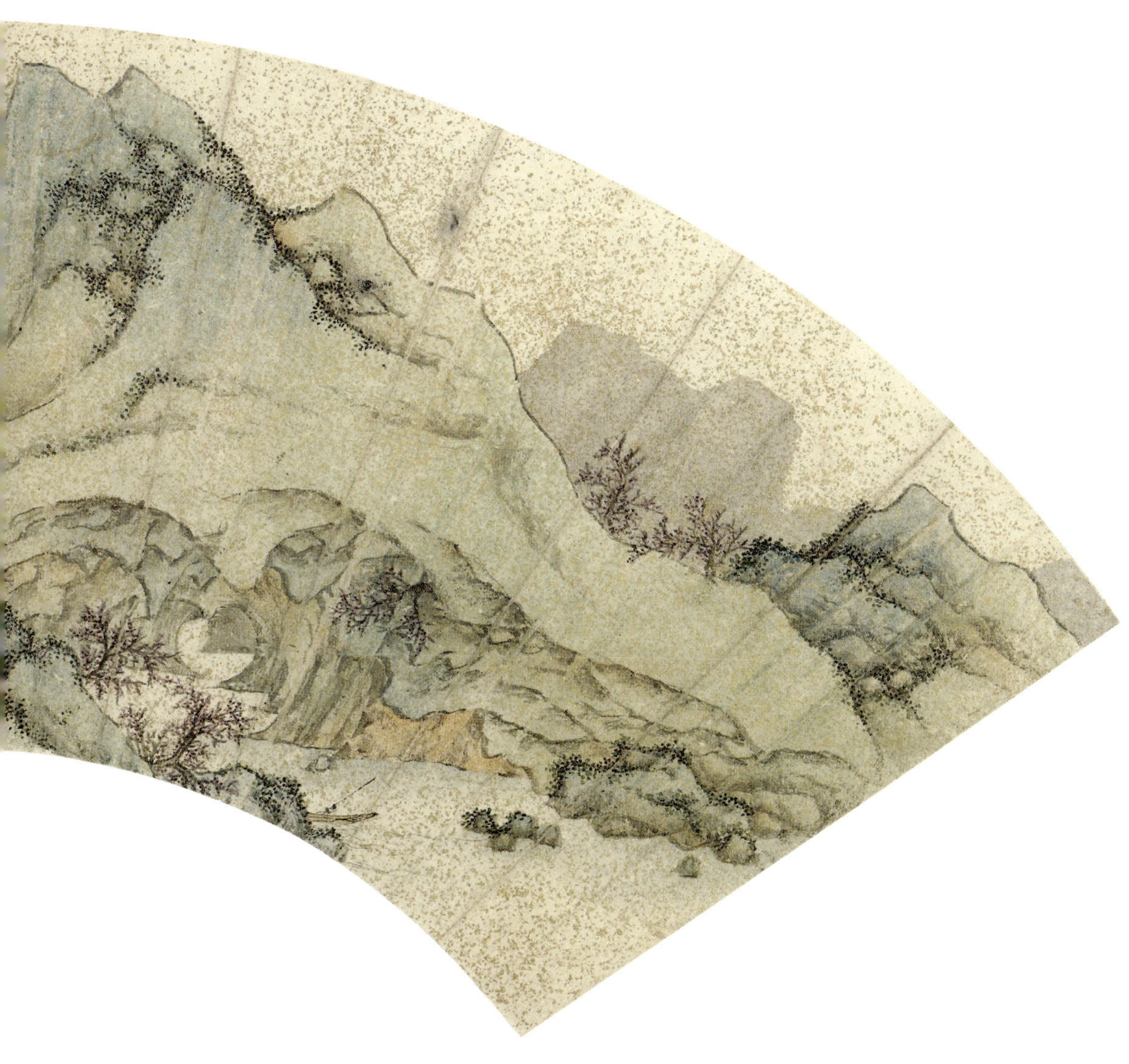

8

清 顧符稹 《桃源圖軸》

Gu Fuzhen (1634–after 1716)
Peach-blossom Spring
Dated 1706
Hanging scroll; ink and colours on silk
34.1 × 46.7 cm

Tao Yuanming advocated the idea of 'standing aloof from the world' (*yu shi wu zheng*), which had a huge influence on traditional Chinese culture. Poets and artists alike revered him, and his 'spiritual Eden' was ardently sought after by Chinese men of culture.

This painting is one of many depictions of Tao Yuanming's 'Tale of the Peach-blossom Spring'. In this artist's powerful imagination, the Peach-blossom Spring is shrouded in clouds amidst towering green peaks. The village beyond is set off by green trees and red flowers, with abundant fields and orderly houses, like a fairytale land cut off from the hunger and bitter struggles of the world. In this place, people live like the immortals, enjoying leisurely lives and the riches nature has to offer.

The artist uses decorative outlines to render the mountain structures which, combined with the verdant greens, create the supernatural atmosphere of the Peach-blossom Spring.

Gu Fuzhen was from Xinghua, Jiangsu Province. A specialist in landscape painting, he worked in the tradition of the early Tang blue-and-green landscapist Li Zhaodao, creating a style that is both delicate and fine.

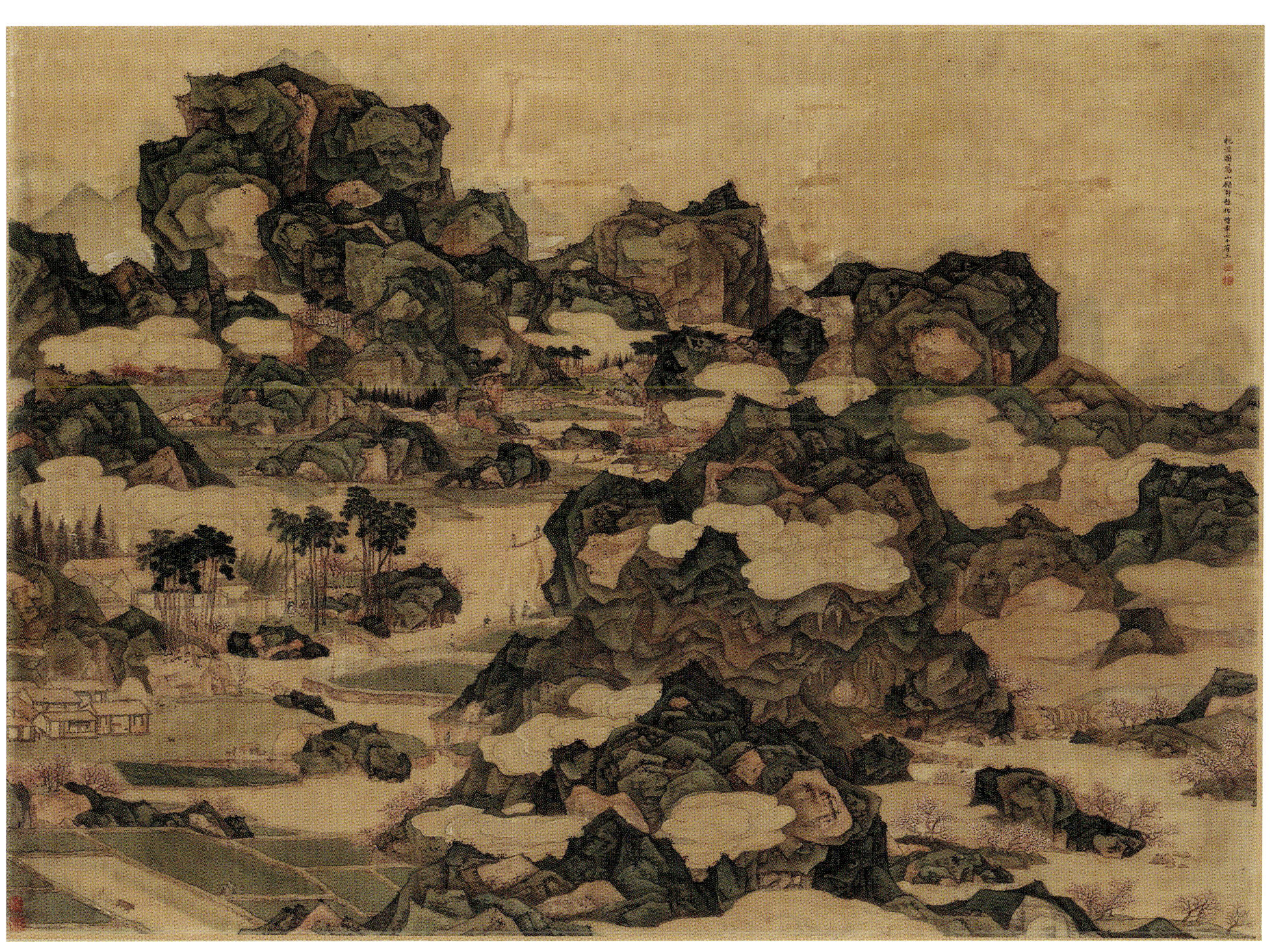

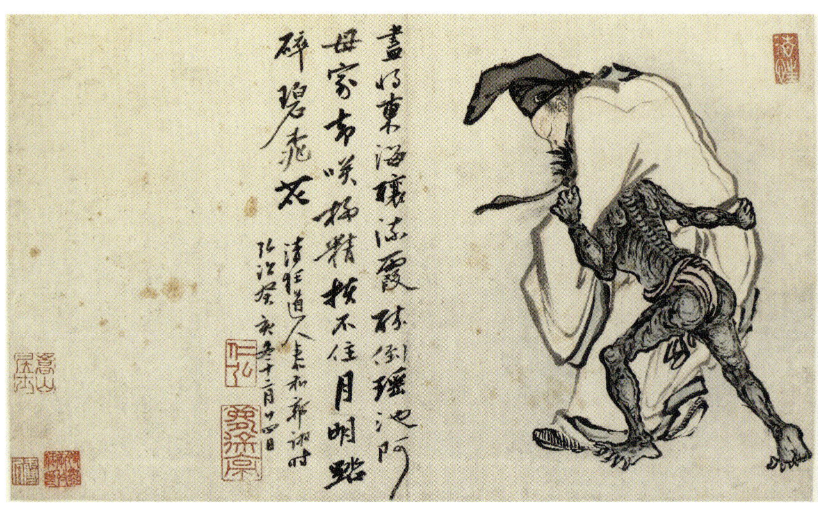

3

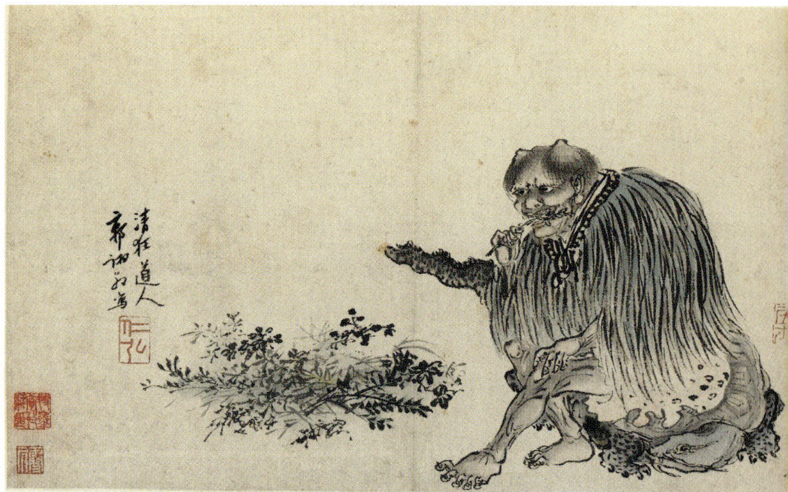

2

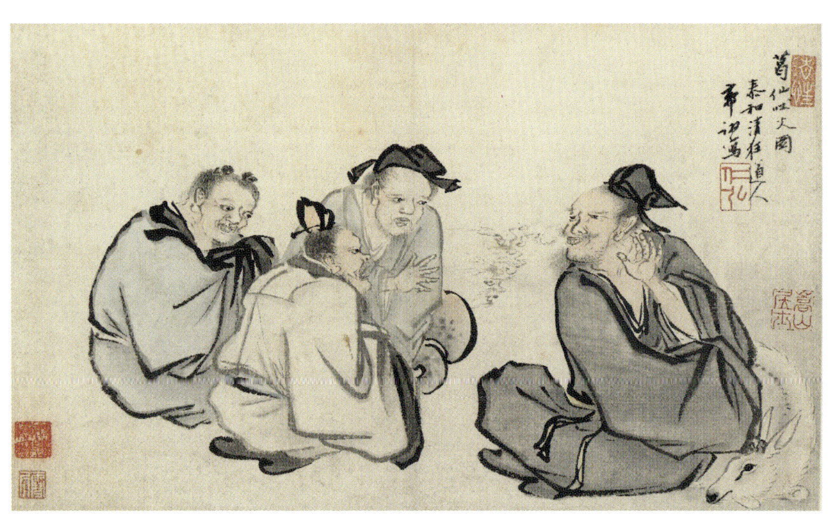

7

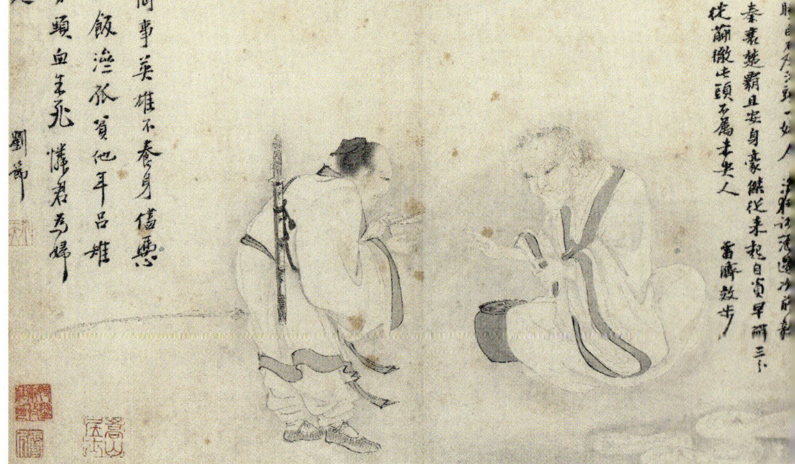

6

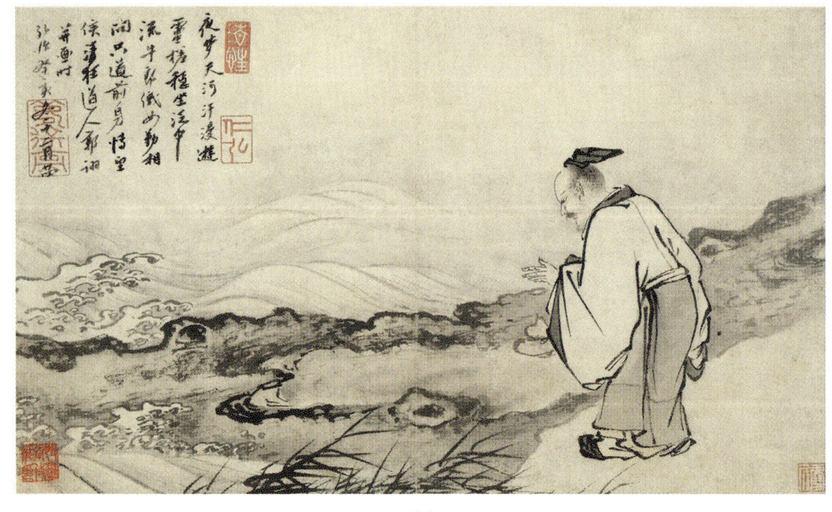

11

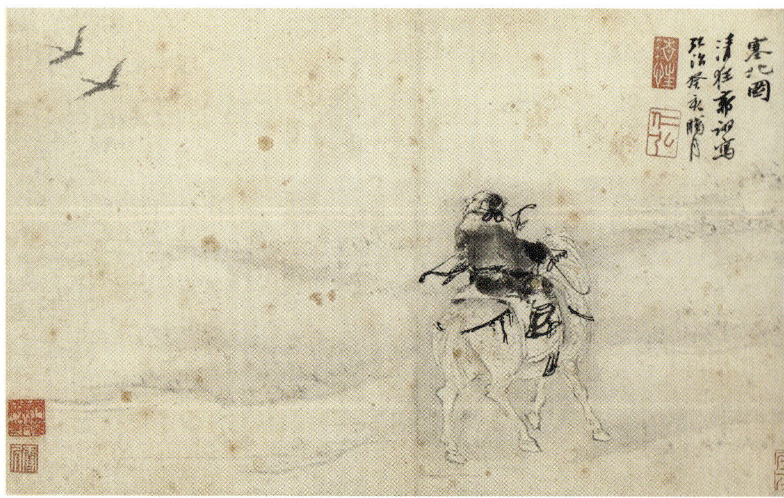

10

9

明 郭詡《人物圖冊》

Guo Xu (1456–*c.*1529)
Album of Various Subjects
Dated 1503
Album of eleven leaves; ink and colours on paper
29.8 × 49.3 cm

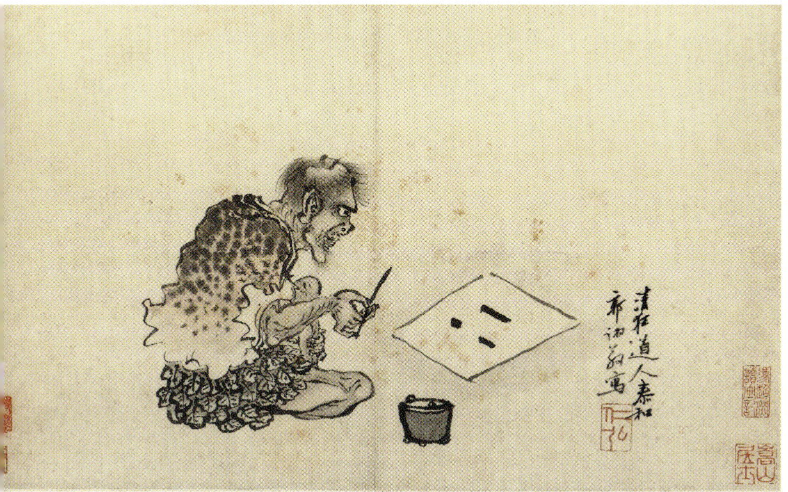

1

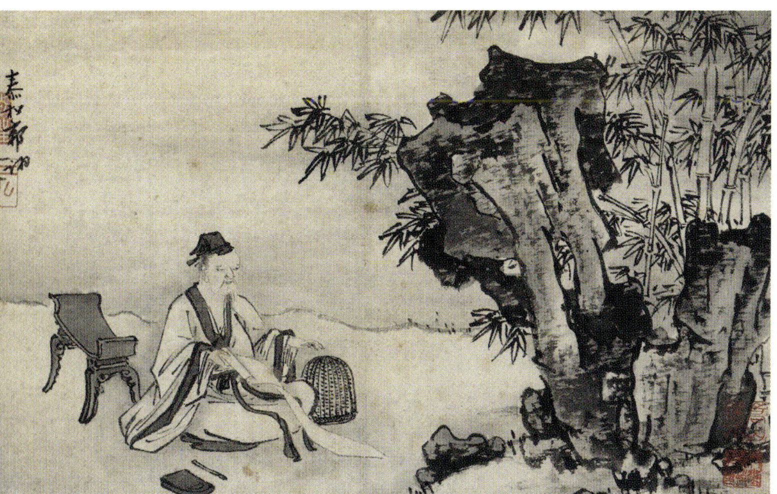

5

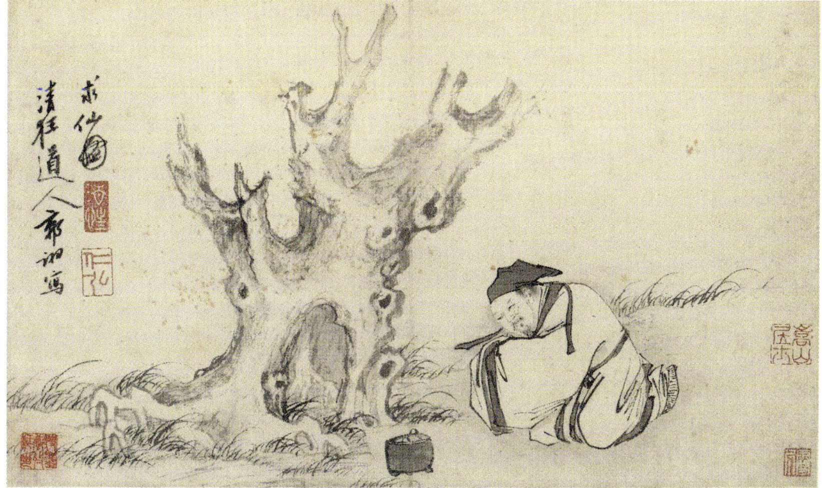

4

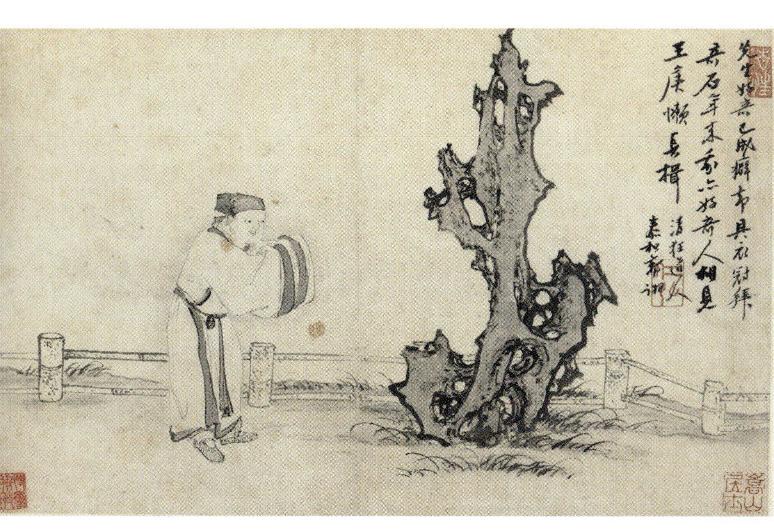

9

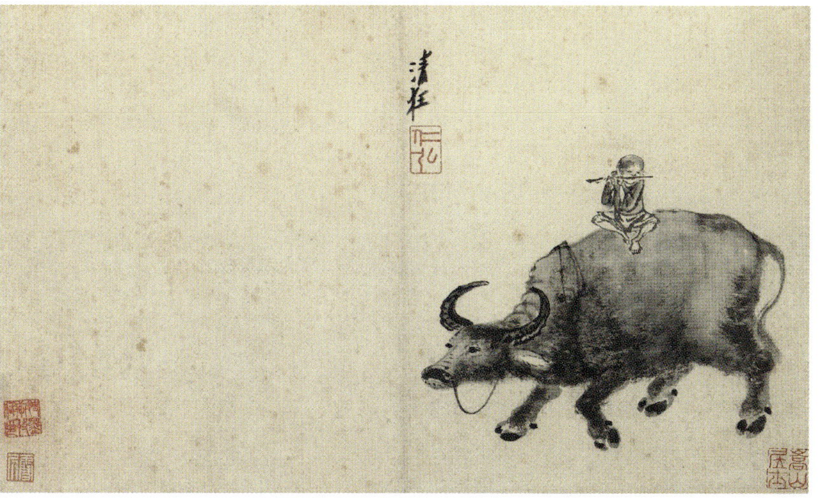

8

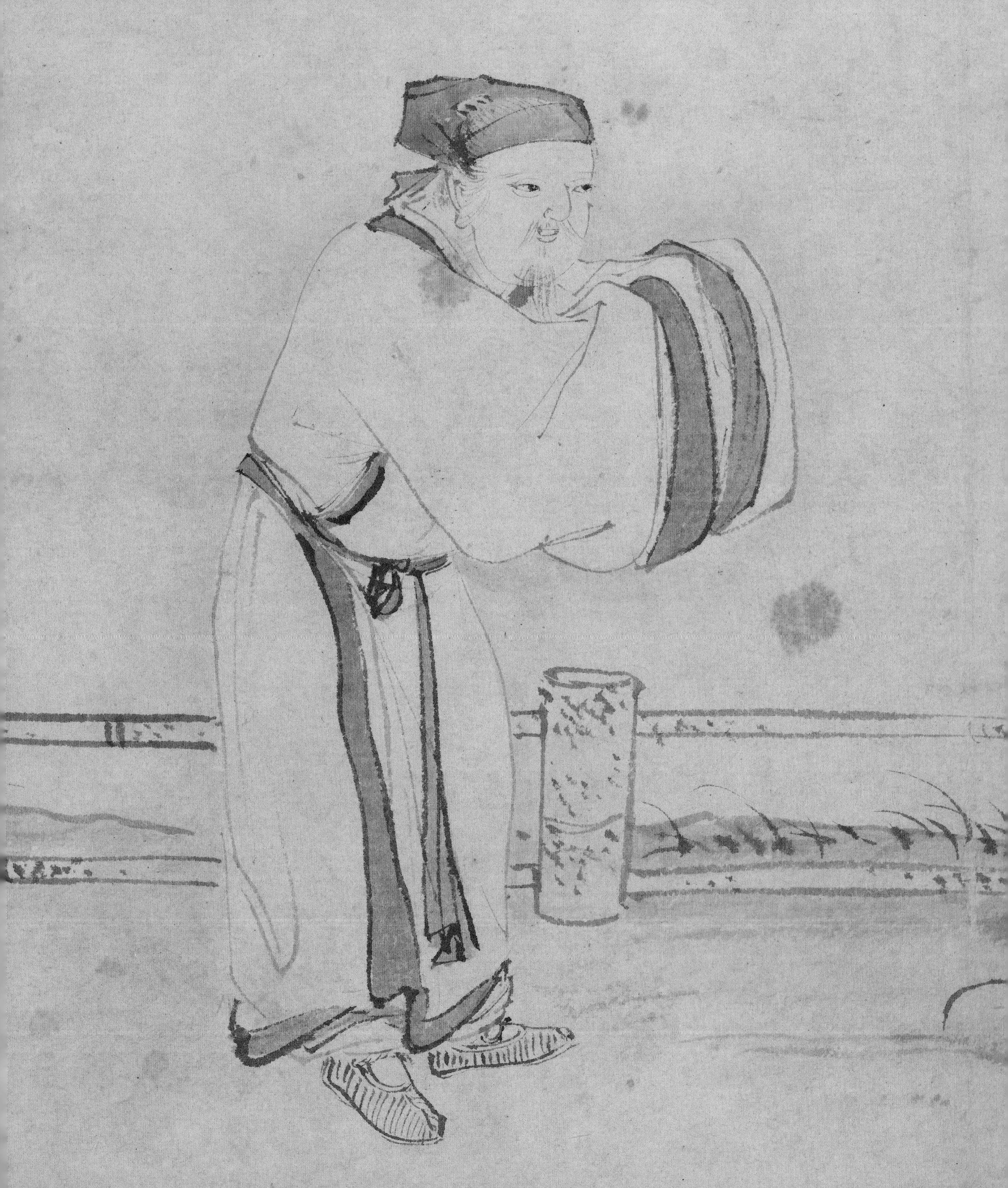

The calligrapher Mi Fu paying his respects to a strangely shaped rock, detail, leaf 9

This figural album contains eleven leaves, each painting depicting either an immortal or historical figure, or illustrating a facet of traditional Chinese culture.

The mythological figures include Fuxi (1) and Shennong (2). In ancient Chinese mythology, Fuxi and Shennong (the Divine Farmer) were the founders of the human race. Fuxi created the universe and civilisation, and together with Nüwa created humans. Shennong invented agriculture and taught humans to plough and grow the Five Grains. He was also the god of medicine, and used herbal remedies to treat illness. The subject of 'Immortal Ge spitting fire' (7) is Ge Xuan, a famous Daoist master during the Three Kingdoms period (220–80). He was a magician and adept at making elixirs of immortality, later becoming an immortal himself. He could perform magic, such as breathing fire from his mouth and spitting out food that transformed itself into bees. 'Night's dream – river of Heaven' (11) depicts the legend of the Cowherd and the Weaver Girl (see Cats 6 & 35).

Of the historical figures, there is Mi Fu in 'Mi Fu admiring a rock' (9). He was a famous Northern Song-dynasty (960–1127) painter and calligrapher who loved rocks and believed they had souls. This became something of an obsession, so that when he saw an interesting rock he bowed before it in worship. 'An old lady feeds a hero' (6) is a story about the great minister Han Xin, who helped Liu Bang unify China and establish the Han dynasty. Before Han Xin rose to prominence, his family was poor and he often went hungry. One day, a washer-woman saw Han Xin by the river and pitied him, so she gave him food. Han Xin told her that he would repay her when he was successful, but the washer-woman was unhappy to hear this, saying she did not help him for a reward.

The other leaves include 'Immortal Qiu' (4), 'Seeking a suitable phrase' (5), 'Playing a flute, riding a buffalo' (8), 'Northern frontier' (10) and 'Drunken immortal' (3). Even though these do not contain specific figures, they embody Daoist thought and folk customs, giving life to the philosophical thinking of traditional Chinese culture.

Guo Xu was from Taihe in Jiangxi Province. He excelled at expressive (*xieyi*) figure painting and used vigorous brushstrokes to create elegant, classical images. His fascinating works seem effortless at times.

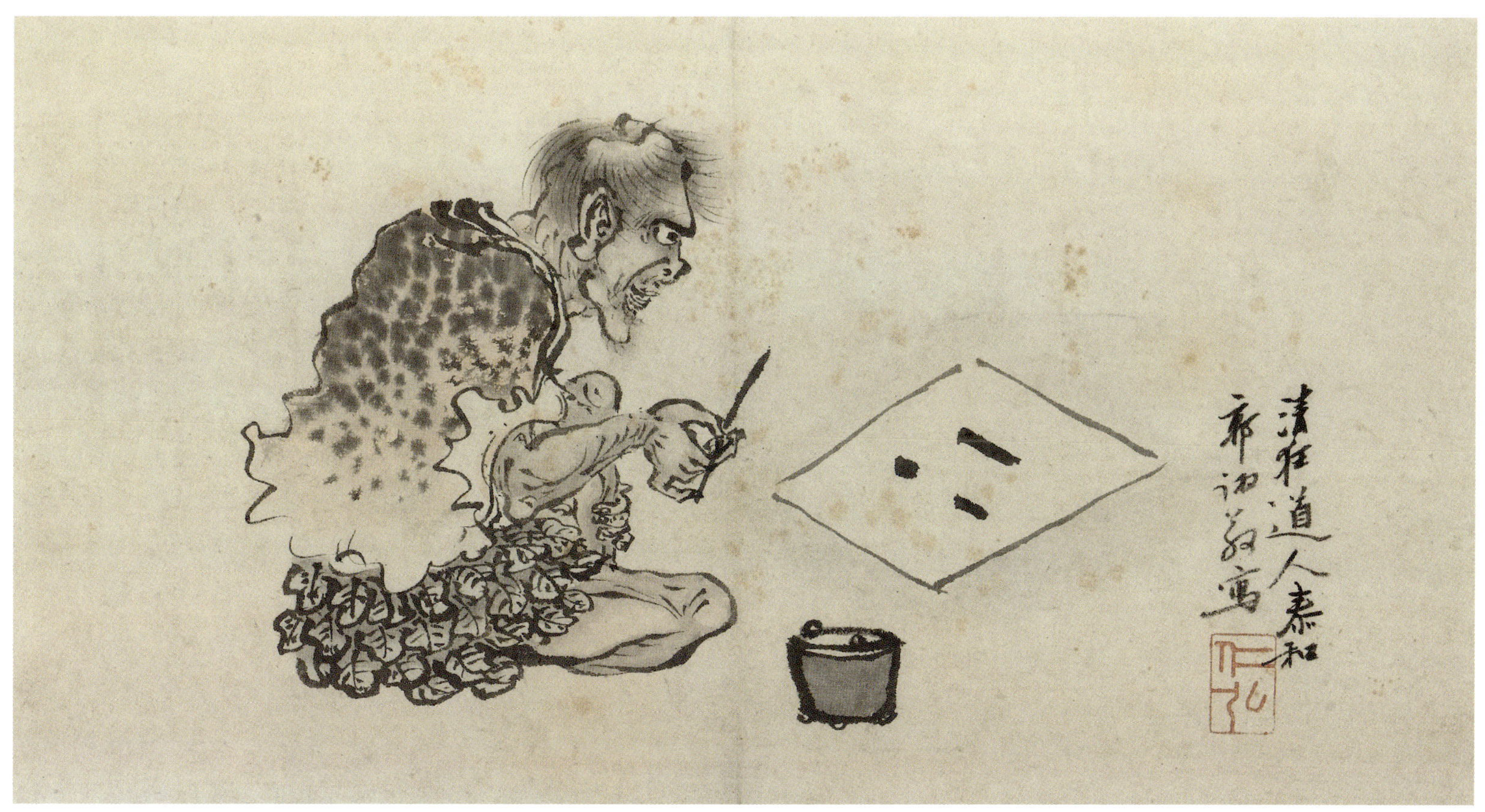

The legendary inventor of writing, Fuxi, creates a trigram, detail, leaf 1

10

清 胡玢《隔江相爭圖軸》

Hu Fen (active Qing dynasty, 1644–1911)
Quarrelling on Two Sides of a River
Hanging scroll; ink and colours on silk
163 × 65 cm
Donated by the Ching Banlee family

This is a genre painting that wonderfully conjures the atmosphere of life in rural China. There is a story behind it, common enough in country villages, which begins with two innocent children at play coming to blows. When one of them starts crying, what started as a disagreement between two children turns into a fight between the parents, as they intervene to defend their offspring. This in turn develops into a bitter clash between the people of the neighbouring villages, who take up their hoes and pitchforks in a tense situation that is dangerously close to becoming a battle.

Each of the figures strikes a different pose in the painting. A small stream separates the two families and there are babies crying, people shouting and gesturing wildly – even a barking dog eager to join in. Some of the women show more self-restraint and hold their enthusiastic husbands back. This charming, lively scene is a humorous one, and reveals the painter's astute observations of village life and his aptitude for lively characterisation. The artist was Hu Fen (an alternate pronunciation of Fen is Bin), whose biography is unknown.

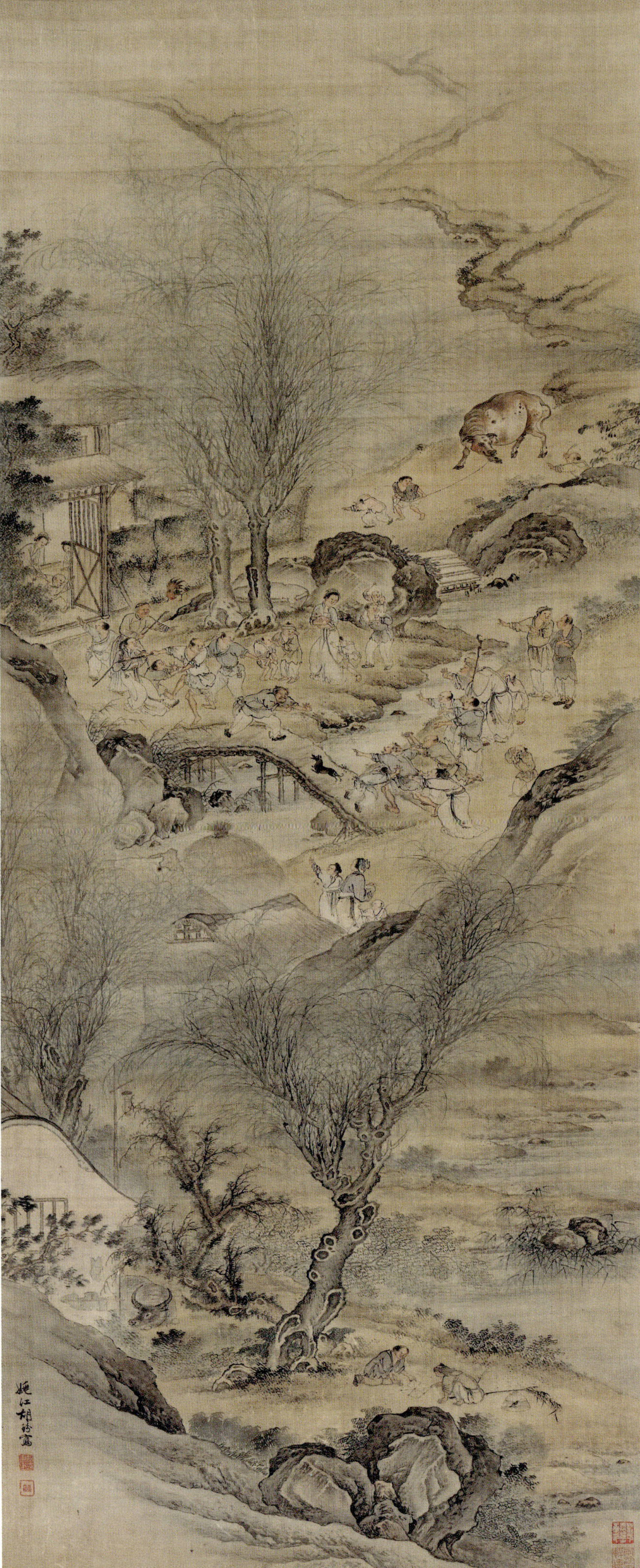

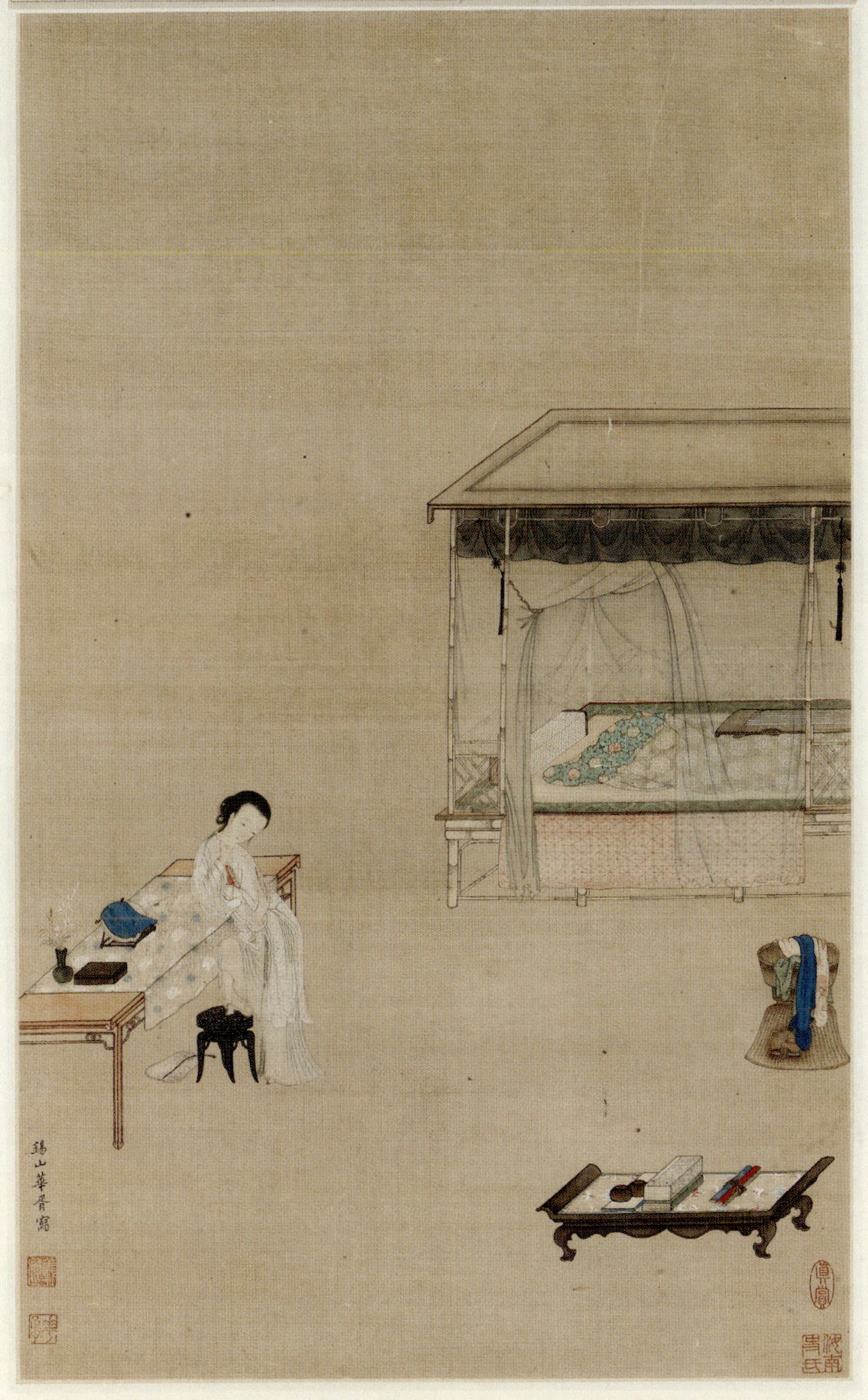

11

清 華胥《甄妃晨妝圖軸》

Hua Xu (active *c.*1799)
Consort Zhen at her Morning Toilette
Hanging scroll; ink and colours on silk
61.6 × 37.1 cm

Consort Zhen refers to Zhen Mi, the empress of Cao Pi of Wei in the Three Kingdoms period (220–80) (see Cat. 23). This painting presents a vivid picture of Lady Zhen at her dressing table, about to perform her morning toilette. Her graceful pose stands in sharp contrast to the hardwood furniture. The books and papers on her table highlight her cultured upbringing, while the dishevelled blankets on the bed, the casually strewn clothing and uncovered mirror reveal the artist's keen perception and close attention to detail. The painter captures Consort Zhen's melancholic mood and her longing for her lover, Cao Zhi – the emperor's brother.

Hua Xu, whose style-name is Xiyi, lived during the Qianlong (1736–95) and Jiaqing (1796–1820) reigns. A painting dated 1799 is extant. From Wuxi in Jiangsu Province, he was mainly a figure and landscape painter.

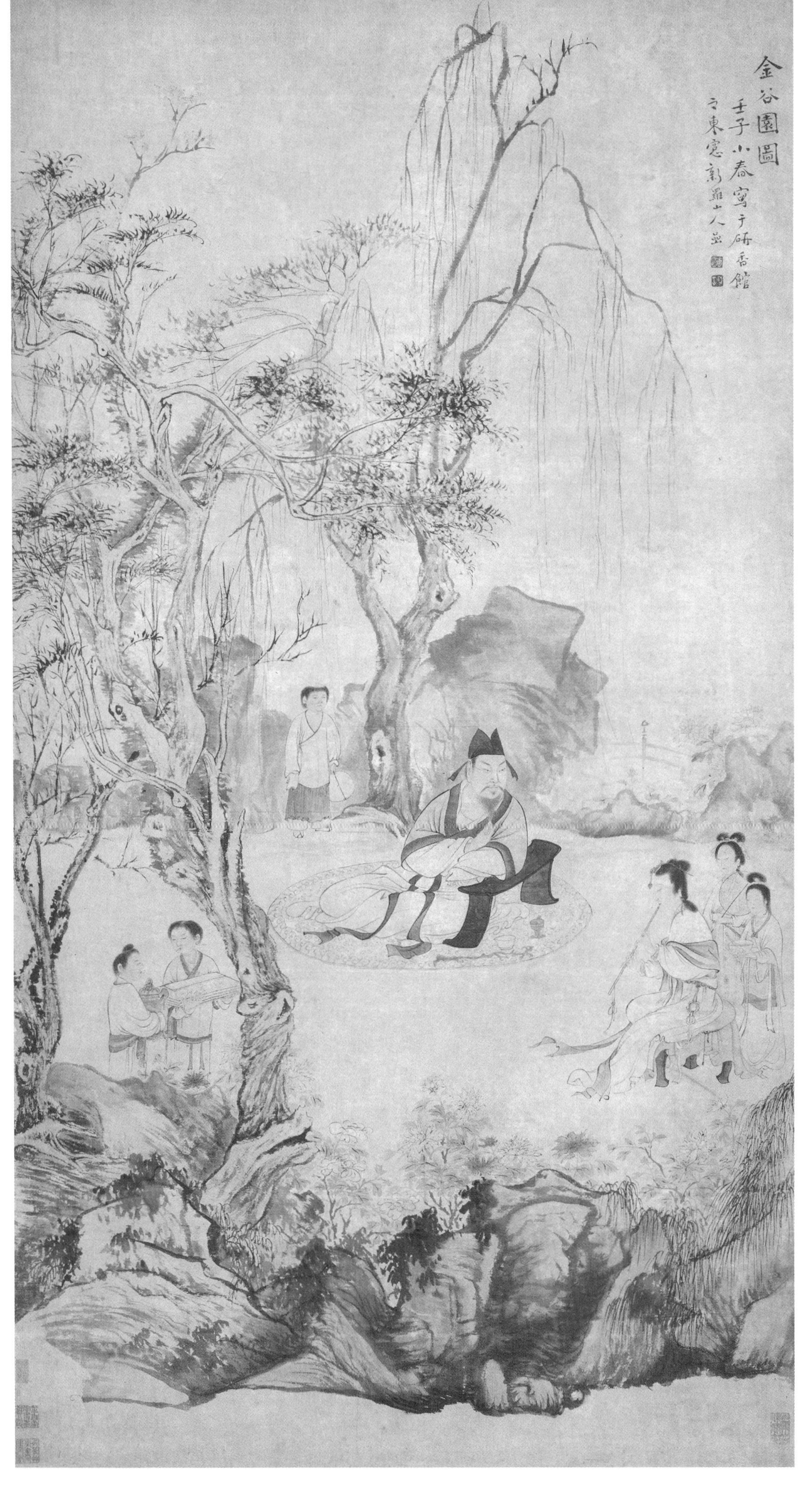
金谷園圖
壬子小春寫于研香館
之東窓新羅山人喦

12

清 華嵒 《金谷園圖軸》

Hua Yan (1682–1756)
Golden Valley Garden
Dated 1732
Hanging scroll; ink and colours on paper
178.9 × 94.1 cm

During the Wei-Jin period (3rd–6th century), China was divided among the feudal lords, and in a constant state of war – it was the most bloody and turbulent period in the country's history. The nobility lived extravagantly and flaunted its wealth. The Golden Valley Garden was a luxurious villa built at great expense by Shi Chong of the Western Jin dynasty (265–317) in Henan. Shi Chong was a local official who used his military power to steal from merchants and terrorise the people. Over 1,000 servants and courtesans lived at the villa, where banquets were often held in the garden. Shi Chong's courtesans would sing and dance for the guests at these banquets, but if he thought they had performed poorly, he would cut off their heads on the spot. Such excessive violence embodied the chaos of this period in the country's history.

In the Golden Valley Garden, the most famous courtesan (and Shi Chong's favourite) was Green Pearl, exceptional not only for her beauty but also for her talent as a brilliant flautist. These qualities led to a tragic sequence of events. Because he refused to give her up to a powerful rival, Shi Chong was implicated in a plot. When soldiers came to arrest him, Shi Chong said to Green Pearl, 'I am in this trouble because of you. What's to be done?' She replied, 'I must kill myself now before your eyes. I cannot let him have what he wants.' She then jumped to her death from a high tower in the garden. Despite Shi Chong's cruel and extravagant nature, Green Pearl loved him loyally, and her story – portrayed in elegiacs and paintings down the ages – came to embody the virtue of wholehearted devotion.

This painting shows the enchanting Golden Valley Garden, with Green Pearl concentrating on playing her flute, while Shi Chong listens at his leisure. Hua Yan was from Ninghua, Fujian Province. He excelled at bird-and-flower and figure painting. His style combined both realistic (*gongbi*) and expressive (*xieyi*) brush techniques, and he painted both high-brow and vernacular subjects. He was an outstanding Yangzhou School artist.

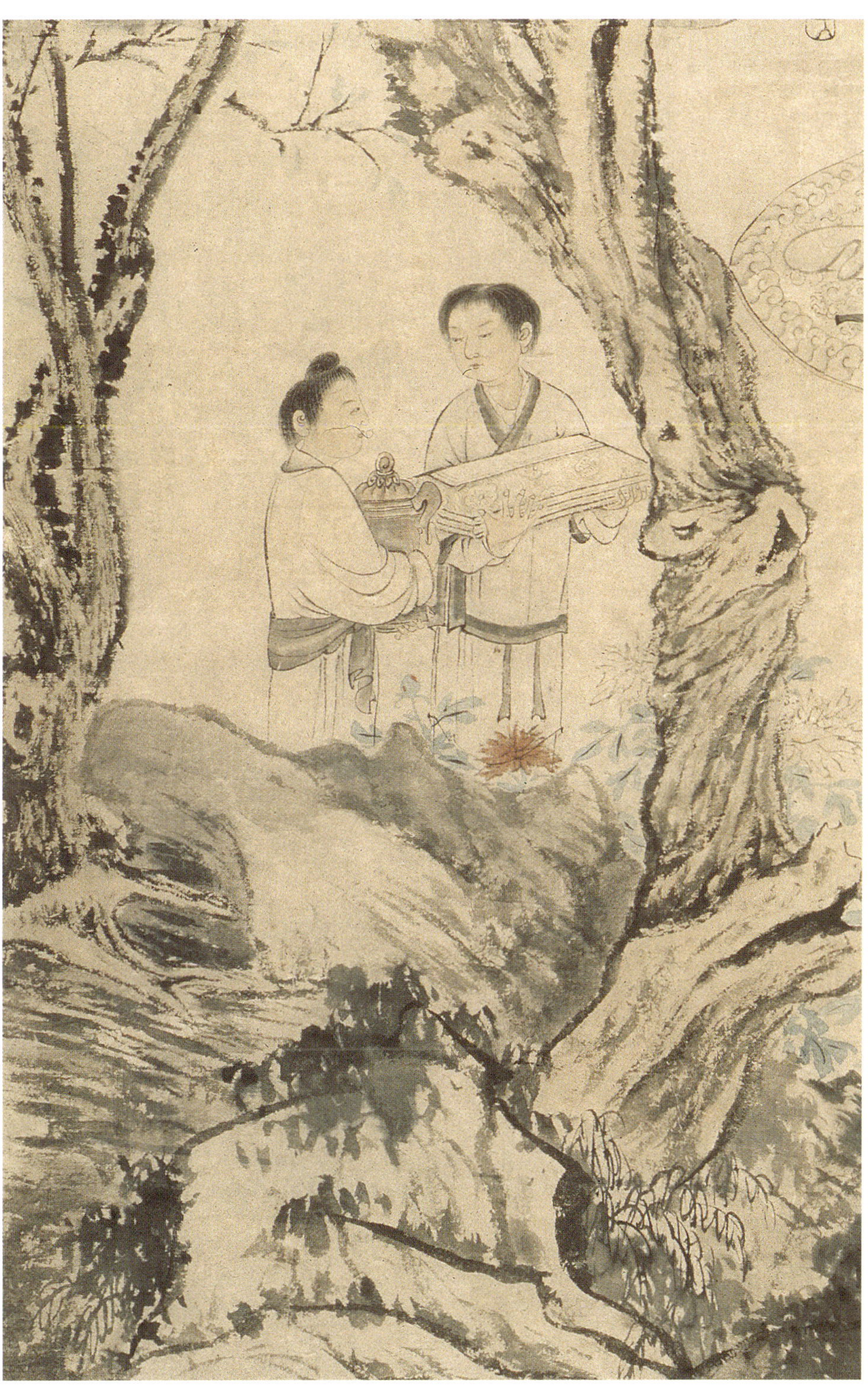

13

明 黄卷 《嬉春圖卷》

Huang Juan (active 1630–56)
Women Enjoying the Spring Festival
Dated 1636
Handscroll; ink and colours on silk
38 × 311.2 cm

In the late Ming and early Qing period (17th century), the freedom of women to leave their homes to travel or otherwise entertain themselves was restricted by rites and customs. Women of the upper classes had more opportunity to come together socially – although this was still by no means common. This period saw many talented courtesans who could compose poetry and paint, start to challenge social conventions, courageously interacting with men in the upper levels of society and heralding a new type of feminine identity. These women typically went on group outings, taking every opportunity to engage with eminent men of the day, recite poetry and make paintings. Courtesans were also invited to the literati's elegant gatherings to help with the festivities. The songs they sang were often about their daily activities, such as outings with friends, readings and poetry discussions, calligraphy and painting, burning incense and tasting tea, and making music together.

This painting illustrates just such an outing of women during the Ming–Qing transition, with towers and pavilions amidst brilliant peach trees and willows creating a festive spring atmosphere. The finely dressed women are vividly and carefully depicted – some have stopped on a path to read, while others drink tea, play the zither and flute, or recite poetry on a boat.

Huang Juan, whose style-name was Shengmo, lived during the Wanli (1573–1620) to Chongzhen (1628–44) reigns in the late Ming dynasty. He was from Putian in Fujian Province. Although a landscape painter, his forte was the genre of elegant women.

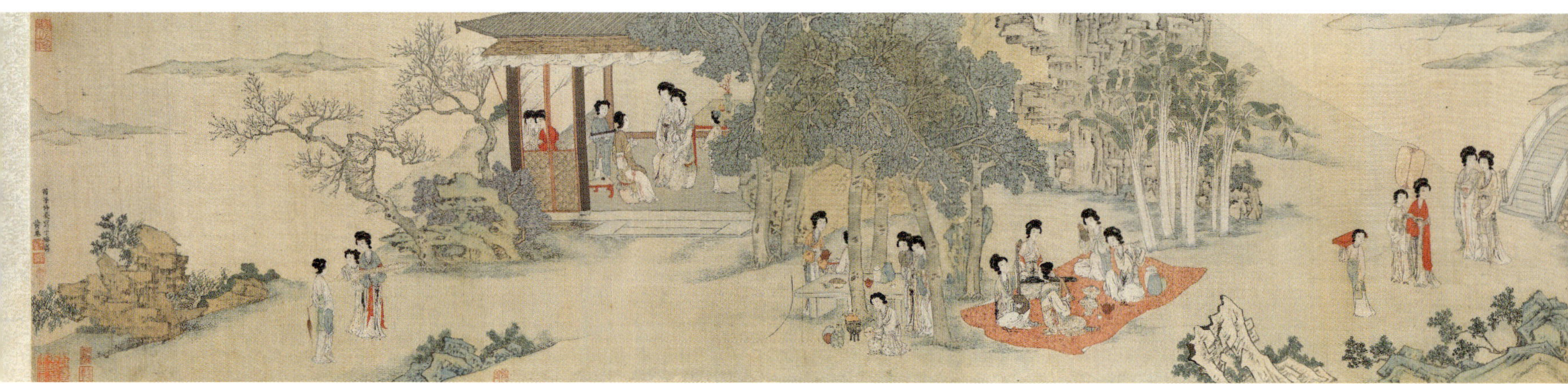

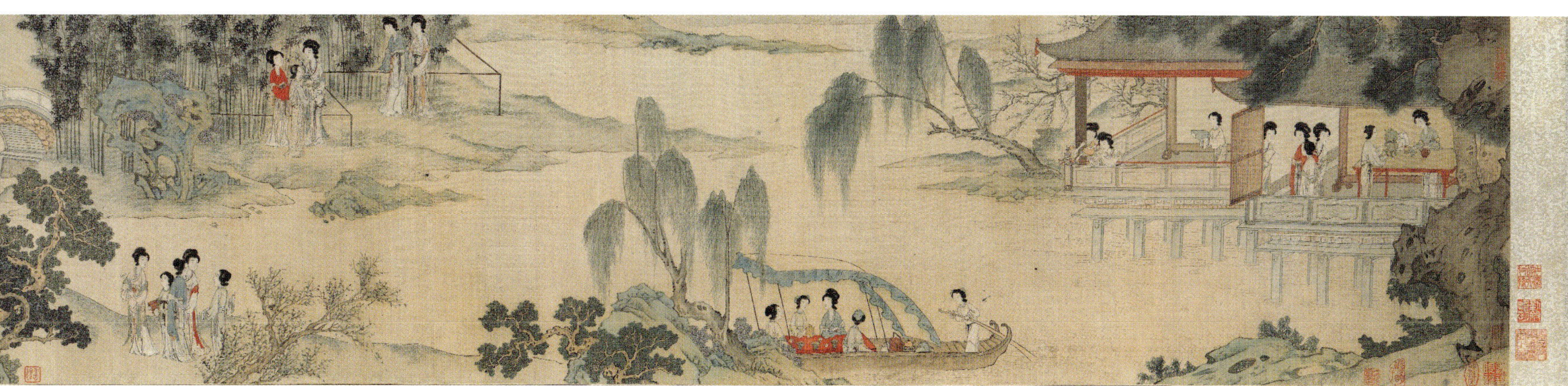

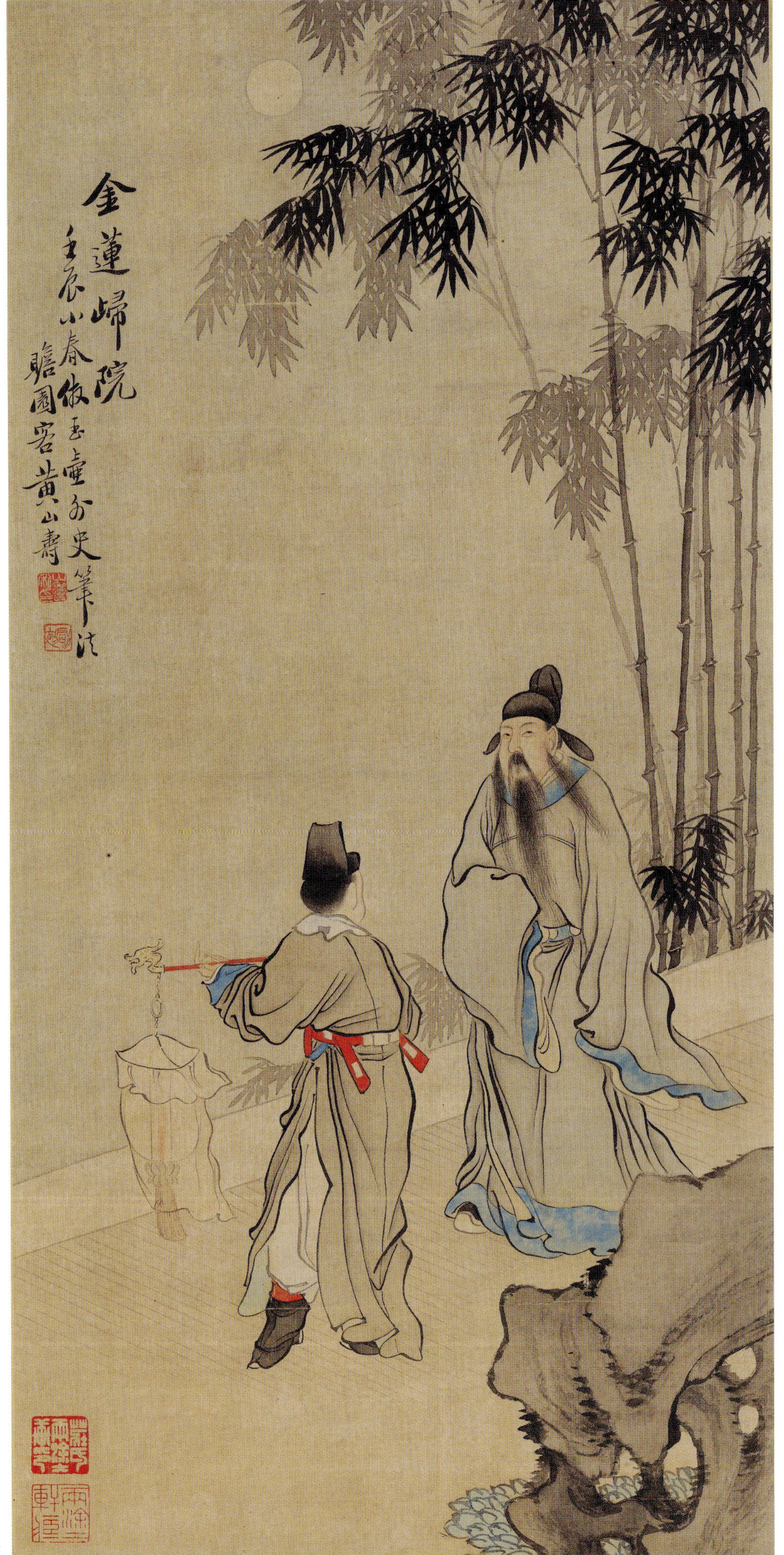
金蓮歸院
壬辰小春倣玉壺外史筆法
瞻園客黃山壽

14

清 黃山壽 《金蓮歸院圖軸》

Huang Shanshou (1855–1919)
Returning to the Academy by
'Golden Lotus' Lamplight
Dated 1892
Hanging scroll; ink and colours on silk
59.6 × 28.6 cm
Donated by the Ching Banlee family

The 'Golden Lotus' in the title of this painting refers to a type of lotus-shaped lantern with gold decoration that was reserved exclusively for use by the emperor of China. Here, 'Academy' refers to the offices within the Imperial City occupied by the great scholar-officials in the Tang (618–907) and Song (960–1279) dynasties. The story 'Returning to the Academy by "Golden Lotus" Lamplight' originated with Linghu Tao, a Hanlin academician and chief minister in the late Tang dynasty. A man of broad learning and many talents, also a master of strategic thinking, he enjoyed the close confidence of the emperor. On one occasion the emperor summoned him during the night to discuss a pressing matter of state. A lively debate followed, which lasted until the candles had burnt themselves out. At this point, the emperor commanded his servants to escort Linghu Tao back to the Academy in his personal carriage, using Golden Lotus lanterns. When the scholar-officials in the Academy saw these lights approaching, they assumed the emperor was visiting.

So, this story came to stand for the special treatment a ruler might endow on a minister. A total of six scholars received this accolade during the Song dynasty, including the great literatus Su Shi (see Cats 15 & 28). He had gone to see the emperor, who repeatedly cried out, 'such remarkable talent!' while reading his writings. The emperor then had him escorted back to the Academy by the palace's Golden Lotus lantern, which moved Su Shi to tears.

This special treatment showed the emperor's acknowledgement and admiration of the talents of these scholar-officials, and it would have been the greatest social recognition they could receive.

This painting depicts a servant holding the lantern and leading a scholar-official dressed in his official clothes back to the Academy at night. From Changzhou in Jiangsu Province, Huang Shanshou was principally a landscapist.

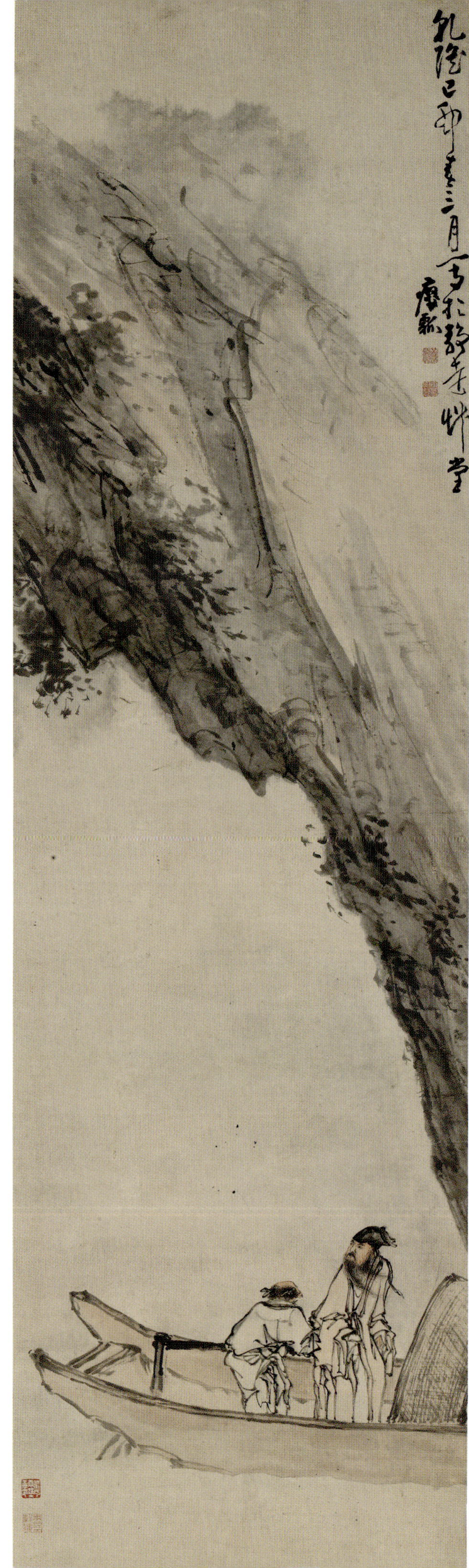

15

清 黃慎 《赤壁夜遊圖軸》

Huang Shen (1687–after 1770)
Night Excursion to the Red Cliffs
Dated 1759
Hanging scroll; ink and colours on paper
181.7 × 52 cm
Donated by the Ching Banlee family

In the winter of 208, the notorious northern commander Cao Cao led a navy of 200,000 sailors and marines southward to attack and invade the kingdom of Eastern Wu. The Eastern Wu king, Sun Quan, adopted a stratagem of Zhuge Liang's (see Cat. 2) by allying himself with Liu Bei of the state of Shu and attacking with fireboats. Cao Cao's warships were all tethered together, and with the help of the wind, there was soon a raging inferno, and a great many of the enemy officers, men and warhorses drowned. The most famous example in Chinese history of 'the few defeating the many', this battle took place at the Red Cliffs, in present-day Huanggang, Hubei Province (some say it was in the northwest of Puqi County, Hubei).

On the sixteenth day of the seventh month of 1082, China's greatest poet, calligrapher and writer, Su Shi, was disgraced and demoted to a post near the Red Cliffs. During his time in exile, he visited the cliffs in a small boat at night and thought of the battle that had taken place there 800 years before. This stirred his emotions and a feeling of connection with the past, leading him to write the celebrated work of Chinese literary history, the 'Former Red Cliff Ode'. Three years later, after visiting the spot again, he composed his 'Latter Red Cliff Ode'. (Both are in the collection of the Taipei Palace Museum.)

This painting depicts the moving scene of Su Shi alone in his boat at night under the towering cliffs. The painting technique is bold and uninhibited, reflecting Su Shi's heroic temperament.

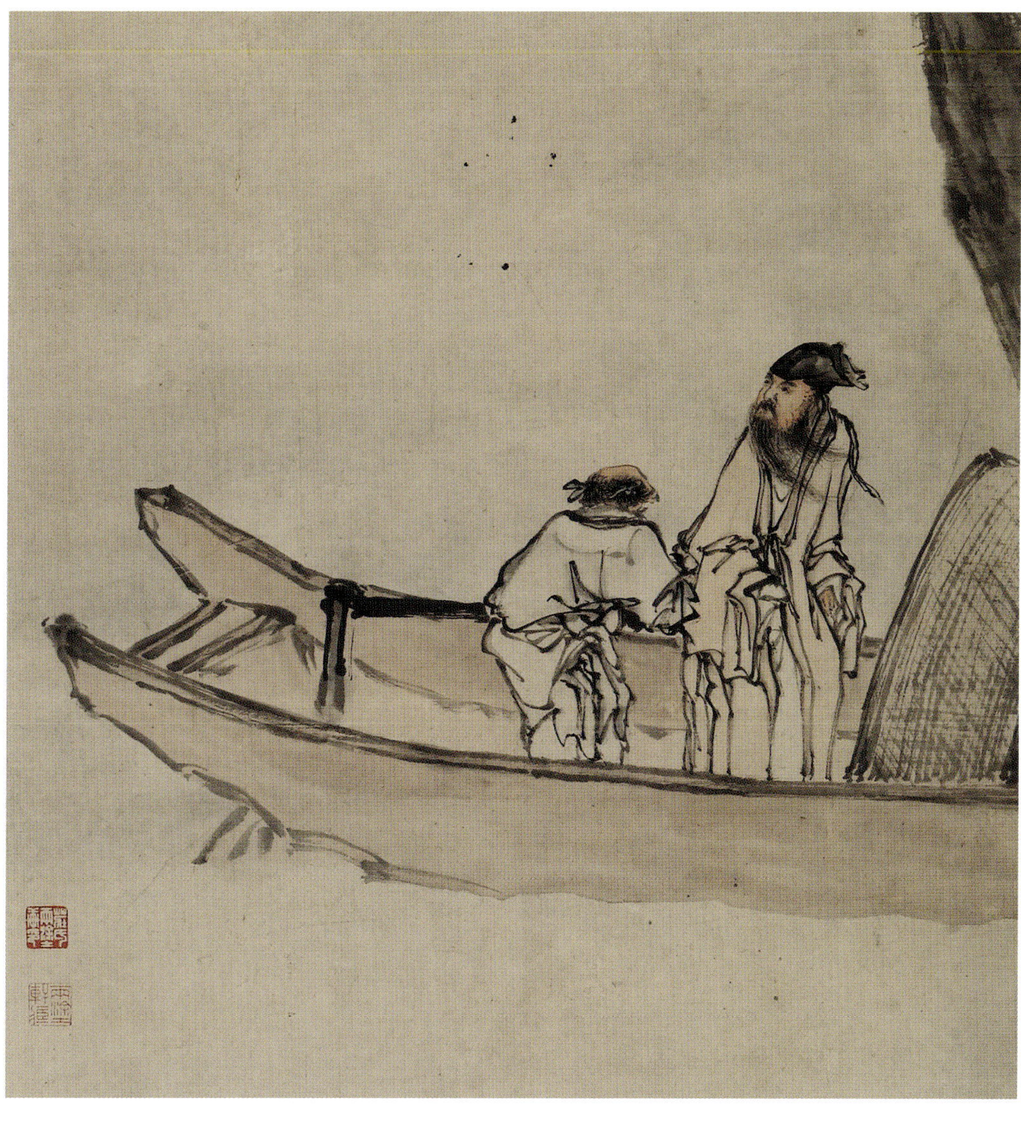

16

清 黄慎 《蘇武牧羊圖軸》

Huang Shen (1687–after 1770)
Su Wu Tending Sheep
Hanging scroll; ink and colours on paper
94.2 × 101.2 cm

'Su Wu tending sheep' is a classic Chinese story of patriotism and of maintaining one's ethnic integrity. The events in the story took place almost 100 years before Wang Zhaojun was married off to a Xiongnu chieftain (see Cat. 32). At this time, relations between the Han Chinese and Xiongnu peoples were extremely delicate. In 101 BC, there was a period of détente, and the Xiongnu chieftain (*Shanyu*) proposed reconciliation, releasing captive Han officials to show goodwill. In response, Han emperor Wu (Wudi) sent his commanders Su Wu and Zhang Sheng to escort detained Xiongnu emissaries back home. When they arrived at their destination, Zhang Sheng hatched a plot to kidnap the Xiongnu chieftain's mother and take her back to China, but the plan was foiled, and Su Wu was implicated instead. Su Wu, not willing to be disgraced, tried to kill himself but he failed. The Xiongnu chieftain respected Su Wu for this and urged him to surrender, offering him gold and an official post in return. Su Wu rejected his offer so the chieftain punished him by imprisoning him in a cellar without food. When Su Wu survived this, the chieftain sent him into the wilderness to herd sheep, and he lived on wild grasses and fruits buried by field mice. He was discovered six years later, still alive, and it was thought to be a miracle.

In 81 BC, the Xiongnu made peace with the Chinese and the Han court requested that Su Wu be released. In all, Su Wu was detained by the Xiongnu for nineteen years without compromising his character, and he became an example of the virtue of maintaing one's ethnic integrity.

This painting was made in an expressive, free-hand style (*xieyi* – literally, 'written ideas'), with concise lines that represent Su Wu's persevering nature. The background has been left as a large blank space – to represent the harsh and desolate desert environment.

Huang Shen was from Ninghua, Fujian Province, in southeastern China. His principle subjects were the lives of gods and immortals, and of cultural luminaries from the past. An outstanding figure painter, with a bold and unrestrained handling of brush and ink, he is a representative of the Yangzhou School of painting.

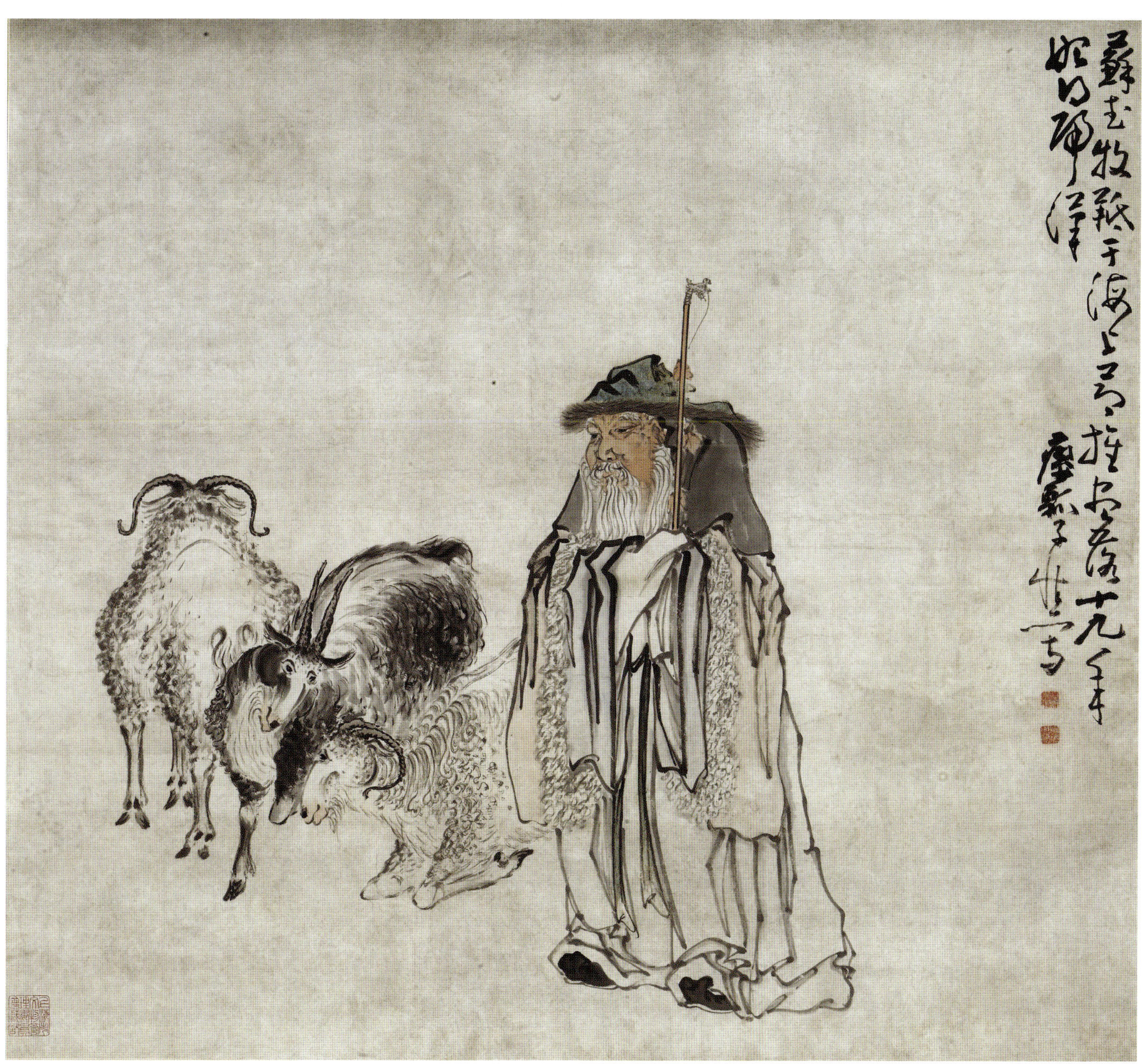

17

明 李麟 《布袋慈尊十八子圖卷》

Li Lin (1558–after 1636)
The Laughing Buddha Budai Surrounded by Children
Dated 1636
Handscroll; ink on paper
29.8 × 138.5 cm

At the centre of this painting is the monk Budai. He has a broad grin, long earlobes and a round belly, and his chest is exposed. With a cloth bag at his side, he is surrounded by eighteen lovely children holding gold and jade (ancient Chinese money), who are playing around him. This charming scene shows why Maitreya Buddha is often called the Laughing Buddha or Happy Buddha. He is also regarded as a symbol of luck, and known as the Lucky Buddha.

Budai, or literally the 'cloth-bag monk', lived during the Five Dynasties period (907–60) at the Yuelin Temple in Ningbo, Zhejiang Province. His real name was Qieci (?–916), and it was said that the cloth bag he carried around on a pole was enough to hold everything he owned. With his unconventional appearance, he wandered here and there, often lying down and frequently laughing at things in a manner others thought inappropriate. His giant belly is meant to reflect his generous spirit, and his cloth bag (*budai*) represents his deeply benevolent nature, as well as his limitless power. Believed to bring fortune and hope to the world and rid it of its woes, people came to believe he was a reincarnation of Maitreya Buddha, the Buddha of the future.

The painter Li Lin was from Ningbo in Zhejiang Province, but little else is known about his life. He specialised in painting religious figures such as these.

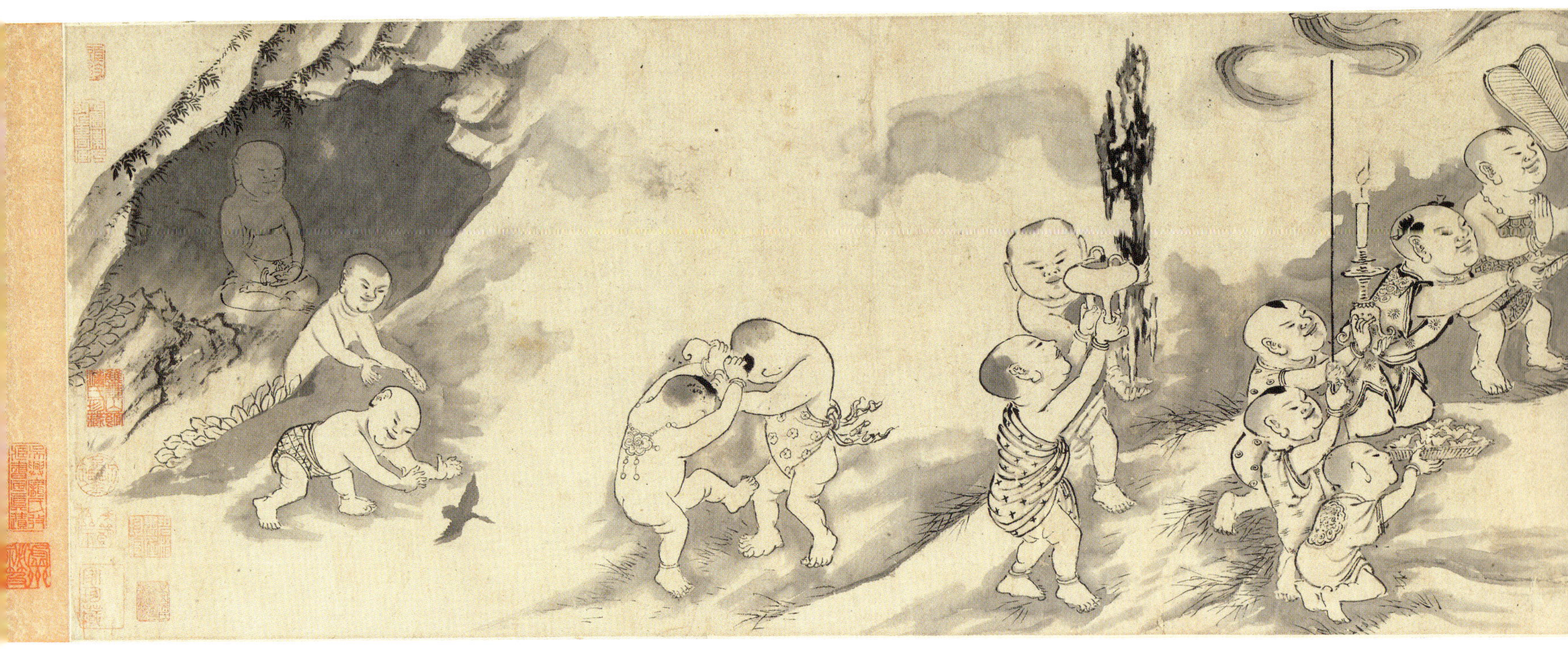

布代慈尊十八子圖

嚴繩孫題

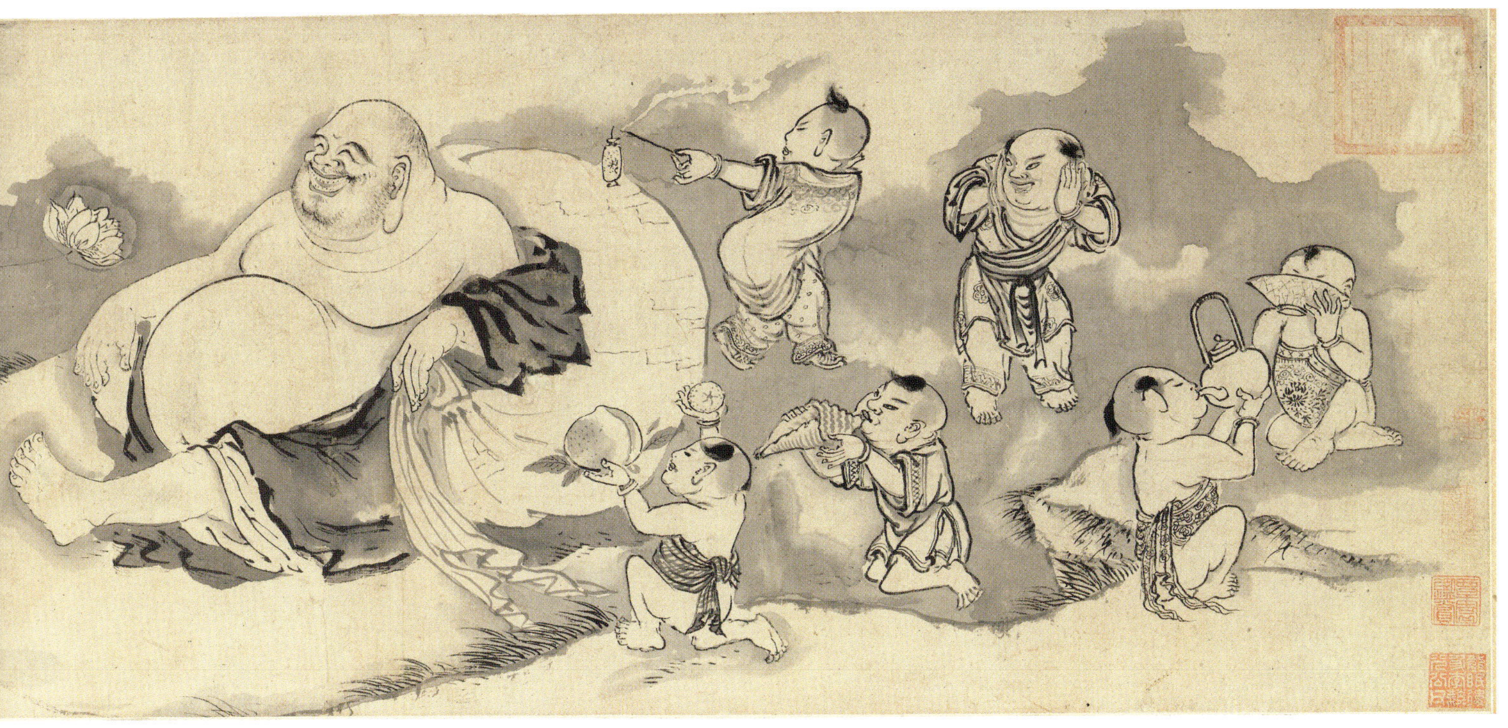

18

明 李士達 《竹林七賢圖卷》

Li Shida (1550–after 1623)
Seven Worthies of the Bamboo Grove
Dated 1616
Handscroll; ink and colours on silk
25.4 × 157.2 cm
Donated by Zhang Zhenfei

It was during the time of the extreme political and social injustices of the Wei-Jin period (3rd–6th century) in China that a number of educated recluses emerged, advocating freedom and spiritual independence. *Seven Worthies of the Bamboo Grove* features this group – Ruan Ji, Xi Kang, Shan Tao, Wang Rong, Xiang Xiu, Liu Ling and Ruan Xian – each of whom had literary and musical talents. They were dissatisfied with social inequities, and pondered over the problems of human freedom and other humanistic concerns. They advocated behaving in a direct and sincere way, were unwilling to cooperate with their rulers and resisted the unfair systems that operated around them. These beliefs were often expressed through unusual actions or phrases such as Ruan Ji's 'crying at the end of the road': Once, he was following a wooded mountain road when it

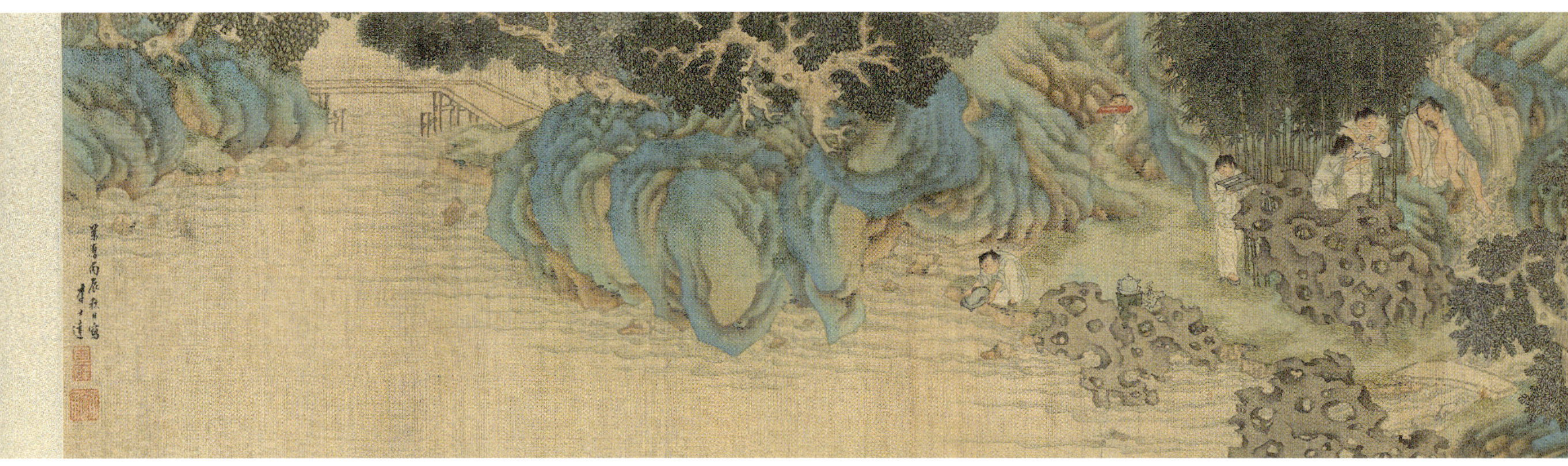

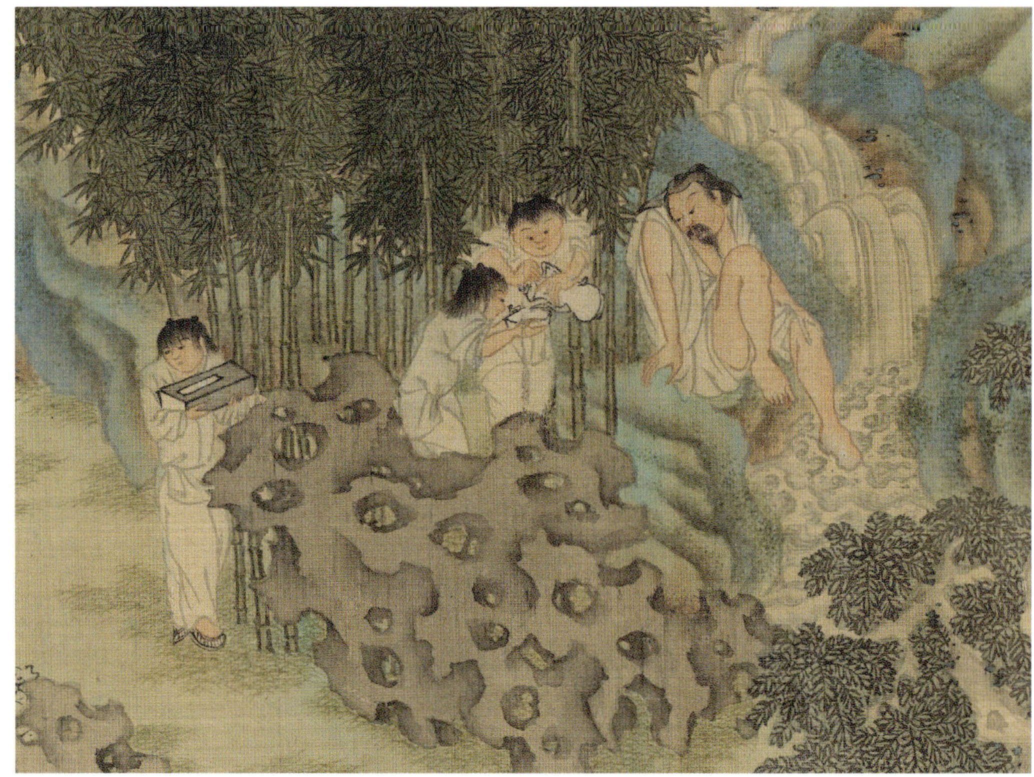

suddenly ended, so he started wailing. The wine-lover Liu Ling once got roaring drunk at home and took off all his clothes. Someone scolded his impropriety, to which he replied, 'The world is my home, and my home is my pants. What are you all doing in my pants?'

On the one hand they satirised social unfairness, and on the other they behaved in these strange ways to avoid being executed. It was unfortunate that Xi Kang, a skilled musician, offended an official and was beheaded. Before his execution, not only was he not afraid but he calmly requested a zither to play his song *Guangling Melody (Guangling san)*. When he was finished he said, 'Thus the *Guangling Melody* ends', and resignedly went to his execution.

Stories abound of the Seven Worthies, and it is clear their words and actions sparked a period of 'human awakening' in Chinese history. Their free-thinking inspired men of culture for generations to come.

This painting portrays the Seven Worthies variously playing the zither and reciting poetry in a secluded bamboo forest, each striking a different pose. Li Shida was from the city of Suzhou in Jiangsu Province.

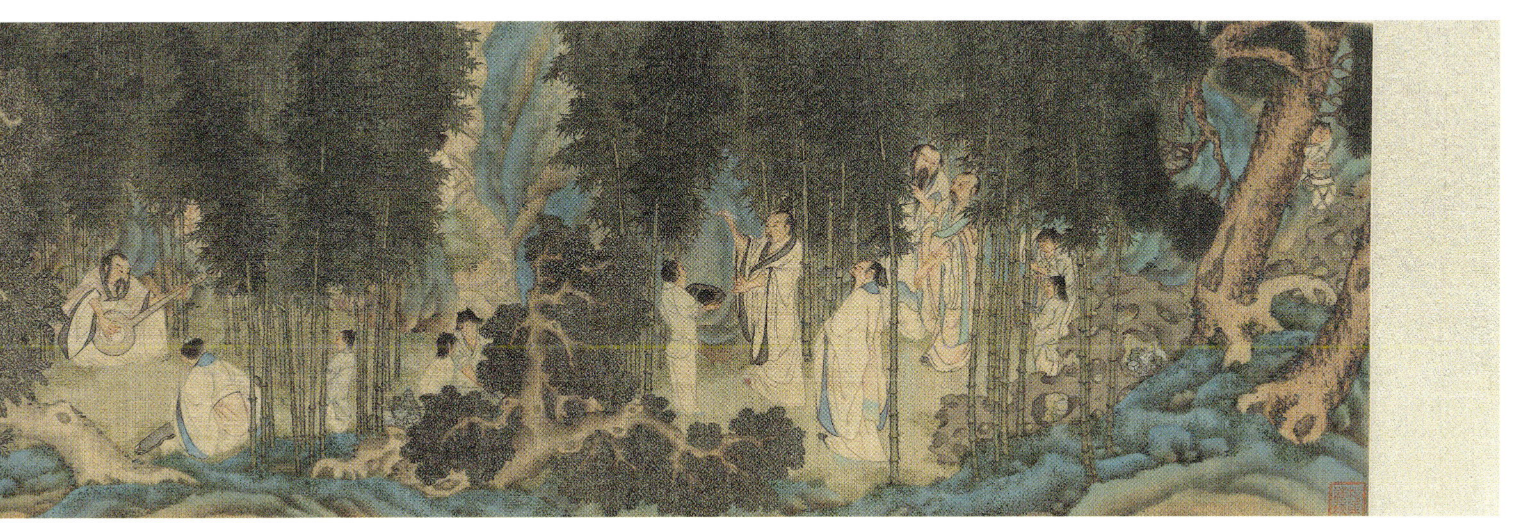

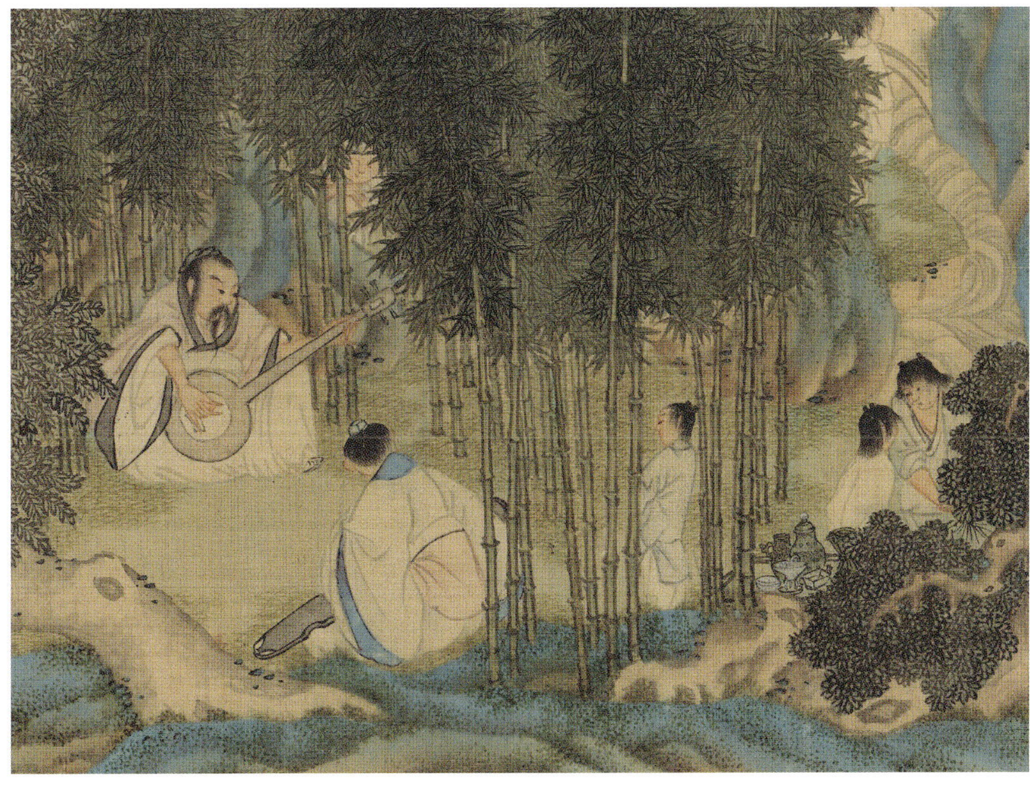

19

清 李瑶 《文姬歸漢圖軸》

Li Yao (active 1736–95)
Wenji Returning to China
Dated 1766
Hanging scroll; ink on paper
98.5 × 29.2 cm

Cai Yan (also known as Wenji) was the daughter of Cai Yong, a scholar during the Eastern (or Later) Han dynasty (25–220). She was an accomplished and broad talent in her own right, who excelled in literature, writing and music. Her first marriage was to Wei Zhongdao, during a period of perpetual war in China. During the ongoing conflict, her father was jailed by his Chinese enemies, and died in captivity. Cai Wenji herself was captured in a raid by foreign troops, ending up among the Southern Xiongnu, where she was forced into a marriage that resulted in two sons. The Eastern Han dynasty fell and the warlord Cao Cao gradually gained control of the north. Out of fondness for his old friend Cai Yong, Cao Cao sent gold and jade to buy Wenji back from the Xiongnu. The Xiongnu agreed that Wenji could return home, but her two sons could not. She missed her homeland deeply, and with a heavy heart Wenji returned to China without her sons. She later married Dong Si and, using her broad learning, she compiled over 400 chapters of a book which had been left unfinished by her father, thereby completing the *Continuation of the Han History (Xu Han shu)*.

The story 'Wenji returning to China' became the subject of many works of literature, drama, art and song. This painting is one such example. Its delicate brushstrokes evoke the sorrow and beauty of Cai Wenji leaving her husband and children to return home.

Li Yao was from Wu County, Jiangsu Province. A specialist in figure painting, he was active during the Qianlong reign (1736–95) of the Qing dynasty.

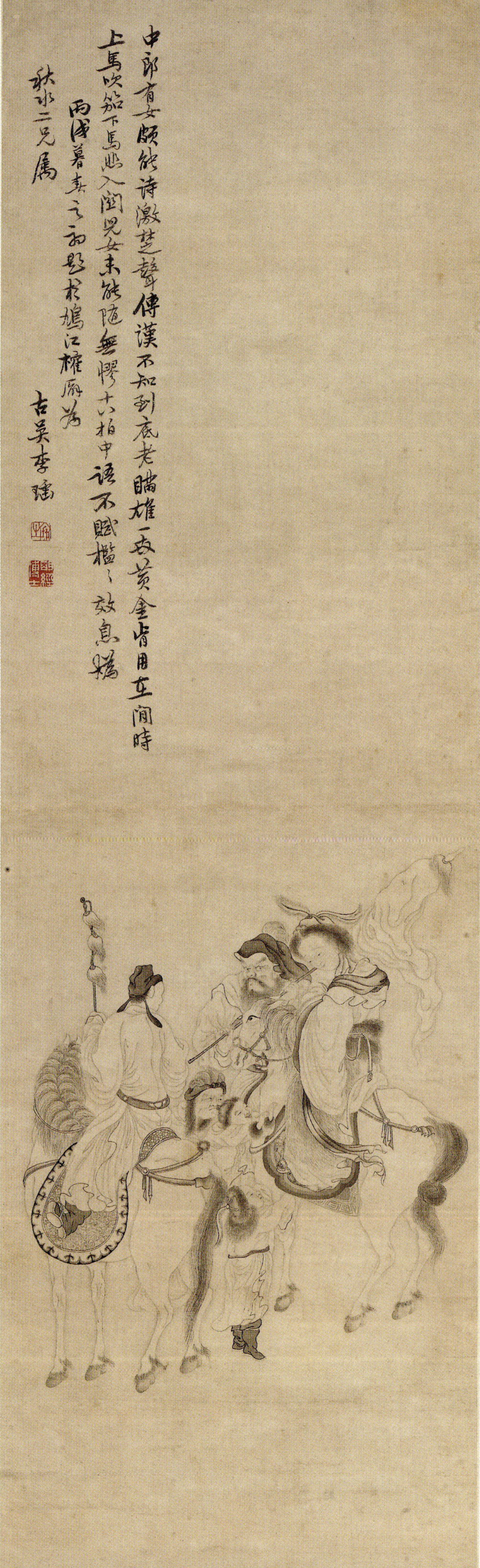

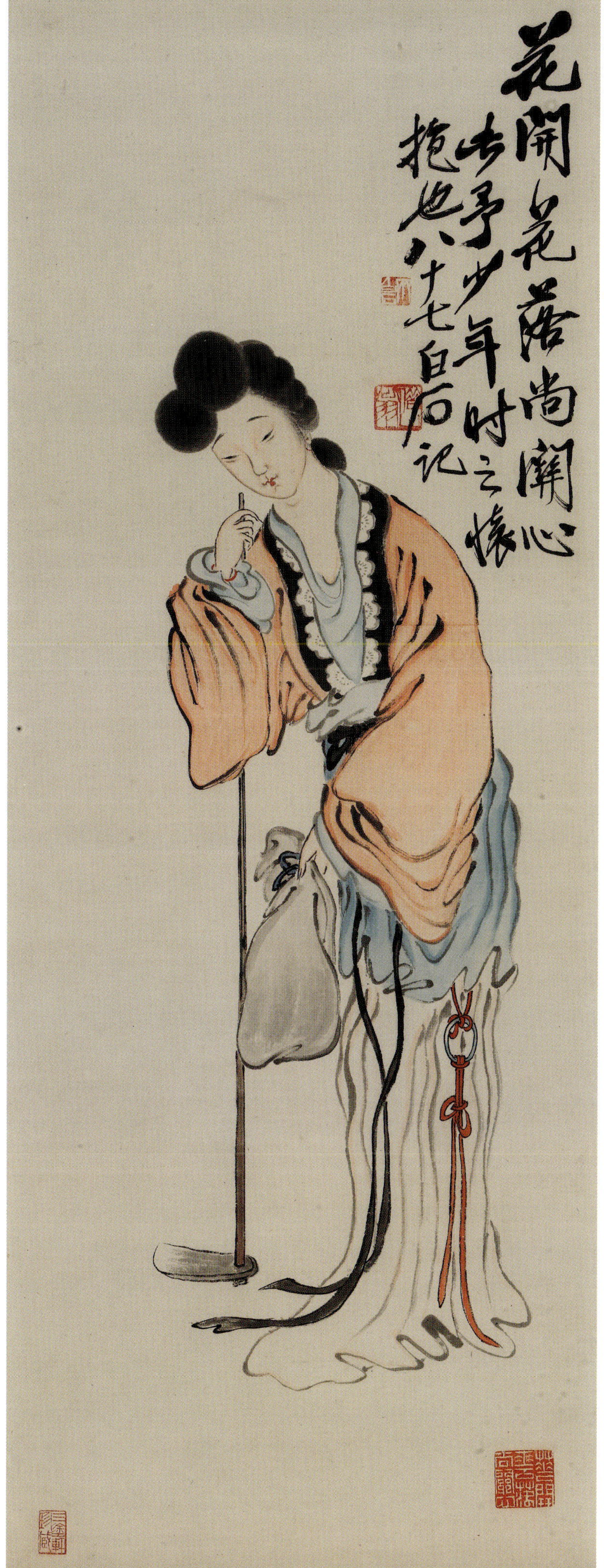

20

現代 齊璜 《黛玉葬花圖軸》

Qi Huang (Qi Baishi; 1864–1957)
Daiyu Buries Flowers
Dated 1950
Hanging scroll; ink and colours on paper
91.4 × 33.3 cm
Donated by the Ching Banlee family

The subject of this painting comes from the eighteenth-century novel, *Dream of the Red Chamber (Honglou meng)*, one of the 'four great works of literature' in China. The book is about a large, traditional Chinese family and its complicated internal conflicts, but also reflects upon the decadence and decline of feudal society as a whole. The story unfolds through the doomed romance between the protagonists Lin Daiyu and her cousin Jia Baoyu, to show how traditional feudal society destroys true love and even human nature.

Lin Daiyu and Jia Baoyu are rebels against this feudal thinking. Daiyu, a talented and beautiful young woman with a penetrating intellect but a weak constitution, moves in with the Jia family, bringing with her the view that everyone should have the right to freedom and independence. She believes, for example, that Green Pearl should not have committed 'chaste' suicide for the sake of Shi Chong (see Cat. 12). In the end it is her rebellious nature that prevents her from being with Baoyu, and she tragically falls into a decline and dies.

Lin Daiyu pities the lot of flowers, as they represent purity but are surrounded by the filth of the world. She compares the flowers to herself, and the Jia family and even all feudal society to the mire. She is unwilling to be consumed by feudal values, but also cannot break free, so when she sees the fallen flowers that represent her future (for her beauty will fade just as flowers wilt), she buries them in the ground to preserve their purity. Going from crying over flowers to burying them is an advancement in her thinking. Her 'Burying Flowers Song' shows her anxious and sentimental nature and resigned attitude towards love, but also her resolve to break free from feudal ideology. Though her story is tragic, the novel's author Cao Xueqin meant for it to show hope for the democratic ideas of individual liberty and freedom in marriage.

Here, the elegant and dejected Lin Daiyu holds a hoe, her head lowered while she sings softly. Qi Huang excelled at freehand (*xieyi*) painting. His achievements make him one of modern China's finest painters.

21

清 闕嵐 《李白吟詩圖軸》

Que Lan (1758–1844)
Li Bai Chanting Poetry
Hanging scroll; ink on paper
111.4 × 42.7 cm

The subject of this painting, Li Bai, was one of China's greatest poets. He and his fellow Tang-dynasty poet, Du Fu, are commonly referred to as 'Li and Du'. Possessed of an extraordinary poetic imagination and unrestrained emotions, Li Bai is representative of the romantic poets. He was highly influential and deeply loved historically, earning him the respectful moniker, 'poet immortal'.

Li Bai lived the life of a wanderer and loved wine so much that he would not write poetry without it, resulting in the nickname, 'drunken immortal'. Wine nurtured his poetic imagination, so that Du Fu wrote of him: 'When Li Bai drinks one jug of wine, he can compose one hundred poems.' Often drunk, Li Bai would spend his nights in the inns of the Tang capital Chang'an, unwilling to leave even if the emperor summoned him to an audience. He called himself the 'immortal of wine' (*jiuzhong xianren*) to show his disdain for authority and his unbending pride in being a man of culture. It is no surprise, therefore, that the image people have of him is of someone perpetually inebriated, wandering around reciting poetry.

This painting illustrates a lively scene of palace ladies making music and dancing, while Li Bai drinks and writes poetry. Que Lan was an artist during the Qianlong reign (1736–95), but little else is known about his life.

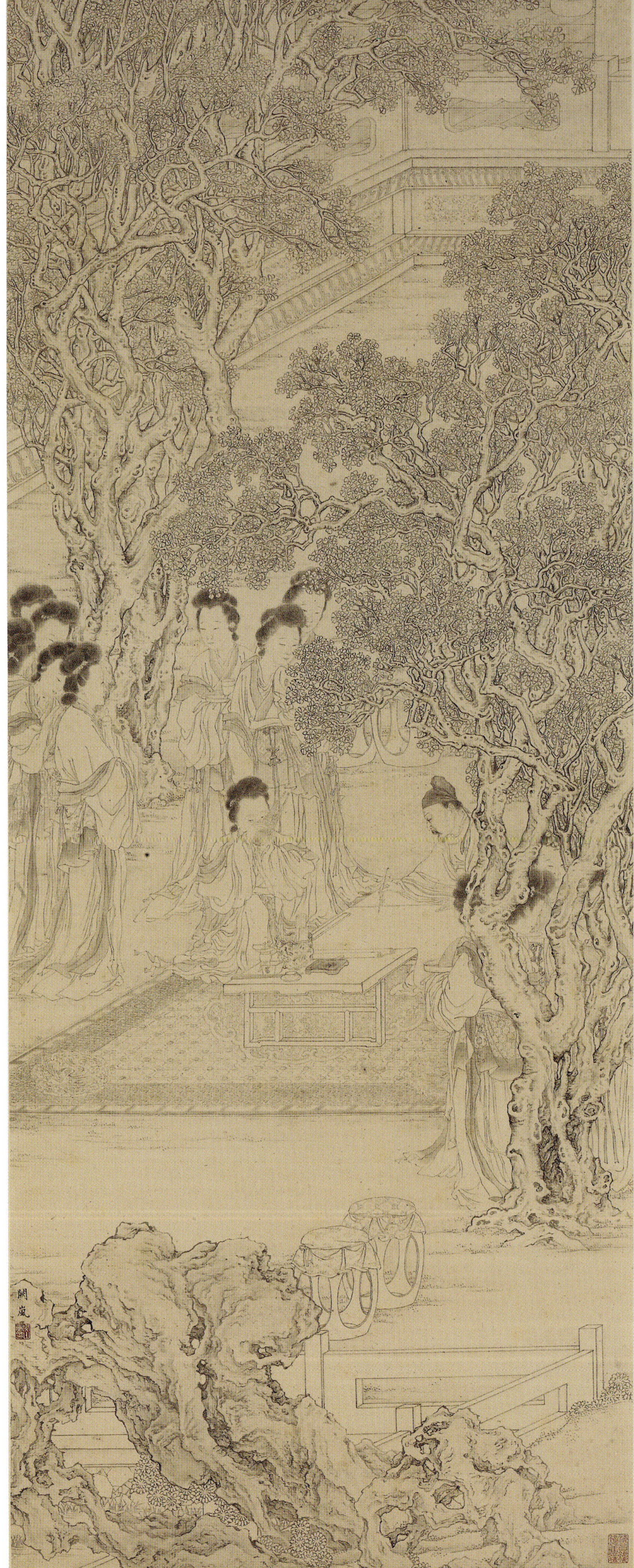

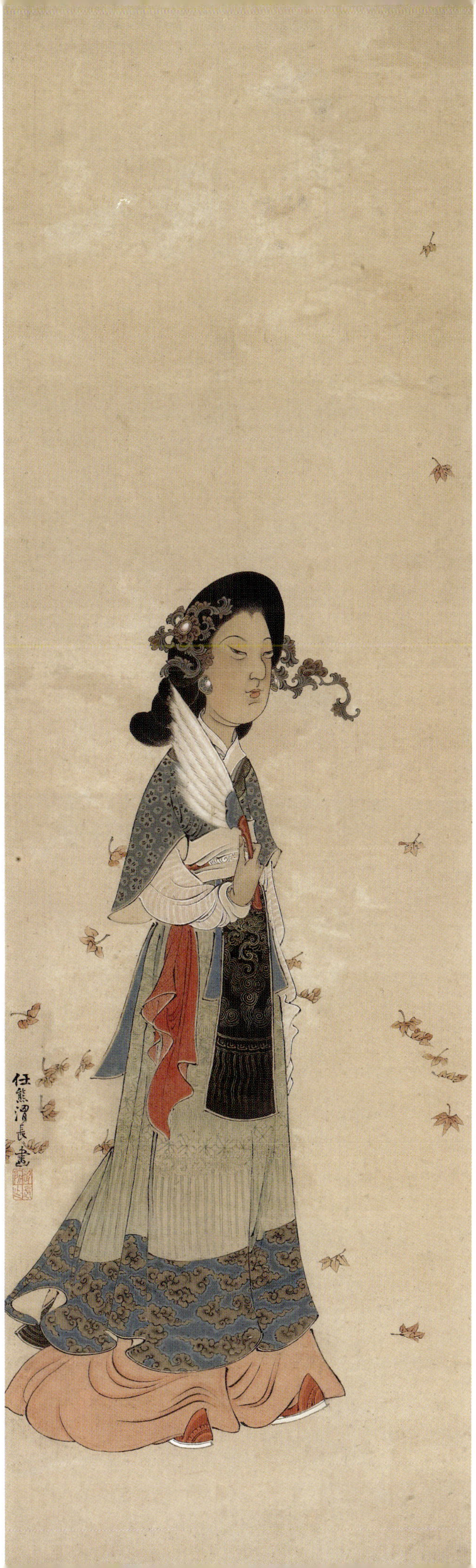

22

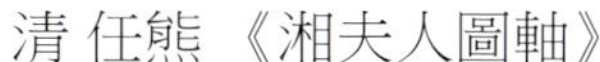

清 任熊《湘夫人圖軸》

Ren Xiong (1823–57)
Lady of the Xiang River
Hanging scroll; ink and colours on paper
121.4 × 35.3 cm

This painting illustrates a figure from a famous poem in antiquity by Qu Yuan, who was a minister of the state of Chu during the Warring States period (475–221 BC). A patriot and a loyal follower of the king, he advocated 'benevolent government' (*mei zheng*), specifically creating policies based on the needs of the people and eliminating special privileges for the nobility. The ruling class opposed his views and plotted against him, resulting in King Huai of Chu dismissing him from office. After Qu Yuan left, the state of Chu fell. He became increasingly worried about the state of his country and its people but there was no way for him to make his voice heard. Sinking into a deep depression at his helpless state, Qu Yuan drowned himself in the Miluo River to show his loyalty to the king. This event is the origin of China's Dragon Boat Festival, celebrated each year on the fifth day of the fifth month in the lunar calendar. Also known as Duanwu or the Double Fifth, on this day people hold dragon-boat races and throw rice dumplings into the Miluo River to remember Qu Yuan.

Qu Yuan's name has been synonymous with patriotism throughout Chinese history, but he was also one of China's greatest writers. He expressed his concern for his nation and his people through his poetry. For example, his poem, 'The Lament' (*Li sao*), is full of contradictions between the real and the ideal, revealing his frustration and ambition. Another poem, 'Lord of the Xiang' (*Xiang jun*), describes the longing of the Lady of the Xiang – the Xiang River goddess – for her husband, the Lord of the Xiang. Qu Yuan compares himself to the Lady of the Xiang and her husband, the Lord of the Xiang, to King Huai of Chu, articulating his hope that the King of Chu will cast off his petty advisors and make use of great men such as himself.

This painting depicts the Lady of the Xiang's beautiful attire, and also her melancholic nature. The painting technique clearly shows the influence of the 'transformative' figural style of the late Ming, pioneered by leading lights such as Chen Hongshou (see Cat. 4) but, here, the outlines and the colouring also have a decorative quality.

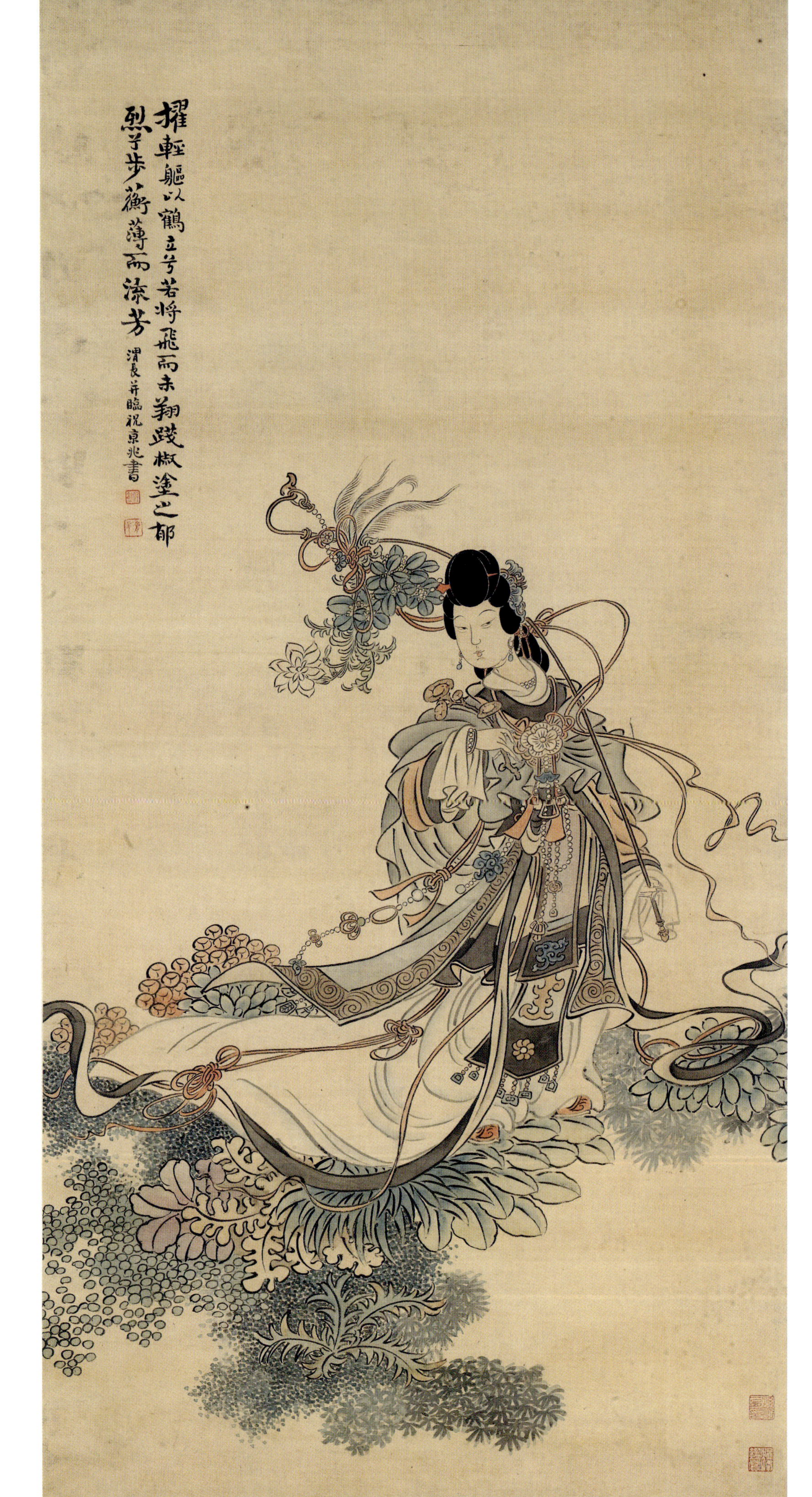
擢輕軀以鶴立兮若將飛而未翔踐椒塗之郁
烈步蘅薄而流芳
渭長并臨祝京兆書

23

清 任熊《洛神像軸》

Ren Xiong (1823–57)
The Goddess of the Luo River
Hanging scroll; ink and colours on silk
110.1 × 53 cm

In Chinese mythology, the goddess of the Luo River was the daughter of Fuxi (who, along with Nüwa, created humans). One day, when she was playing by a riverbank, she accidentally fell in and drowned – which led to her becoming known as the 'goddess of the Luo River'. In the Three Kingdoms period (220–80) she was the female character in ancient China's most romantic love story, described in a ballad by Cao Zhi entitled the 'Goddess of the Luo River Ode' (*Luoshen fu*).

The poet Cao Zhi was the son of a powerful northern warlord Cao Cao. Cao Zhi was in love with Zhen Mi (see Cat. 11), but for various reasons she was forced to marry Cao Zhi's elder brother Cao Pi. Cao Pi later became the Prince of Wei, and in 220, he proclaimed himself emperor Wendi (r. 220–26). Zhen Mi was installed as his empress but soon tired of the complicated palace intrigues. Beautiful but aloof, she was later implicated by a rival and Cao Pi ruthlessly forced her to commit suicide.

When Consort Zhen died, Cao Zhi went to Luoyang to see Cao Pi. He happened to obtain his former lover's pillow; seeing it brought back old memories and he was devastated by her loss. Returning home, he passed by the Luo River, where he had a dream in which Zhen Mi appeared to him. They each spoke of their sorrow at being separated. Upon waking, Cao Zhi was fuelled by his emotions to compose a rhapsody – using the figure of the goddess of the Luo River to commemorate his former love. The poem became the most classic love story in the history of Chinese literature.

This painting shows the alluring and sensual goddess of the Luo River amidst wild grasses and flowers, a sorrowful, wistful look in her eyes.

Ren Xiong was from Xiaoshan, Zhejiang Province. He worked in all painting genres, from landscape and figure to bird-and-flower painting. Technically, his brushwork is bold, being greatly influenced by Song-dynasty methods. He was especially accomplished in figure painting, in which he used a smooth but vigorous technique to depict exaggerated, 'lofty and ancient' figures. He is an important representative of the Shanghai School.

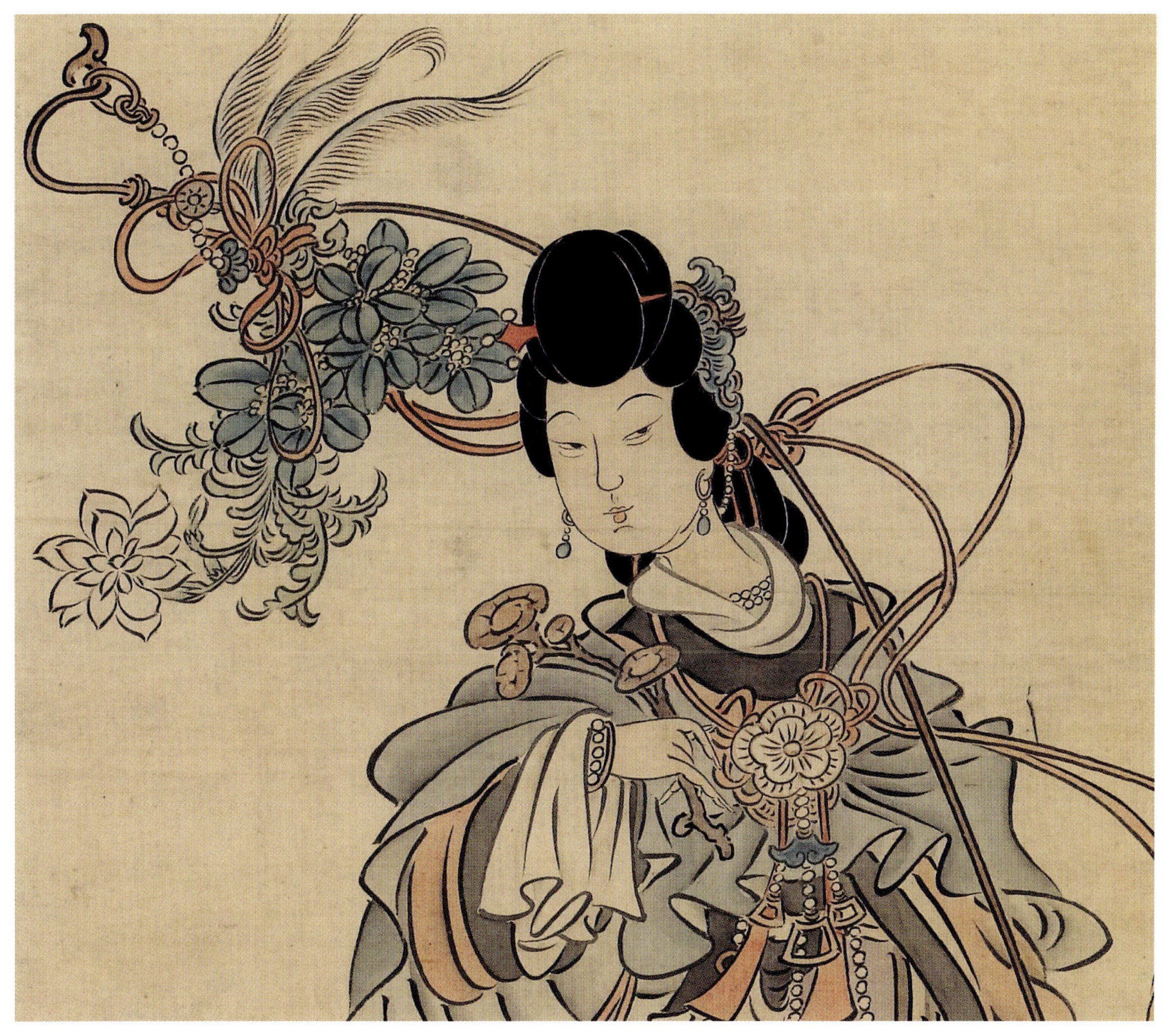

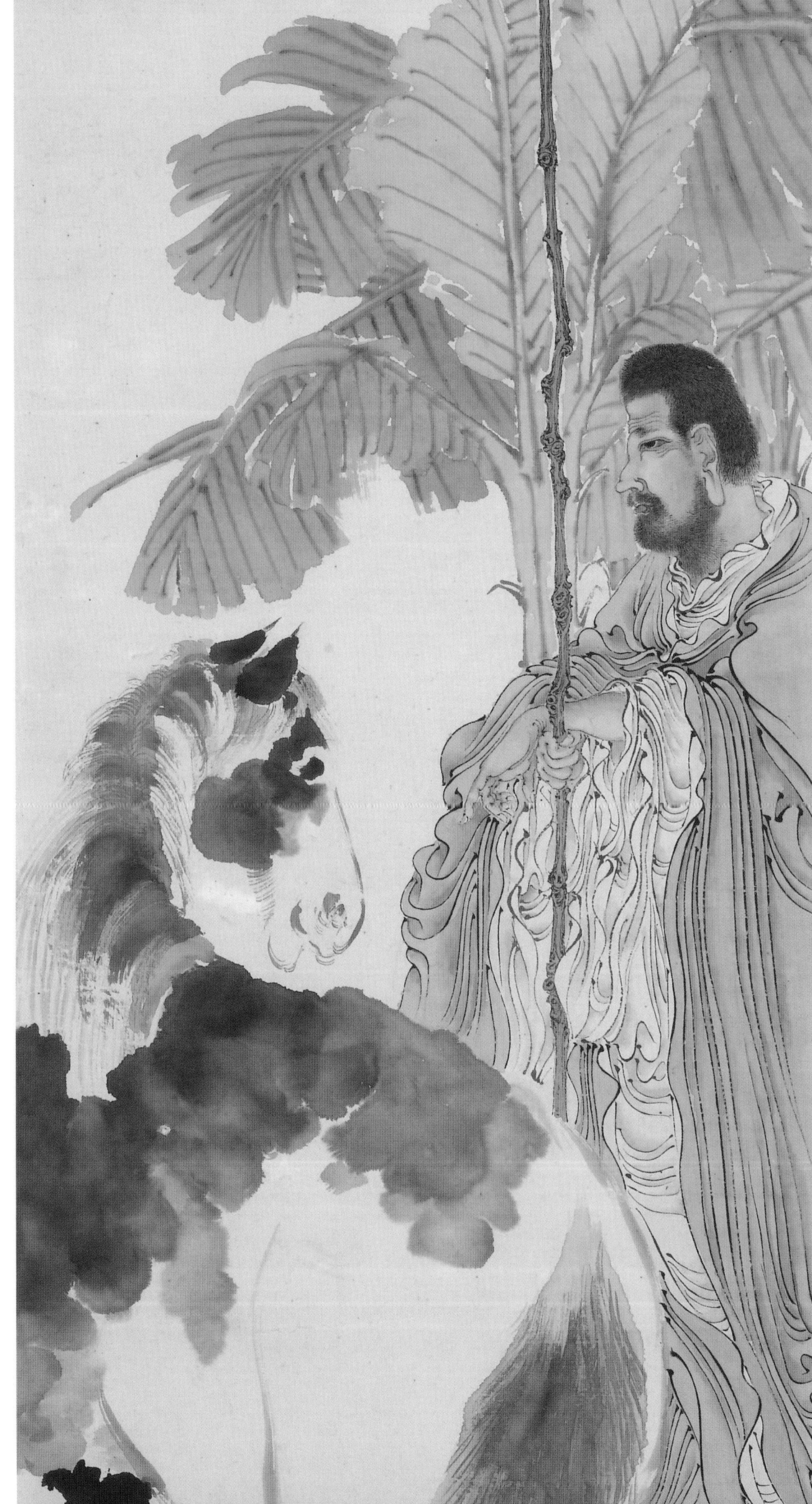

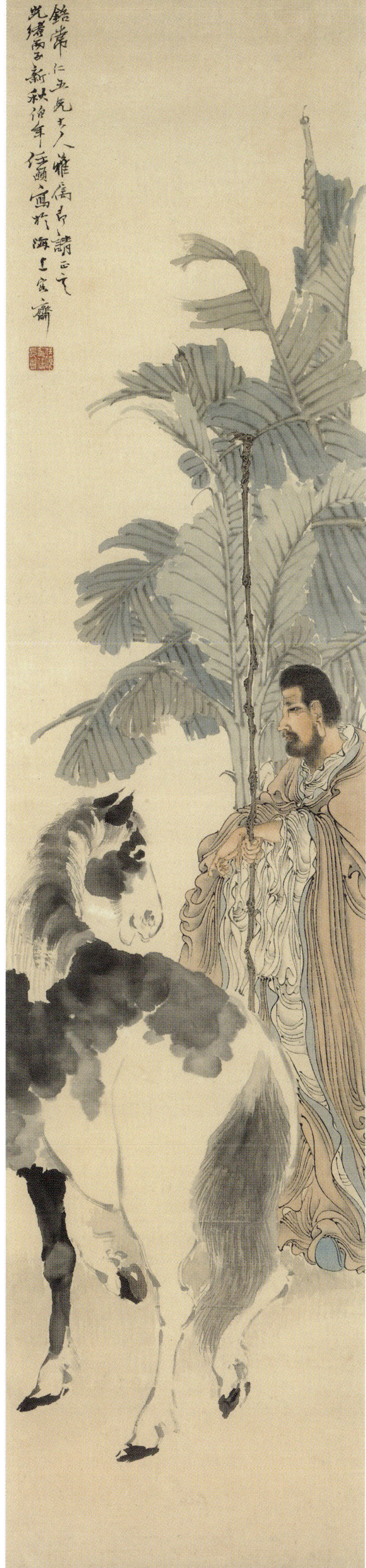

24

清 任頤 《支遁愛馬圖軸》

Ren Yi (Bonian; 1840–96)
The Monk Zhidun Admiring a Horse
Dated 1876
Hanging scroll; ink and colours on paper
135.5 × 30 cm

Zhidun was an eminent monk during the Eastern Jin dynasty, a period celebrated in Chinese history for its art, style and learning. A master of both Buddhism and Daoiṣm, he advocated the view that 'all material existence is empty', and established the study of the Perfection of Wisdom (*Banruoxue*). His thinking is representative of a branch of philosophy popular during the Wei-Jin period (3rd–6th century). During this period, men of culture enjoyed the practice of 'pure talk' (*qingtan*), which involved the use of pithy phrases full of wisdom and religious meaning. Stories about Zhidun's love for horses and cranes also became popular.

In his later years, Zhidun lived as a recluse in a temple, where he raised many fine horses. Once, a friend thought that a horse Zhidun had raised lacked charm, and deliberately let it run free. When Zhidun found out he laughed and said that what he loved about horses was their divine quick-wittedness; and that it did not matter who raised a horse, provided it had as fine a spirit as his beloved animals did. He loved cranes too. In another anecdote, it is said he once cut off the wing feathers of one of his cranes to stop it flying away, but when the feathers grew back he let the crane go. When people questioned him about this, he said, 'Cranes are meant to fly high in the sky; who are we to make them our playthings?' Such stories illustrate Zhidun's open-mindedness, as well as his profound philosophical thinking on the dialectic links between the human mind within, and things without.

This painting is based on these stories. It shows Zhidun standing with his staff, surrounded by banana leaves, while admiring one of his fine horses. Raising a hoof, the horse turns its head, seemingly returning Zhidun's gaze and expressing his gratitude.

Ren Yi was from Shaoxing in Zhejiang Province. A student of Ren Xun, he excelled at figure, bird-and-flower, and landscape painting. One of the leading masters of the Shanghai School, he pioneered a refreshing painting style and he was technically highly original.

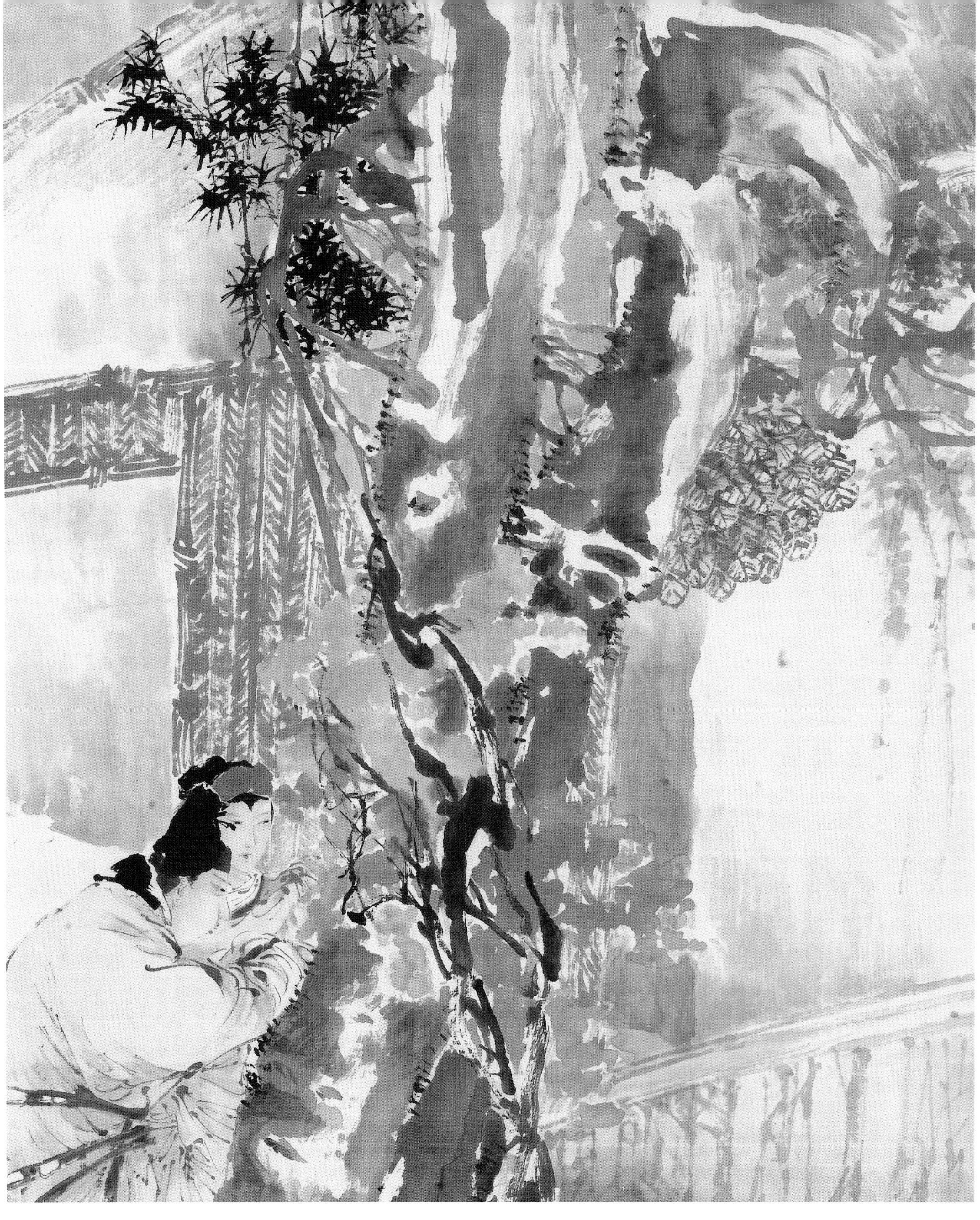

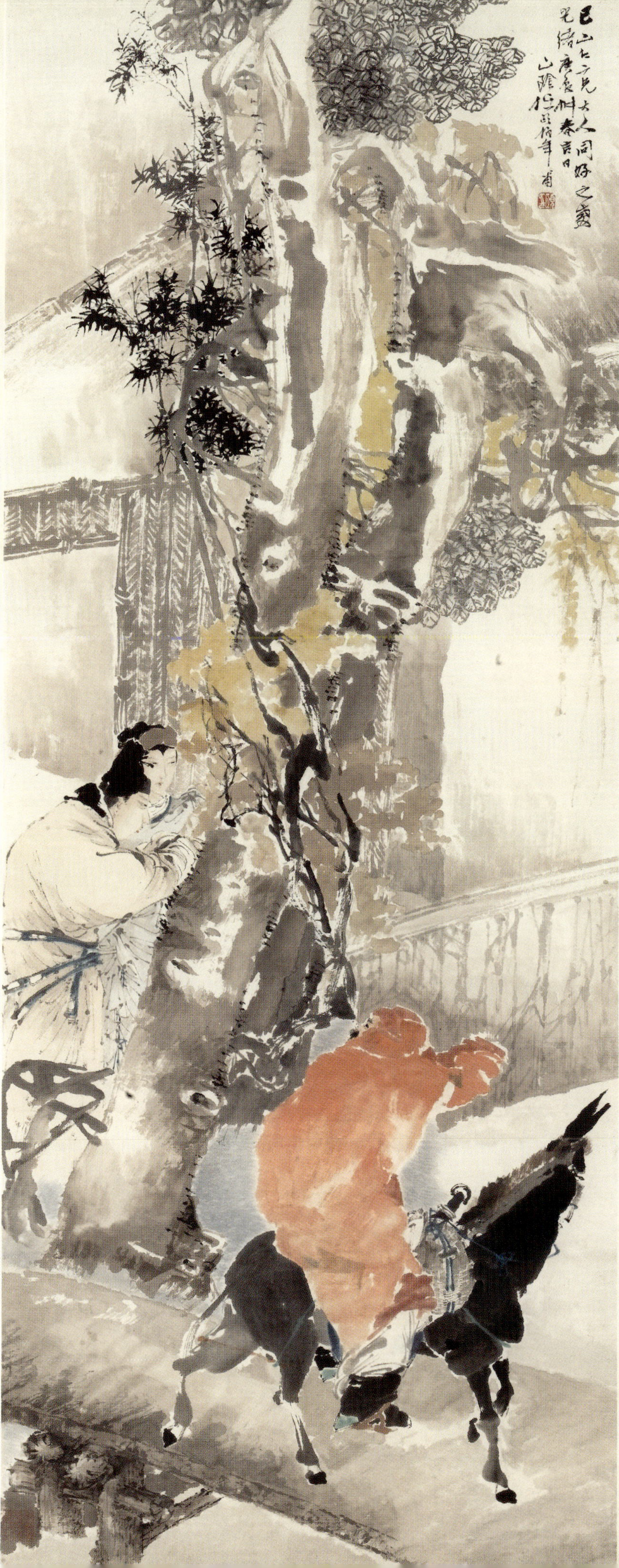

25

清 任頤 《風塵三俠圖軸》

Ren Yi (Bonian; 1840–96)
Three Knights in Wind and Dust
Dated 1880
Hanging scroll; ink and colours on paper
122.7 × 47 cm

'Romance of the Red Dust' (*Fengchen sanxia*) comes from a Tang-dynasty short story, 'Tale of the Curly-bearded Stranger' (*Qiuran ke zhuan*), which features the three knights-errant, Li Jing, Hongfu nü (Red Duster lady) and 'Curly-bearded Stranger'. (*Fengchen sanxia* means literally 'three knights-errant of the dusty wind'.) An accomplished military strategist who had won more battles than all his peers, Li Jing was the single greatest contributor to the founding of the Tang dynasty in 618. Red Duster was a courtesan of the arrogant Yang Su, a powerful official. When Yang Su received Li Jing, he was extremely contemptuous towards him, but Red Duster, who was at Yang Su's side, perceived Li Jing's heroic character and fell in love with him at first sight. She disguised herself and fled with Li Jing to become his wife. The bizarrely named Curly-bearded Stranger was a great knight-errant, a man of tremendous resolve who fought evil wherever he found it.

Li Jing and Red Duster were on their way to see Li Shimin – the later Tang emperor Taizong – when they chanced upon Curly-beard, who was captivated by Red Duster's beauty. She was equally struck by his heroic temperament and they became sworn brother and sister. She introduced him to Li Jing, and the three of them rode off together into the dusty wind. When they got to Chang'an, Li Jing and Red Duster went to find Li Shimin. Meanwhile Curly-beard gave all of his money to them, entreating Li Jing to do his best to help Li Shimin while he rode off with his wife and servant, saying that he was a king from a distant land. Li Jing helped Li Yuan (later Tang emperor Gaozu, r. 618–26) and his son Shimin to pacify the Jiangnan region in the south, thereby founding the Tang dynasty. Li Jing was ennobled as Duke-of-state of Wei, and Red Duster was made a lady of the first rank.

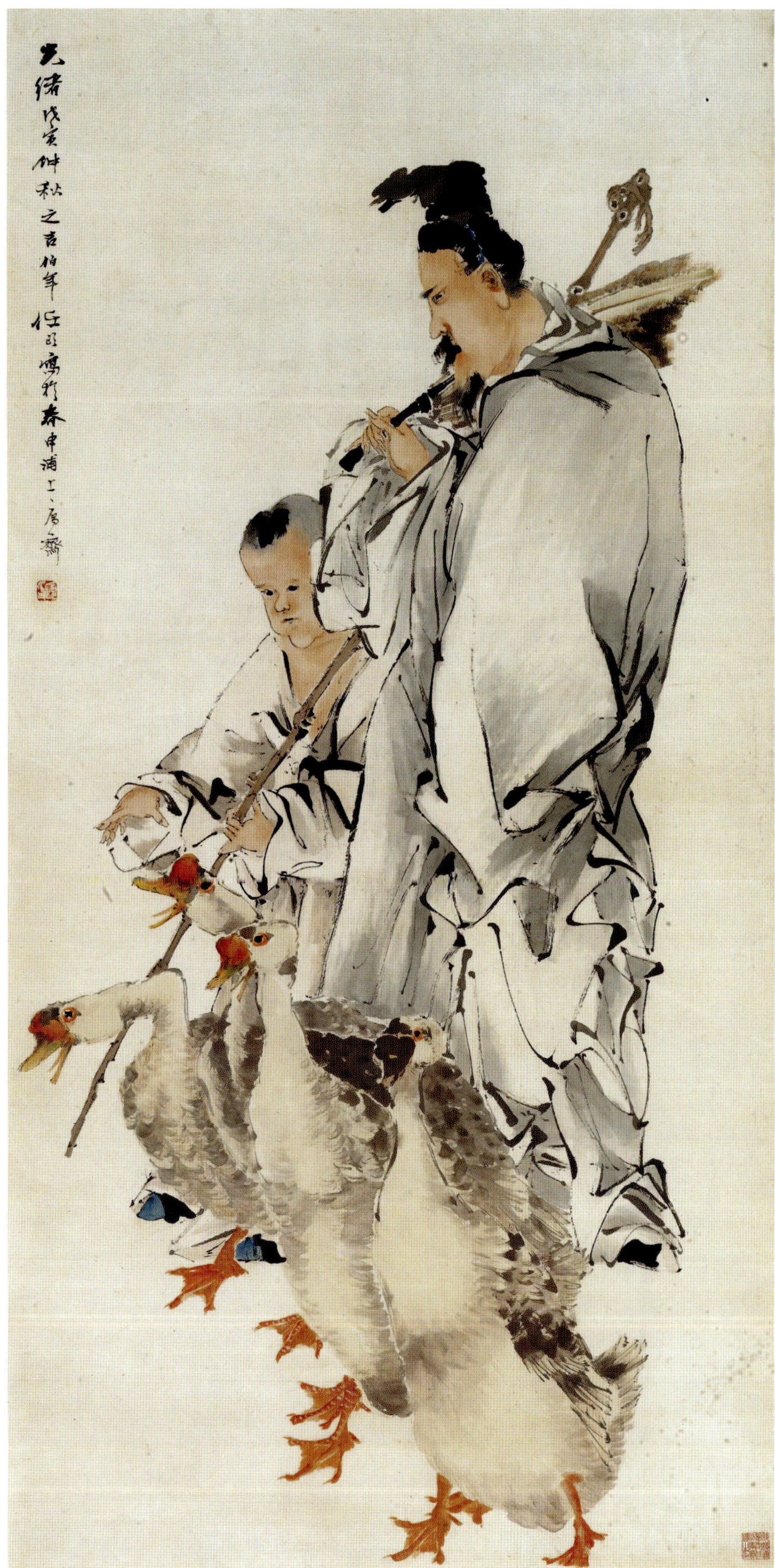

26

清 任頤 《羲之愛鵝圖軸》

Ren Yi (Bonian; 1840–96)
Wang Xizhi Admiring Geese
Dated 1878
Hanging scroll; ink and colours on paper
133.4 × 65.9 cm

The inspiration for Chinese calligraphy often comes from the natural world. Wang Xizhi, known as the 'sage of calligraphy', transformed the art form by introducing many life-like and natural elements – things he learned from his close observation of, for example, the agile movement of the necks of geese. It is well known that Wang Xizhi admired geese – not only for their gracefulness but just as much as a delicacy to eat.

Legend has it that there was once a Daoist from Shaoxing in Zhejiang who wanted to obtain one of Wang Xizhi's treasured works of calligraphy. He knew that Wang Xizhi loved geese to the point of obsession, so he prepared some plump, tall, white geese to offer in exchange. When Wang Xizhi saw the geese he spent half a day writing out a classical text for the Daoist and happily accepted the geese in exchange. The text he transcribed was *The Way and its Power* (*Dao de jing*), which also came to be called *Manuscript Exchanged for Geese (Huan'e tie)*. The story known as 'Wang Xizhi admiring geese' has been passed down the generations ever since.

The painting shows a boy holding a bamboo pole, trying to lead the geese home before nightfall. His expression is both innocent and charming, in contrast to the figure of Wang Xizhi, who focuses intently on the white goose, imitating it in his calligraphy.

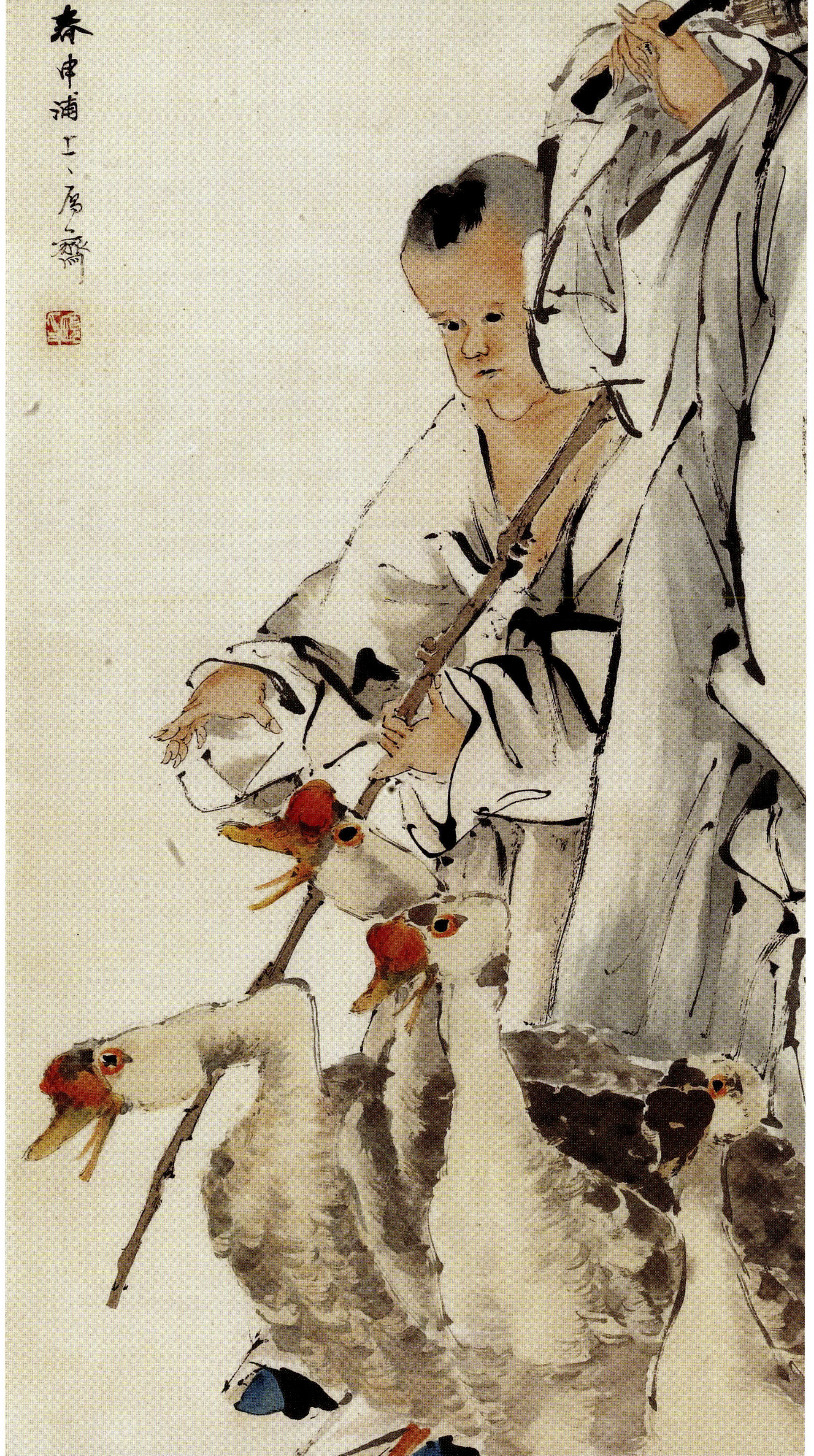

27

清 沈韶 《三仙圖軸》

Shen Shao (active 1662–1722)
Three Immortals
Dated 1677
Hanging scroll; ink and colours on paper
99.5 × 57.5 cm

The two laughing figures holding brooms, with gourds tied around their waists, are the Two Immortals of Harmony (*Hehe erxian*) – Chinese gods of love.

The Two Immortals of Harmony are the famous Tang-dynasty poet Hanshan (literally, 'Cold Mountain') and the monk Shide (literally, 'Foundling'), who, it is said, were brothers. One day, the elder brother went on a long journey whilst on military duty, causing his mother to cry with worry for him. The younger brother went to look for him, and the whole ten-thousand-*li* journey took him only one day, so people called him 'myriad return' (*wan hui*), to signify family reunion. The two brothers later became monks, with names meaning Cold Mountain and Foundling. Because of their unwavering friendship and cheerful outlook in the face of adversity, they became known as the Two Immortals of Harmony, standing for peace, harmony and success. The qualities of love, gentleness, peace and harmony are central to traditional Chinese culture, and in folk legend, the pair eventually became gods of love, symbolising harmonious marriage. Often, their likenesses are displayed at weddings to wish the newlyweds a long and happy marriage.

The figure holding the fishing rod in this painting is Liu Haichan, the god of wealth. There was such an historical figure who lived during the Five Dynasties period (907–60), and who later became an immortal. Tradition has it that Liu Haichan liked to play with a golden toad, an animal regarded in folk legend to be a spirit that spat gold coins (see Cat. 36). Liu Haichan would fish for the toad with a string of gold and then give away to humans the gold that the toad spat out. It is said he is a joyful, fat little man with dishevelled hair, who puffs out his chest and goes barefoot. People pray for wealth and prosperity by playing with a string of gold coins held in their hands.

The painter Shen Shao was from Jiaxing, Zhejiang Province, and lived during the Kangxi reign (1662–1722) of the Qing dynasty. He was a student of the portrait master Zeng Jing (1568–1650) and was an adept portraitist.

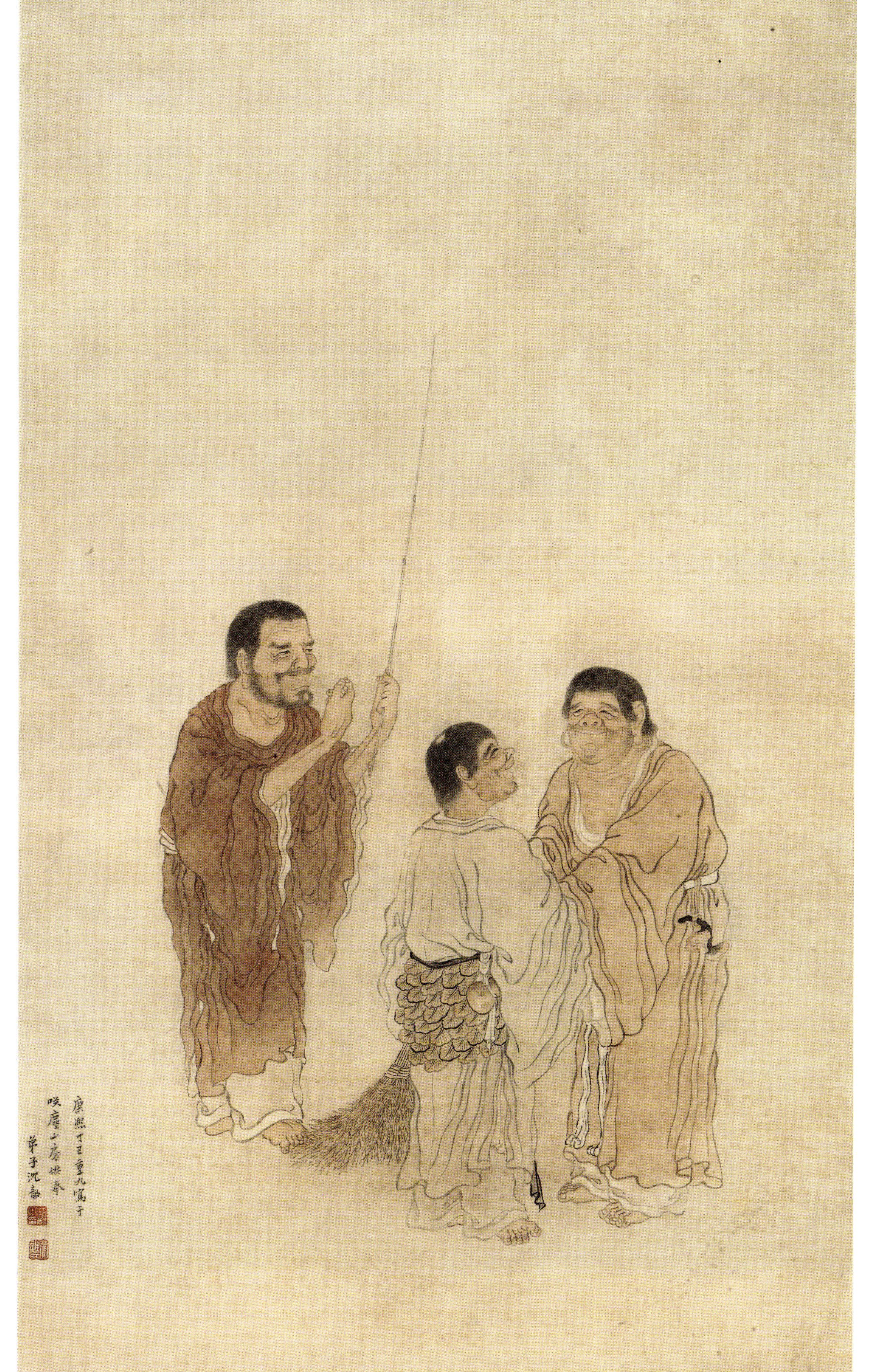
康熙丁巳重九寫于
咲塵山房供奉
弟子沈韶

28

清 石濤《西園雅集圖卷》

Shitao (1642–1707)
Elegant Gathering in the West Garden
Handscroll; ink and colours on paper
36.4 × 328 cm

During the Northern Song dynasty, Wang Shen (1048–1104), a son-in-law of emperor Yingzong (r. 1063–67), and also an eminent painter, held a party in his garden. This 'elegant gathering' (*yaji*) was seen as a classic example of the charmed lives of the elite. The event became well known not only for its distinguished hosts and guests but also because it resulted in a remarkable painting, Li Gonglin's *Elegant Gathering in the West Garden*.

Among the sixteen guests were the top painters, calligraphers and writers of the late Northern Song dynasty, including Su Shi, Mi Fu, Li Gonglin and Qin Guan. Here, in Shitao's painting, they are shown drinking, composing poetry and playing the

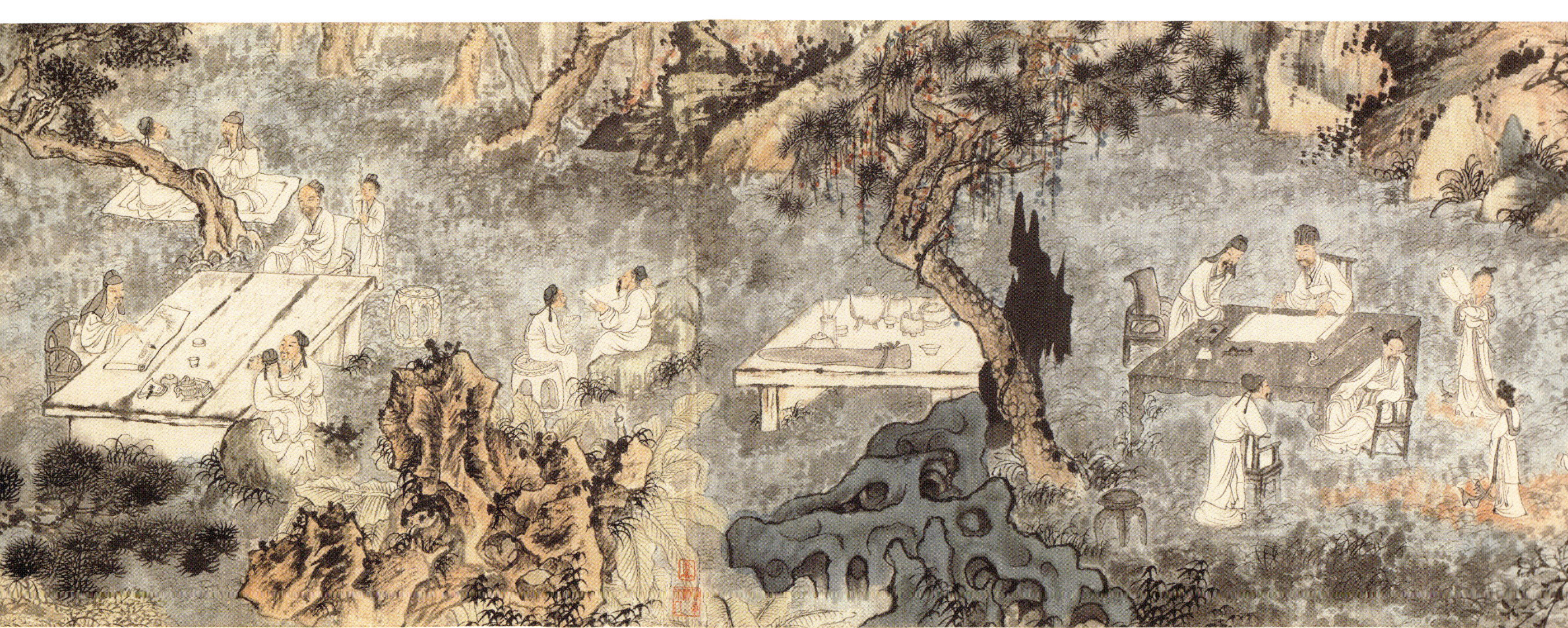

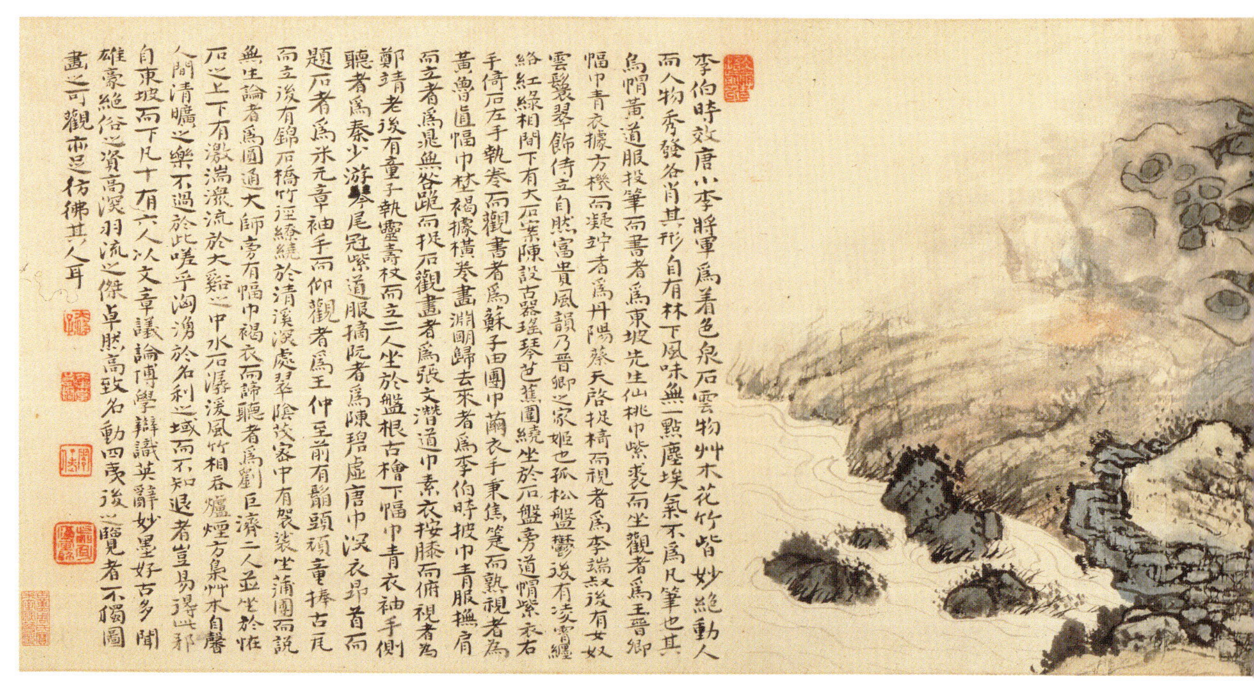

zither. Li Gonglin's recorded painting of this scene inspired many artistic recreations and represented quintessential literati life.

This painting uses a combination of realism and freehand drawing, with agile brushwork and lively forms. Shitao was one of the Four Great Monk Painters of the Qing dynasty (1644–1911), and excelled at landscape, figure and flower paintings. He was in tune with the changing cycles of nature, in which he found artistic inspiration.

FOLLOWING PAGES: The great literatus Su Shi (writing) with his host Wang Shen (seated) and friends

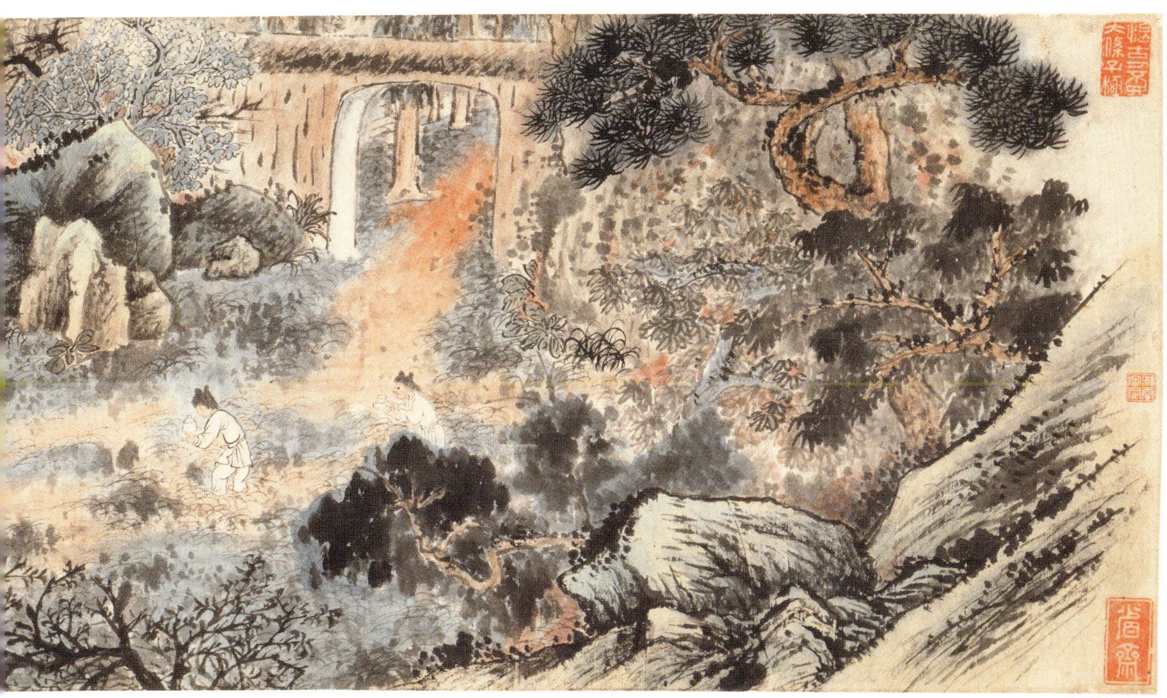

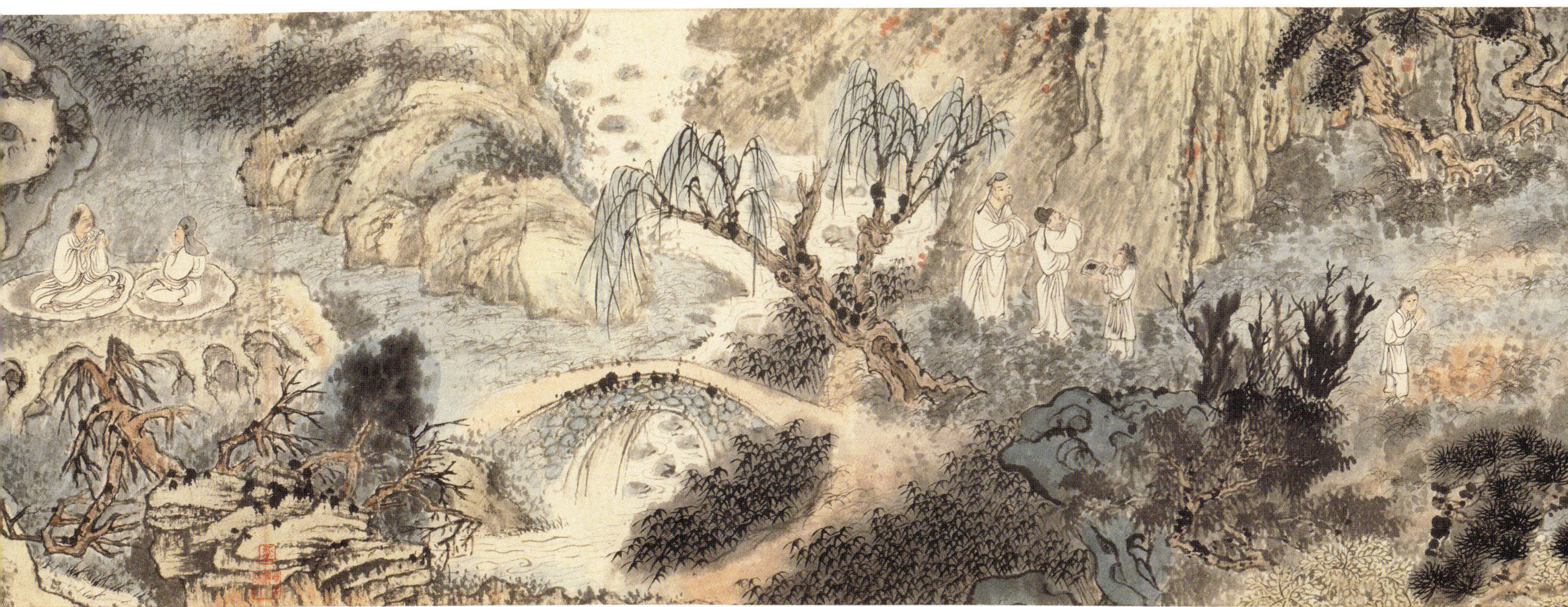

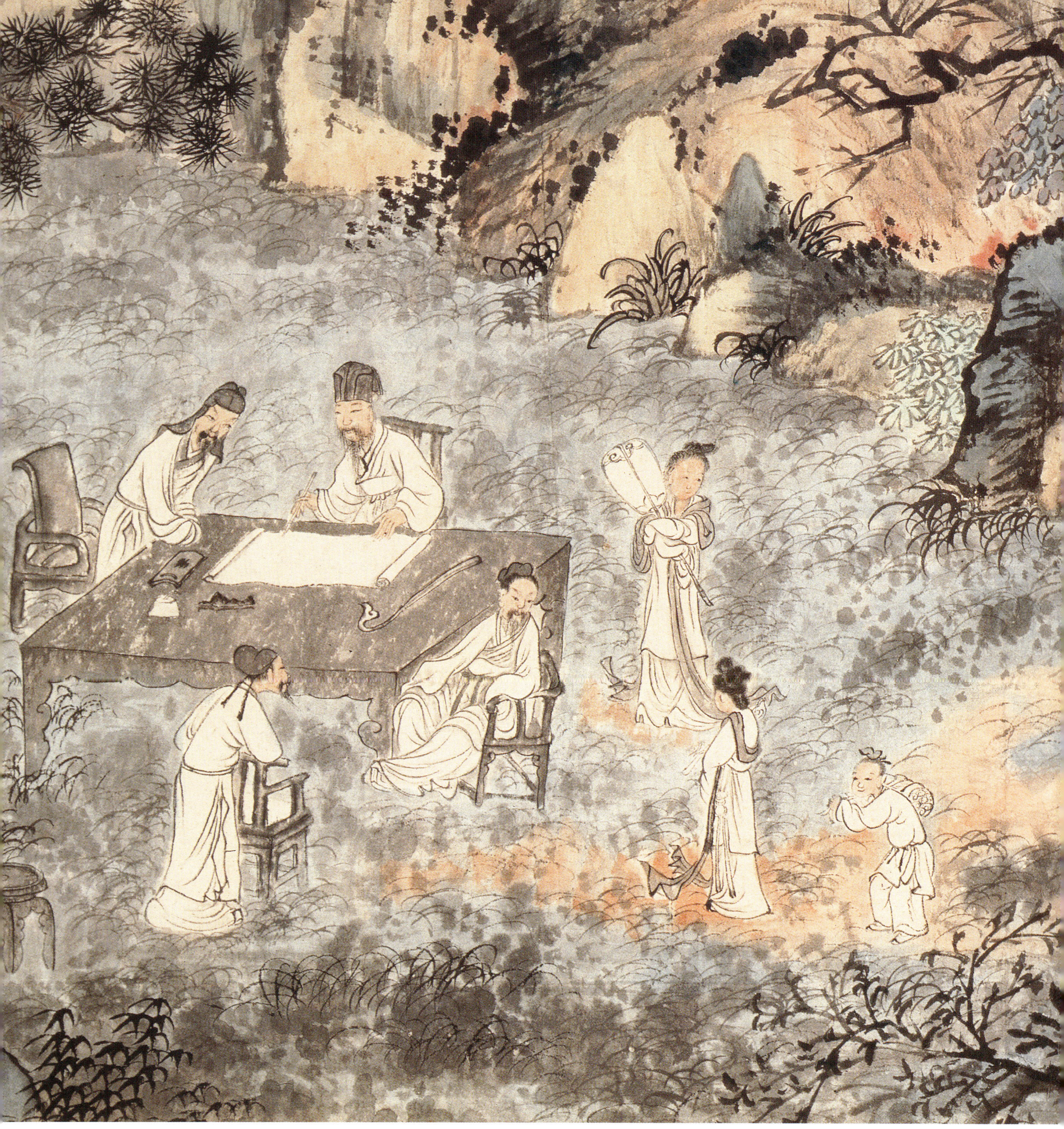

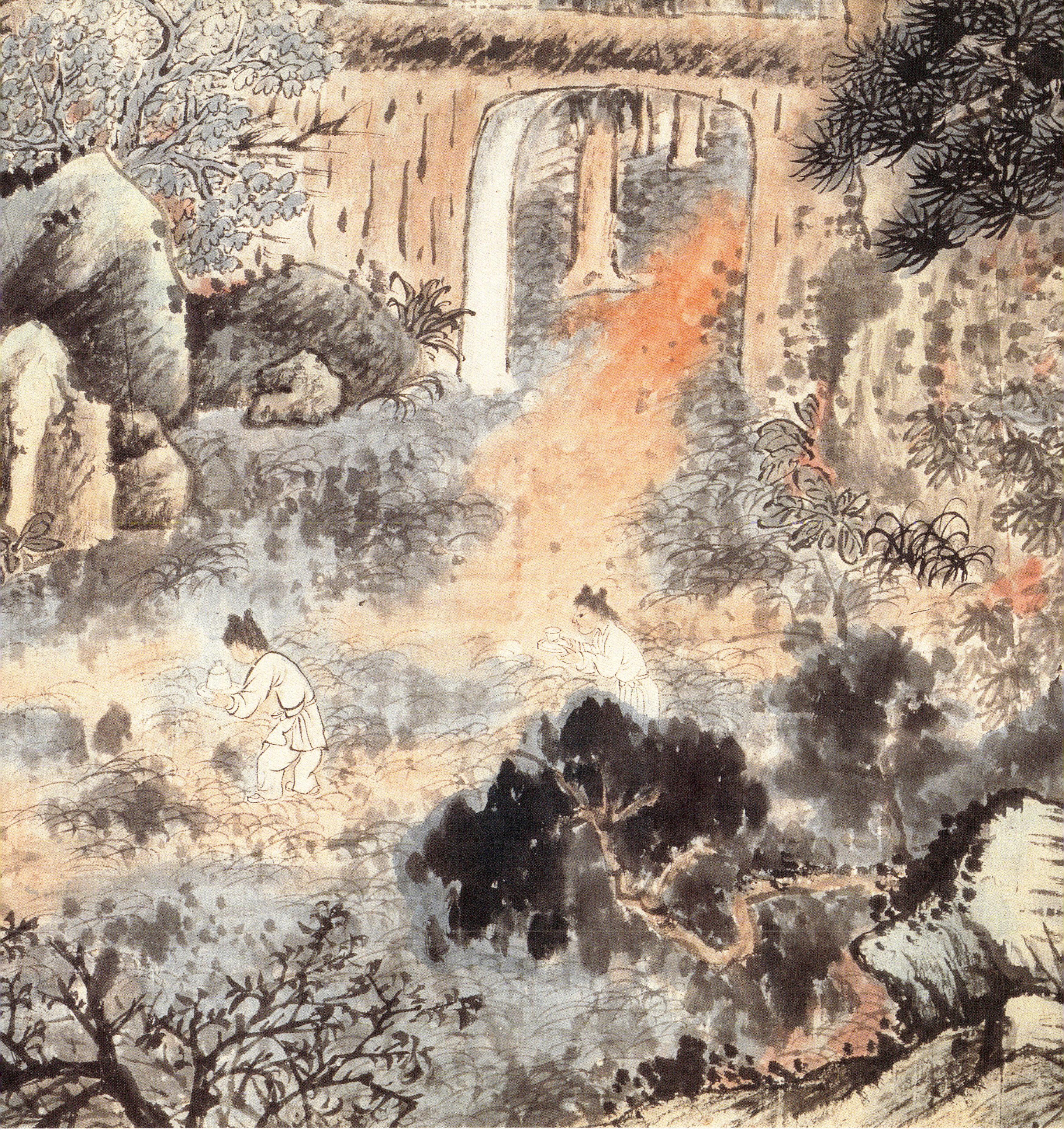

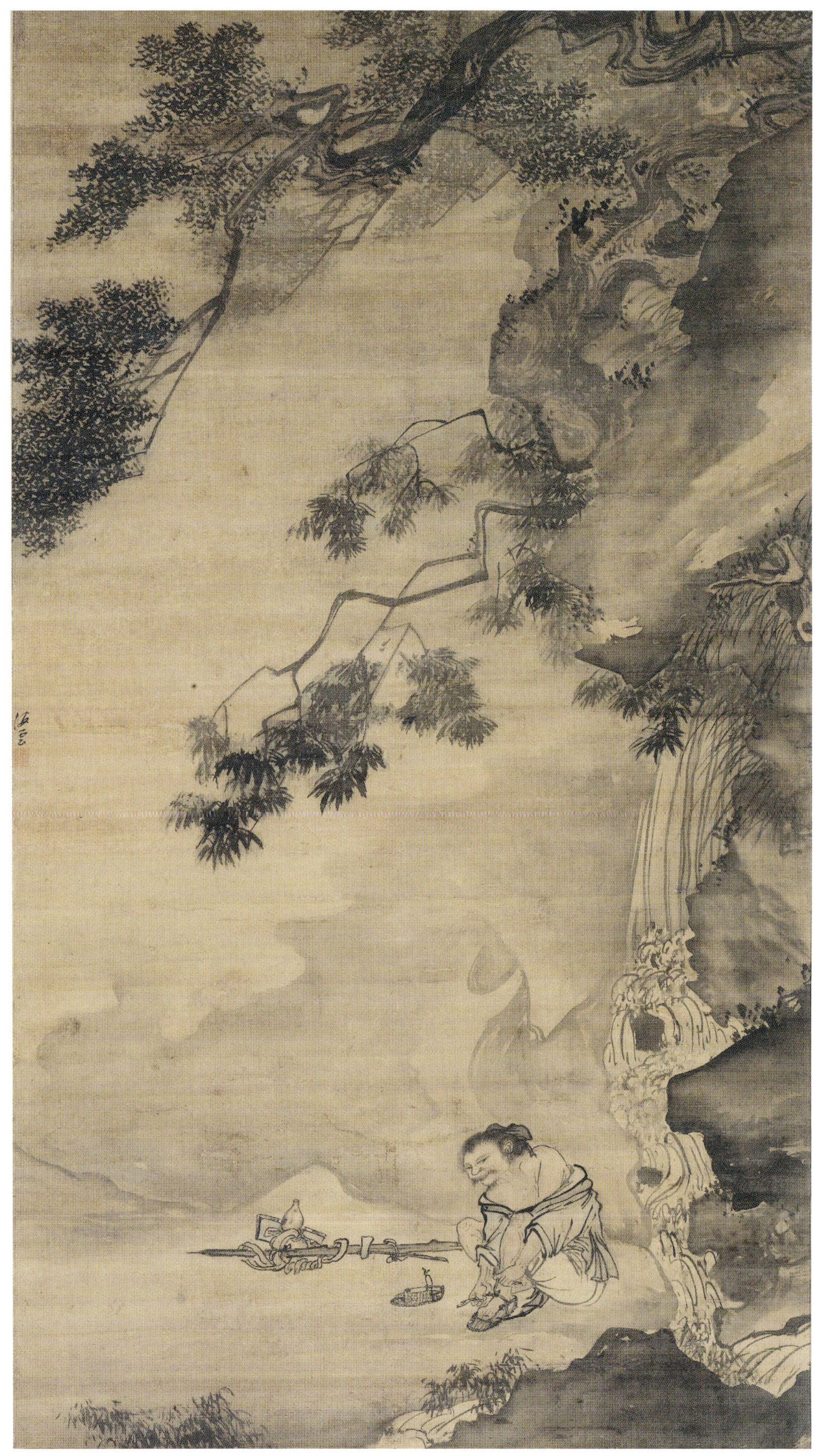

29

明 汪肇 《拐仙圖軸》

Wang Zhao (active 1506–21)
Iron-crutch Li
Hanging scroll; ink and colours on silk
133.9 × 74.1 cm

Iron-crutch Li (Li Tieguai) was one of the Eight Immortals. Originally a handsome young man who practised self-cultivation as a recluse on Mount Dang, he was transformed into an immortal by the ancient Daoist sage and patriarch, Laozi. One day, he was invited by Laozi to travel in spirit to Mount Hua. Before leaving, Li left an instruction with a young Daoist priest who helped him by doing odd jobs: 'If my spirit does not return in seven days, cremate my body.' On the sixth day, Li's soul had not returned, but the priest decided nevertheless to burn his body. That night, Li's spirit returned but could not find his body. His wandering soul happened upon the corpse of a starved man, and in his haste he jumped into the body, returning it to life. He didn't realise that the blackened, shrivelled corpse belonged to a lame man who could only walk with the aid of an iron crutch. Thereafter, he became known as Iron-crutch Li. He had an unkempt appearance and was lame, and he carried a gourd with him that contained medicine, which he would use to cure people he met on his way. His story gave hope to people facing the inevitability of death through sickness or old age.

Wang Zhao was active during the Zhengde reign-period (1506–21) of the Ming dynasty, and was from Xiuning, Anhui Province. He excelled at bird-and-flower, landscape, and figure painting. He was a painter of the later Zhe School.

30

清 王震《達摩面壁圖軸》

Wang Zhen (1867–1938)
Bodhidharma Meditating Before a Wall
Dated 1923
Hanging scroll; ink and colours on paper
145 × 41.5 cm
Donated by the Ching Banlee family

Buddhism flourished in China following its arrival from India during the Eastern Han, and Liang emperor Wu (502–49) of the Southern Dynasties was a devout follower. Bodhidharma was the third son of King Sugandha of India. He became a monk after his father died, and later became known as the 28th Patriarch of Indian Zen, who was sent by Prajnatara to China to teach the Dharma. Bodhidharma came eastward over the seas and travelled from Guangzhou to the Liang-dynasty capital in Nanjing. Liang emperor Wu received the eminent monk, and in their discussions Bodhidharma advocated the teachings of not reciting sutras, not building temples, and not recording Buddhist sutras and texts. He also advocated 'nirvana in nothingness' (*kong wu ji mie*), which would directly show men's hearts, but emperor Liang Wudi did not care for these teachings, so Bodhidharma travelled north to continue his work.

It is said that he came to the Shaolin Temple in Henan, where he gathered all the monks and taught them Chan (Japanese: Zen). He once sat facing a wall day and night in complete silence. Birds built their nests on his shoulders and he continued to sit. He remained in silent thought like this for nine years, and was named 'Bodhidharma meditating before a wall' (*Damo mian bi*). His teachings were later incorporated into Chinese culture, giving rise to China's own type of Buddhism – Chan. Chan deeply influenced Chinese thinking, and Bodhidharma became its patriarch. The term 'Bodhidharma meditating before a wall' came to be used to describe diligent study and high achievement.

This painting places Bodhidharma by a lonely cliff, his spirit focused. The brushstrokes are succinct and emphatic. Wang Zhen excelled at figure and flower paintings. He was a student of the late Qing-dynasty scholar-painter Wu Changshuo (1844–1927) and was a representative of the Shanghai School.

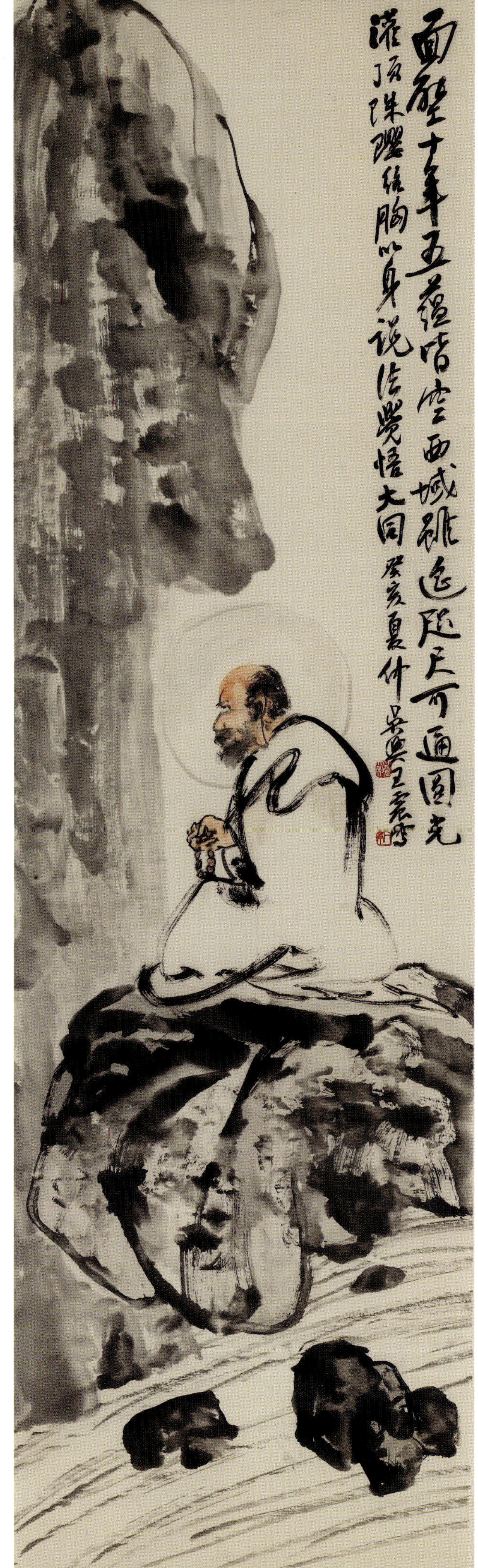

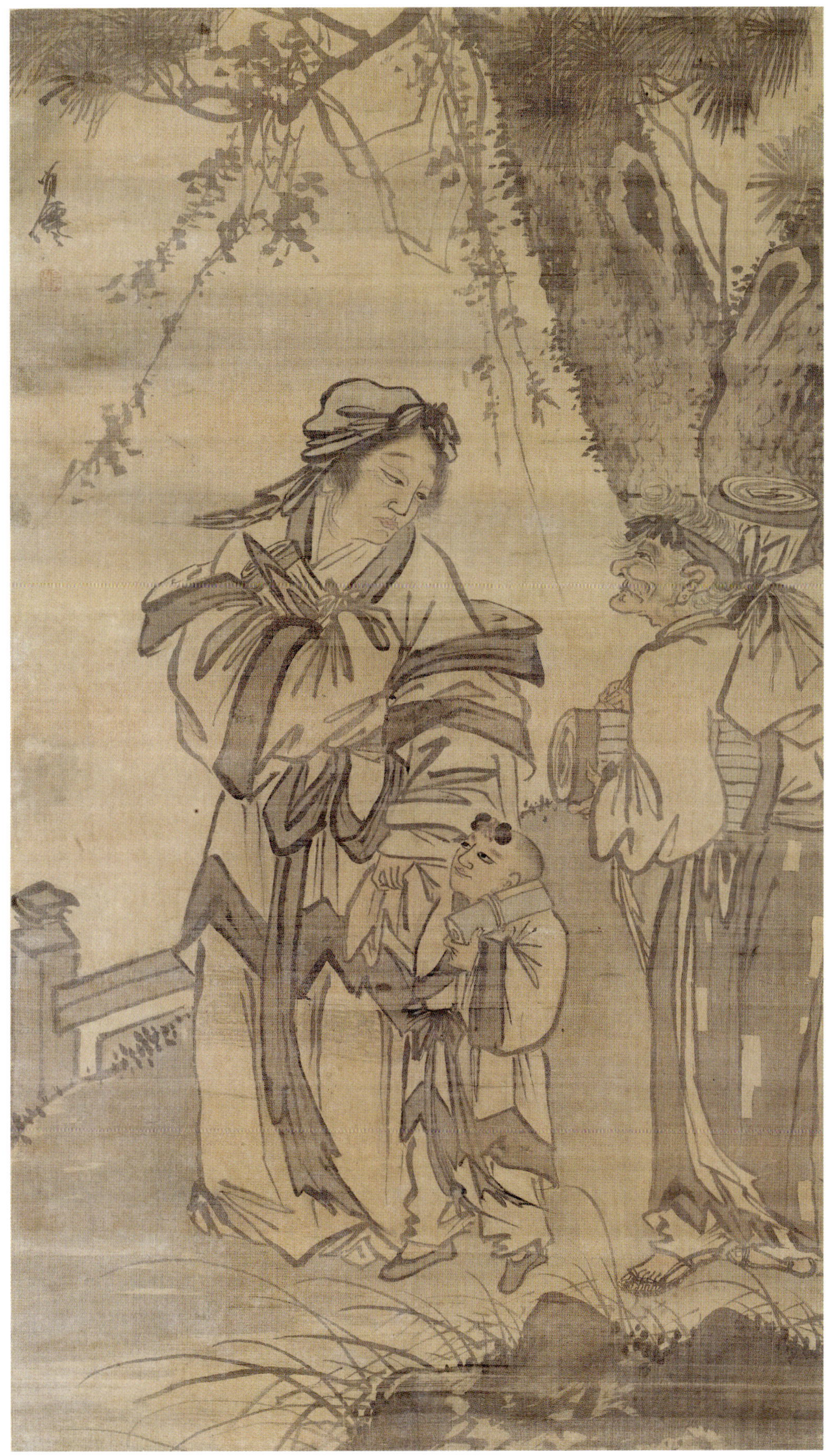

31

明 吴世恩 《教子圖軸》

Wu Shien (mid-Ming, 15th–16th c.)
Educating a Son
Hanging scroll; ink and colours on silk
154 × 85.7 cm

In ancient Chinese society, great importance was attached to the education of children, both among the nobility and the population in general (of course, this was mainly the education of boys). This gave rise to 'the culture of children's education'.

'Mencius's mother educates her son' is the most well-known story relating to this. Mengzi, known in the west by his Latinised name, Mencius, was a Confucian philosopher during the Warring States period (475–221 BC). His father died when he was young, and thereafter, his mother, who wove cloth for a living, took her son's education extremely seriously. Once, Mencius became distracted while reciting poetry and stopped in mid flow. His mother was furious, and to teach him a lesson she tore up the cloth that she was in the middle of weaving. Another time, seeing him fighting with a boy from a neighbouring family, she decided that they should move house, as their environment was not conducive to her son's education. At their new home, on finding that the blacksmith who lived next door created so much noise pounding his metal, they moved again, this time to a remote area. They moved three times in all, and the story came to be known as 'Mencius's mother's three moves'.

This painting shows Mencius, his mother, and their servant, each carrying tools for learning. They resolutely push forward on the difficult road to their new home. Wu Shien was Wu Wei's (1459–1508) son. One of the representatives of the Zhejiang School, his paintings have a bold and unrestrained style.

32

明 尤求 《昭君出塞圖卷》

You Qiu (active 1553–83)
Lady Zhaojun Leaves China
Dated 1554
Handscroll; ink on paper
25.8 × 376.9 cm

Wang Zhaojun is a household name from Chinese history, renowned not only for her incomparable beauty but also revered for the patriotic spirit she showed when she travelled across the desert to honour her duty to marry a Xiongnu chieftain. By 33 BC, the brutal war between Han China and the Xiongnu to the north had finally died down, and the Han court adopted a policy of political marriages (*heqin*). To solidify friendly relations between the two peoples, palace ladies acting as princesses were sent out to marry Xiongnu chiefs. The palace ladies were reluctant to go, but Wang Zhaojun summoned her courage and agreed to make the long journey to marry the Xiongnu chieftain, Hu Hanxia.

She got along well with the Xiongnu and discouraged their chief from waging war, at the same time introducing them to Chinese culture. During her sixty years in Xiongnu lands there was peace between the two peoples, and her story came to symbolise unity between different ethnic groups.

This handscroll painting illustrates Zhaojun's arduous journey and her grand welcome by the

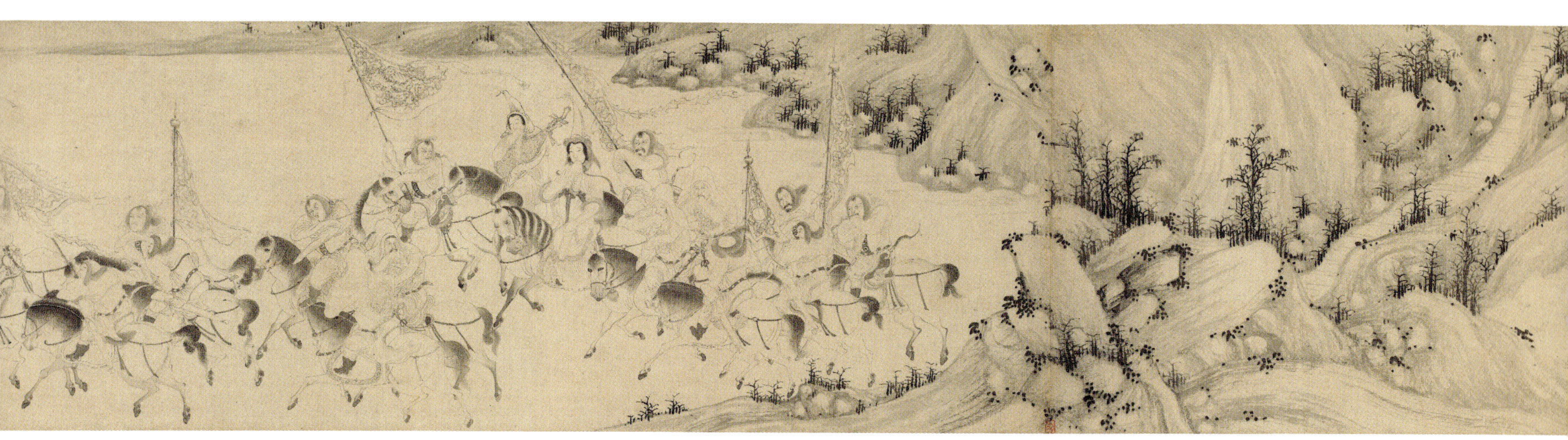

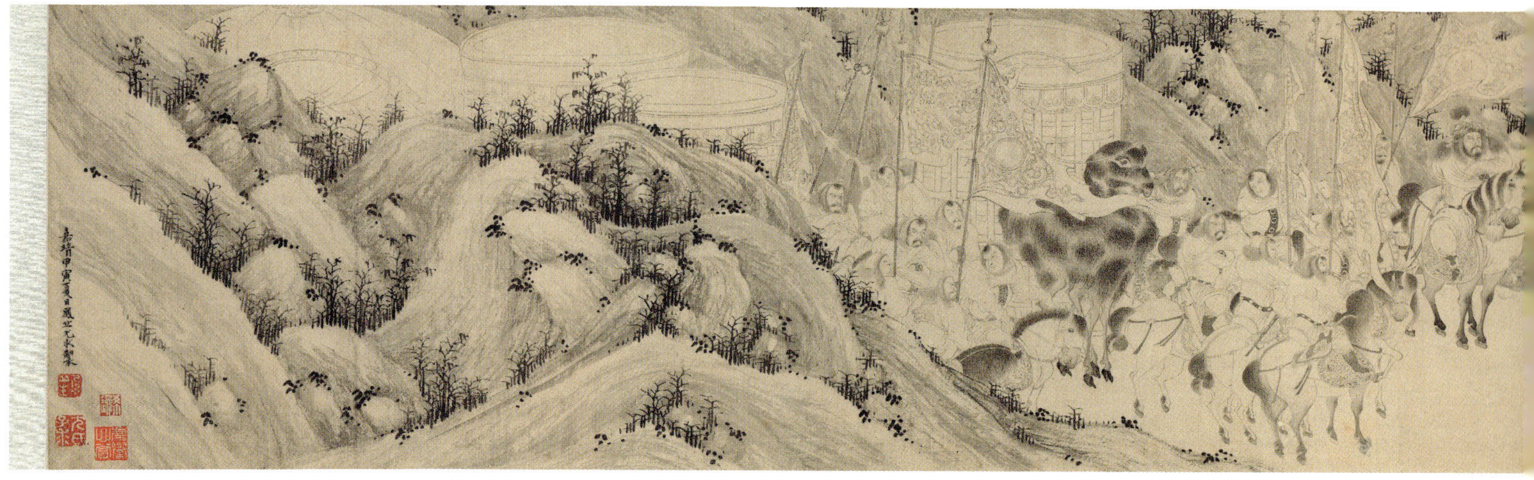

Xiongnu. The painting is incisive and skilfully executed, with life-like figures and vivid gestures.

The artist You Qiu was active from 1553 to 1583 in Wu County, Jiangsu Province – in the Suzhou region. He was a skilled painter of female figures, at his best painting in the ink-outline (*baimiao*) technique seen here, for which he made his name. He can be said to have followed in the footsteps of the earlier Suzhou master, his father-in-law Qiu Ying (*c.*1494–1552).

FOLLOWING PAGES: Lady Zhaojun and her nomad escort arriving on the steppe

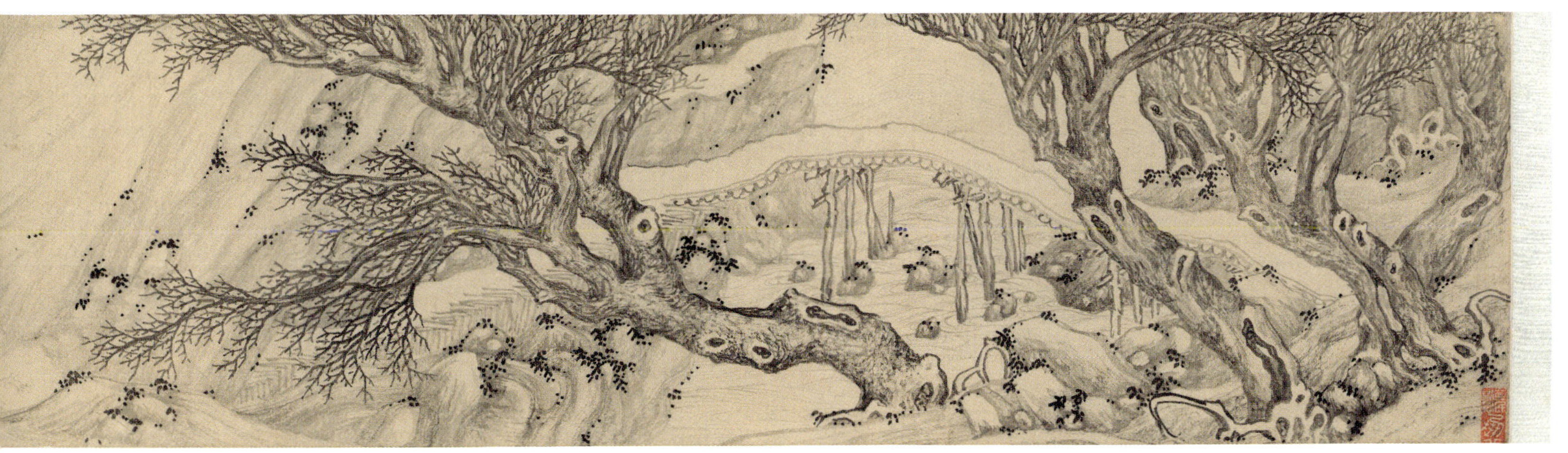

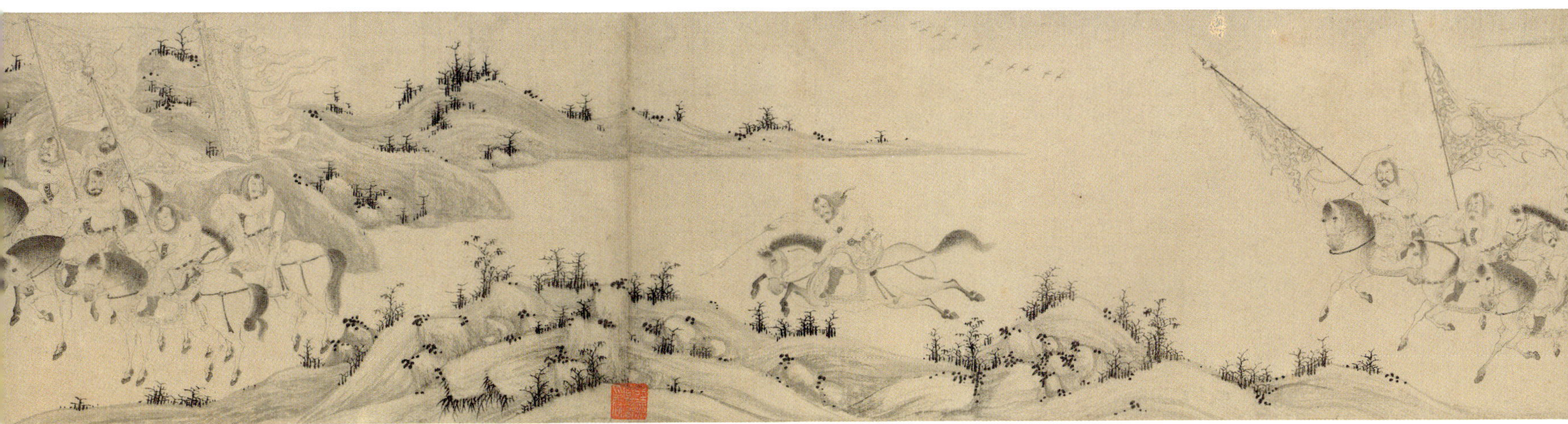

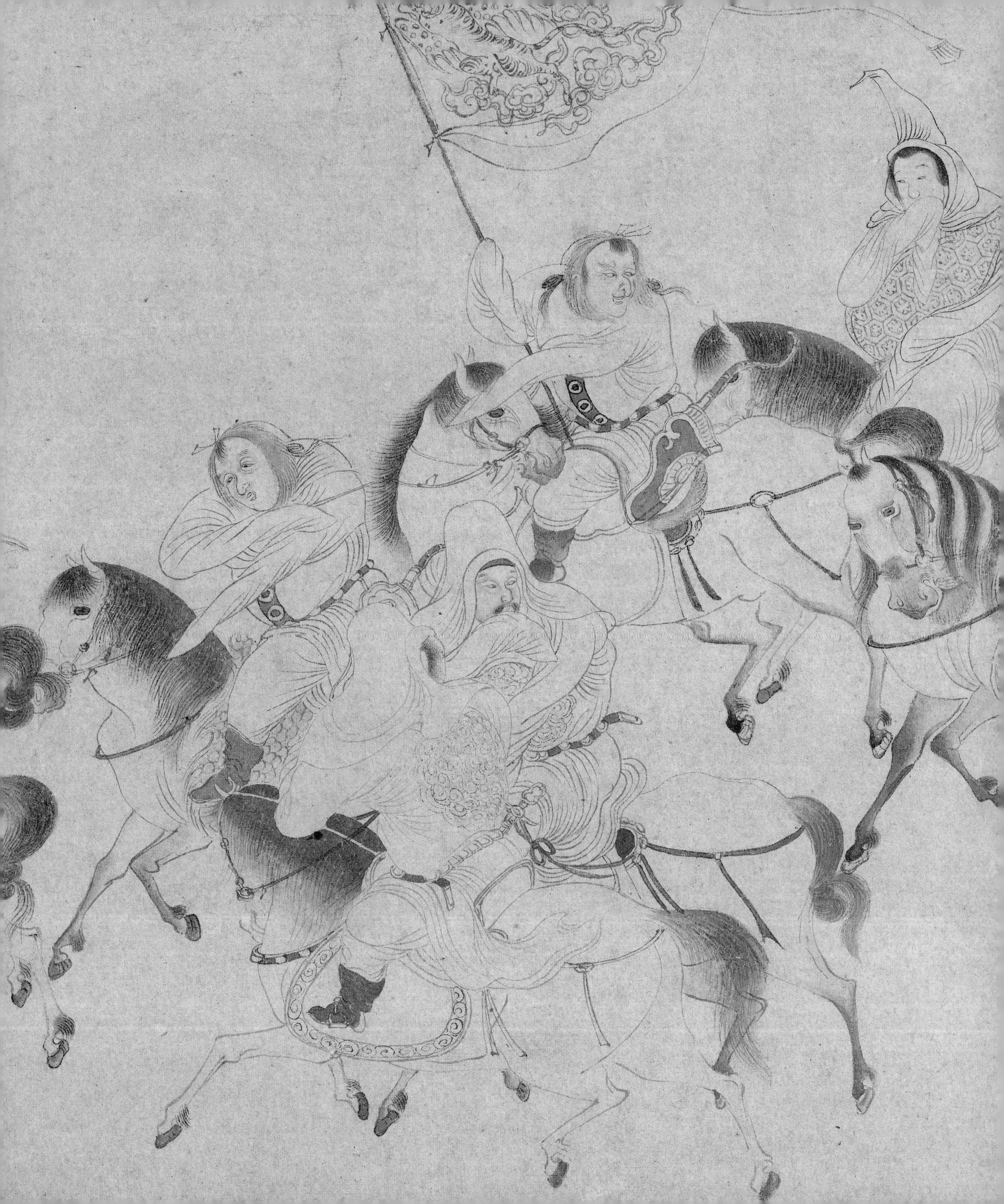

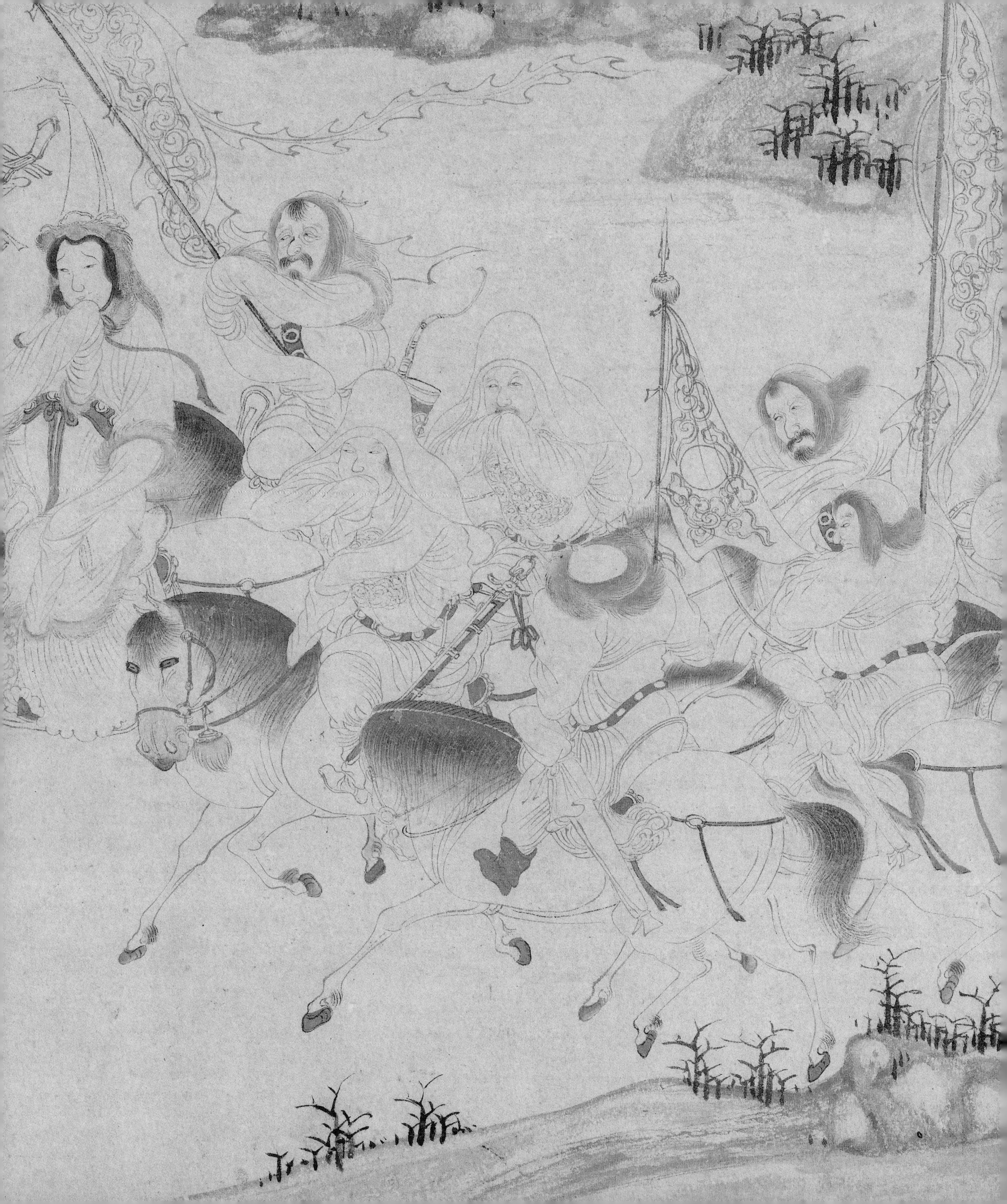

33

明 尤求《漢宮春曉圖卷》

You Qiu (active 1553–83)
Spring Morning in the Han Palace
Dated 1568
Handscroll; ink on paper
24.5 × 801.3 cm

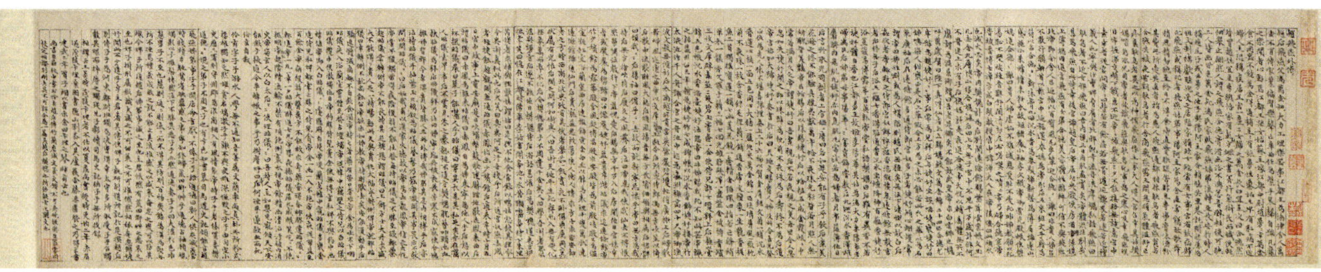

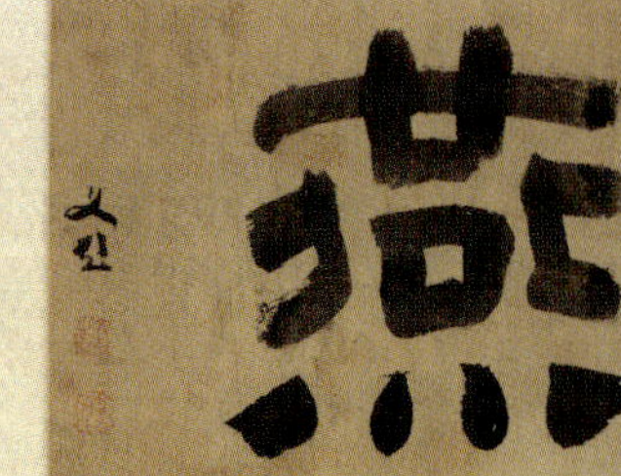

b

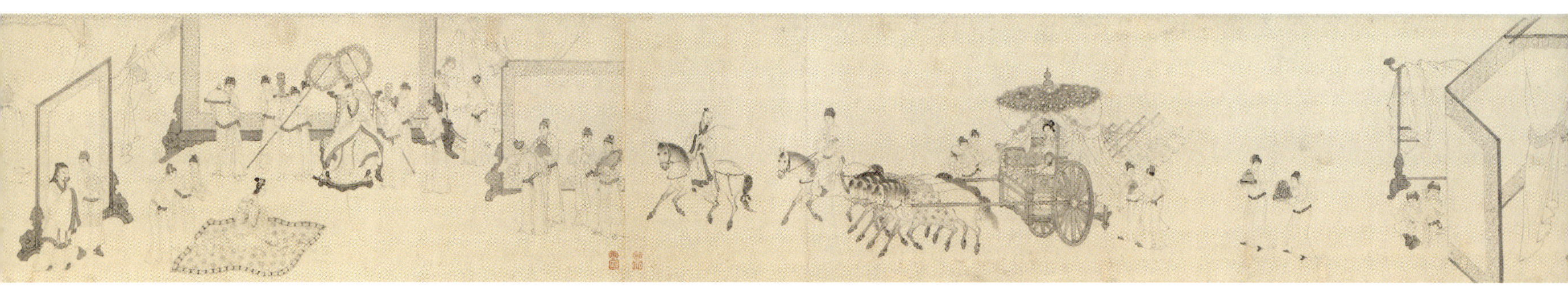

5

4

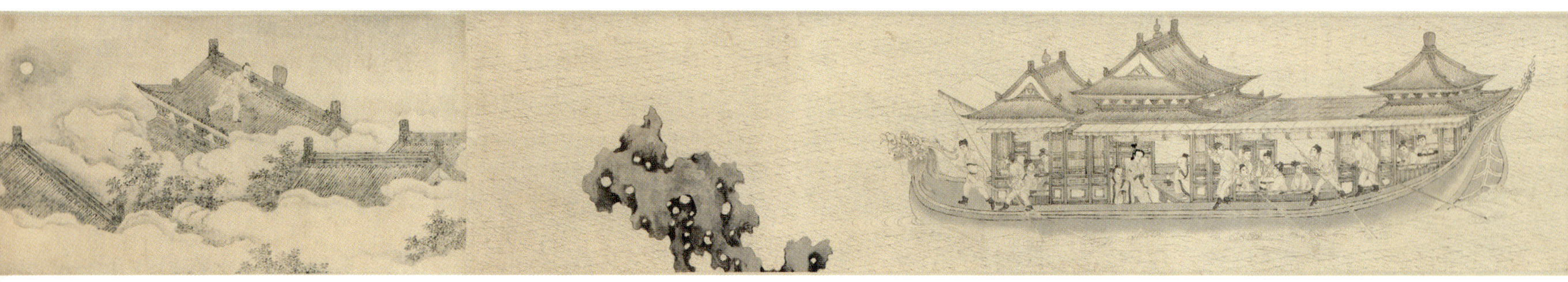

9

8

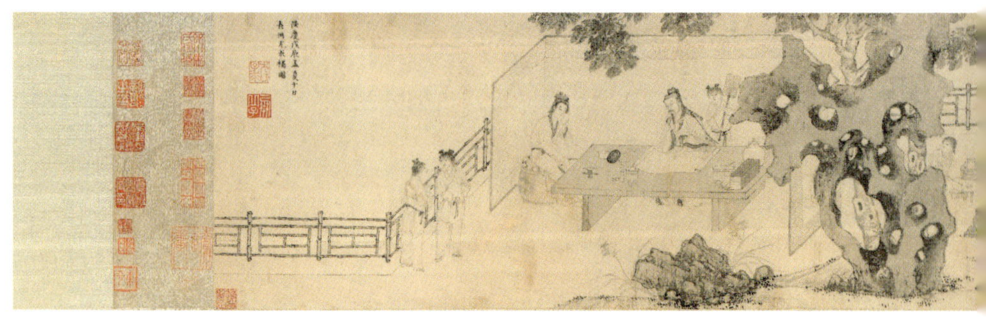

12

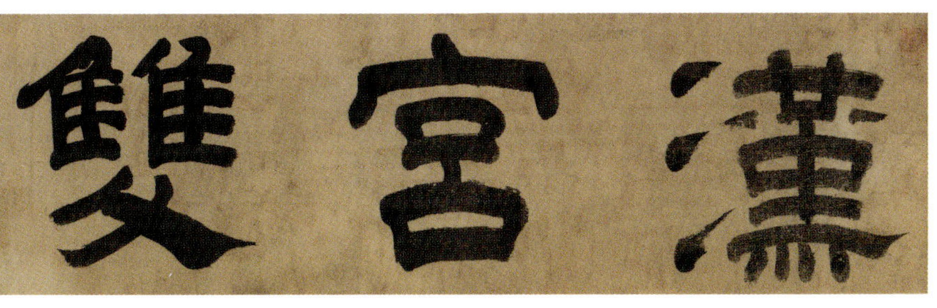

a

a Title panel: 'A Pair of Swallows in the Han Palace'
b Calligraphy by Wen Zhengming (1470–1559)
1 The Zhao sisters serve in the household of Princess Yang'a
2 Zhao Feiyan and the huntsman
3 The emperor and Feiyan in the bedchamber
4 Zhao Hede is summoned to the palace
5 The emperor receives Hede
6–7 The sisters assume positions of great honour in the back palace
8 A pleasure outing by barge
9 A lover visits the sisters by night
10 The sisters make up
11 The emperor secretly watches Hede bathing by candlelight
12 The emperor and Hede at leisure before his death from an overdose of aphrodisiac

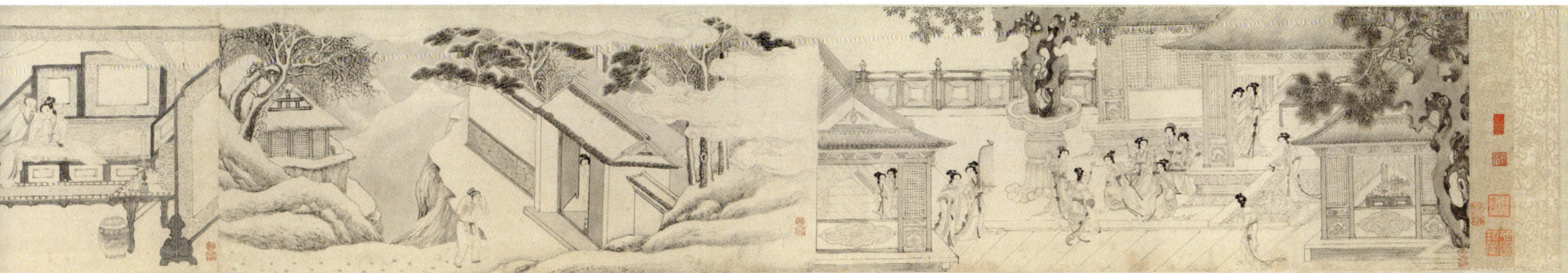

2 1

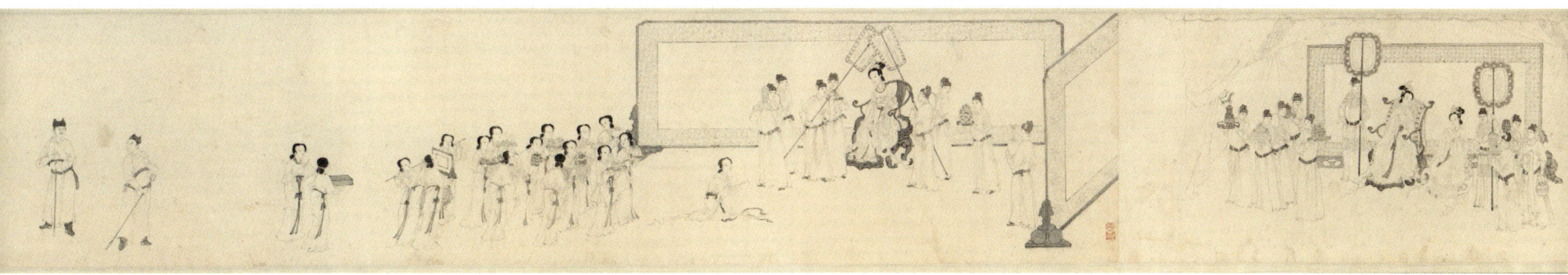

7 6

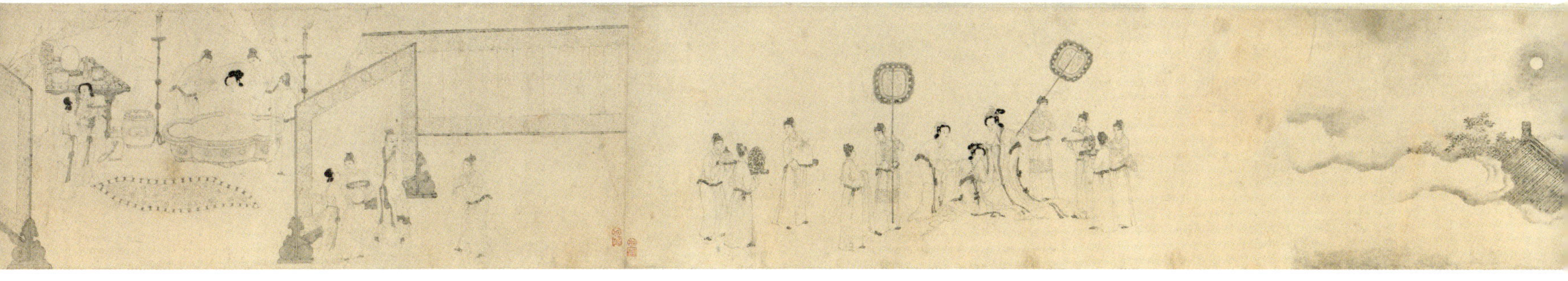

11 10 9 continued

The Han dynasty continually grew in power after the consolidation of the empire by emperor Wudi (r. 140–87 BC). During emperor Chengdi's reign (32–7 BC), however, political power fell into the hands of the royal family's in-laws, and emperor Chengdi himself did little but remain in his palace indulging in wine, music and women. The story known as 'Pair of swallows in the Han Palace' refers to his beloved beauties, Zhao Feiyan (Zhao the Flying Swallow) and her younger sister, Zhao Hede. Born into the serving class, they were both extraordinarily beautiful, while one was plump and the other slender, and they could both sing and dance. As soon as emperor Chengdi spotted them, he had them brought to the palace, where he doted on them more every day. He even deposed the empress, installing Zhao Feiyan in her place, and he elevated Zhao Hede to the rank of Bright Consort, a standing second only to the empress.

The two sisters enjoyed the emperor's favour for over ten years. To ensure that her son, when she had one, would become heir to the throne, Zhao Feiyan pressed the emperor to kill off his only other son (by another imperial consort). In fact, she never gave birth to a son herself, but in order to maintain her position, she took a bribe from Prince Kang and urged the emperor to name his

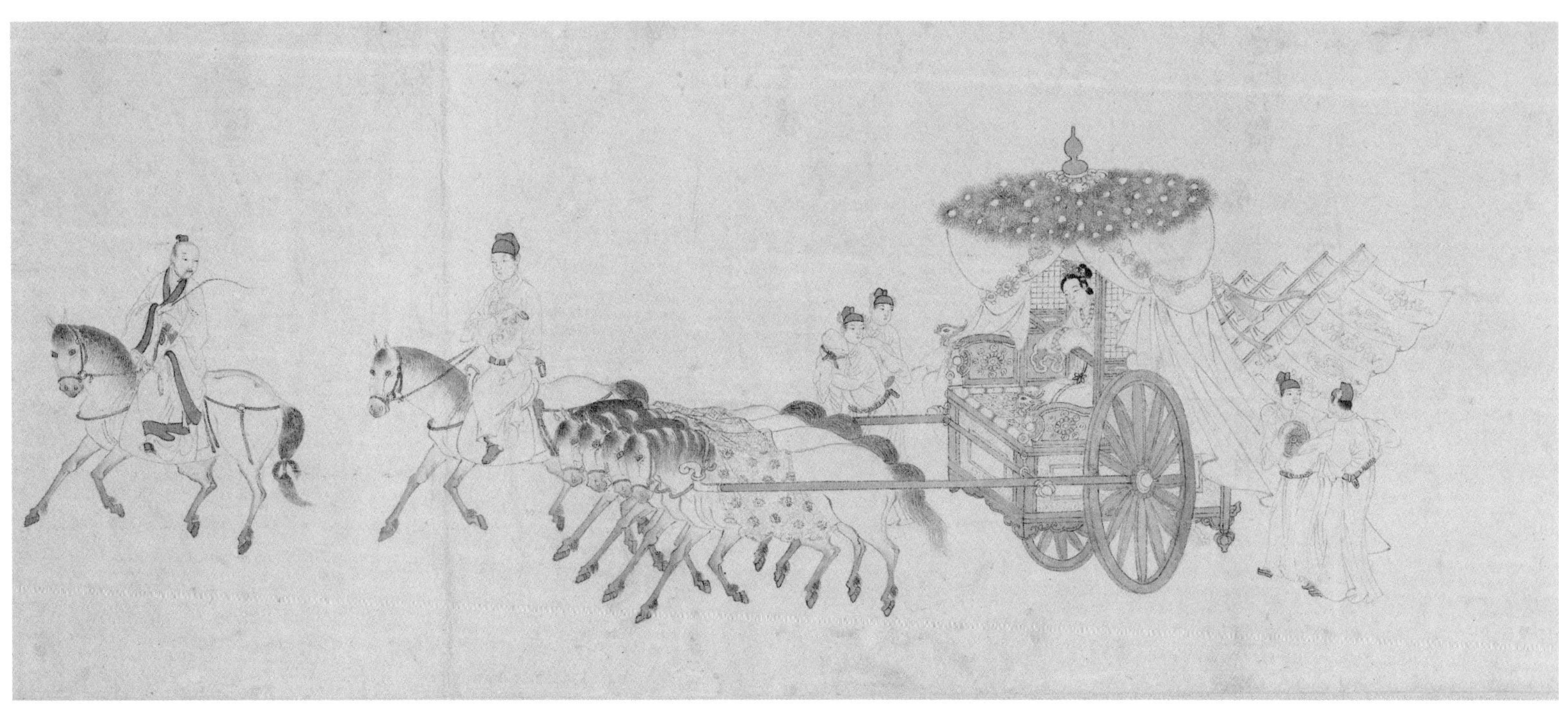

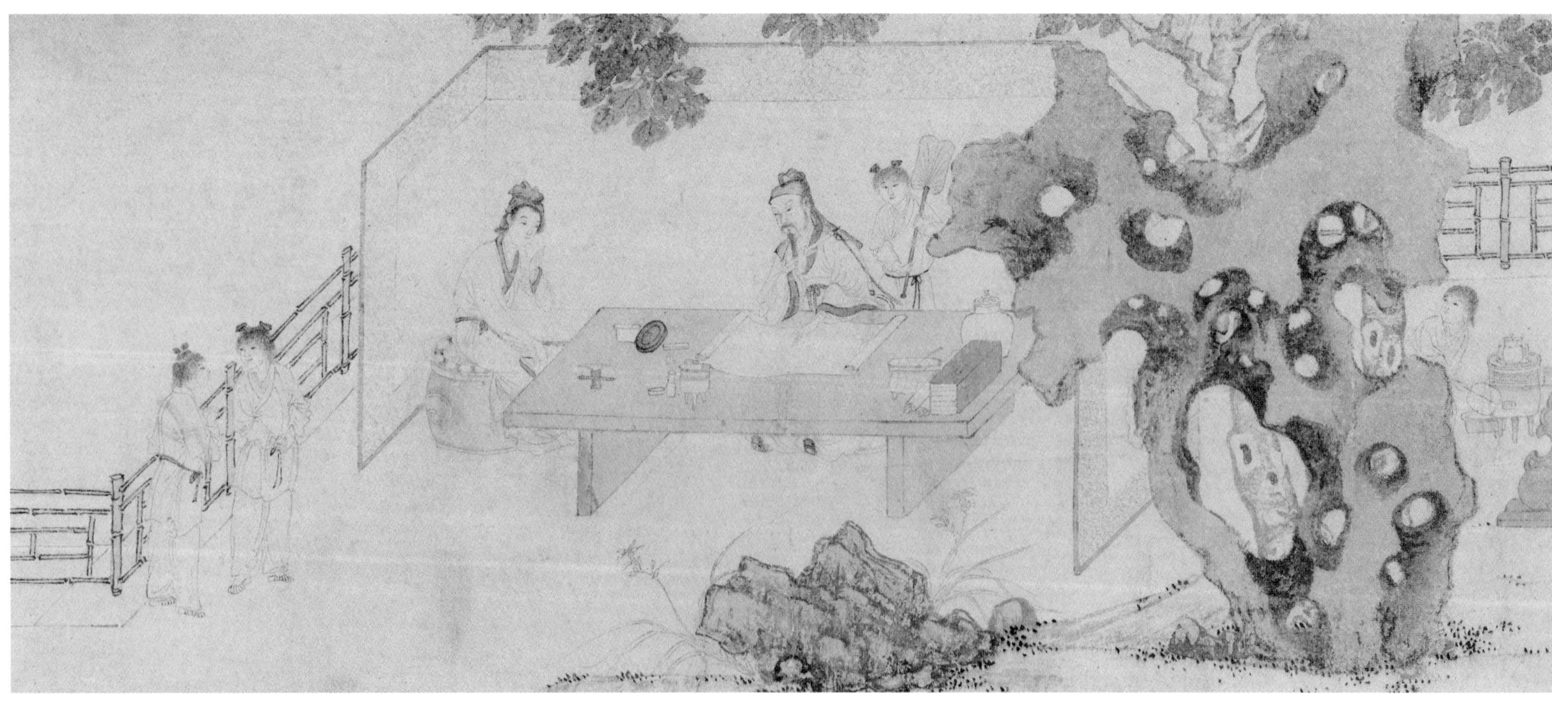

nephew, the prince's son (Liu Xin, the Prince of Dingtao), as his heir. Liu Xin did later accede to the Han throne as emperor Aidi (r. 6–1 BC).

The fact that emperor Chengdi had no son caused consternation in the palace, a situation exploited by the courtier Wang Mang, who wanted the throne for himself. He helped the Empress Dowager, Liu Xin's mother, to investigate the conduct of the Zhao sisters, which resulted in Zhao Hede's suicide. As Zhao Feiyan had helped Liu Xin come to power, he pardoned her and named her Empress Dowager. After emperor Aidi died, Wang Mang stripped Zhao Feiyan of her title and forced her to kill herself. The story of the two Zhao sisters, 'Spring morning in the Han Palace', became a coded reference in Chinese history to emperors who let the sensual pleasures of music and beauty bring disruption to their domains.

This painting is divided into nine or more individual scenes, broadly: Han Chengdi's first encounter with Zhao Feiyan; Feiyan entering the palace and receiving the emperor's favour; the sisters being elevated to consorts; the emperor and his consorts on a boat outing; the empress unable to bear rejection; and the emperor as a voyeur peeping at his consort bathing.

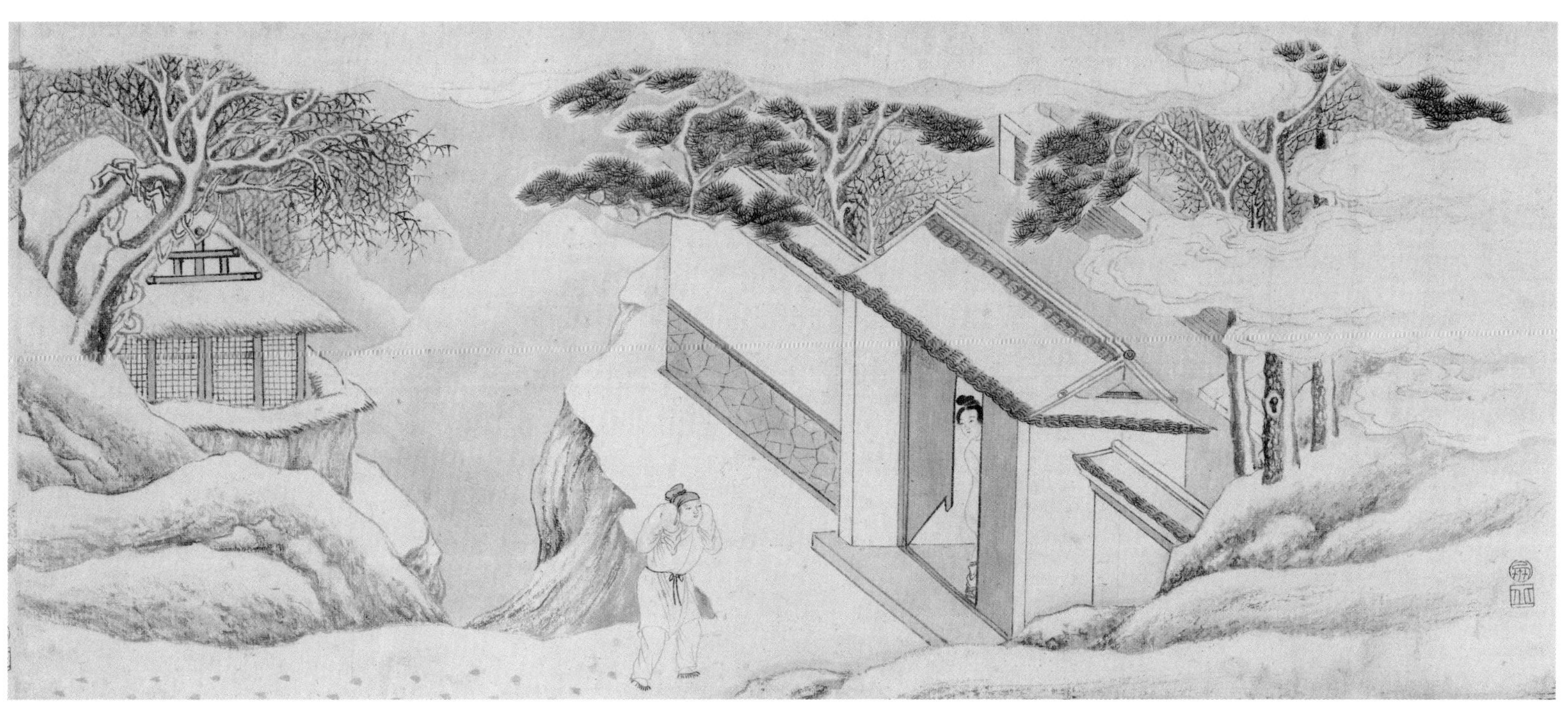

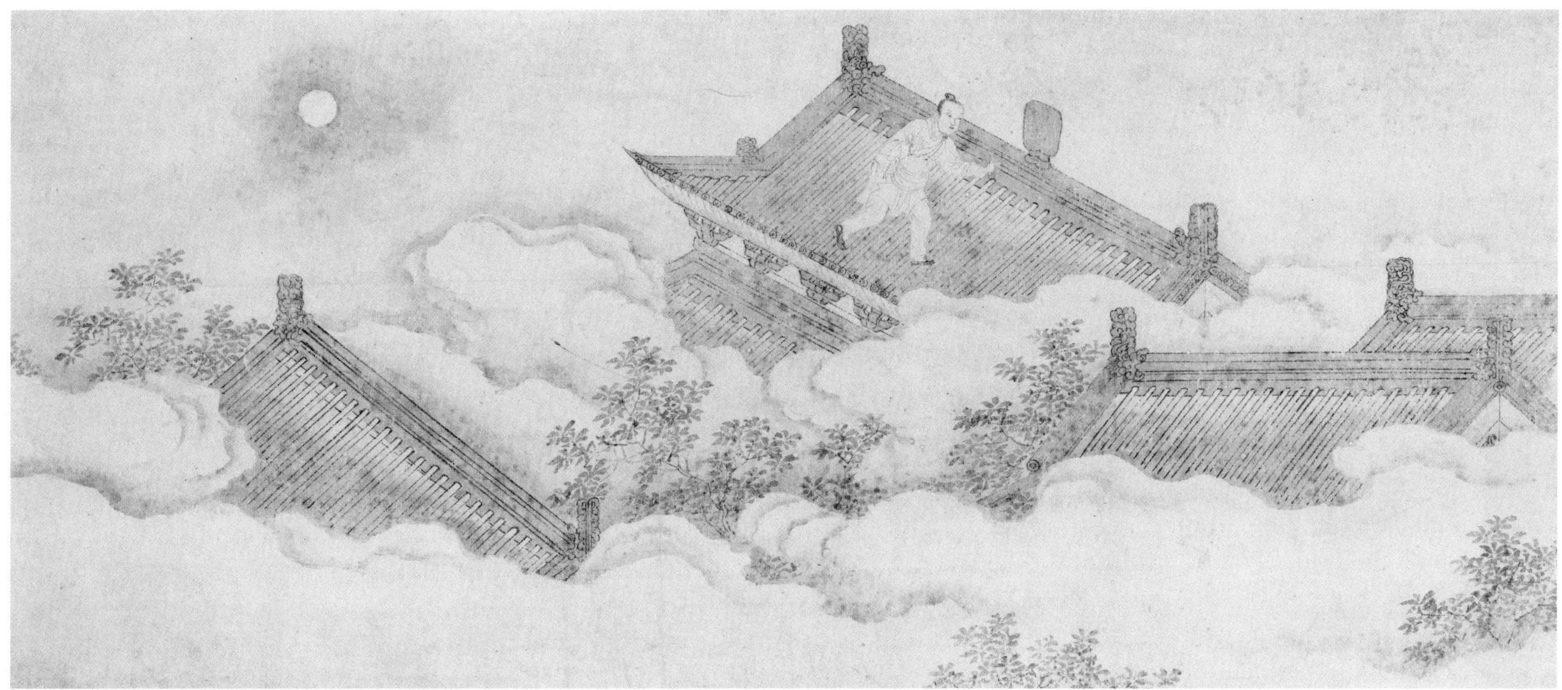

34

清 尤詔、汪恭《隨園女弟子圖卷》

You Shao and Wang Gong (active 1796–1820)
The Female Disciples of Master Suiyuan
Dated 1796
Handscroll; ink and colours on silk
41 × 308.4 cm

Harmony Garden, or Suiyuan, was a villa in the city of Nanjing belonging to the famous Qing-dynasty poet Yuan Mei, also known as 'Mr Harmony Garden'. Yuan Mei's poetry was known throughout China, and he received countless students. What was remarkable about this was that a large number of his followers were women. In feudal society, women had limited opportunities for a cultured education but Yuan Mei boldly challenged the social convention that 'women [should] not have learning but rather be virtuous' (*nüzi wucai bian shi de*). He opened his doors to both men and women, creating a new climate for learning that had far-reaching implications.

There are thirteen female disciples in this painting, including Yun Feng, Yun He and Liang Peilan, as well as Yuan Mei's sister and grand-daughter. The others are mostly the daughters of

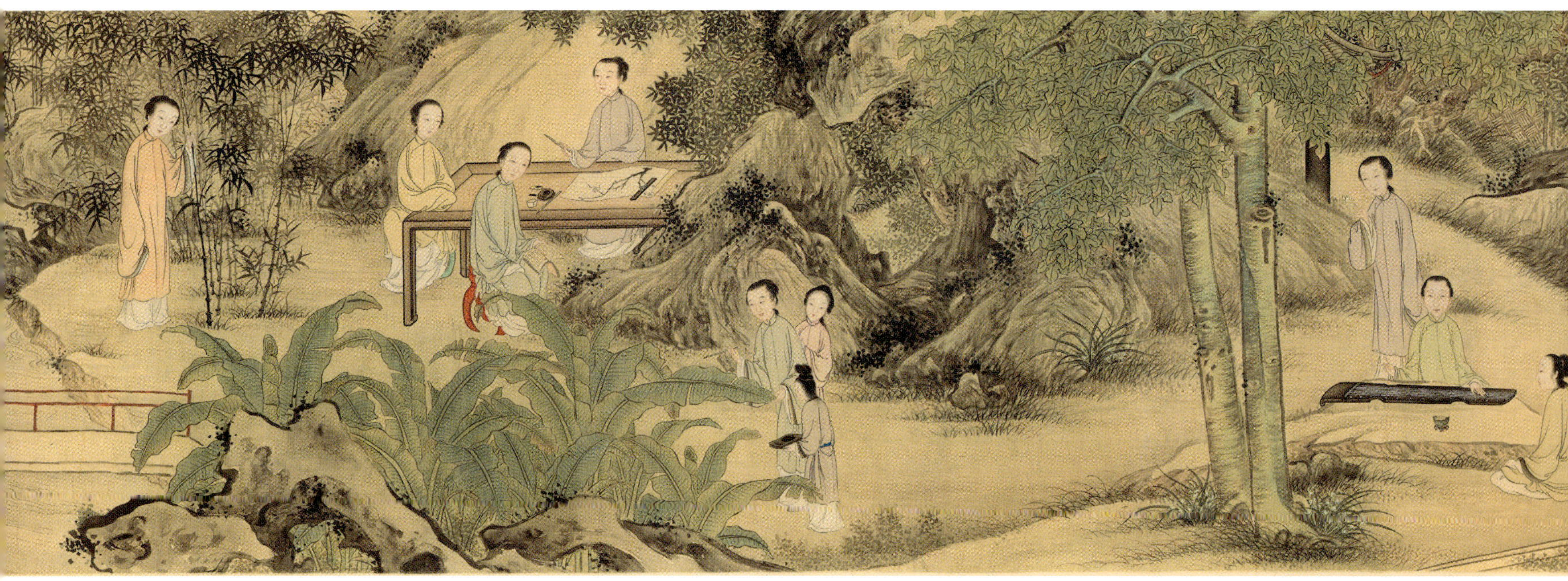

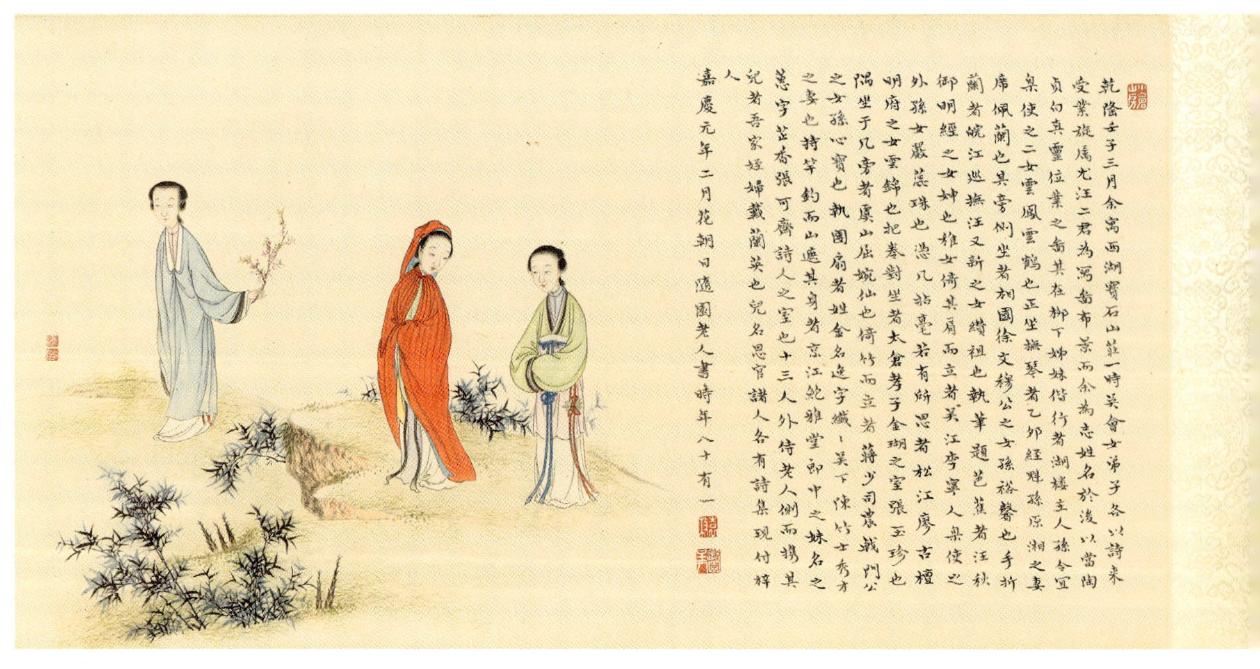

prominent families, both restricted by the custom that 'men are honoured, women serve', as well as lacking the means to interact with the outside world or reap the benefits that Chinese culture had to offer. Yuan Mei created an atmosphere of equality between the sexes at the Harmony Garden and personally taught his female followers, developing their talents for poetic and literary composition. He achieved a certain success, and later in his life Yuan Mei compiled his students' poetry into *Female Disciples of Harmony Garden: Selected Poems (Suiyuan nüdizi shixuan)* to honour them and expand their influence. It was well received by contemporary literati and helped to promote women's poetry in the Qing dynasty.

Wang Gong, who painted the landscape setting, was active during the Jiaqing reign (1796–1820). He was from Xiuning, Anhui Province, and specialised in figure painting. The portratist You Shao's biography is unknown.

FOLLOWING PAGES: Detail of Yuan Mei's female disciples, including Wang Shen (inscribing a bamboo leaf), Liao Yunjin (painting) and Jin Yi (holding a fan)

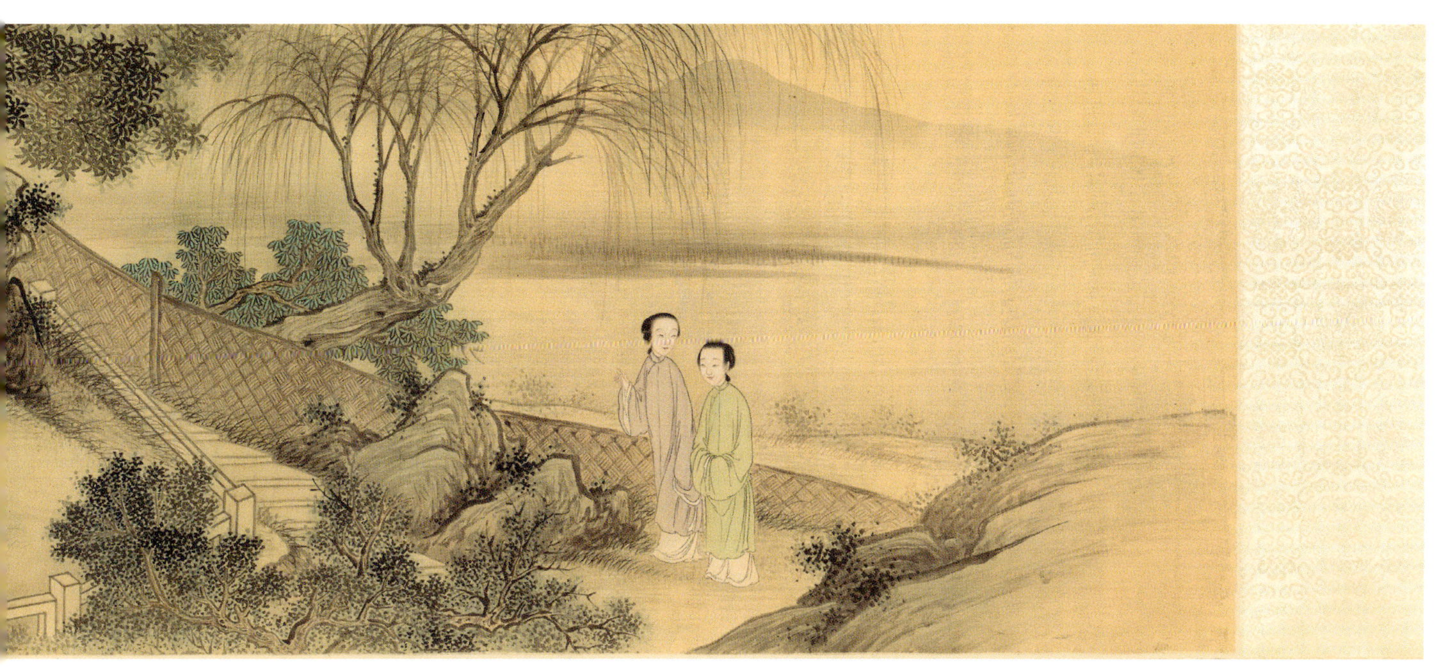

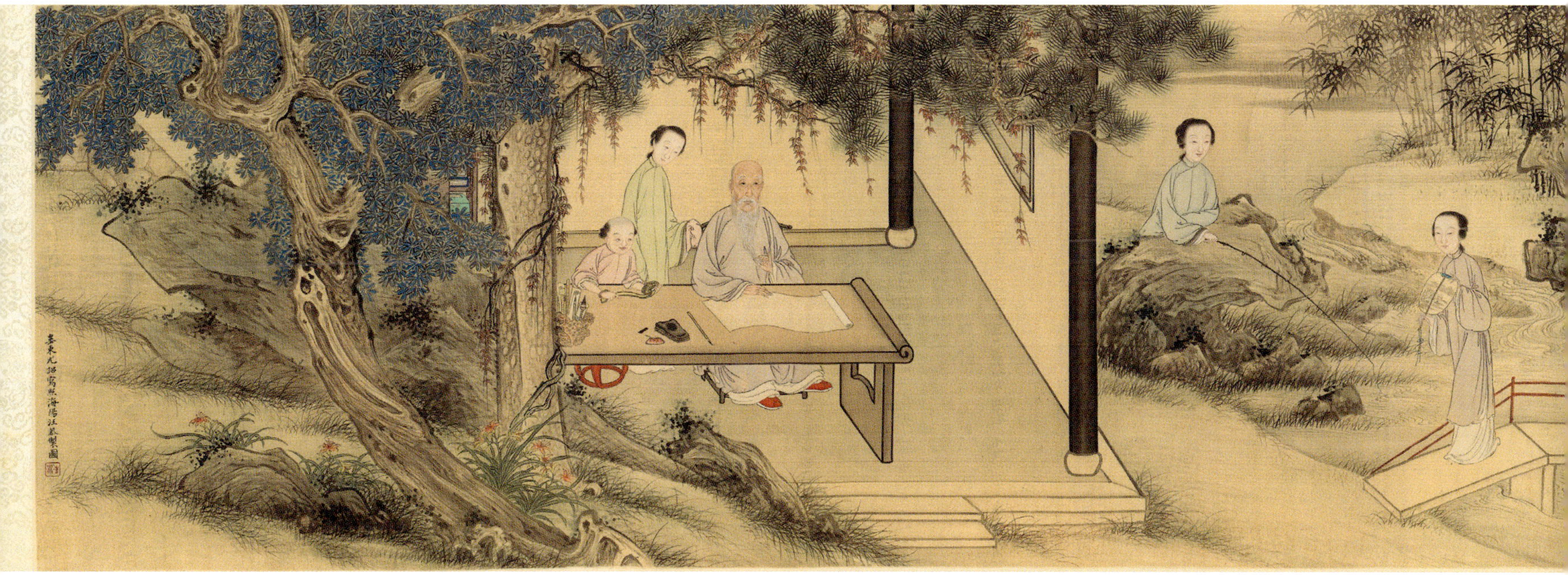

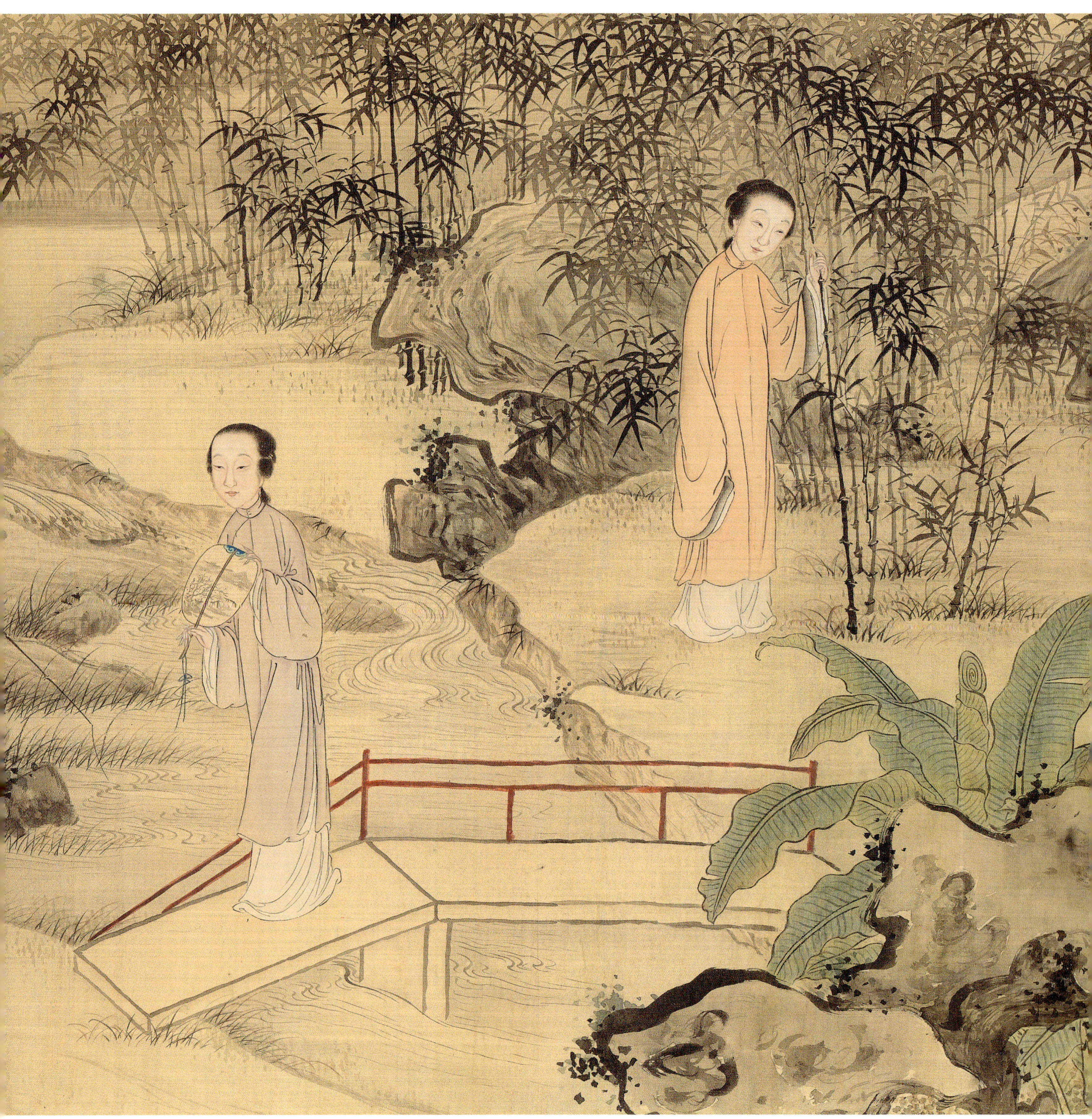

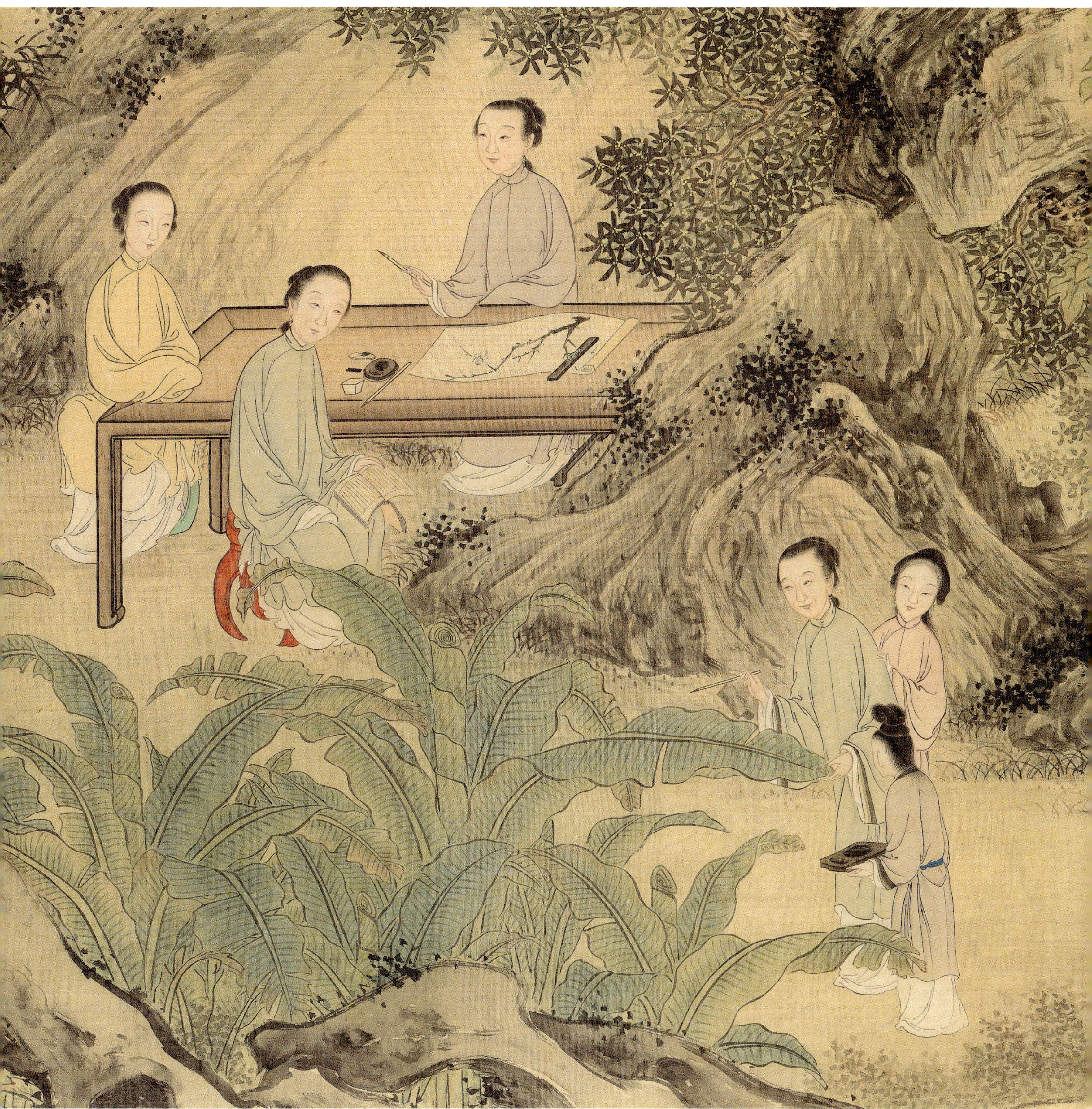

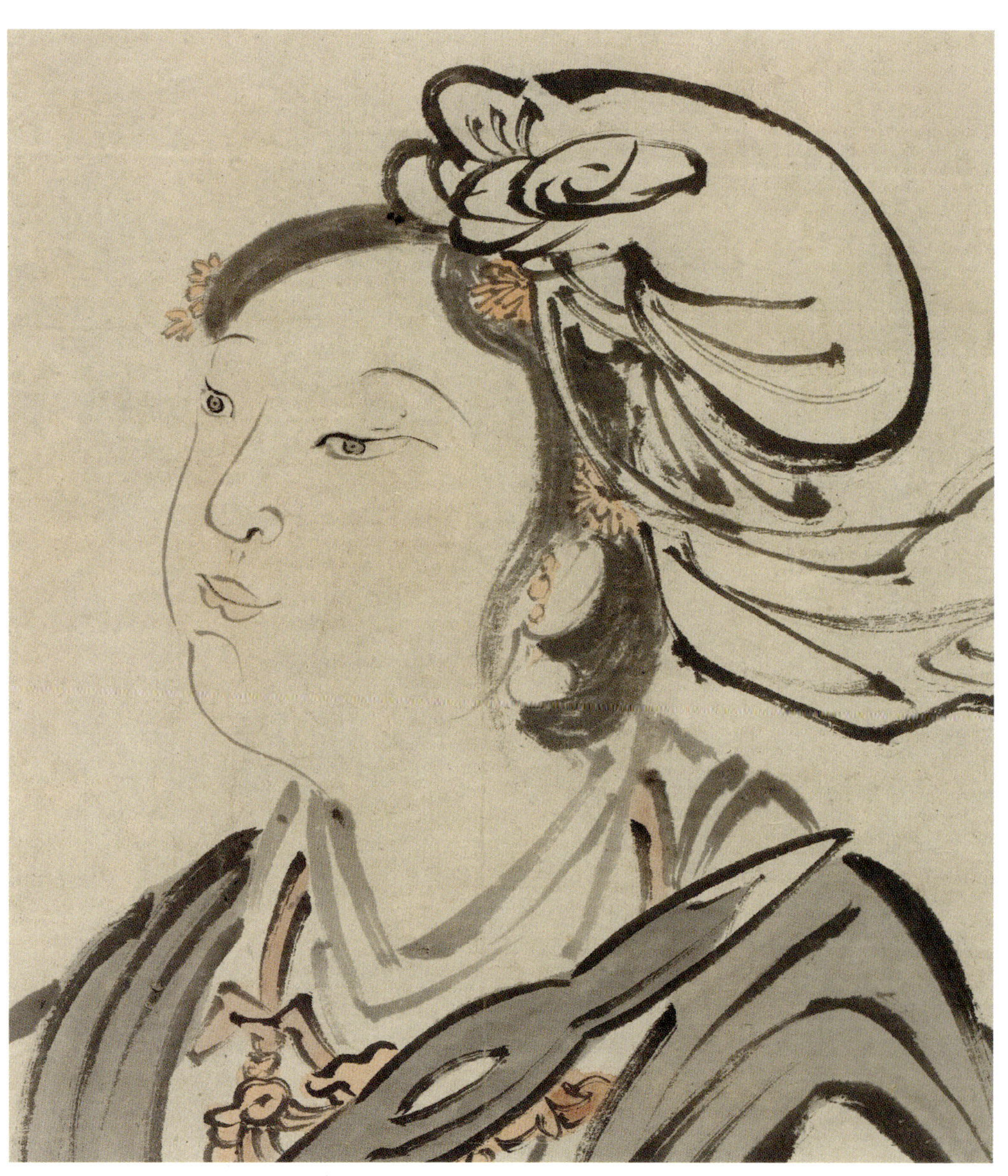

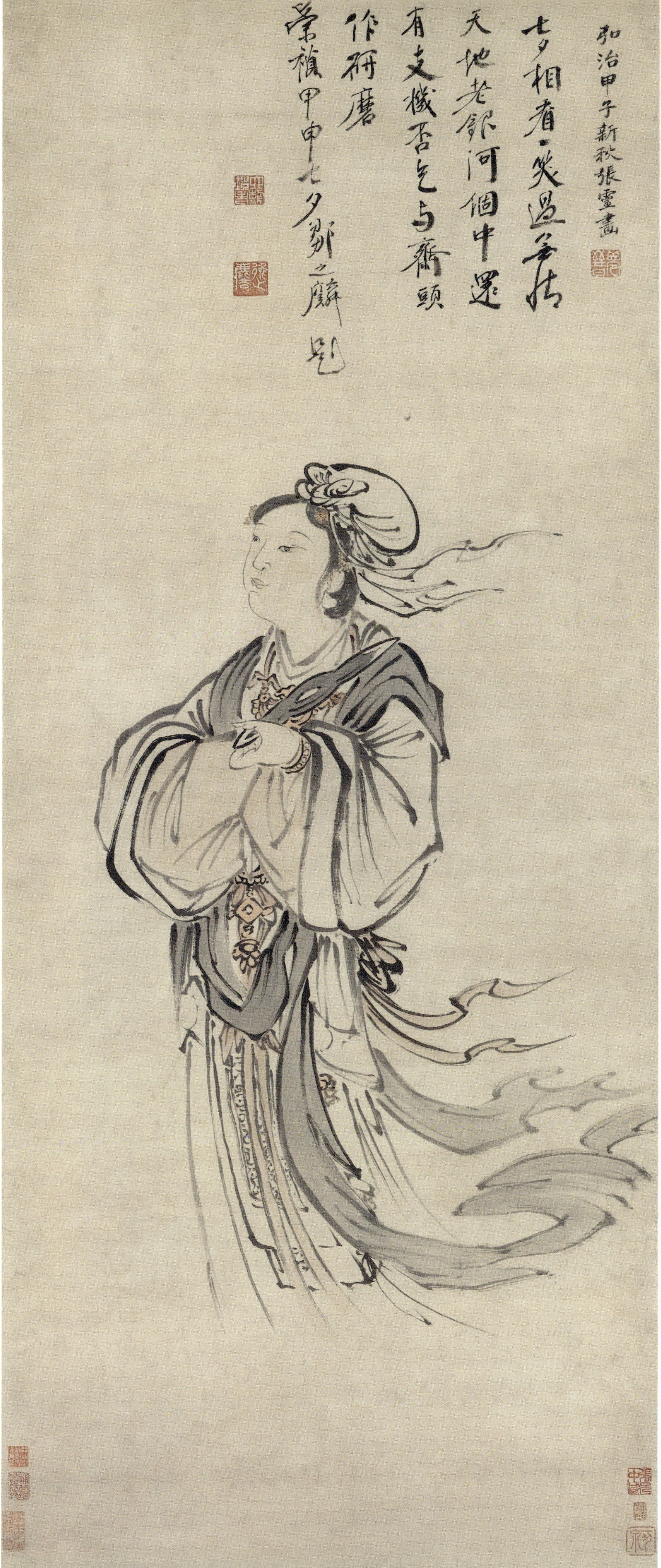

35

明 張靈 《織女圖軸》

Zhang Ling (?–before 1529)
The Weaver Girl
Dated 1504
Hanging scroll; ink and colours on paper
136.4 × 56.4 cm
Donated by Liu Jingji

In ancient Chinese folklore, the Weaver Girl (Zhinü) was a star that was separated from the Cowherd star (Niulang) by the Milky Way. In the Han dynasty they became literary figures that represented a man and a woman in love, and throughout the ages they have been featured in many romantic stories of reunion and parting. Legend has it that the Cowherd and the Weaver Girl met at the Magpie Bridge every year on the seventh day of the seventh month of the lunar calendar, which is variously called the Night of Sevens, the Double Seventh or the Festival to Plead for Skills, and can be likened to Valentine's Day in the west.

The woman in this painting is wearing a headscarf and a long silk stole. She treads lightly, as if walking on air, and she holds a shuttle in her hands. Her concentrated expression as she looks forwards seems to indicate she is waiting to meet her lover.

Zhang Ling was from the city of Suzhou in Jiangsu Province. He was friends with two of the great Suzhou scholar-artists, Tang Yin and Wen Zhengming, and excelled at figure and landscape painting. The artist's inscription in the top right corner of this painting indicates that it was executed in 1504. The second inscription, above the figure, was made by the later scholar-painter Zou Zhilin (1606–85) in 1644.

36

明 張路《雜畫圖冊》十八開

Zhang Lu (1464–1538)
Daoist Immortals and Natural Symbols
Album of eighteen leaves; ink and colours on flecked paper
Each leaf 31.6 × 59.3 cm

In Daoism, it is believed one can attain immortality through continual self-cultivation, thereby obtaining perpetual life and powerful abilities. In ancient China, man aspired to attain the free and unattached life of a deity or an immortal. Deities (*shen*) performed divine functions, being gods of the earth and elements, whereas immortals (*xian*) lived forever, roaming and redressing wrongs among humankind. Any person with the propensity to become an immortal could become one.

This album features relatively well-known Daoist deities, including gods of the seas (1), mountains (2), good fortune (3) and long life (4), as well as immortals and other figures: Liu Haichan (5), White Deer Immortal (6), Master Lie (7), the Four Elders (8), The Five Planets (*Wu lao*) (9), Immortal Woman Ma (10), Iron-crutch Li (11), Xiangzi (12), Royal Uncle Cao (13), Zhongli (14), Lü Chunyang (15), Lan Caihe (16), elder Zhang Guo (17) and Green Goat Immortal (18). The grouping known as the Eight Immortals (who, in fact, number more than eight) is especially well known and loved throughout China. Daoist thought was also transmitted through stories about them. In one story, known as 'The Eight Immortals cross the sea, each revealing his divine powers', they use their various talents to avert disaster and cure sickness, and to bestow long life, prosperity and long family lineages.

These paintings are made with succinct lines that create slightly exaggerated figures. Zhang Lu, from Kaifeng, Henan Province, excelled at landscape as well as figure painting, and had an 'unruly' style that used free-flowing brush strokes. He was one of the Zhe School masters.

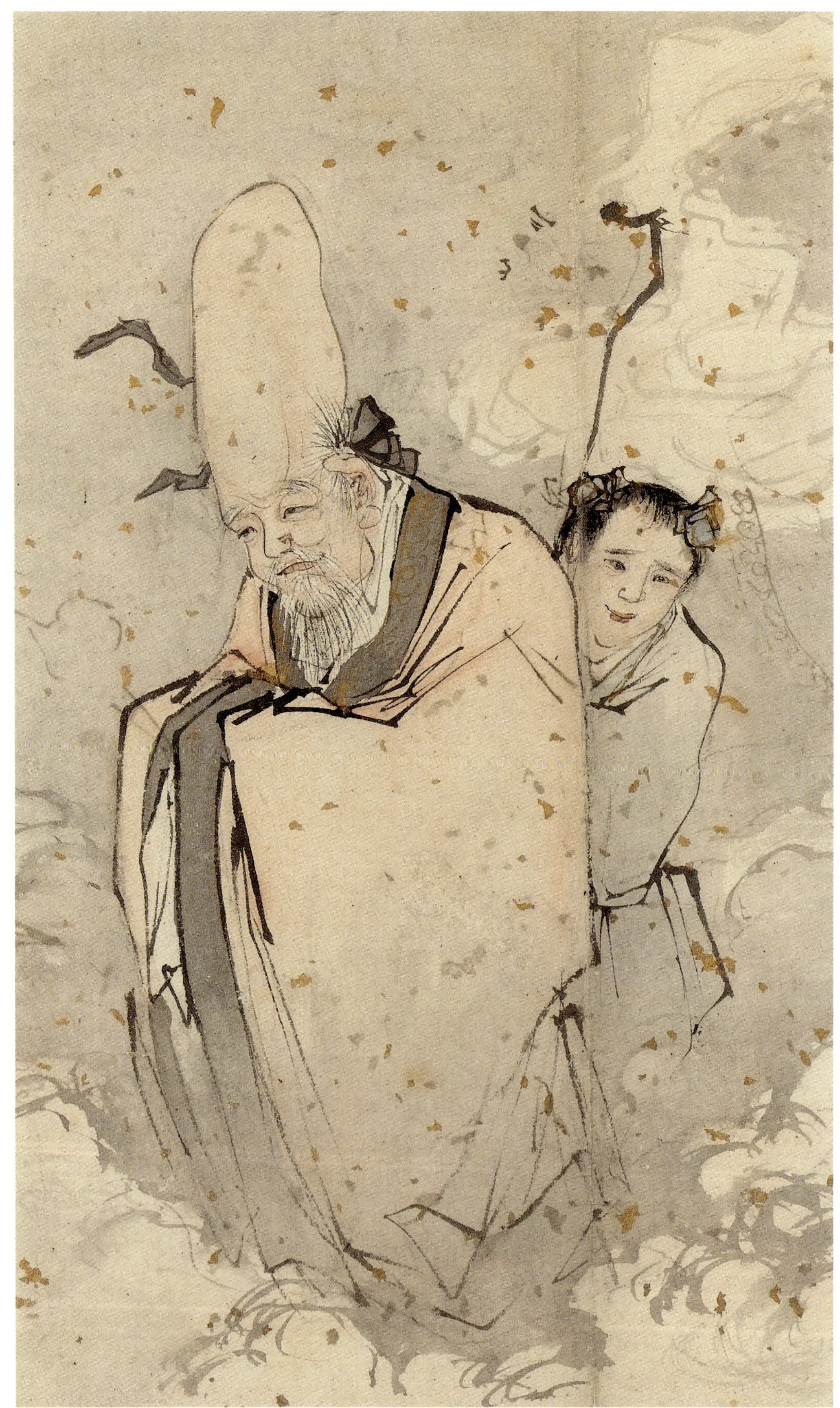

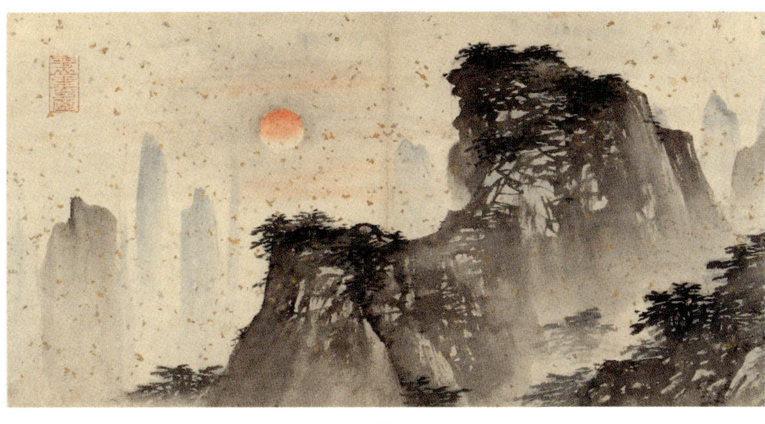

2

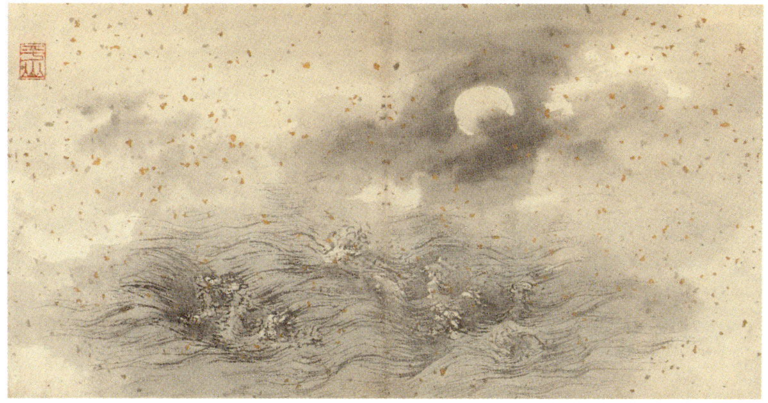

1

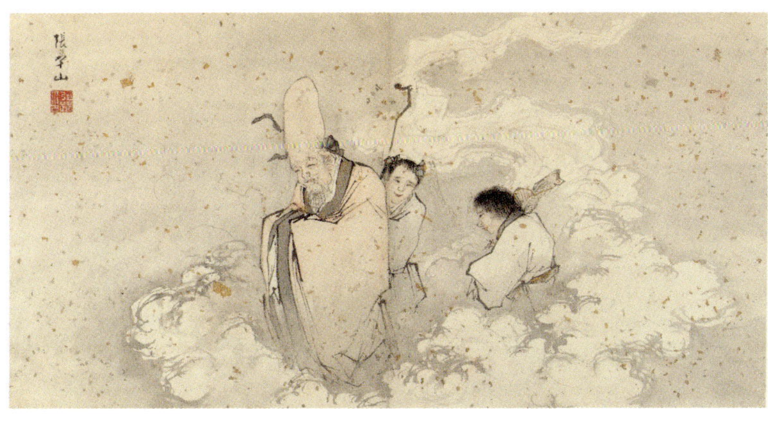

4

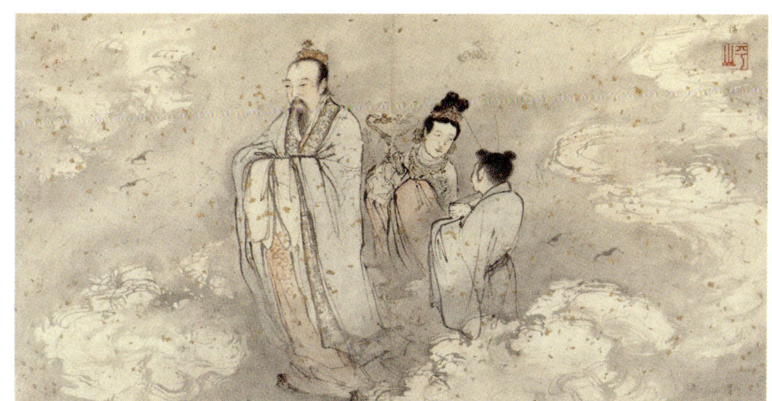

3

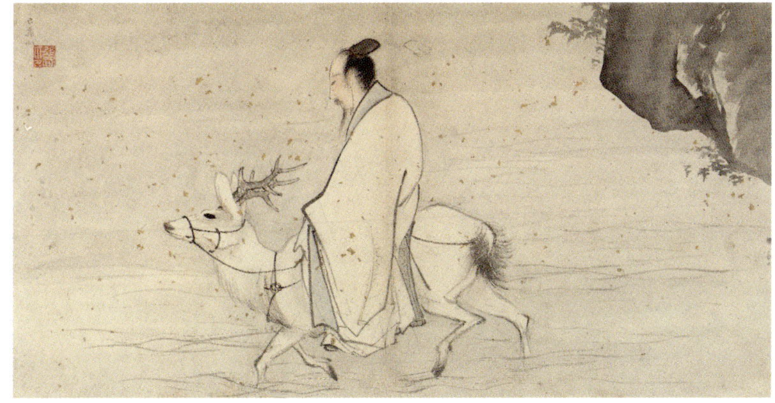

6

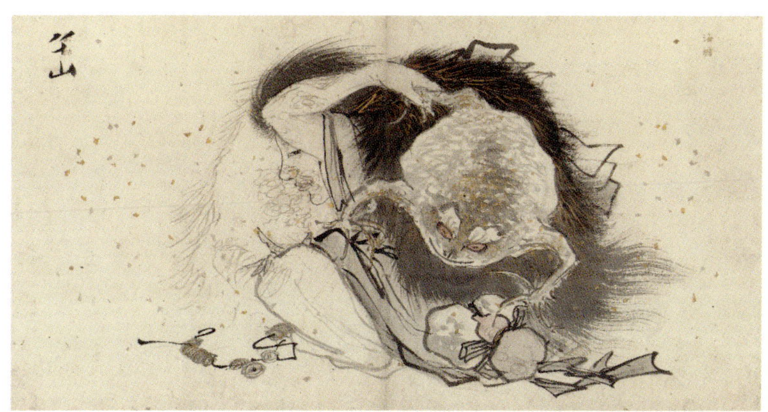

5

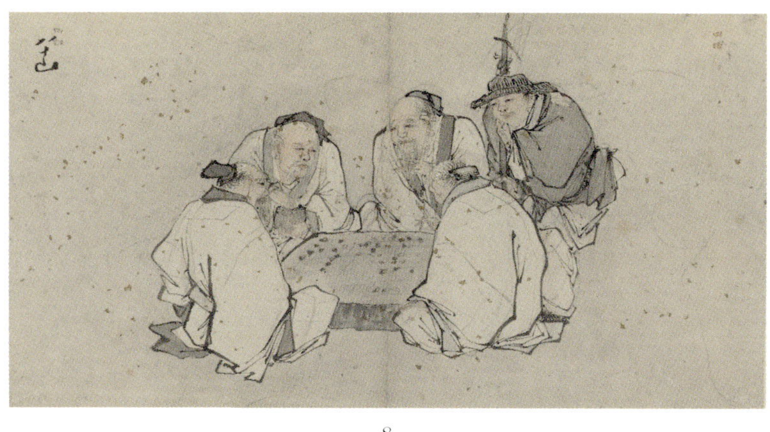

8

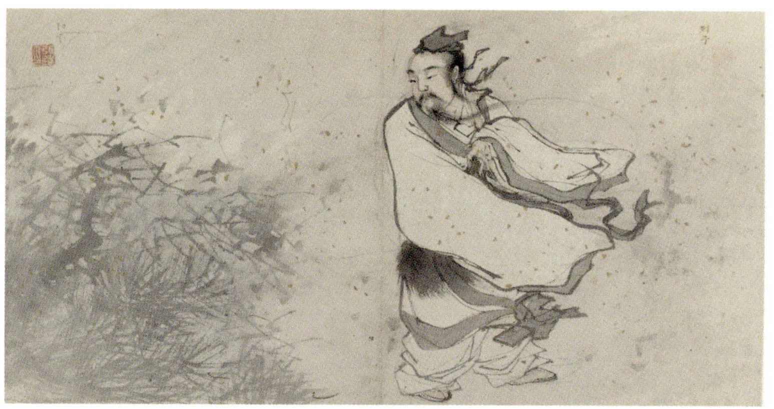

7

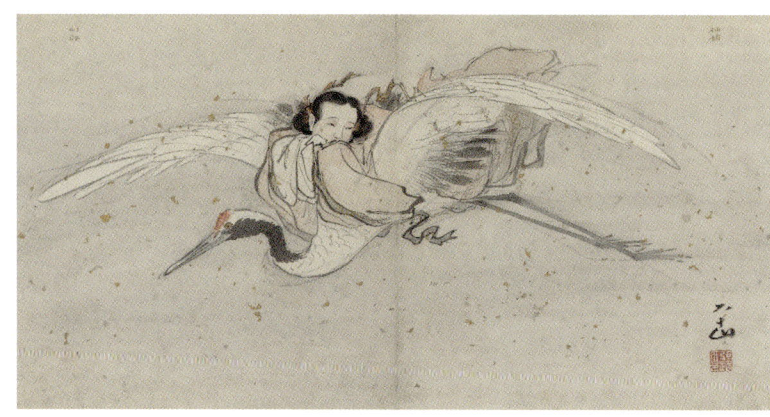

10

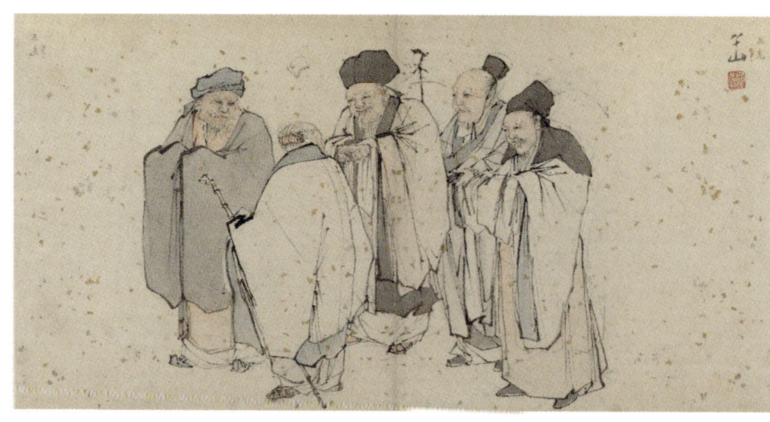

9

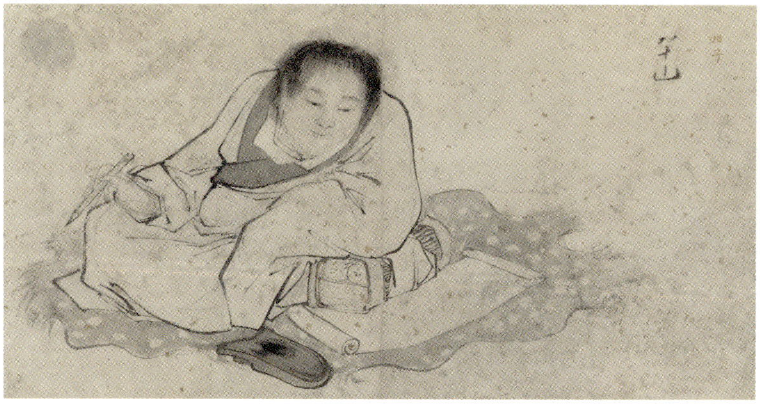

12

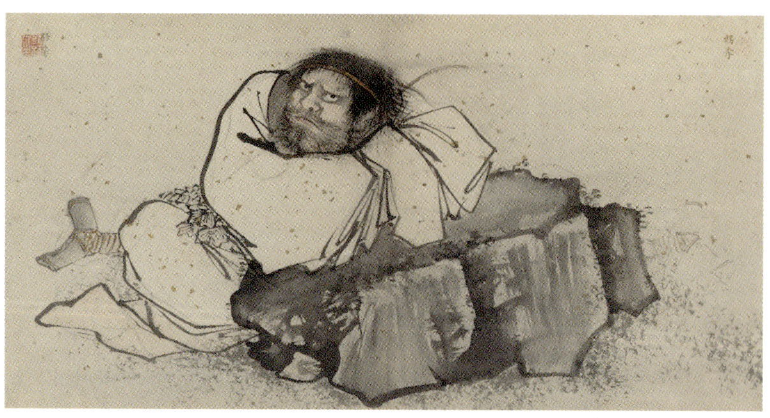

11

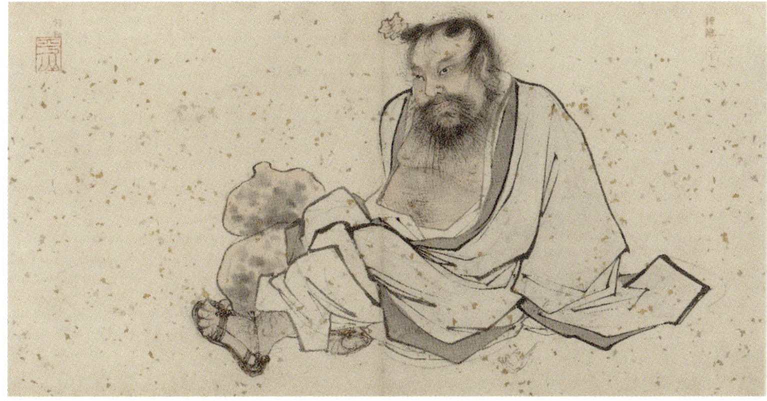

14

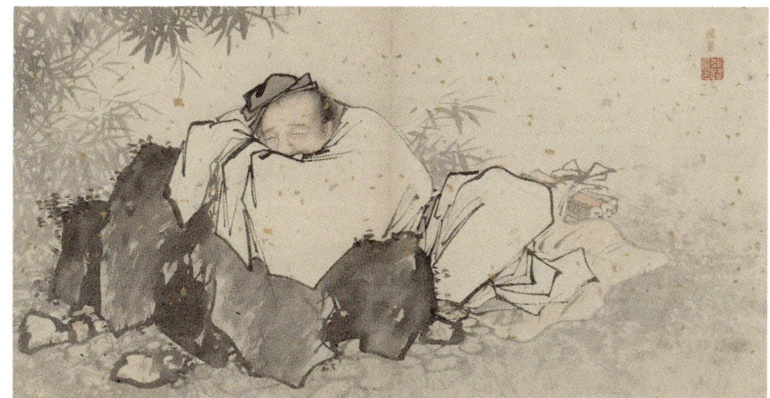

13

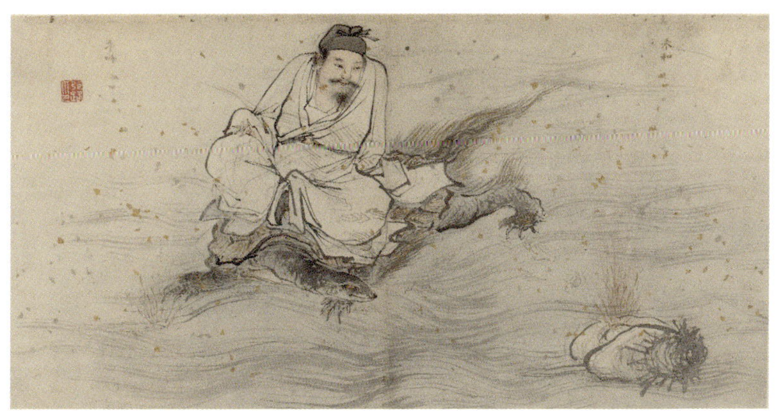

16

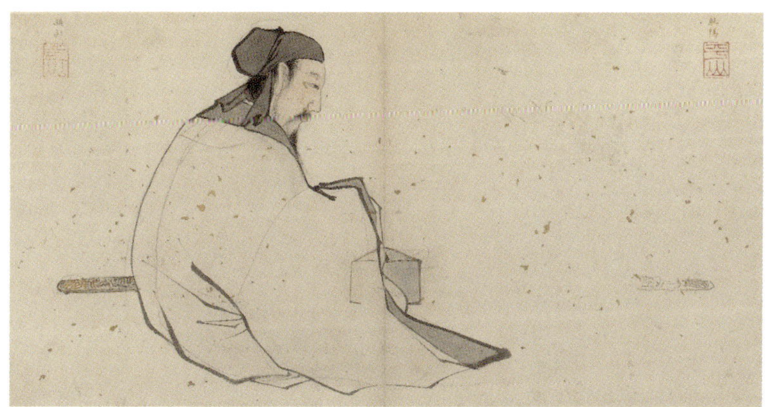

15

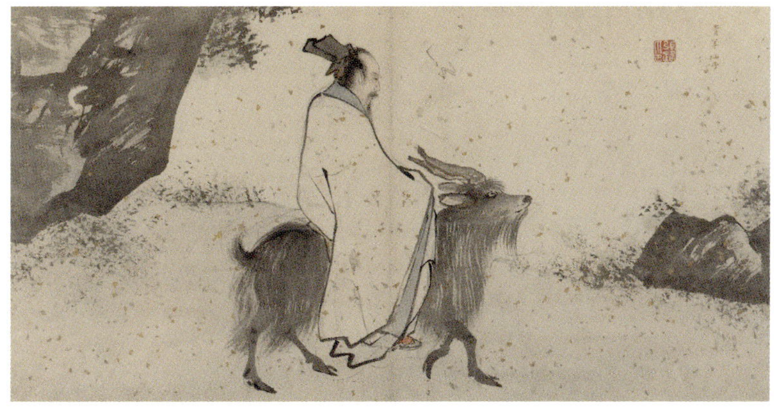

18

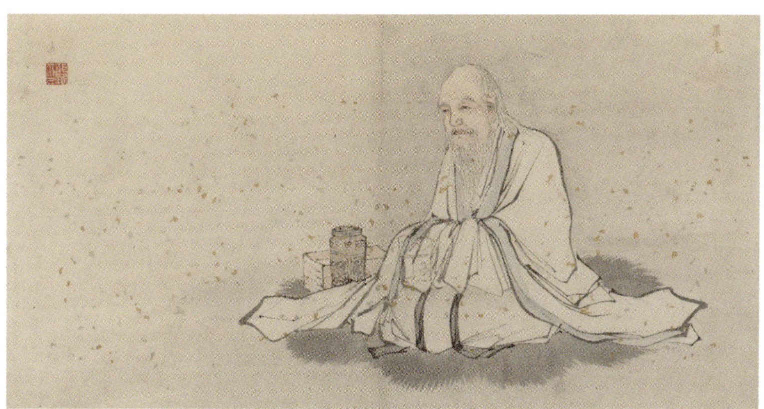

17

37

清 周璕 《張天師圖軸》

Zhou Xun (1649–1729)
Celestial Master Zhang
Dated 1685
Hanging scroll; ink and colours on paper
116.7 × 55.4 cm

Celestial Master Zhang is the name for a Daoist patriarch, and it is passed down from generation to generation. There have been sixty-four generations so far, the first one being Zhang Daoling of the Han dynasty. After travelling to Sichuan, he said that Laozi (the ancient Daoist patriarch) 'gave him the True Law of the Three Heavens' (*jiao yi santian zhengfa*). People called him Celestial Master Zhang (Zhang Tianshi) and his teaching was called 'Way of the Celestial Masters' (*Tianshi dao*), which he set out in a book of magic writing. The 'Way of the Celestial Masters' sect flourished under the Yuan dynasty, and its leader gradually evolved from a Daoist figure into a folk deity that could control the rain, subdue demons and bestow good fortune upon humans. In the Ming and Qing dynasties, Celestial Master Zhang gained more magical powers, including the ability to extract poison. People are fond of attaching his image to their doors during the Dragon Boat Festival.

Swords (*jian*) and magic symbols (*fu*) were important tools used by the Heavenly Master to perform magic. These symbols, resembling a cross between Chinese characters and pictures, were written on yellow paper or silk, and were understood as a form of secret writing from the gods. This magic writing originated in ancient shamanism and was used in early Daoism to pass on magic. These talismans composed of magic writing could enact the will of the gods by summoning gods, commanding ghosts, subduing demons, curing illness and averting disaster.

In this painting, Celestial Master Zhang is wearing a long robe and holding a sword, while his eyes are intensely fixed on a bat. As 'bat' is a homonym for 'magic symbol' (both are pronounced *fu*), this means he is creating prosperity in the world by bringing rain, stopping floods, subduing demons and dispelling sickness.

Zhou Xun was from Nanjing. He excelled at figure and animal painting.

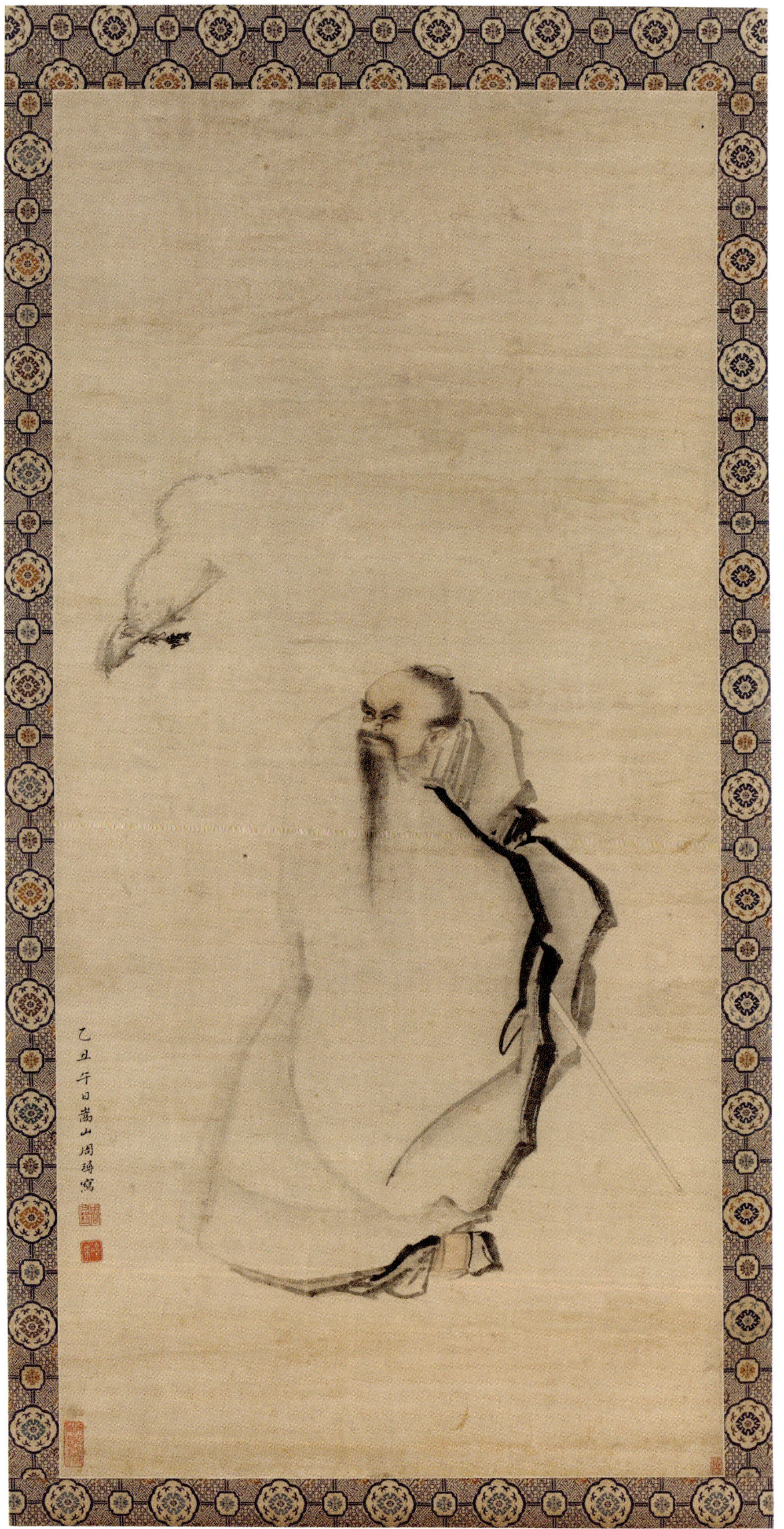

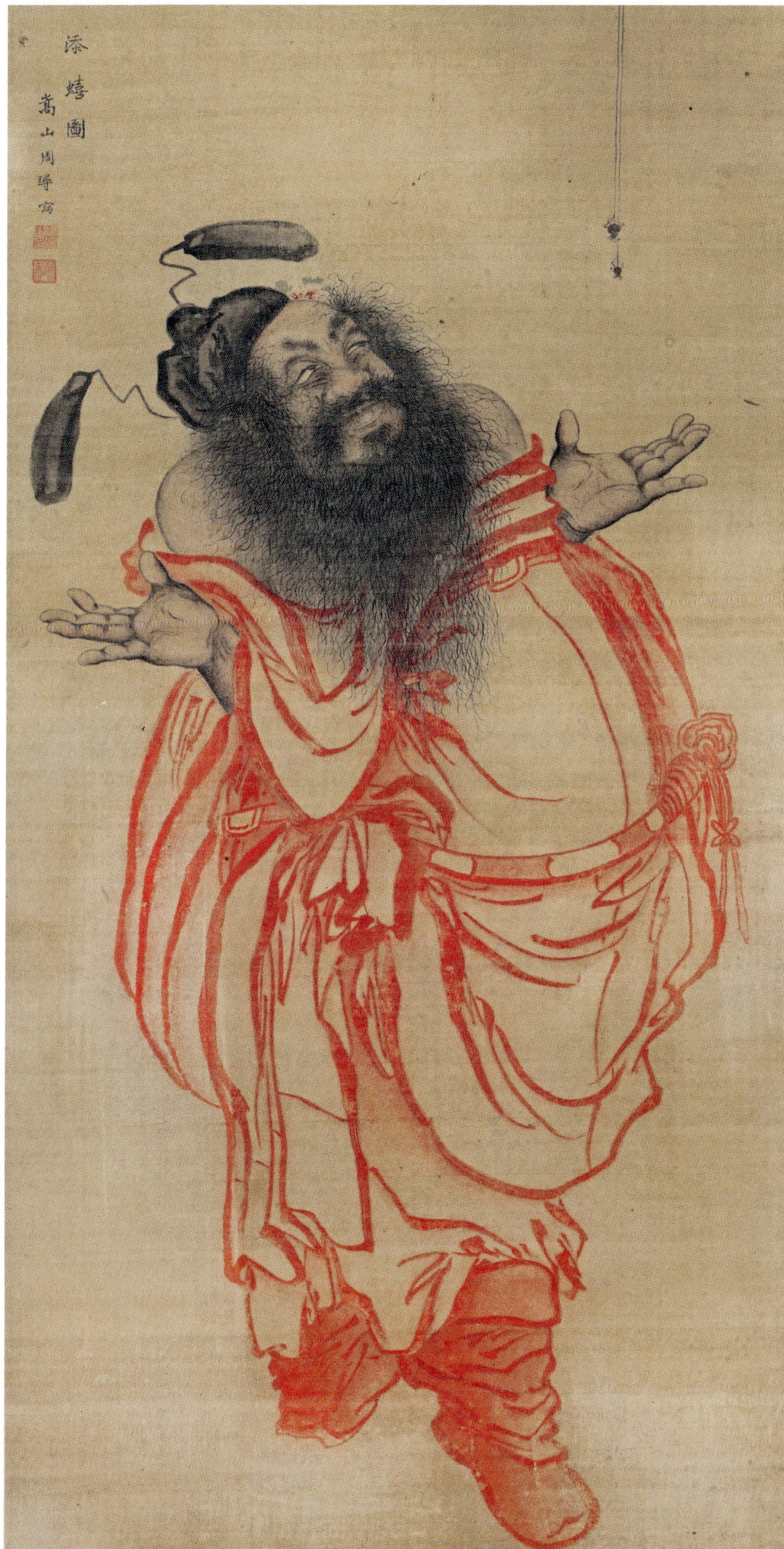

38

清 周璕《添蟢圖軸》

Zhou Xun (1649–1729)
Zhong Kui and Spiders
Hanging scroll; ink and colours on silk
128.6 × 64.4 cm

The title of this painting in Chinese – *tianxi* (literally 'adding spiders') – is a homophone for 'joyful things'. In Chinese, the word *xi* refers to a type of small spider that spins its web by water or in trees. In Chinese folk culture, it is an auspicious creature that can bring about propitious events. For example, during the Western (or Former) Han dynasty (206 BC–AD 8), it was believed that if a person saw several of these spiders together, it meant that he or she was about to experience a joyful event, which was why they were also called 'joyful spiders'. In Chinese, *xi* can also mean 'happiness' and 'joy'. The custom of the Joyful Spiders is still alive in some parts of China today. The phrase 'adding spiders' (*tianxi*) means to offer glad tidings to someone, and in some regions, such as Fengtai, Shandong Province, it refers to having children. In modern China, when a woman becomes pregnant, it is referred to as 'having joy' (*youxi*).

The figure in the painting is Zhong Kui, who according to tradition was skilled at catching ghosts and driving away demons. People hang his image above their doors to protect their homes, as he is an auspicious door god.

With his thick beard and red robe, he cuts an imposing figure. The custom of portraying him with a piercing glare is not followed in the painting, which instead shows him gazing benignly at the 'joyful spiders' dangling before him. This is a happy metaphor for 'joy coming down from heaven' (*xi cong tianxia*).

Zhou Xun was from Nanjing, and excelled at figure and animal painting.

Select bibliography

Ancients in Profile: Ming and Qing Figure Paintings from the Shanghai Museum. Exh. cat. Hong Kong: University Museum and Art Gallery, University of Hong Kong, 2001.

Andrews, Julia F. et al. *Between the Thunder and the Rain: Chinese Paintings from the Opium War through the Cultural Revolution, 1840–1979.* San Francisco: Echo Rock and Asian Art Museum of San Francisco, 2000.

Barnhart, Richard M. *Painters of the Great Ming: The Imperial Court and the Zhe School.* Exh. cat. Dallas: Museum of Art, Dallas, 1993.

Barnhart, Richard M. *Peach Blossom Spring: Gardens and Flowers in Chinese Painting.* Exh. cat. New York: Metropolitan Museum of Art, 1983.

Brown, Claudia, and Ju-hsi Chou. *Transcending Turmoil: Painting at the Close of China's Empire, 1796–1911.* Exh. cat. Phoenix: Phoenix Art Museum, 1992.

Cahill, Suzanne. *Transcendence and Divine Passion: The Queen Mother of the West in Medieval China.* Stanford: Stanford University Press, 1993.

Cao Xueqin (tr. David Hawkes). *The Story of the Stone.* London: Penguin, 1980

Chang Kang-i Sun and Haun Saussy (eds). *Women Writers of Traditional China: An Anthology of Poetry and Criticism.* Stanford: Stanford University Press, 1999.

Chou, Ju-hsi, and Claudia Brown (eds). *Chinese Painting Under the Qianlong Emperor, 1735–1795.* Exh. cat. Phoenix: Phoenix Art Museum, 1985.

Chou, Ju-hsi, and Claudia Brown (eds). *Chinese Painting Under the Qianlong Emperor: The Symposium Papers in Two Volumes. Phoebus: A Journal of Art History* 6, no. 2 (1991).

Clunas, Craig. *Pictures and Visuality in Early Modern China.* London: Reaktion Books, 1997.

Egan, Ronald C. *Word, Image and Deed in the Life of Su Shi.* Cambridge: Harvard University, 1994.

Elman, Benjamin A. *From Philosophy to Philology: Intellectual and Social Aspects of Change in Late Imperial China.* Cambridge, Mass.: Council on East Asian Studies, Harvard University, 1984.

Finnane, Antonia. *Speaking of Yangzhou: A Chinese City, 1550–1850.* Cambridge, Mass.: Harvard University Asia Center, 2004.

Fong, Wen C. *Between Two Cultures: Late-Nineteenth- and Early-Twentieth-Century Chinese Painting from the Robert H. Ellsworth Collection.* New York: Metropolitan Museum of Art; New Haven: Yale University Press, 2001.

Fong, Wen C., and James C.Y. Watt. *Possessing the Past: Treasures from the National Palace Museum, Taipei.* Exh. cat. New York: Metropolitan Museum of Art, 1996.

Green, Alexandra (ed.). *Rethinking Visual Narratives from Asia: Intercultural and Comparative Perspectives.* Hong Kong: Hong Kong University Press, forthcoming.

Hawkes, David (tr.). *Ch'u Tz'u: The Songs of the South, an Ancient Chinese Anthology.* Boston: Beacon Press, 1959.

Hawkes, David (tr.). *The Story of the Stone.* 3 vols. London and New York: Penguin, 1973–.

Hay, Jonathan. *Shitao: Painting and Modernity in Early Qing China.* Cambridge: Cambridge University Press, 2001.

Highlights of Ancient Chinese Figure Paintings from the Liaoning Provincial Museum and the Shanghai Museum; see *Shimao fengqing: Zhongguo gudai renwuhua jingpin ji.*

Hightower, James R. *The Poetry of T'ao Ch'ien.* Oxford: Clarendon, 1970.

Hsü, Ginger Cheng-chi. 'The Drunken Demon Queller: Chung K'uei in Eighteenth Century Chinese Painting'. *Taida Journal of Art History* 3 (1996), pp. 141–75.

Lai Yu-chih. 'Remapping Borders: Ren Bonian's Frontier Paintings and Urban Life in 1880s Shanghai'. *The Art Bulletin* 86 (September 2004), pp. 550–72.

Laing, Ellen Johnston. 'Erotic Themes and Romantic Heroines Depicted by Ch'iu Ying'. *Archives of Asian Art* 49 (1996), pp. 68–91.

Laing, Ellen Johnston. 'Neo-Taoism and the "Seven Sages of the Bamboo Grove" in Chinese Painting'. *Artibus Asiae* 36, nos 1–2 (1974), pp. 5–54.

Lawton, Thomas. *Chinese Figure Painting.* Exh. cat. Washington DC: Smithsonian Institution, Freer Gallery of Art, 1973.

Li Zhujin [Chu-tsing Li] and Wan Qingli. *Zhongguo xiandai huihua shi (History of Modern Chinese*

Painting). 2 vols. Taipei: Rock Publishing International, 2001.

Liangtuxuan shuhua jicui (Liangtu Studio Calligraphy and Painting Collection). Shanghai: Shanghai shuhua chubanshe, 2002.

Little, Stephen, with Shawn Eichman. *Taoism and the Arts of China.* Chicago: Art Institute of Chicago, 2000.

McCausland, Shane, and Matthew P. McKelway. *Chinese Romance from a Japanese Brush: Kano Sansetsu's Ch gonka Scrolls in the Chester Beatty Library.* London: Scala Publishers, 2009.

McCausland, Shane (ed.). *Gu Kaizhi and the Admonitions Scroll.* London: British Museum Press, 2003.

Mather, Richard B. (tr.). *A New Account of Tales of the World by Liu I-ch'ing.* Ann Arbor: Center for Chinese Studies, University of Michigan, 2002.

Minford, John, and Joseph S. M. Lau (eds). *Classical Chinese Literature: An Anthology of Translations.* New York: Columbia University Press; Hong Kong: The Chinese University Press, 2000-.

Murray, Julia K. *Mirror of Morality: Chinese Narrative Illustration and Confucian Ideology.* Honolulu: University of Hawai'i Press, 2007.

Murray, Julia K. 'What is "Chinese Narrative Illustration"?', *The Art Bulletin* 80, no. 4 (December 1998), pp. 602–15.

Olivová, Lucie, and Vibecke Bordahl (eds). *Lifestyle and Entertainment in Yangzhou.* Copenhagen: NISA Press, 2009.

Owen, Stephen (tr. and ed.). *An Anthology of Chinese Literature: Beginnings to 1911.* New York and London: W.W. Norton & Co, 1996.

Rorex, Robert A., and Wen C. Fong. *Eighteen Songs of a Nomad Flute: The Story of Lady Wen-chi.* New York: Metropolitan Museum of Art, 1974.

Shimao fengqing: Zhongguo gudai renwu hua. Hong Kong: Hong Kong Wenwei Publishing, 2008.

Shimao fengqing: Zhongguo gudai renwu hua guoji shuxue yantaohui (*Customs and Manners: An International Scholarly Symposium on Ancient Chinese Figure Painting*). Shanghai: Shanghai Museum, 2008.

Shimao fengqing: Zhongguo gudai renwu hua jingpin ji (Highlights of Ancient Chinese Figure Paintings from the Liaoning Provincial Museum and the Shanghai Museum). 3 vols. Shanghai: Shanghai guji chubanshe, 2008.

Stuart, Jan, and Evelyn S. Rawski. *Worshiping the Ancestors: Chinese Commemorative Portraits.* Stanford, CA: Stanford University Press, 2001.

Watson, Burton (tr.). *Courtier and Commoner in Ancient China: Selections from the History of the Former Han by Pan Ku.* New York and London: Columbia University Press, 1974.

Weidner, Marsha (ed.). *Latter Days of the Law: Images of Chinese Buddhism, 850–1850.* Exh. cat. Lawrence: Spencer Museum of Art, University of Kansas, in association with University of Hawai'i Press, 1994.

Weidner, Marsha et al. *Views from Jade Terrace: Chinese Women Artists, 1300–1912.* Exh. cat. Indianapolis: Indianapolis Museum of Art; New York: Rizzoli, 1988.

Weng Wange [Wan-go Weng]. *Chen Hongshou: His Life and Art.* 3 vols. Shanghai: Shanghai renmin meishu chubanshe, 1997.

West, Steven, and Wilt Idema (tr.). *The Story of the Western Wing.* Berkeley: University of California Press, 1995.

Wu Hung and Katherine R. Tsiang (eds). *Body and Face in Chinese Visual Culture. Harvard East Asian Monographs.* Cambridge, Mass.: Harvard University Asia Center, 2005.

Zhongguo gudai shuhua tumu (Illustrated Catalogue of Selected Works of Ancient Chinese Painting and Calligraphy). Multiple vols. Beijing: Wenwu chubanshe, 1990-.

Index

First published in 2010 by
Scala Publishers Ltd
Northburgh House
10 Northburgh Street
London EC1V 0AT, UK
www.scalapublishers.com

In association with the Chester Beatty Library, Dublin
Generously supported by the E. Rhodes and
Leona B. Carpenter Foundation

ISBN: 978 1 85759 604 5

Edited by Sandra Pisano
Designed by Andrew Shoolbred
Index by Joan Dearnley

Printed in Singapore

10 9 8 7 6 5 4 3 2 1

p. 1: Zhang Ling, *The Weaver Girl* (Cat. 35, detail)
pp. 2–3: Li Shida, *Seven Worthies of the Bamboo Grove* (Cat. 18, detail)
pp. 4–5: Shitao, *Elegant Gathering in the West Garden* (Cat. 28, detail)

Acknowledgements
The Chester Beatty Library acknowledges the support and encouragement of John and Julia Curtis in the publication of this catalogue. Special thanks are due to the Library's staff, including Paula Shalloo, Sinéad Ward and Laura Muldowney, and to the editorial and production team at Scala, including Sandra Pisano and Claudia Varosio.